BUREAU OF INTERNATIONAL RESEARCH

HARVARD UNIVERSITY AND RADCLIFFE COLLEGE

BARRIERS TO WORLD TRADE
A Study of Recent Commercial Policy

THE MACMILLAN COMPANY
NEW YORK · BOSTON · CHICAGO · DALLAS
ATLANTA · SAN FRANCISCO

MACMILLAN AND CO., LIMITED
LONDON · BOMBAY · CALCUTTA · MADRAS
MELBOURNE

THE MACMILLAN COMPANY
OF CANADA, LIMITED
TORONTO

BARRIERS TO WORLD TRADE

A Study of Recent Commercial Policy

By MARGARET S. GORDON

6776

THE MACMILLAN COMPANY

New York *1941*

PRINTED IN THE UNITED STATES OF AMERICA
NORWOOD PRESS—NORWOOD, MASS., U.S.A.

TO MY PARENTS

ACKNOWLEDGMENTS

This study was undertaken in 1937 with the assistance of a grant of funds from the Bureau of International Research of Harvard University and Radcliffe College. The author wishes to express her deep sense of gratitude to the Bureau and to the individual members of the committee in charge who gave generously of their time in helping to guide the work. Dean John H. Williams, of the Harvard Graduate School of Public Administration, encouraged the author in the initial stages of the project and helped to outline the study. Later, Professor Gottfried Haberler took over the work of guiding the author and read the manuscript in various stages of its evolution. Professor Sidney B. Fay, Chairman of the Bureau, and Miss Edith D. Haley, its Secretary, have been of great assistance at all times.

The author is indebted to a number of United States Government officials whose expert knowledge of various aspects of commercial policy proved an invaluable aid and who provided access to material and information not available in published sources. Among those who should be mentioned particularly are the Honorable Henry F. Grady, Assistant Secretary of State; Mr. William A. Fowler, of the Trade Agreements Division of the State Department; Mr. Henry Chalmers, of the Bureau of Foreign and Domestic Commerce; and the Honorable Oscar B. Ryder, of the United States Tariff Commission.

For whatever merits the book may possess in its final form, much credit must be assigned to the many competent individuals who read the manuscript and offered valuable criticisms and suggestions. Special mention should be made of Professor John B. Condliffe of the University of California and Mr. Henry J.

Tasca, his assistant, both of whom read the entire manuscript with great care. Professor Howard S. Ellis read a portion of the manuscript and provided the author with access to valuable material on exchange control in Hungary. The author is likewise indebted to Drs. Michael A. Heilperin and Joseph Coppock, who offered a number of helpful suggestions. The sections on control of trade in agricultural commodities owe much to the expert knowledge of Dr. Joseph S. Davis and other members of the Food Research Institute of Stanford University.

Last but not least, the author wishes to mention her long-suffering husband, who has been forced to spend many a dinner hour during the course of the last three years discussing the technicalities of exchange control, clearing agreements, and similar subjects. He has scrutinized the manuscript down to the last comma. For all expressions of opinion, and for any defects or errors which have crept into the final version of the book, the author alone is responsible.

Berkeley, California   MARGARET S. GORDON
November, 1940

CONTENTS

PART I. INTRODUCTION AND BACKGROUND

PART II. THE CONTROL OF INTERNATIONAL PAYMENTS

ix

CONTENTS

CONTENTS

PART I

INTRODUCTION AND BACKGROUND

CHAPTER I

INTRODUCTION

Before the World War, the study of commercial policy revolved around questions of tariffs and tariff bargaining. The outbreak of hostilities in 1914 changed all this, bringing into being a host of direct governmental restrictions on imports and exports. Exchange controls and licensing systems adjusted the flow of commodities to the exigencies of the war. Although these regulations were gradually removed after the Armistice, it was not so very long before they were reimposed. The onslaught of the "great" depression, and more particularly the chaos brought on by the international financial crisis of 1931, caused nations to turn once more to the foreign trade controls which they had learned to employ during the World War.

This time, however, the objectives of control were somewhat different. Defense of the currency, to be sure, was again a predominant issue, especially in 1931 and 1932. But the wartime concern with conserving resources for military purposes and strangling the trade of the enemy had been replaced by a desire, first and foremost, to protect the domestic market from the impact of rapidly falling world prices. The achievement of internal price stability became virtually a universal aim, and in the pursuit of this end many nations developed trade control systems which far exceeded in rigidity and complexity the restrictions of the World War period.

As trade began to recover from the great depression the newly adopted weapons of trade restriction were not laid aside.[1]

---

[1] This is not to deny that exchange restrictions, and even import quotas, were relaxed in many countries, but there were few cases in which the power to control and direct trade was abandoned.

3

In place of the former emphasis on drastic limitation of imports, however, there was an increasing tendency to utilize import restrictions as bargaining instruments in order to secure concessions for exports in foreign markets. As the prospects for multilateral relaxation of trade barriers appeared more and more hopeless, bilateral negotiations were undertaken on an unprecedented scale. More and more countries sought to equalize the balance of trade with every other country; and the whole battery of trade control weapons—exchange restrictions, import quotas, export subsidies, and the like—was utilized, often in discriminatory fashion, to achieve this end. Trade tended to be rigidly canalized in bilateral streams, its movements responding, not to changes in prices or shifts in demand, but to the decisions of governmental authorities.

This trend toward bilateral balancing of imports and exports has been resisted by a number of countries, notably the United States, with its Reciprocal Trade Agreements Program based on the most-favored-nation principle; and up to the outbreak of war in 1939, a substantial portion of world trade remained subject to no limitation other than tariffs. The tense international situation which preceded the opening of hostilities, however, did not encourage adherence to laissez-faire principles of commercial policy. The trend toward rigid governmental control of exports and imports became increasingly difficult to resist in an atmosphere of growing economic nationalism and military preparedness. During 1937 and 1938 it became more and more clear that a vital struggle was being waged between the proponents of a multilateral system based on tariffs and the most-favored-nation clause, on the one hand, and the proponents of controlled bilateral canalization of trade, on the other.

At the moment, it is difficult to predict what the eventual outcome of this struggle will be. The outbreak of a second world war meant the spread of rigid trade controls to countries which had previously tended on the whole to avoid such measures. The wartime restrictions are not likely to be immediately abandoned with the return of peace. In any event, one thing is clear. An understanding of the newer methods of trade control has become an essential part of the economist's equipment. So long as tariffs remain the primary weapon of commercial policy, the world price system remains intact. Every country is linked to every other country in such a way that the effect of localized changes in economic conditions spreads throughout the world, through the media of prices and exchange rates. As soon as quantitative methods of control become widely prevalent, the old system is robbed of its essential characteristics. Domestic price movements become divorced from price movements abroad, and the balance of payments no longer adjusts itself automatically to altered situations (if, in fact, it ever did). Every adjustment must be controlled and directed by the proper authority. Planned control of the entire economic system gradually develops, if the movement is allowed to go far enough. Governmental control of international trade may be, in fact, and frequently is, merely one aspect of a larger movement in the direction of more and more complete public control of the economic system.[2]

The aim of the present study is to trace the outstanding trends in commercial policy since 1931, with particular emphasis on the technique of the newer methods of trade control. No attention will be paid to the effects of the measures studied, from either a theoretical or statistical point of view, except in so far as such an analysis is essential in order to explain the nature of the restrictive devices or the ways in which they have been revised as a result of experience. The study is not confined to any geographical region or group of countries, since one of its objects is to present a picture, even though necessarily somewhat incomplete, of the extent to which the movements of world trade as a whole have come to be influenced

[2] Cf. G. Haberler, *Liberale und planwirtschaftliche Handelspolitik* (Berlin, 1934), *passim*.

by measures of restriction other than tariffs. Because of the broad scope of the book, discussion of the policies of any one country must inevitably be somewhat superficial. The reader who is interested in developments in a given country or region should turn to more specialized studies. It is hoped that whatever the present study lacks by way of intensive analysis of particular situations is compensated by the comprehensiveness of the picture presented.

Finally, no attempt has been made to trace developments in the field of commercial policy since the outbreak of war in September, 1939. New decrees are constantly being issued by the belligerent countries, and any summary of the current situation would become out of date almost as rapidly as it was written. The year 1931 marked the beginning of the last stage in the development of commercial policy after one great war; 1939 marks the conclusion of this stage and the beginning of another great military conflict. This study confines itself, except for a necessary introductory survey of developments during the nineteen-twenties, to an analysis of commercial policy between these two significant dates.

CHAPTER II

COMMERCIAL POLICY DURING AND AFTER THE
WORLD WAR

1. *Abnormal Measures Necessitated by the War*

During the greater part of the nineteenth century and in the early years of the present century, customs duties constituted the only important barrier to international trade.[1] Import and export prohibitions and other restrictive devices which had been widely used during the mercantilist period had by this time largely disappeared. To be sure, the free trade movement, which had got under way with the signing of the Cobden Treaty between France and England in 1860, had been superseded by growing protectionism in Continental Europe from the seventies on. Nevertheless, the general level of customs duties at the outbreak of the war in 1914, as compared with the level to which the post-War generation has become accustomed, was not excessively high.[2] Most of the important trading nations of the world were bound together by a network of commercial treaties which provided for substantial reductions from general or maximum statutory tariff rates. Since the majority of these treaties embodied the unconditional most-favored-nation clause, a large number of countries generally benefited from any reductions which were included in each new treaty.[3] Thus,

---

[1] The volume and direction of flow of international trade were affected also by the shipping regulations enforced by certain countries. All questions relating to shipping policy, however, lie outside the scope of this book.

[2] See League of Nations, International Economic Conference, *Tariff Level Indices* (Geneva, 1927).

[3] The unconditional and unlimited most-favored-nation clause has been formulated in a number of different ways since the seventeenth century, when

7

although tariff bargaining was widely carried on, discrimination among countries in tariff matters was rare. Furthermore, England and Holland still adhered to their free-trade position in 1914, while the Latin American countries had not yet gone in for protection to any significant extent, and a number of Asiatic countries were prevented from imposing any but the most moderate revenue duties through treaties which had been forced on them by western powers. In the United States, the Underwood Tariff of 1913 called for substantial reductions from the rather high rates previously in force.

Perhaps most important of all, commercial policy before the War exhibited a marked degree of stability, as compared with the rather chaotic situation which has generally prevailed since 1914. Tariff rates were frequently consolidated in commercial treaties for periods as long as ten years.[4] Moderate revisions were naturally considered essential from time to time because of changing economic circumstances and because of the desire to encourage the development of new industries, but only in the cases of a few relatively unimportant countries were tariff rates ever robbed of their effectiveness almost overnight by currency upheavals and violent price fluctuations.

---

it began to make its appearance in commercial treaties, and the wording of the clause has tended to become more complicated with the passage of years. In demanding the inclusion of the clause in commercial treaties, countries have always had one purpose in mind—the protection of their exports from discriminatory treatment in foreign countries. Essentially, the form now generally in use provides that imports into one of the contracting countries from the other contracting country shall not be subject to any duties or charges higher than those imposed on the like products of any third country, and that any advantages or privileges granted by either contracting party to any third country shall be immediately and gratuitously extended to the like products of the other contracting party. For the model formulation of the clause, drawn up by the League of Nations Economic Committee in 1929, see League of Nations, *Recommendations of the Economic Committee Relating to Commercial Policy* (Geneva, 1929), pp. 12–13.

[4] We shall hear more of consolidated rates at a later stage. See, especially, pp. 228n., 245 below. Rates are said to be consolidated against increases when a country agrees in a treaty with a second country not to raise the duties on certain commodities for the duration of the treaty.

All this was suddenly changed by the outbreak of war in 1914. In the first place, commercial treaties existing between belligerent countries were automatically denounced, and commercial relations with the enemy were prohibited.[5] Furthermore, in order to prevent supplies from reaching the enemy through neutral countries, both the Allies and the Central Powers soon after the outbreak of the War published long lists of goods to be considered "contraband of war." Neutral countries could not export goods coming under this category to belligerents without violating the duties of neutrality.[6] Thus, new channels of trade had to be built up to replace those destroyed by this economic warfare, and nations were in many instances thrown back on their own resources for supplies which had formerly been imported from abroad.

This disrupting of the peacetime channels of trade, combined with the tremendous pressure placed upon every belligerent country to conserve its own resources and utilize them in the manner best calculated to secure the furtherance of military ends, resulted in the enactment of a host of trade restrictive measures. Of these, export prohibitions were among the most important. It was forbidden to export arms, essential raw materials, and various other articles without securing a license from the proper authorities. At first, the lists of commodities affected by these regulations were relatively short, but as time went on, various additions were made, occasionally involving goods which would help some important industry in enemy territory if they were eventually to find their way there.[7]

One would expect that the same factors tending to bring about a restriction of exports would have led to the removal of barriers to imports. It is true that imports, especially of indispensable commodities, were encouraged to some extent by

[5] Cf. O. Delle Donne, *European Tariff Policies since the World War* (New York, 1928), pp. 56–57, 60.

[6] *Ibid.* There is no need to dwell here on the many serious difficulties which arose from attempts to enforce these measures relating to contraband of war.

[7] Cf. *ibid.*, pp. 61–68.

the lowering of tariff rates. For a number of reasons, however, it was found necessary to restrict certain types of imports, especially in the later years of the War. In order to help prevent depreciation of the exchanges, an effort was made to limit the purchase abroad of luxuries and nonessential articles. Thus, available supplies of exchange could be utilized for the more essential foreign expenditures. Tariffs were increased in some instances to accomplish this end, but, in general, greater reliance was placed on import prohibitions. As in the case of export prohibitions, licenses to import the commodities concerned were granted in occasional instances. Import prohibitions were adopted for other reasons as well. One of the most vital wartime problems was the conservation of shipping space for the transportation of men and important supplies. Consequently, we find that restrictions were placed on the import of certain bulky articles which required much shipping space but which were of no particular importance for the conduct of the War. Further, although it must be emphasized that protection of domestic industry was not of prime importance in inducing measures of import restriction during the War, there were an appreciable number of cases in which tariffs were increased or import prohibitions imposed in order to protect from foreign competition some new or old industry which was of importance from a military point of view and which was too weak to stand on its own feet.[8] Finally, in view of the heavy budgetary requirements of the War, it is not surprising that tariffs were in some instances increased for the purpose of securing revenue.

Along with all these measures of trade control went ex-

---

[8] It has sometimes been charged that the McKenna Duties introduced by the British Government in 1915 were actually intended to be protective in effect. They were levied on luxury goods with the object of yielding increased revenue, protecting the sterling exchanges, and relieving shipping but were unaccompanied by excise duties on like products of domestic origin, so that they did, in fact, discriminate in favor of home production. Cf. J. H. Richardson, *British Economic Foreign Policy* (London, 1936), pp. 87–88.

change regulations, which were adopted as precautionary measures at the outbreak of the War and tended to be applied with
increasing severity as time went on. In the beginning, these
measures were aimed at preventing the flight of capital to
neutral countries. Later on, exchange restrictions were utilized,
in conjunction with the import prohibitions already mentioned,
to keep the excess of imports from becoming unduly large.
Meanwhile, foreign balances were built up through the enforced sale of foreign securities. The situation was everywhere
complicated by the fact that huge governmental expenditures
were leading to internal inflation, with its inevitable threat to
the exchanges. Neutral countries could not but be affected by
the general rise in prices and, for this and other reasons, were
forced in their turn to inaugurate some degree of control over
the exchanges and foreign trade.

It is important to emphasize the fact that the administration
of wartime trade restrictions was guided by the exigencies of
the War. For the belligerent countries, one consideration—the
winning of the War—outweighed all others, whether it was a
question of commercial policy or of any other matter. Consequently, while the technique of trade regulation in many
instances resembled that employed in recent years, the spirit
in which it was exercised was often radically different. The
belligerent countries could not afford to concern themselves to
any important degree with the seeking of concessions for their
exports. Thus, much of the bargaining which plays so large
a part in peacetime commercial policy was absent from the
scene. Discrimination, in so far as it entered in at all, was of a
very special sort, involving primarily attempts to strangle the
trade of the enemy, not only through the prohibitions against
dealings with enemy countries, but also through the special
regulations applying to trade with neutral countries situated
near to hostile territory.[9]

[9] To cite an example, goods affected by England's export prohibitions were
divided into three classes: (1) goods the exportation of which was prohibited

2. *Trade Restrictions after the War*

The close of the War in 1918 was not accompanied by a
speedy return to normalcy in the economic world. The exigencies of reconstruction and the inevitable adjustments required
in the transition from an economy geared to satisfy wartime
needs to a peacetime economy involved a continued need for
governmental intervention. Controls had to be maintained in
the sphere of foreign trade as well as in the sphere of domestic
economy. On the one hand, unusually large imports of certain
commodities were required until European agriculture and industry could be made to function normally, while, on the other
hand, certain industries which had been sheltered by wartime
restrictions or which had suffered from lack of capital replacement during the War could not immediately be subjected to
competition from abroad.

Exchange restrictions and import and export prohibitions
might have been more speedily relaxed had it not been for the
marked currency fluctuations which characterized the earlier
years of the nineteen-twenties. As it was, only limited progress
was made in this direction until about 1925, the year of England's return to the gold standard. Foreign trade after the
War in some instances reopened "with the simplest form of
barter, transactions being in the nature of exceptions permitted
under a general regime of prohibitions." [10] The exchange regulations which had been introduced during the War were continued in effect in most countries until after their currencies
were stabilized. Currencies which had been pegged during the
War, however, in some cases with the help of foreign loans,
were allowed to depreciate after the return to peace. In other

to all destinations; (2) goods whose exportation was prohibited only to countries outside the British Empire; (3) goods whose exportation was prohibited
only to neutral countries bordering the enemy nations. (Delle Donne, *op. cit.*,
pp. 67–68.) Exports to enemy countries were, of course, prohibited altogether.
  [10] United States Tariff Commission, *Extent of Equal Tariff Treatment in
Foreign Countries* (Washington, 1937), p. 3.

words, no attempt was made to enforce an official rate of exchange.[11] The exchange restrictions were aimed at limiting the extent of depreciation through preventing the flight of capital and speculation in the exchanges. The restriction of imports was accomplished, for the most part, through import prohibitions rather than through exchange regulations. In a few countries exchange restrictions have been enforced continuously since the first World War or shortly thereafter, but by the end of the nineteen-twenties the majority of countries had returned to a free gold standard or to some form of a gold exchange standard.[12]

In Western Europe, import and export prohibitions were relaxed at a relatively early stage. By May, 1919, exports from the United Kingdom were practically unrestricted.[13] The attempt to do away with import restrictions in England encountered considerable opposition from industrialists, but even these regulations were abandoned in August, 1920.[14] A French governmental decree of June 13, 1919, provided for the abolition of the major portion of France's wartime import prohibitions,[15] although some of these were revived later during the inflation period. Foreign trade control in Germany was actually tightened up in some directions during the period of inflation, and it was not until after the coming into force of a revised customs tariff on October 1, 1925, that the Reich Commission for Import and Export Licenses was dissolved and trade restrictions were largely given up.[16] Other countries

---

[11] League of Nations, International Financial Conference, Brussels, 1920, *Papers of the Conference, Exchange Control*, No. XI (London, 1920), pp. 3–5.

[12] Bulgaria has enforced exchange control continuously since 1918, while Portugal maintained control from October, 1922, to October, 1937. Otherwise, the restrictions enforced in recent years date, for the most part, from 1930 and later years. See Table III (p. 54).

[13] Delle Donne, *op. cit.*, p. 101.

[14] The importation of dyestuffs, however, was prohibited except under license by the Dyestuffs Act, promulgated in 1920 and in effect ever since. See Richardson, *op. cit.*, p. 88.

[15] Delle Donne, *op. cit.*, p. 143.

[16] *Ibid.*, pp. 210–11.

in Central and Eastern Europe were even slower than Germany in returning to normalcy. In some cases, the licensing regime for imports and exports was never abolished, and, while the system was administered in a relatively unrestrictive manner in the latter part of the nineteen-twenties, it was an easy matter to broaden the application of the license requirements when conditions seemed once more to call for such action, as they did in 1931 and 1932.[17]

An unsuccessful attempt was made to do away with trade restrictions through multilateral action following the World Economic Conference of 1927. An international conference in October of the same year resulted in the drawing up of a Convention for the Abolition of Import and Export Prohibitions and Restrictions, in accordance with which the participating states were to undertake to abolish such prohibitions and restrictions within a period of six months after the coming into force of the convention.[18] Certain qualifying articles were, however, included, several of which later served to weaken substantially the value of the convention. States were to be permitted to retain prohibitions or restrictions which, "on grounds other or more imperative than economic grounds," might be regarded as indispensable.[19] Resort might be had, further, to measures of restriction under "genuinely extraordinary and abnormal circumstances." Finally, provision was made for temporary exceptions with regard to certain specified products, among which were coloring matter, scrap iron and scrap of other metals, and coal. Although the Convention was ratified by nineteen countries, it did not enter into force in July, 1930, as had been planned. Its application was made

[17] Among the countries in which import licensing systems were in effect continuously from the World War on were Austria, Czechoslovakia, and Hungary.

[18] League of Nations, International Conference for the Abolition of Import and Export Prohibitions and Restrictions, Oct. 17 to Nov. 8, 1927, *Proceedings* (Geneva, 1928), pp. 7–17.

[19] League of Nations, Economic Organization, Consultative Committee, *Application of the Recommendations of the International Economic Conference,* Report for May, 1927–May, 1928 (Geneva, 1928), p. 24.

conditional on the adherence of certain states, and when Poland failed to ratify, a group of countries with closely interdependent trade relations withdrew their ratifications. This left only seven countries adhering unconditionally to the convention, and significantly enough, these were all countries whose exports and imports were, with few exceptions, unaffected by prohibitions or other restrictions.[20]

3. *Tariff History, 1918–1929*

As the abnormal trade controls of the War period were gradually relaxed, nations returned once more to tariffs as their chief weapon of commercial policy. Tariff changes were predominantly upward during the nineteen-twenties, in spite of the conclusion, in the latter half of the decade, of a large number of commercial treaties calling for duty reductions. Numerous factors, many of them closely inter-related, were responsible for this upward movement.

By 1918, as a result of the world-wide inflation which had taken place during the War, prices were in many cases two or three times as high as they had been in 1914. This meant that the specific duties which were extensively employed on the European Continent had lost much of their effectiveness as measures of protection. Prices were still far above their pre-War levels even after the world-wide deflation which took place in 1920 and 1921. Because of the chaotic currency situation and general economic instability of the early nineteen-twenties, however, most countries postponed thoroughgoing tariff revisions until 1925 or thereabouts.[21] In the meantime,

---

[20] The countries concerned were Great Britain, Denmark, the United States, Japan, Norway, the Netherlands, and Portugal. See League of Nations, Economic Work of the League of Nations, *Report and Draft Resolutions Presented by the Second Committee to the Assembly* (Geneva, 1930), p. 3, and Economic Committee, *Report to the Council on the Work of the Thirty-third Session*, Oct. 27 to Nov. 1, 1930 (Geneva, 1930), p. 4.

[21] Thus we find Germany undertaking a tariff revision in 1925 (cf. p. 13

existing tariff rates were adjusted through the adoption of certain flexible devices designed to "correct" for price changes or currency fluctuations.

One such expedient was the system of "coefficients of increase," adopted by France and certain other European countries. Almost immediately after the removal of French import prohibitions in June, 1919,[22] this system was inaugurated to secure for French industry the degree of protection which it had enjoyed before the War. The specific duties contained in the pre-War tariff were multiplied by a coefficient or multiplier, calculated in each case to represent the ratio of the official valuation of the commodity in 1918 to its corresponding valuation in 1913.[23] The maximum coefficient, which was applied to most manufactured goods, was three. Agricultural products were not at first affected by this law, but later the system was extended to include cereals and sugar products.[24] As time went on and French prices soared higher during the inflation period, the coefficients were in many cases increased, until the rates on some commodities were seven or eight times as high as they had been in 1914.[25] Other countries to apply similar devices, in connection with all or only part of their tariff schedules, were Greece, Italy, Belgium, and Czechoslovakia.[26]

A comparable device, which aimed at "correcting" for currency depreciation, consisted in expressing the tariff rates in terms of gold and requiring the payment of an equivalent sum in the national currency. Thus the duties actually paid would fluctuate with the premium on gold. This has been a practice of long standing in certain Latin American countries and was

---

above), while France did not make much progress toward revising the old tariff schedule of 1910 until 1927.

[22] Cf. p. 13 above.

[23] Delle Donne, *op. cit.*, p. 144.

[24] *Ibid.*, pp. 144–45.

[25] *Ibid.*, p. 148.

[26] See W. Röpke, *Die internationale Handelspolitik nach dem Kriege* (Jena, 1923), pp. 42–43.

adopted shortly after the War by Germany, Estonia, Yugo-slavia, Latvia, Austria, Poland, Portugal, Rumania (for certain luxury goods), and Hungary.[27]

It is rather intriguing to note that, while countries with weak currencies found it necessary to compensate for depreciation by adjusting tariff rates upward, certain other countries whose currencies were *relatively* stable felt themselves impelled to protect their industries from the competition of the weak-currency countries. Thus, surtaxes on the products of countries with depreciated currencies were introduced to supplement existing tariffs. The same end was sometimes achieved, under another name, by the enactment of anti-dumping legislation, which covered cases of so-called exchange dumping as well as those of ordinary dumping.[28]

Of more permanent and fundamental importance in its influence on post-War tariff policy was the fact that the War had demonstrated the vulnerability of nations which were cut off from normal sources of supply of essential commodities. Thus we find an increasing emphasis on economic preparedness, manifesting itself in the protection of industries which had been of strategic importance during the War. One of the first

[27] *Ibid.*, p. 42. Clearly, in so far as costs of production in the country experiencing currency depreciation failed to rise in proportion to the extent of depreciation of the currency, "correction" by this method would actually result in an enhanced degree of protection for the commodities concerned.

[28] A considerable number of anti-dumping measures were introduced during the early nineteen-twenties. Cf. H. Chalmers, "The Post-War Drift in European Commercial Policy," *American Economic Review*, XIV, Supplement (March, 1924), 17. The British Safeguarding of Industries Act of 1921 (see p. 217 below) contained, in addition to tariffs for the protection of key industries, provisions for the imposition of special duties, by order of the Board of Trade, in cases of exchange dumping and of ordinary dumping. (Richardson, *op. cit.*, p. 88, and Delle Donne, *op. cit.*, pp. 94–113.) If dumping is defined as price-discrimination between two markets, then so-called exchange dumping does not constitute dumping in the strict sense. Cf. G. Haberler, *The Theory of International Trade* (London, 1936), p. 300, and F. D. Graham, *Protective Tariffs* (New York and London, 1934), pp. 91–94. It may be noted, further, that in so far as export prices in the depreciated-currency country rise in proportion to the extent of depreciation, any tendency for that country's exports to be stimulated disappears.

measures which was clearly motivated by this consideration was the Safeguarding of Industries Act, enacted by the British Parliament in 1921. This measure provided for duties, equal in the majority of cases to 33⅓ per cent ad valorem, to be applied to the protection of certain "key" industries, considered essential from the point of view of national defense and industrial security.[29]

Since the importance of easy access to supplies of foodstuffs had been demonstrated during the War, the program of economic preparedness extended to increased protection for agriculture. Another consideration, which had exercised an important influence on French and German tariff legislation even before the War, was also involved here. On the Continent of Europe, the peasantry was looked upon as a stable and desirable element in the population. With the growth in strength of radical parties after the War, the attempt to encourage the maintenance of the peasantry as a bulwark against the overthrow of existing institutions was intensified and gave rise to increased protection to agriculture. This movement was to some extent forestalled during the reconstruction period, because countries in which agriculture had been interrupted during the War through destruction of territory or shortage of labor were in no position to produce an adequate supply of foodstuffs internally and recognized their need for cheap imports from abroad.[30] Once the process of rehabilitation had made progress, however, the agricultural-importing countries of Europe began to lay greater emphasis on the necessity of protection from the competition of lower-cost areas abroad. A

[29] Richardson, op. cit., p. 88. Among the commodities affected by the new rates were scientific instruments and glassware, optical glass, certain chemicals, wireless valves, etc. See also Delle Donne, op. cit., pp. 110–11. Many of these commodities had been imported from Germany up to 1914, and Britain had found herself handicapped by her inability to procure them during the War.

[30] Practically all restrictions on the importation of agricultural products into Germany had been removed at the outbreak of the War, in order to mitigate anticipated food shortages. Cf. W. Röpke, German Commercial Policy (New York, London, and Toronto, 1934), p. 56.

substantial degree of protection was considered essential in view of the tendency for agricultural prices to fall on world markets. Overseas agricultural countries had increased their production during the War and were now geared to maintain this higher level of production despite the tendency for European markets for imported agricultural staples to contract. Further, production costs were being lowered in Canada, the United States, Australia, and Argentina as a result of increasing mechanization. These factors tended to give rise to a chronic condition of over-supply on the world market.

Agrarian protectionism in Europe began to be increasingly evident from 1925 on. This was the first year in which European wheat production (excluding that of Soviet Russia) exceeded the average of the five years before the War.[31] It was also the year in which Germany undertook a general revision of her tariff and decided to reimpose high duties on foodstuffs.[32] Other countries to grant increased protection to agriculture in 1925 were Austria and Czechoslovakia, which put into effect sliding scale duties on wheat, and Italy, which in that year commenced its "battle of the grain."[23]

In addition to all these factors making for higher tariffs, the peace treaties had established new political units, all desirous of erecting their own autonomous tariff systems. The number of separate customs units in Europe was increased by the War from 20 to 27, while political frontiers were lengthened by about 12,500 miles.[34] The old Austro-Hungarian Empire with its more or less balanced agricultural and industrial economy

[31] See League of Nations, Economic Committee, *Considerations on the Present Evolution of Agricultural Protectionism* (Geneva, 1935), p. 16.

[32] The protection granted to agriculture in the tariff act of August, 1925, however, was somewhat more moderate than that which had been in force before the War. Cf. Röpke, *German Commercial Policy*, p. 56.

[33] League of Nations, *Considerations on the Present Evolution of Agricultural Protectionism*, p. 16.

[34] See League of Nations, The World Economic Conference, *Final Report* (Geneva, 1927), p. 29, and H. Chalmers, "The World Economic Conference," *American Year Book*, 1927, p. 298.

had been severed into parts, some of which were predominantly agricultural and some of which were predominantly industrial. Each of the new units tried to develop a rounded economy by granting high protection to its weaker industries. Thus pre-War channels of trade were broken up and replaced by narrower, more restricted channels.

But four years of struggle had resulted in far-reaching industrial changes, even in countries whose political boundaries were not altered by the peace treaties. On the Continent of Europe, important industries had suffered from capital depletion during the War, and increased protection was granted in order to encourage the rebuilding of these weakened industries. Overseas countries, on the other hand, had been forced to encourage the production within their own borders of finished commodities formerly imported from Europe. Thus infant industries had been started which could be, and, in many cases, were, maintained after the War only through protective tariffs. This was particularly true of such immature industrial countries as Canada, Australia, and Argentina, which had imported manufactured goods extensively before 1914 from Europe, and especially from England. Japan and China also made notable advances in the direction of industrialization. Even in the United States, however, one of the arguments for sharp tariff increases in 1922 was based on the existence of the so-called "war babies," industries which had experienced a mushroom growth during the abnormal trading conditions of the War and which were held to require protection to survive once they were subjected to competition from countries which had supplied the commodities involved before the War.[35] The rise of new industries abroad had much to do with the fact that British exports never succeeded in regaining the dominant position in world markets which they had occupied in 1914. The bearing of this and other factors, such as the over-valuation of the

---

[35] F. W. Taussig, *The Tariff History of the United States* (7th ed.; New York, 1923), p. 451.

pound sterling after 1925, on Britain's eventual resort to protectionism will be discussed in Chapter VIII.

Of considerable importance, moreover, as a force behind the
world-wide trend toward higher tariffs in the post-War period
was the violence of financial crises, leading as they did to severe
unemployment. It is highly significant that the United States
enacted the Fordney-McCumber and Smoot-Hawley Tariff
measures shortly after the crises of 1921 and 1929 respectively.

In many instances, tariffs were increased in the post-War
period far more than was necessary to provide an adequate
degree of protection. The explanation of this lay in the fact
that everywhere new commercial treaties had to be negotiated
to replace those which had been denounced or had ceased to
operate during or immediately after the War. Tariff rates were
consequently set at abnormally high levels purely for "bargaining" purposes. The higher a country's tariffs were at the outset
of trade negotiations, the more easily it could demand large
concessions by offering substantial duty reductions in return.
These tactics had been employed before the War, but in the
nineteen-twenties bargaining duties tended to be higher in relation to the degree of protection actually desired than had
formerly been the case.[36]

The desire to increase revenue was not altogether absent as
a motive for raising tariffs in Europe, where strained budgets
were a prominent characteristic of the post-War decade. This
factor tended, however, to play a relatively more important
rôle in Latin America, where upward tariff revisions were quite
frequent in the nineteen-twenties. Most of the Latin American
countries were, nevertheless, beginning to adjust their tariff
schedules in such a way as to encourage the expansion of manu-
facturing. This was apparent both in increased protectionism
to infant industries and in the reduction of duties on machinery

---

[36] For an illuminating discussion of this question, see League of Nations,
Economic and Financial Section, *Memorandum on European Bargaining Tariffs,*
by W. T. Page (Geneva, 1927).

and industrial equipment.[37] Tariff revisions in Japan and India showed similar tendencies, while elsewhere in the Orient considerable progress was made toward a greater degree of tariff autonomy.[38]

After the conclusion of the World Economic Conference of May, 1927, it looked for a time as though the declarations of the conference in favor of lower tariffs would have some influence on governmental policies.[39] A League of Nations report, issued about a year later, pointed out that, while tariffs were on the whole higher than those in force the preceding May, the increases which had actually been carried out were not as great as those which had been contemplated at the time the conference met.[40] Furthermore, numerous tariff reductions had been arranged in commercial treaties concluded during the course of the year. On balance, the opposing tendencies toward higher or lower tariffs in a number of countries seemed to be about equally matched, and the report expressed the opinion that in these cases much would depend on the prospects for success of the lower tariff movement in the world as a whole.[41]

But the turn of events proved definitely unfavorable for tariff reductions. The unsound agricultural situation grew more critical in 1928 and 1929.[42] A further decline in agricultural prices on world markets led to an intensification of agrarian pro-

---

[37] See H. Chalmers, "Current Trends in Foreign Commercial Policy," *The Annals of the American Academy of Political and Social Science*, CL (1930), 141–42.

[38] *Ibid.*, pp. 143–44. Freedom to alter tariffs in China, and certain other Oriental countries, had previously been restricted in commercial treaties with western powers. (Cf. p. 8 above.)

[39] The Conference recommended tariff reductions through unilateral, bilateral, and multilateral action. In the interests of greater tariff stability, states were also urged to refrain from sudden and violent tariff changes and to make a wide use of duty consolidations in commercial treaties, such treaties to be concluded for relatively long periods. See League of Nations, The World Economic Conference, *Final Report*, pp. 26–27, 29–32.

[40] League of Nations, *Application of the Recommendations of the International Economic Conference*, Report for May 1927–May 1928, p. 8.

[41] *Ibid.*

[42] See pp. 29–30 below.

tectionism in the food-importing countries of Europe, a development which became more marked with the outbreak of the world depression in the fall of 1929. Not only were tariffs on agricultural commodities increased, but other measures were adopted to encourage home production and to control prices. This movement found its most thorough expression in Germany, but all the important food-importing countries of Europe shared in it to a considerable extent.[43] Meanwhile, the agricultural countries of Central and Eastern Europe, "crushed between the strong competition from the large-scale cereal and meat producers of the newer lands such as Canada, Australia, and the Argentine, and the progressive closing of their neighboring markets," [44] turned to higher protection on their part.

Once the world depression really got under way, all hopes for a modification of tariff barriers grew very dim. Faced with shrinking markets for their exports, and with domestic production threatened by falling prices abroad, the majority of countries attempted to stave off the impact of the downward

[43] The sudden upward surge in import duties on wheat from the middle of 1929 on, as compared with the rather moderate increases which had taken place up to that time, is brought out clearly in a table to be found in League of Nations, *The Course and Phases of the World Economic Depression* (Geneva, 1931), p. 324. The following indices of import duties on wheat have been calculated from this table. The countries for which indices are given here are among those in which tariffs increased especially markedly.

Indices of Import Duties on Wheat from Countries
Enjoying Most-Favored-Nation Treatment
(January 1, 1913 = 100)

	Jan. 1, 1928	July 1, 1929	July 1, 1930	Nov. 8, 1930
Germany	91.0	116.6	272.5	454.3
France	101.6	101.6	232.0	232.0
Greece	100.0	71.7	175.0	175.0
Italy	100.0	186.7	220.0	220.0

The restrictions other than tariffs which were adopted from 1929 to 1931 will be discussed in later sections of this book.

For indices of European tariff levels in 1913, 1927, and 1931, see H. Liepmann, *Tariff Levels and the Economic Unity of Europe* (London, 1938), pp. 413 ff.

[44] League of Nations, *World Economic Survey, 1931–32* (Geneva, 1932), p. 280.

spiral of deflation outside their borders by raising import duties. We shall deal with this movement in the next chapter.

4. *Commercial Treaties in the Post-War Period*

Such treaties as had not been abrogated during the War were, for the most part, denounced after the War. It was natural that governments should wish to render themselves free of treaty obligations in order to adjust their tariff schedules to altered economic circumstances. Relatively few new treaties of a permanent nature were negotiated during the early nineteen-twenties, while currency conditions were still unsettled. Countries which delayed tariff revisions until the return of greater stability were naturally not ready to commit themselves to treaty obligations of a long-run nature.

During this unsettled period, however, the *status quo* was frequently maintained through a temporary *modus vivendi* which prolonged the relations set up in the old treaty until new negotiations could be carried through.[45] Countries maintaining import prohibitions signed bilateral "contingent" agreements under which each agreed to admit fixed amounts of specified commodities from the other.[46] The duration of such agreements was short, generally not exceeding a year, but they were frequently prolonged for additional periods, often in a slightly revised form to take account of altering circumstances.

The wave of tariff revisions which set in about 1925 was accompanied by the negotiation of a whole series of commercial treaties of a more permanent nature. For a time, it was doubtful whether the unconditional and unlimited form of the most-favored-nation clause would be restored to the position of general favor which it had enjoyed before the War.

[45] See Chalmers, "The Post-War Drift in European Commercial Policy," p. 18.

[46] These agreements were quite similar to some of the quota agreements of recent years; for illustrations, see Röpke, *Die internationale Handelspolitik nach dem Kriege,* p. 49.

France and Spain had taken the lead in restricting the application of the clause.[47] On the other hand, the United States, which had adhered to the conditional form of the clause before the War, definitely swung over to the unconditional form in 1923.[48] The declaration of the World Economic Conference of 1927 in favor of the unconditional most-favored-nation clause apparently had some influence on the future course of treaty negotiations. It was followed, in August, 1927, by the signing of the Franco-German commercial treaty, which was based on a mutual grant of unconditional and unlimited most-favored-nation treatment.[49] Since it called for numerous reductions and consolidations of rates, which were made applicable to all most-favored-nation countries,[50] the treaty provided the basis for greatly enlarged imports into these two great markets of Continental Europe. It had a wider importance, however, in that it marked the return of France to acceptance of the unlimited form of the most-favored-nation clause and was followed by the conclusion throughout Europe of a network of treaties, embodying tariff reductions which were extended to all countries entitled to most-favored-nation treatment.

As a result, the strangling effects on international trade of the greatly increased post-War tariffs were to some extent mitigated, and it began to look as though commercial policy would henceforth follow pre-War lines. Certain differences were in evidence, however. The practice of including in treaties, as an exception to the most-favored-nation clause, a provision reserving the right to grant special favors to certain third countries, generally neighboring countries, was more common

[47] Chalmers, "The Post-War Drift in European Commercial Policy," p. 19.

[48] See W. S. Culbertson, *International Economic Policies* (New York, 1931), pp. 92–95.

[49] The operation of the most-favored-nation clause was subject to temporary restrictions and limitations but was to become complete as from December 15, 1928. See League of Nations, *Application of the Recommendations of the International Economic Conference,* Report for May 1927–May 1928, p. 10.

[50] Except in so far as the reductions applied to commodities France had excepted from most-favored-nation treatment in earlier post-War treaties.

than before the War.[51] A new feature of some of the treaties
was a provision specifically extending the application of the
most-favored-nation clause to import and export restrictions,
which had generally been regarded as outside the application
of the clause.[52] In certain cases, also, the applicability of the
clause to goods arriving indirectly via third countries was
recognized.[53]

The negotiation of commercial treaties by Latin American
countries in the post-War period was much less common than
among European countries. Most of the republics of Latin
America maintained, like the United States, single-column tariff
schedules, which did not allow for conventional duty reductions.[54] Furthermore, the greater part of their trade was carried on, not with each other, but with European nations. Thus,
most Latin American treaties concluded during this period
were with European countries and provided simply for mutual
most-favored-nation treatment.[55] A number of agreements,
however, were concluded between countries of the American
Continent, providing for simplification of customs procedure.[56]

The approach of the depression was not accompanied by
any marked cessation of activity in the negotiation of commercial treaties. The treaties concluded in 1929, however,
tended to provide for fewer tariff reductions than those of
earlier years.[57] This tendency was to become decidedly more
noticeable as the depression deepened and as permission to increase rates previously consolidated began to be sought.

---

[51] Cf. League of Nations, *Memorandum on European Bargaining Tariffs*, p. 9.
[52] Cf. H. Chalmers, "Current Trends in Foreign Commercial Policy,"
pp. 132–33.
[53] *Ibid.*, p. 133.
[54] See H. Chalmers, "Control of Foreign Trade," *American Year Book*, 1927,
p. 308.
[55] *Ibid.*
[56] Chalmers, "International Trade Control," *American Year Book*, 1929,
p. 320.
[57] *Ibid.*, p. 318.

CHAPTER III

The Depression and the Breakdown of the Gold Standard

1. *The Contraction of World Trade from 1929 On*

The causes of the world depression have been discussed at such length in the writings and speeches of economists and statesmen that a thorough analysis of the question here would be superfluous. It will be useful for our purpose, however, to review some of the more significant of the international developments which had a direct bearing on the severity of the contraction of world trade in the early years of the depression.[1]

A factor of first importance was the abnormal nature of post-War capital movements, both short-term and long-term. Capital was exported in large amounts from the United States and England, and in lesser amounts from other creditor countries, to Central Europe, Latin America, and some of the British Dominions. Table I affords some indication of the size and direction of these movements. Germany was by far the largest borrower, requiring foreign capital not only for internal reconstruction but also to help her pay reparations.

On the whole, long-term capital movements, though about as large as before the War, were considerably less steady.[2] Owing largely to the monetary instability of the post-War era, short-

---

[1] For more detailed analyses, consult Lionel Robbins, *The Great Depression* (New York, 1934); Sir Arthur Salter, *Recovery: The Second Effort* (New York, 1932); and the two League of Nations publications, *Course and Phases of the World Economic Depression,* and *World Economic Survey, 1931–32.*

[2] Cf. League of Nations, *Course and Phases of the World Economic Depression,* p. 35.

TABLE I

A. Exports of Capital from the Principal Creditor Countries [a]

(in millions of dollars)

	1923	1924	1925	1926	1927	1928	1929	1930
United Kingdom [b]	700	380	261	− 127 [c]	386	569	574	112
France [d]					503	237	− 20 [c]	− 252 [c]
Switzerland		23	43	28				
Belgium-Luxemburg and Congo [e]						69		
Sweden	1	10	20	33	65	18	71	26
Czechoslovakia			17	55	61	61	24	50
United States	− 104 [c]	590	642	173	580	1,099	206	196

B. Imports of Capital to the Main Debtor Countries [a]

(in millions of dollars)

	1924	1925	1926	1927	1928	1929	1930
Germany	421	857	151	1,072	1,007	553	148
Hungary	27		26	89	91	38	24
Poland	48	69	+ 72 [f]	82	124	67	
Yugoslavia			8	23	27	+ 13 [f]	
Argentina [g]	[h]	[h]	226	122	181	4	243
Australia [i]	220	110	170	257	193	166	187
Canada	107	277	173	51	164	+ 87 [f]	+ 160 [f]
India [j]	71	+ 69 [f]	178	120	67	36	
Japan	226	74	128	50	80	+ 9 [f]	+ 128 [f]
Dutch East Indies		+ 187 [f]	+ 45 [f]	+ 57 [f]	0	66	34
New Zealand [k]	22	33	67	+ 3 [f]	+ 5 [f]	53	49
South Africa	5	34	20	72	26	46	65

[a] Source: League of Nations, *World Economic Survey, 1931–32*, pp. 39–40. The figures are indirect estimates calculated on the basis of figures relating to merchandise, gold, and services. Reparation receipts and payments are included with merchandise and services. The reader should bear in mind the fact that estimates such as these may be subject to wide margins of error, especially in years characterized by currency instability, as were some of the years covered in this table.
[b] Excluding Government capital transactions.
[c] Imports of capital.
[d] Including the French overseas territories, except Indo-China. The amortization of inter-Allied debts is excluded.
[e] Excluding amortization of inter-Allied debts.
[f] Exports of capital.
[g] Economic years, ending September 30th.
[h] September, 1923, to September 31, 1925: 87.
[i] Economic years, ending June 30th.
[j] Economic years, beginning March 31st.
[k] The figures for 1927 and later years refer to economic years, beginning April 1st.

term capital movements formed a considerably more important proportion of the total capital flow than had been the case before the War. Many of the loans to Central and South-eastern European countries, in particular, were made on a short-term basis. Out of a total foreign indebtedness of 29.7 billion marks in July, 1931, Germany owed 13.1 billions on short term.[3] In addition, European banks and investors tended to hold, in London, New York, and other financial centers, large short-term balances which they shifted about from place to place in response to actual or anticipated changes in money market conditions or exchange rates.

When, toward the latter part of 1928, the flow of capital from creditor countries, especially the United States and France, began to dwindle, and the New York stock market became a center of attraction for investible funds from European financial centers, debtor countries found their access to foreign capital considerably impaired.[4] Interest payments on their foreign debts could, accordingly, no longer be met from the proceeds of fresh borrowings, and, since radical readjustments were required before adequate export surpluses could be developed, many of these countries were forced to export large amounts of gold.

Certain of the agricultural and raw material exporting countries were the first to be "hit" by this transfer problem. Unfortunately for them, the slowing up of the stream of capital imports occurred at a time when over-production of a number of basic commodities was beginning to constitute a serious problem. The factors, already discussed in connection with post-War tariff developments,[5] which were tending to create a condition of maladjustment in world agriculture were coming to a head, and, for a number of reasons, abnormally large stocks

[3] *Wirtschaft und Statistik*, XIV (1934), 134. These estimates are somewhat higher than those of the Wiggin Committee, owing to the fact that they are based on later and more authentic information.

[4] Cf. League of Nations, *World Economic Survey, 1931–32,* p. 42.

[5] Cf. pp. 19, 22 above.

of certain raw materials were beginning to accumulate. It was this combination of circumstances which forced Argentina and Australia off the gold standard and led to a decline in the Brazilian milreis late in 1929.[6]

Closely related to the abnormal capital movements and monetary instability of the post-War period were the large and irregular gold flows which characterized the nineteen-twenties. The widespread adoption of the gold exchange standard, the high tariff policy of the United States in spite of its newly acquired creditor position, and the stabilization of currencies at values which were inconsistent with internal price levels played especially important rôles in bringing about heavy gold movements. From 1928 on, a two-way drain of gold to France and the United States gradually led to a shortage of gold reserves in most other countries.[7]

Factors making for rigidity of industrial prices tended to be somewhat more prominent in the post-War economic world than they had been before the War. Such developments as the spread of large-scale industry and increasing prevalence of monopolistic competition, the more complete cartellization of industry in Europe, and the enhanced strength of trade unionism must be taken into account here. When agricultural prices began to fall sharply in the early stages of the depression, industrial prices remained relatively stable, so that the terms of trade turned sharply against the agricultural countries.

The pressure of debtor countries to increase their exports simultaneously enhanced the tendency for prices of basic foodstuffs and raw materials to fall. Creditor countries responded by raising tariffs rather than by opening their markets to the products of the distressed producers of basic commodities. By 1931, the gold value of world trade amounted to only 57.9 per

[6] See L. Smith, "Suspension of Gold Standard in Raw Material Exporting Countries," *American Economic Review*, XXIV (1934), 430–49. See also Table II, p. 40.

[7] League of Nations, *World Economic Survey, 1931–32*, pp. 190–92.

cent of its 1929 level.[8] Much of this decline was attributable
to the rapid fall in gold prices, which by 1931 had decreased to
67.5 per cent of their 1929 level.[9]

2. *Commercial Policy, 1929–31*

We have noted that the intensification of agricultural protection from 1928 on cut short the movement for lower trade
barriers which had got under way following the World Economic Conference of 1927. During the first two years of the
depression, tariffs were raised all over the world to protect home
industries, especially agriculture, from falling world prices, to
improve the trade balance, or to provide additional revenue.
The movement was cumulative, for, as tariffs were raised in
other countries, protectionists seized on a new line of argument,
to the effect that the closing of foreign markets to exports
necessitated the restriction of imports.

The resentment aroused abroad as a result of the passage of
the Hawley-Smoot Tariff Act by the United States Government in June, 1930, has now become a well-known matter of
historical record.[10] Protectionist forces in Congress paid little
heed to the argument that a great creditor nation must be
willing to accept imports if it expects to receive payment on its
debts. Rates were raised well above the high levels of 1922.
The new tariff act embodied increases on 250 agricultural items,
while various branches of industry obtained substantial additional protection.[11] Tariff revisions followed in Canada, Cuba,

[8] League of Nations, *Review of World Trade, 1935* (Geneva, 1936), p. 10.
Indices of gold value are of questionable significance when most of the countries of the world are off the gold standard, but the widespread abandonment
of gold did not start until September, 1931, so that the employment of an
index of gold value is reasonably legitimate up to the end of 1931.

[9] *Ibid.*

[10] For a full treatment of this subject, see J. M. Jones, Jr., *Tariff Retaliation:
Repercussions of the Hawley-Smoot Bill* (Philadelphia, 1934).

[11] See League of Nations, *Evolution of Economic and Commercial Policy
(Autonomous, Contractual and Collective) since the Tenth Assembly* (Geneva,
1931), p. 4.

Mexico, France, Italy, Spain, Australia, New Zealand, and other countries.[12] In the British Dominions, increased margins of imperial preference were granted in the new tariff schedules.[13]

Bilateral agreements based on the most-favored-nation clause continued to be negotiated during the early years of the depression, but they contained few tariff reductions and their duration rarely exceeded a year. A number of these agreements were supplementary to treaties previously concluded and provided for the "unbinding" of duties consolidated in the original treaties.[14]

The years 1930 and 1931 were marked by a succession of regional and multilateral conferences, mainly in Europe, for the purpose of arresting the upward tariff movement, but these attempts at collaboration accomplished little of a concrete nature. In September, 1929, the Assembly of the League of Nations had adopted a resolution calling for the convening of a conference to consider the conclusion of a tariff truce to stabilize customs duties for a period of two or three years, during which negotiations for the reduction of tariff barriers might be conducted. Under existing circumstances, however, the Preliminary Conference with a View to Concerted Economic Action, which met in Geneva early in 1930, was obliged to drop altogether the proposal for a tariff truce. The participating nations merely agreed upon a multilateral undertaking to prolong existing commercial agreements until April 1, 1931, and, *before raising tariffs,* to provide opportunity for negotiations with other countries whose interests might be affected.[15] In-

[12] *Ibid.*

[13] *Ibid.*

[14] *Ibid.* See also H. Chalmers, "Foreign Tariffs and Trade-Control Movements, 1930–1931," U. S. Department of Commerce, *Commerce Reports,* April 20, 1931, p. 133.

[15] See League of Nations, Preliminary Conference with a view to Concerted Economic Action, Feb. 17 to Mar. 24, 1930, *Commercial Convention (with Protocol); Protocol Regarding the Programme of Future Negotiations; Final Act, Mar. 24, 1930* (Geneva, 1930). The Protocol Regarding the Programme of Future Negotiations concerned tentative plans for cooperation in connection with certain pressing European problems, in particular the means of adjusting economic relations between industrial and agricultural countries.

nocuous as this Convention was, it was never put into force. Later conferences, called primarily for the purpose of deciding on a date for the coming into force of the Convention, failed to reach any agreement. Several of the more important European countries delayed their ratifications for months, and in the meantime the economic situation rapidly deteriorated.[16] In the intervals between conferences, nations were busily at work revising their tariffs upward.

Meanwhile, M. Briand's proposal for a "United States of Europe" was attracting considerable attention. Early European reactions to the scheme were favorable, but, as the discussions proceeded, various objections began to be raised to the economic and political implications of the plan.[17] The whole problem was referred in September, 1930, to a Commission of Enquiry for European Union, but the impracticability of the scheme, under existing circumstances, had become all too apparent before the Commission got very far with its investigations. The storm created by the Austro-German announcement, in March, 1931, of a proposed customs union between the two countries served to emphasize the political obstacles in the way of European economic *rapprochement* and did much to destroy all hopes for the conclusion of any sort of comprehensive European tariff union in the near future.

On the economic side, the complete failure of every attempt to secure multilateral action in the sphere of commercial policy in 1930 and 1931 resulted in large part from the unwillingness of nations to commit themselves to international obligations which would limit their freedom to combat the depression through autonomous measures. The problem of *reducing* tariffs

[16] See League of Nations, *Proceedings of the Second International Conference with a View to Concerted Economic Action (1st sess.)*, Geneva, November 17–28, 1930 (Geneva, 1931), and *Proceedings of the Second International Conference with a View to Concerted Economic Action (2d sess.)*, Geneva, Mar. 16–18, 1931 (Geneva, 1931).

[17] Cf. H. Chalmers, "Foreign Tariffs and Trade-Control Movements, 1930–31," p. 133.

through multilateral agreements, with all its attendant diffi-culties,[18] hardly entered into the picture at this time. All that was sought, at least for the immediate future, was some meas-ure of international cooperation to forestall the upward move-ment of duties—and even this failed.

The fact that attention was being centered on the necessity for inter-European collaboration, however, played a part in promoting attempts to secure regional agreements in various parts of Europe. On December 22, 1930, a convention was signed at Oslo by Norway, Sweden, Denmark, Holland, and Belgium, obligating the signatories to refrain from increasing their customs tariffs except upon due notice. In a protocol regarding future negotiations, the participants declared their willingness to support future international efforts to diminish obstacles to world trade.[19] A series of conferences of the agri-cultural countries of Eastern Europe was held at Warsaw (August, 1930), Bucharest (October, 1930), Belgrade (Novem-ber, 1930), and Warsaw (November, 1930) to explore the possibilities for relieving the depressed condition of agriculture, and especially of cereal-growing, in the countries represented.[20] The need for setting up national organizations to supervise the export of agricultural products was recognized, but the most important result of these meetings was a request for preferential treatment of European cereals imported into the industrial countries of Western Europe.[21] While some of the importing countries concerned adopted a sympathetic attitude toward this proposal, prompt action was impeded by the necessity of

[18] Cf. pp. 427–34 below.
[19] *Commerce Reports,* January 12, 1931, p. 120. It was further agreed to investigate possibilities for extending the application of the principle on which the above agreement was based to other matters affecting mutual economic relations.
[20] League of Nations, *World Economic Survey, 1931–32,* p. 284. Bulgaria, Estonia, Hungary, Lithuania, Poland, Rumania, Czechoslovakia, and Yugo-slavia participated.
[21] *Ibid.* Also League of Nations, *Evolution of Economic and Commercial Policy (Autonomous, Contractual and Collective) since the Tenth Assembly,* pp. 4–5.

proceeding cautiously with arrangements which involved the recognition of an exception to the most-favored-nation clause and which threatened to arouse the resentment of overseas agricultural countries.[22]

To sum up, then, commercial policy in these first two years of the depression was dictated by the fact that every country was seeking to "save its own skin"—to shelter itself from the impact of world deflation by keeping out foreign goods. Consequently, concessions to other countries, whether through bilateral or multilateral action, were deemed out of the question. In the desperate drive to stave off the effects of falling world prices, resort was had, in a few instances, even to quantitative measures of trade control, measures which were to become common after the financial crisis of 1931. Discussion of these latter devices, however, must be reserved for later chapters.

3. The Financial Crisis of 1931

The growing financial weakness of the borrowing countries in 1931 finally led to a virtual breakdown in the international monetary system during the course of that year. The warning signal was sounded by the collapse of the Credit-Anstalt in Vienna in May. Although this institution played an extremely important part in the credit structure of Austria and other Succession States,[23] the repercussions of its failure were out of

[22] For the later history of this proposal, see pp. 447–50 below. It was pointed out in the numerous discussions on this question that the quantities of cereals exported to Western Europe by the Eastern European nations were "insignificant in comparison with those arriving from overseas countries" and that, accordingly, overseas agricultural countries would not be materially injured. (Cf. *ibid.*, p. 5.) Among the factors which might be expected to induce the countries of Western Europe to consider seriously the granting of such special treatment were (*a*) the influence of the various contemporaneous proposals for a European tariff union, and (*b*) the prospect of securing in return concessions for their exports in markets which, for a number of the Western European countries (especially Germany), were of considerably greater importance than markets in overseas agricultural countries.

[23] At the time of its downfall, it was carrying on about 70 per cent of the

all proportion to the seriousness of the disaster. A wholesale withdrawal of short-term funds from other countries of Central Europe set in. Germany had already been exposed to a drain of her foreign short-term funds in the autumn of 1930, but now a renewed run began on the Reichsbank. The position of Germany was especially vulnerable, because it was widely suspected that with the fall in world prices it was becoming increasingly difficult for the country to meet its foreign obligations. The German banks had been using short-term credits for financing medium-term transactions,[24] and the continuing withdrawal of short-term funds was placing some of them in an embarrassing position. Neither the securing of a large international credit nor the announcement of the Hoover moratorium in June succeeded in forestalling the crisis.[25] Panic conditions developed during the first week of July, involving an outbreak of internal hoarding. The reserves of the Reichsbank were beginning to approach their legal minimum, and efforts to secure further international credits proved fruitless. The failure of the Danat bank (one of the largest of the German banks) on July 13th was followed by the declaration of a general banking holiday on July 14th. Exchange restrictions were introduced on July 13th.[26] When the banks finally reopened, the withdrawal of foreign deposits was prohibited.[27] Meanwhile, a series of international conferences led to the conclusion of a "standstill" agreement between Germany and her foreign creditors providing "for the continuation of credits to the German debtors up to the total then outstanding for a period of six months."[28] For the most part it was the sums owed to

banking business of Austria and had large outstanding loans in Hungary and Czechoslovakia. Cf. *The Economist*, CXII (1931), 1370.

[24] Cf. P. Einzig, *World Finance, 1914–1935* (New York, 1935), p. 219.

[25] The delay of France in ratifying the Hoover moratorium did much to destroy the beneficial psychological effect initially produced by the news of the proposal.

[26] See Table III, p. 54.

[27] C. R. S. Harris, *Germany's Foreign Indebtedness* (Oxford, 1935), p. 16.

[28] League of Nations, *World Economic Survey, 1931–32*, p. 76.

foreign banks and financial houses which were covered by the standstill agreements,[29] the total amount involved equalling 6.3 billion marks, or less than half the total of Germany's short-term liabilities.[30] Thus, even after the conclusion of these agreements, further withdrawals of short-term capital would doubtless have taken place in the absence of exchange restrictions.

The outbreak of the crisis in Germany simply rendered the problems of other Central European countries more acute. Not only did foreign creditors become panicky about the safety of their short-term loans, no matter to whom they had been made, but Germany herself had been forced to call on the outstanding credits which she held in other Central European countries. Moreover, for many countries of Central Europe, Germany's plight meant the paralyzing of one of their most important export markets. Hungary was especially vulnerable because of her large outstanding short-term foreign debts. She introduced exchange control on July 17, but this did not prevent a deepening of the crisis which eventually led to the declaration of a transfer moratorium at the end of the year. Numerous banks in Central and Eastern Europe were forced to close their doors.

4. *The Breakdown of the Gold Standard*

By this time banks all over the world were engaged in a scramble for liquidity, which was destined to have far-reaching results. The next victim was England, which was subjected to a persistent drain of gold throughout the summer of 1931. The publication of the Macmillan Report,[31] which revealed the extent of London's short-term indebtedness and indicated that the pound had been over-valued since 1925, undoubtedly came

---

[29] Harris, *op. cit.*, p. 19.
[30] Cf. p. 29 above.
[31] Committee on Finance and Industry, *Report*, Cmd. 3897 (London, 1931).

at an unfortunate time, coinciding as it did with the crisis in
Germany. Of even greater influence, perhaps, was the appearance of the May Report, which demonstrated the weakness
of Britain's budgetary position.[32] Furthermore, the fact that
London was known to be carrying large frozen assets in
Central Europe added to the general feeling of uncertainty
about the future of the pound. Sizable credits placed at the
disposal of the Bank of England by the Bank of France and
the Federal Reserve System, and also by private interests, did
not suffice to stop the drain of gold.[33] Mr. MacDonald's
National Government, formed at the end of August, was finally
forced to announce the suspension of the gold standard on
September 20, after a sharp acceleration in the rate of gold
withdrawals.[34]

The effect of this action on the rest of the world can best be
appreciated if one stops to consider not only the importance
of Great Britain as a trading country but the fact that a very
large part of the world's trade was financed through London.
Furthermore, countries which adhered to the gold exchange
standard tended to carry large balances in London. Thus we
find that the countries which were most tempted to follow England off gold were those (like Japan) whose export trade was
highly competitive with that of Great Britain and would be
adversely affected by a depreciated pound, those (like Denmark) which were especially dependent on the British import
market, and those which, for one reason or another, held large
balances in London or carried on their trade in terms of sterling.
Table II (p. 40) indicates the dates at which countries have
suspended the gold standard since 1929. Within the British
Empire, Australia was already off gold, New Zealand's currency had depreciated, the Indian rupee was pegged to sterling
and automatically followed the pound, Canada succumbed in

[32] Committee on National Expenditure, *Report*, Cmd. 3920 (London, 1931).
[33] League of Nations, *World Economic Survey, 1931–32*, p. 77.
[34] *The Economist*, "A Diary of the Crisis," CXIII (1931), 554–55.

October, while South Africa continued to adhere to the gold standard until the end of 1932. The three Scandinavian countries were quick to announce suspension because of their close financial and economic ties with Great Britain. Many of the South American countries were forced off gold in the autumn of 1931 or the early months of 1932 for similar reasons.[35] The coincidence of the outbreak of the Manchurian crisis with Britain's departure from gold rendered reimposition of the gold embargo by Japan in December doubly certain.[36]

Thus, by the end of 1931, the international currency situation had become extremely unstable. Each time another country departed from the gold standard and confidence was shaken anew, there was a tendency for gold prices to decline still more, and the position of countries trying to adhere to the gold standard grew more precarious. One by one, new recruits swelled the ranks of countries with depreciated or devaluated currencies. When the United States finally left the gold standard in April, 1933,[37] it began to look as if it would be merely a matter of time before pre-depression par values became altogether a thing of the past. The experience of France, the most important of the gold *bloc* countries, perhaps best illustrates the inevitability of the final outcome. The *Banque de France* was in an extremely strong position in 1931, and its position grew stronger after the crisis of that year. The Paris money market was flooded with capital seeking refuge from insecurity elsewhere. But, economically, the position of France deterio-

[35] Ninety per cent of the foreign exchange business of Bolivia, for example, was carried on in terms of sterling. The depreciation of the pound so disrupted dealings in foreign exchange in that country that, for a short period following England's departure from the gold standard, no exchange was sold by the banks. The country suspended the gold standard on September 25th. Cf. United States Bureau of Foreign and Domestic Commerce, *Foreign Financial News: Special Circular*, No. 388 (February 20, 1933), pp. 7–8.

[36] The embargo imposed during the War had not been removed until the end of 1929. Japan experienced a serious flight of domestic capital during the autumn of 1931.

[37] The question as to whether or not the United States was *forced* off the gold standard is one which is still being debated.

TABLE II

Dates of Measures Affecting Exchange Rates, 1929–38, Inclusive [a]

Year and Country	Official Suspension of Gold Standard (Dates in Parentheses Refer to Introduction of New Gold Parity)	Depreciation or Devaluation in Relation to Gold
1929		
Uruguay	December	April
Argentina	December 17	November
Paraguay	c	November
Brazil		December
Australia	December 17	
1930		
Australia		March
Bolivia		March
New Zealand		April
Venezuela		September
1931		
Mexico	July 25	
United Kingdom	September 21	August
British India	September 21	September
British Malaya	September 21	September
Egypt	September 21	September
New Zealand	September 21	September
Palestine	September 21	
Colombia	September 25	September
Bolivia	September 25	
1931 (cont.)		
Irish Free State	September 26	September
Norway	September 28	September
Sweden	September 29	September
Denmark	September 29	September
Austria		September
El Salvador	October 9	
Finland	October 12	October
Canada	October 19	October
Nicaragua	November 13	September
Japan	December 13	October
Portugal	December 31	October
1932		
Colombia		January
Nicaragua		January
Ecuador	February 8	June
Chile	April 20	April
Greece	April 26	April
Siam	May 11	June
Peru	May 14	May
Yugoslavia		July
South Africa	December 28	

Dates of departure from the gold standard and of currency changes[a]

1933–1935

Country	Date	Month
1933		
South Africa		January
Austria	April 5	April
United States	April 20	April
	(January 31, 1934)[b]	
Guatemala	[c]	April
Honduras		April
Panama		June
Philippines		April
Estonia	June 28	
Cuba	November 21	
	(May 22, 1934)[b]	
1934		
Czechoslovakia	(February 17)	February
Italy		March
Austria		April
1935		
Belgium	March 30	March
	(March 31, 1936)	
Luxemburg	(April 1)	March
Danzig	(May 2)	May
Rumania		July

1936–1938

Country	Date	Month
1936		
U.S.S.R.	[c]	April
France	September 27	September
Netherlands	September 27	September
Netherlands Indies	(September 27)[b]	September
Switzerland	September 28[b]	September
Latvia	(October 8)[b]	September
Italy	(October 9)[b]	October
Czechoslovakia		October
1937		
France		June
1938		
France		May
Sterling area currencies[d]		
China[d]		
Argentina[d]		
Bolivia[d]		
Peru[d]		
Uruguay[d]		

[a] This table is compiled primarily from that published by the League of Nations in *Money and Banking, 1937–38*, Vol. I, *Monetary Review* (Geneva, 1938), p. 107. It has been brought up to date (to Jan. 1, 1939) from other sources: League of Nations, *World Economic Survey, 1937–38* (Geneva, 1938), p. 153, and *World Economic Survey, 1938–39* (Geneva, 1939), pp. 182–84.
[b] Provisional parity.
[c] Brazil, Honduras, and the U.S.S.R. have not adhered to a free gold standard since the War. This holds true, also, for Iran, Spain, and Turkey, which do not appear in the Table.
[d] Depreciation during course of year. In Chile, the peso declined on the free market, but not on the official market, for the year as a whole.

rated more and more as time went on. Her power to withstand the competition of a widening circle of depreciated currency countries grew progressively weaker, until finally her monetary position itself was threatened by a loss of confidence.[38] A prolonged gold drain in 1935, and especially in 1936, led to the announcement on September 25, 1936, of the Government's decision to devalue the franc on the following day. The upper and lower limits of devaluation were, shortly thereafter, fixed at 25.19 per cent and 34.35 per cent respectively below the old parity.[39] Switzerland and the Netherlands, which had experienced heavy gold withdrawals in 1935, followed France, the former by devaluing its currency and the latter by suspending specie payments and placing an embargo on gold exports.[40] Of the remaining gold *bloc* countries, Belgium had devalued its currency in March, 1935, while Italy and Poland had adopted exchange control in May, 1934, and April, 1936, respectively.[41] On October 5, 1936, following the depreciation of the French, Swiss, and Dutch currencies, the gold value of the Italian lira was provisionally lowered to 59.06 per cent of its 1927 parity.[42]

The devaluation of the franc was effected as part of the so-called Tripartite Monetary Agreement of September 25, 1936, an informal arrangement calling for cooperation in currency matters among the British, French, and American Governments. Great Britain and the United States reaffirmed their intention to continue to pursue policies aimed at maintaining "the greatest possible equilibrium in the system of international exchange," while all three Governments declared their intention

[38] Budgetary difficulties played their part, as well.

[39] See League of Nations, *Money and Banking, 1936–37*, Vol. I, *Monetary Review* (Geneva, 1937), p. 28.

[40] *Ibid.*, pp. 27–29. In the Swiss case, as in the French, upper and lower limits to the devaluation were fixed.

[41] *Ibid.*, pp. 26–27.

[42] *Ibid.*, p. 29n. Certain other currency readjustments took place in exchange-control countries at the same time. Latvia officially abandoned the gold standard and reëstablished parity with the pound sterling on September 28, while Czechoslovakia devalued its currency for a second time on October 9. (*Ibid.*) See Table I.

"to continue to use the appropriate available resources so as to avoid as far as possible any disturbance of the basis of international exchanges resulting from the proposed readjustment" of the franc.[43] The application of the agreement was soon broadened by the adherence of the Belgian, Swiss, and Dutch Governments.[44] It remained in effect at the outbreak of war in 1939, in spite of the further devaluations of the French franc which occurred in 1937 and 1938 and the later weakness of the pound sterling.[45]

There were a few countries which maintained their currencies nominally at par up to September, 1939, by imposing drastic exchange restrictions. Germany was by far the most important of these. Her reasons for pursuing this course of action will be discussed in the next chapter. As we shall see, however, much of Germany's trade came to be conducted on the basis of depreciated exchange rates.

Before leaving the subject of currency adjustments, it should be noted that, in spite of successive realignments of various important currencies, there was a substantial degree of exchange stability *within* certain currency *blocs* throughout most of the period between 1931 and 1939. First and foremost in importance among these currency *blocs* was the so-called "sterling area," which accounted for more than a third of the total value of world trade in 1936.[46] Developing informally after Britain's departure from gold, the sterling area gradually

[43] See texts of the statements announcing the agreement issued to the press by the French Government and the British and American Treasuries, as given in Bank for International Settlements, *Seventh Annual Report* (Basle, 1937), Annex VII. A few weeks later, statements were issued announcing the conclusion of certain technical arrangements for the purchase and sale of gold through stabilization funds of the three countries. See *New York Times*, October 13, 1936.

[44] See League of Nations, *World Economic Survey, 1936–37* (Geneva, 1937), pp. 7–8.

[45] For brief summaries of French currency developments since the autumn of 1936, see League of Nations, *World Economic Survey, 1937–38*, pp. 152–156, and *Money and Banking, 1937–38*, Vol. I, pp. 27–30.

[46] *Ibid.*, p. 27.

came to include, in addition to the United Kingdom, a group of about fifteen countries whose currencies were linked more or less firmly with sterling. This group was actually rather loosely defined, but it may be said to have consisted (*a*) of certain British Dominions and colonies (not including Canada), whose currencies were definitely pegged to sterling "through the operation of a sterling exchange standard," [47] and (*b*) of a number of independent countries, including the four Scandinavian countries, Egypt, Estonia, Latvia, Portugal, and Siam, whose currencies were so managed as to be kept stable in terms of sterling.[48] In addition, there was a third category of countries, sometimes grouped with the sterling *bloc* and sometimes not, in which official exchange rates exhibited a considerable degree of stability in terms of sterling, while open-market rates deviated more or less from official rates. In this latter group might be included Argentina, certain other South American countries, and Japan.[49]

Of less importance was the dollar *bloc,* including, in addition to the United States, the Philippines, Cuba, and certain Central American countries, which followed the United States off gold in 1933. Finally, mention should be made of the gold *bloc,* which is now of little more than historical interest.

In the summer of 1937, apart from the weakness of the

---

[47] League of Nations, *World Economic Survey, 1934–35* (Geneva, 1935), p. 193.

[48] Cf. *ibid.* and League of Nations, *Money and Banking, 1937–38*, Vol. I, p. 23. Most of the countries in the sterling area followed Britain off gold in the autumn of 1931.

[49] Richardson, in *British Economic Foreign Policy*, p. 55, mentions Argentina and "other South American countries" as belonging to the sterling area. On multiple exchange rates in Latin America, see pp. 102–11 below. In Japan, the Yokohama Specie Bank T. T. selling rate on London did not deviate from 1s. 2d. from November, 1934, on, whereas the Tokyo open market rate fluctuated above and below this point to some extent up to August, 1937, after which time it was fixed at 1s. 2d. See *Oriental Economist,* III (1936), 36 and V (1938), 43, 764. The Yokohama Specie Bank carries out the official policy of the Japanese Government in exchange matters.

franc, it could be said that a substantial degree of general exchange stability had been achieved. Most currencies had been relatively stable since the beginning of 1934. In the middle of 1937, some weakness began to develop in the currencies of South American and of other raw material producing countries, in consequence of the decline in prices of primary products.[50] Later on, the British pound showed some tendency to decline. The outbreak of war in 1939 naturally proved a disturbing factor and led a number of countries to shift their allegiance from the sterling *bloc* to the dollar *bloc*.

We have emphasized in this chapter only those phases of the great depression which have had the most direct bearing on commercial policy, but enough has been said to indicate that, from 1929 on, the world passed through a period of extreme instability. No country escaped unscathed, and there resulted a growing feeling that international economic interdependence breeds insecurity. Each nation therefore fell back on its own resources and pursued a policy of fostering internal recovery first and foremost. Along with this spirit of isolationism in the economic sphere, and closely tied up with it, went a distressing move in the direction of nationalism in the political sphere. In such an atmosphere, the erection of more and more restrictive trade barriers was a natural and inevitable development.

The attempts at control of foreign trade in recent years have been, broadly speaking, of two main types: those aimed directly at controlling the *making of payments* between countries and those affecting in the first instance the *movements of individual commodities* between countries. The former category includes exchange control and all the various kinds of clearing or payment agreements; the latter, tariffs, quotas, monopolies, prohibitions, and the like. The two types of control overlap

[50] See League of Nations, *World Economic Survey, 1937–38,* pp. 151 ff.

at every stage, however, thus adding to the complications of the subject. We shall discuss first, in the chapters immediately following, the measures affecting payments, and thereafter we shall take up, in Part III, the measures affecting commodity movements. Finally, in the concluding chapters we shall review the whole question of international commercial bargaining.

PART II

THE CONTROL OF INTERNATIONAL PAYMENTS

CHAPTER IV

EXCHANGE CONTROL: INTRODUCTION AND TECHNIQUE

1. *Nature of Exchange Control*

Exchange control in its broadest sense might be said to include all attempts at regulation of the exchange value of a currency. In this sense, the discount policy of the central bank might, for example, be regarded as a mild form of exchange control, since it would have an influence on exchange rates. Active official intervention in the foreign exchange market, say, through a stabilization fund, is a more positive form of control. Finally, attempts to influence the demand or supply of foreign exchange through restricting the range of activity of individuals engaged in purchasing or selling exchange constitute the most direct form of exchange control. The narrower and more common interpretation of the term confines it to this last and most positive form.[1] It would perhaps be less confusing to make use of the frequently employed term "exchange restrictions" in describing this form of control, were it not for the fact that this expression brings to mind

---

[1] Some writers include regulation through a stabilization fund as one form of exchange control proper. See B. Ohlin, "Mechanisms and Objectives of Exchange Control," *American Economic Review*, XXVII, Supplement (March, 1937), 141, and P. T. Ellsworth, *International Economics* (New York, 1938), p. 391. The more usual practice, however, is the one which I have adopted. Cf. Haberler, *The Theory of International Trade*, p. 84, and League of Nations, *Report on Exchange Control* (Geneva, 1938), p. 8. In any event, since the subject of intervention through stabilization funds belongs properly to the field of monetary policy rather than to that of commercial policy, I propose to confine my attention, for purposes of this study, to restrictions on dealings in foreign exchange.

a loose set of regulations, rather than the well rounded "system" of control which frequently prevails. Exchange control, then, as ordinarily understood, means limiting the right of individuals to deal freely in the foreign exchange market, and it is in this sense that we shall use the term.

Wherever currency "management" exists *in any form* (and strictly speaking, we must include here all cases of metallic standards with fixed parities), the rate of exchange tends to be "artificial," in the sense that it does not conform to the rate which would prevail in the case of an absolutely free inconvertible paper currency. Intervention through a stabilization fund might conceivably be aimed at maintaining in effect either an artificially high rate or an artificially low rate;[2] or, on the other hand, the managers of the fund might confine their operations to the (technically very difficult) task of "ironing out" abnormal fluctuations while seeing to it that the rate tended, on the whole, to conform to that which would result from the normal operation of market forces. Exchange restrictions, however, have almost invariably been introduced in order to prevent the value of the national currency in the exchange markets from falling, that is, to maintain its value at an artificially high level. The problems involved are analogous to those which arise in connection with any sort of governmental price-fixing.

If the object of exchange control is to prevent the value of the currency from falling,[3] the demand for foreign exchange must be restricted, and measures must be taken to keep the

---

[2] It is doubtful if an artificial rate could be successfully maintained by this means for a long period, however.

[3] In order that no confusion may arise over terminology, it should be noted here that, if the rate of exchange is expressed (as it usually is in practice) as the number of units of domestic currency which must be given for one unit of foreign currency, then an artificially high value for the national currency means an artificially low rate of exchange. In other words, the German reichsmark is being maintained at an artificially high value in terms of the pound sterling if the rate is fixed at 12 RM to the pound when ordinary market forces would result in a much higher rate, say 16 RM to the pound.

supply of exchange from falling off. A demand for foreign exchange will arise from those wishing to import merchandise, to meet expenses for shipping or other services obtained abroad, or to transfer capital in any form to foreign countries. The supply of foreign exchange will arise from exports of merchandise, services furnished to foreigners, or imports of foreign capital. Thus, a thoroughgoing system of exchange control will have to take account of all items on both sides of the balance of payments. This is usually achieved in practice by setting up a monopoly of foreign exchange dealings in the hands of some governmental agency, such as the central bank. Exporters and all others acquiring balances abroad must sell these balances at the official rate to the control authority, which is charged with the task of allocating this supply of foreign exchange to those wishing to purchase it, according to certain rules of precedence laid down in advance. The fact that the value of the national currency is being maintained at an artificially high level means that the supply of foreign exchange coming into the hands of the government will not be adequate to take care of the total demand—hence the need for rules of precedence or rationing. The task of the authorities will be rendered especially difficult by the fact that it is virtually impossible, under such circumstances, to prevent the development of a "black bourse" (illicit exchange market), through which exporters will be glad to sell their exchange at a premium (over and above the official buying rate) to anyone wishing to transfer money abroad illegally (without the permission of the authorities).

Exchange control is most frequently introduced to meet an emergency situation, when, for one reason or another, abnormal pressure on the exchange market is threatening to drive the country off the gold standard and/or cause a sudden decline in the value of the currency. The abnormal pressure may result from a variety of causes—political (war or internal political instability), economic (severe decline in exports, unaccompanied by corresponding contraction of imports), or financial (cessation of foreign loans, monetary panic, etc.) in nature. In practice, several of these factors may appear in combination, and eventually, a flight of foreign and domestic capital,[4] accompanied by a speculative bear raid on the national currency, is likely to develop. If the pressure on the exchanges is purely temporary in nature, the resort to exchange control may help to tide over a difficult situation. If, however, the country is suffering from a *chronically passive balance of payments on income account* [5] at current exchange rates, the attempt to maintain the currency at an artificially high value through exchange restrictions may prove exceedingly difficult to enforce and will tend to put off the achievement of a fundamental adjustment through price deflation or devaluation of the currency. We shall have more to say about this after we have examined the recent experience with exchange control.

2. *The Spread of Exchange Control from 1931 On*

Exchange control is not a new device. Its counterpart can be found in sixteenth and early seventeenth century England, when all payments to or from foreign countries "passed through the hands of the 'King's Exchanger,' who had a legal monopoly in the transaction of foreign business." [6] It was widely adopted during the World War, and a number of countries, as we have seen, were forced to retain exchange restrictions for a con-

---

[4] Unlike normal foreign investments, a flight of capital may involve a flow of funds from a country with relatively high interest rates to one with extremely low interest rates, since the impelling motive is a search for security. Cf. Haberler, *The Theory of International Trade*, p. 85. Where exchange speculation is involved, it is the anticipation of a change in exchange ratios, not a search for higher profits abroad, that leads to purchases of foreign currencies.

[5] Cf. *ibid.*, for the use of this phrase by Haberler. Such a situation exists when prices are relatively high in relation to prices in other countries. It may be associated with a persistent flight of capital in anticipation of eventual devaluation of the currency.

[6] *Ibid.*, p. 25.

siderable period after the War.[7] By 1930, however, nearly every country had returned to a free gold standard or to some form of a gold exchange standard.

The years from 1931 on witnessed a revival of exchange control on an unprecedented scale. Few indeed were the countries which succeeded in passing through the "great" depression without resort to *some* exchange restrictions, if only for a short period, and in many countries severe and far-reaching systems of control were adopted. The technique of restriction was refined and elaborated, and a complicated mass of administrative regulations grew up. The measures of the World War period appear simple by comparison. In addition, exchange control has, for a number of countries, become a convenient weapon of commercial policy, often discriminatory in nature.

The origins of this epidemic of exchange restrictions must be sought in the situation which grew out of the financial crisis of 1931. A glance at Table III (p. 54) reveals the fact that the epidemic reached its height in the last six months of that year. It will be convenient for our purposes to distinguish between two groups of countries: (1) those which, though unable to maintain a free gold standard, attempted to protect the par values of their currencies by introducing exchange restrictions, and (2) those with depreciated paper currencies.

a. Countries which maintained parity and introduced exchange restrictions. This group is made up almost entirely of debtor countries in Central and Southeastern Europe. Most of them sooner or later resorted to partial or total devaluation in some form, but all tried to forestall such action in 1931 or 1932 by introducing exchange restrictions. Those, like Germany and Hungary, which had incurred short-term foreign debts to any appreciable extent, were caught in the maelstrom of the financial panic of 1931. Those whose exports were primarily agricultural had, by the middle of 1931, experienced an especially severe decline in the value of their exports but

[7] Cf. pp. 12–13 above.

TABLE III

RECENT EXCHANGE CONTROL MEASURES, DATES OF INTRODUCTION AND SUPPRESSION, TO JAN. 1, 1939[a]

Year and Country	Exchange Control Introduction	Exchange Control Suppression
1918		
Bulgaria	[b]	
1922		
Portugal	October 21	October 18, 1937
1930		
Iran	February 25	
Turkey	February 26	May 30, 1933 [c]
1931		
Brazil	May 18	
Spain	May 18 [e]	
Germany	July 13	
Hungary	July 17	
Chile	July 30	
Uruguay	September 7	
United Kingdom	September 22 [d]	March 2, 1932
Colombia	September 25	
Greece	September 28	
Czechoslovakia	October 2 [f]	
Iceland	October 2	
Bolivia	October 3	

Year and Country	Exchange Control Introduction	Exchange Control Suppression
1931 (cont.)		
Yugoslavia	October 7	
Latvia	October 8	
Austria	October 9 [f]	
Finland	October 5 [d]	December 31, 1931
Argentina	October 13	
Norway	October 17 [d]	
Nicaragua	November 13	
Denmark	November 18	
Estonia	November 18	
1932		
New Zealand	January 1 [d]	
Costa Rica	January 16	
Ecuador	May 2	June, 1932 [e]
Rumania	May 18	
Japan	July 1	October 7, 1935 [e]
Paraguay	August	
1933		
U. S. A.	March 6	November 12, 1934
Mexico	May 3 [d]	October, 1933
El Salvador	August	

54

	1934		
Honduras	March 27		
Italy	May 26 ᵍ	July 13, 1934	
Cuba	June 2		
China	September 9	November 23, 1935ᶜ	
	1935		
Belgium	March 18	April 26, 1935	
Luxemburg	March 18	April 26, 1935	
Danzig	June 12		
Lithuania	October 1		
Hong-Kong	November 9		
	1936		
Iran		March 1	July 31, 1937
Poland		April 26	
Ecuador		July 30	
Venezuela		December 12	
	1938		
China		March 14	
Afghanistan		June 16	
New Zealand		December	

ᵃ Compiled primarily from table published by League of Nations in *Money and Banking, 1937–38*, Vol. I, p. 107. Dates of introduction of mild or unofficial regulations, not included in the League list, have been included here. They are based mostly on data taken from Bank for International Settlements, *Foreign Exchange Regulations in the Different Countries* (Basle, 1931–1938), and the *Times*, London. Mild restrictions of an extremely informal nature have also been introduced, usually for short periods, by Australia, Canada, France, the Netherlands, South Africa, Sweden, and Switzerland, though these countries have not been included in our list. The table has been brought up to date on the basis of information published by *The Economist* and U. S. Bureau of Foreign and Domestic Commerce, *Foreign Financial News*.

ᵇ Exchange restrictions in force in Bulgaria and Portugal from 1931 on had been introduced in 1918 and 1922, respectively.

ᶜ Restrictions later reimposed, as indicated in table.

ᵈ Mild restrictions, in some cases of an unofficial or semi-official nature.

ᵉ Exchange control for Nationalist Spain introduced by decree of military authorities at Seville, September 28, 1936. New regulations issued by Burgos Government, November 24, 1936.

ᶠ Austria and the Sudeten area in Czechoslovakia were made subject to German exchange regulations after their absorption into the Reich.

ᵍ Mild restrictions from September 29, 1931.

had had difficulty in effecting a corresponding restriction of imports. All, whether primarily agricultural or primarily industrial, were facing serious transfer problems. The cessation of the stream of capital imports meant that the service on foreign debts could be met only by developing adequate export surpluses, since gold reserves were already low.[8] This was difficult to accomplish in the face of falling world prices, when debts had been incurred on the basis of the higher values ruling in the nineteen-twenties. As the crisis spread from country to country, moreover, banks in Central and Southeastern Europe began to experience a two-way drain on their resources, some depositors preferring to withdraw their money for transfer abroad, others for internal hoarding.

Under such circumstances, these countries had two alternatives to the introduction of exchange restrictions—drastic price deflation or abandonment of any attempt to maintain the par values of their currencies. But deflation of export prices, especially in agricultural countries, had already gone far and had caused much suffering among producers with rigid cost structures. Statesmen were becoming daily more impressed with the difficulties of attempting to narrow the gap between "sticky" internal prices and falling export prices. In Germany political opposition to the Government's deflationary policy was even at this stage beginning to assume significant proportions. Moreover, in view of the facts that the world price level was continuing to fall and that creditor countries were raising tariffs

[8] Strictly speaking, what these countries required was an active balance of payments on income account (except for interest and dividend payments). A number of the countries of Central and Eastern Europe receive some net income from tourist expenditures and most of them receive substantial sums in the form of emigrants' remittances. The majority ordinarily have active service balances (leaving interest and dividend payments out of account), though the sums have recently been of a considerably smaller order of magnitude than in the nineteen-twenties. See League of Nations, *Balances of Payments, 1936* (Geneva, 1937). It should be noted, here, that Czechoslovakia, on balance a creditor country in 1931, constitutes an exception to some of the statements in the text. As we shall see, however (p. 58 n. below), her position was especially difficult because she was surrounded by exchange-control countries.

and introducing other obstacles to imports, the outlook for "improving" trade balances through deflation was not promising.[9] Finally, failure to stop the withdrawal of capital might have caused such severe liquidation in the debtor countries that the payment of debts would have been rendered impossible for some time to come.[10] In fact, this was already beginning to happen.

Currency depreciation, on the other hand, was looked upon with horror in most of these countries as a result of their disastrous post-War experiences. In addition, for debtor countries such as these, the realization that a reduction in the value of their currencies would increase the burden of their foreign debts played some part in decisions to cling to parity. In the German case, the argument was also used that any advantage which could be secured for exports through depreciation would be partially offset by the necessity of paying higher prices for the large quantities of imported raw materials going into the manufacture of many important German exports.[11]

The fact that the real epidemic of exchange control in Central and Eastern Europe did not break out until after England's

[9] There is no need here to go into the well-known theoretical controversy over the transfer problem, which has its roots in nineteenth-century controversies over monetary policy and was revived by Keynes and Ohlin in a series of articles in the *Economic Journal*, XXXIX (1929). For references to the literature on the subject, see Haberler, *The Theory of International Trade*, p. 67 n. See also J. Viner, *Studies in the Theory of International Trade* (New York and London, 1937), Chs. VI and VII. It is sufficient to point out, in the first place, that it is impossible to take into account, in any theoretical analysis, all of the factors which must be considered in order to determine whether, in a concrete case, transfer is possible. (Cf. Haberler, *The Theory of International Trade*, p. 78.) This holds particularly for the analysis of a severe crisis. Secondly, whether we accept the Keynes view or the Ohlin view of the transfer mechanism, debtor countries cannot increase exports if creditor countries are unwilling to permit expansion of their imports.

[10] Cf. T. Balogh, "Some Theoretical Aspects of the Central European Credit and Transfer Crisis," *International Affairs: Journal of the Royal Institute of International Affairs*, XI (1932), 346–63.

[11] Cf. F. Huhle, "Das Clearingswesen im Aussenhandel vom deutschen Standpunkt aus," *Jahrbücher für Nationalökonomie und Statistik*, CXLVI (1937), 172.

departure from the gold standard points to several elements in the situation which have not yet been mentioned. In the first place, the competitive power of countries which tried to maintain the gold standard was greatly weakened by the wholesale depreciation of currencies which took place in the autumn of 1931.[12] Secondly, and perhaps more important, markets in neighboring countries were constantly being further restricted by new exchange regulations. Under this condition, exports resulted to a large extent in an accumulation of frozen credits abroad.[13] It is difficult to see how countries which were not in a strong financial position could respond to this situation, *except* by (*a*) introducing exchange restrictions or (*b*) allowing their own currencies to depreciate. Unfortunately, there emerged in Central Europe an exchange control "war," in which a new series of restrictions in one country was followed by retaliations elsewhere.[14]

b. Countries with depreciated currencies. The course pursued by these countries depended (1) on their financial strength, and (2) on their financial relations with Great Britain. Moderate exchange restrictions were introduced by

[12] European agricultural countries, of course, had already suffered as a result of the depreciation of the currencies of Australia, New Zealand, and various Latin American republics. It may be well, at this stage, to refer once more to a theoretical point, mentioned in an earlier connection (p. 17 n. above), to the effect that, once prices in depreciated-currency countries have risen in proportion to the depreciation of the currency, the exports of such countries no longer enjoy the advantage of an "exchange bounty." Actually, available evidence suggests that the countries which followed England off gold enjoyed an exchange advantage for a considerable period, as a result of a failure of their export prices to rise significantly. See S. E. Harris, *Exchange Depreciation* (Cambridge, Mass., 1936), *passim*.

[13] Cf. pp. 75–76 below. Czechoslovakia, in particular, was affected by this situation. Cf. A. Basch, "Memorandum on Devaluation Experience in Czechoslovakia" in Joint Committee of the Carnegie Endowment and International Chamber of Commerce, *The Improvement of Commercial Relations between Nations* and *The Problem of Monetary Stabilization* (Paris, 1936), pp. 223–24. Austrians complained that available supplies of exchange were being purchased by foreigners who suffered from exchange restrictions in their own countries. This, of course, would be possible only in so far as such foreigners held, or were in a position to acquire, balances in Austria.

[14] Cf. *The Economist*, CXIV (1932), 412.

England for a short period after she left gold, but the strength of the pound made possible their abandonment within six months. The British Dominions and the Scandinavian countries (except Denmark) got along with very mild and, in some cases, temporary restrictions, largely because their practice of maintaining sizable balances in London made it possible for them to peg their currencies to sterling at an early date.[15]

The Latin American countries which preceded or followed Britain off gold, however, were in a far more vulnerable position. Their supplies of gold and foreign exchange were, at this stage, inadequate for any attempt to set up stabilization funds or link their currencies to sterling. Yet they were unwilling to allow their exchanges to fluctuate freely, especially as it was desirable to limit the extent of depreciation in order not to increase the burden of their foreign debts more than was necessary. There was, in addition, the danger of a flight of capital, especially for those countries which were suffering from budgetary difficulties. The significant point of distinction between these countries and the debtor nations of Central and Southeastern Europe was that the former had made no effort to keep their official exchange rates at par.[16] On the contrary, the official rates expressed recognition of substantial degrees of depreciation.[17]

Finally, a word should be included about the countries which managed to escape the exchange control epidemic in 1931 and

[15] Denmark pegged its currency to sterling, but not without the help of relatively severe exchange restrictions. Argentina became a member of the sterling group early in 1934, after having gone through a period of rigid exchange control. Canada's currency has, on the whole, followed the dollar rather than the pound, but Canada's relations with the New York money market are analogous to the relations of the other Dominions with the London money market.

[16] It should be noted, further, that the Latin American republics were not burdened with short-term debts to any appreciable extent, as were many of the European debtor countries.

[17] Cf. pp. 102–11 below. The contagious nature of the exchange control epidemic of the latter half of 1931 is perhaps best illustrated by the case of Argentina, which abandoned the gold standard in December, 1929, but found it unnecessary to introduce exchange restrictions until October, 1931.

1932. As might be expected, these were mostly creditor countries or countries with relatively strong gold reserves. As we have seen in Chapter III, however, all these countries were forced eventually to resort to exchange restrictions or devaluation, or both.[18]

3. *The Technique of Exchange Control*

a. Mild restrictions. There is a vast difference between the relatively mild exchange restrictions which have been enforced, sometimes for brief periods, in certain countries, and the thoroughgoing systems of exchange control which have gradually been evolved elsewhere. Where mild restrictions have been adopted, they have nearly always been introduced immediately preceding or following suspension of the gold standard. For the most part, the countries which have managed to get along with these moderate restrictions have been creditor countries in a relatively strong financial position or countries whose close financial and economic ties with Great Britain made it possible for them to become members of the sterling area at a relatively early date. The object of mild restrictions has been to prevent extreme fluctuations in the exchanges by discouraging speculation and forestalling a flight of capital. In most cases, no attempt has been made to maintain a fixed "official" exchange rate. Sometimes the authorities have relied on the coöperation of the banks to achieve their ends, without having resort to governmental exchange restrictions. This practice was followed in Norway, where the banks coöperated informally with the central bank for the purpose of utilizing the available exchange in the best interests of the country.[19]

Official exchange restrictions were imposed in England by a Treasury Order at the time of departure from the gold standard,

---

[18] Cf. pp. 39–42 above.
[19] U. S. Bureau of Foreign and Domestic Commerce, *Foreign Financial News: Special Circular*, No. 388 (February 20, 1933), p. 22.

but the government relied on the banks to see that the regulations were carried out. Purchases of foreign exchange or "transfers of funds with the object of acquiring such exchange directly or indirectly by British subjects or persons resident in the United Kingdom" were prohibited except for the purpose of financing the following: (1) normal trading requirements; (2) contracts existing before September 21, 1931; (3) reasonable traveling or other personal purposes. Customers who wished to make remittances abroad were to be required by their banks to "certify the purpose for which the foreign currency is required and to declare that the transaction is not in any way against the spirit of the Government recommendation relative to the export of capital from this country."[20] No attempt was made to fix an "official" exchange rate for the pound, which was allowed to seek its own level, subject to the restrictions outlined above.[21] The interference with normal operations on the exchanges proved unpopular, however, since it tended to impair London's power to function as a financial center. In particular, the disruption of the forward exchange market interfered with the financing of foreign trade.[22] The restrictions were removed on March 3, 1932, by which time confidence in the pound had been restored to such an extent that the inflow of capital was becoming "almost embarrassing in volume."[23] Shortly thereafter, the British Government decided to rely on official intervention in the exchange markets to prevent undue fluctuations in sterling, and to this end the Exchange Equalization Fund was set up.

Essentially similar to the British regulations, though differing somewhat in detail, were temporary restrictions introduced by Finland, the United States, Belgium, and Luxemburg. In

---

[20] *The Times,* London, September 23, 1931.

[21] The monetary policy pursued by the Bank of England, of course, affected its movements, as did, less directly, the general financial policy of the British Government.

[22] Cf. *The Economist,* CXIII (1931), 599.

[23] *The Times,* London, March 3, 1932 (editorial).

some cases, the restrictions remained in force for an even shorter period than in Great Britain. Japan and Italy, which maintained mild restrictions similar to the British regulations for considerable periods, eventually adopted more stringent systems of control. In Japan, the system which was in force until January, 1937, did not, like the British regulations, directly prohibit the purchase of foreign securities but simply required permission of the Ministry of Finance for such transactions. Otherwise, the banks could carry on their business in a normal manner, aside from the obligation of submitting detailed records of foreign exchange transactions to the Minister of Finance at frequent intervals.[24] In Italy, previous to the tightening of regulations which took place in May, 1934, exchange could be freely purchased for imports, but it was available only on the presentation of documents showing that the merchandise had actually been received.[25] This provision was designed to forestall attempts to export capital through securing exchange to pay for fictitious imports.

A general supervision of applications to purchase foreign exchange, then, is the most characteristic feature of mild systems of exchange control. Certain supplementary measures are, however, frequently taken, even in countries which impose only mild restrictions. Prohibitions on the export of bank notes and securities are quite common as a means of introducing a further check against capital outflow.[26] Specific measures against dealings in the forward exchanges are frequently adopted in countries with few restrictions, in order to prevent speculation. A decree of September 28, 1931, in Italy, for example, prohibited long-dated sale transactions, unless pre-

[24] Ministry of Finance Ordinance No. 7 of 1933, as amended by Ordinance Nos. 12, 19, and 26 of 1933. (Translation secured from a Japanese official.)

[25] *The Economist*, CXIII (1931), 1232.

[26] A prohibition on the export of gold also constitutes one means of preventing the export of capital, but such action usually constitutes an integral part of the measures taken on suspension of the gold standard.

ceded by a deposit of scrip or of 25 per cent of the sale price. Similarly, long-dated purchase transactions had to be preceded by a deposit of 25 per cent of the purchase price.[27]

Finally, mention must be made of the embargoes on foreign loans which have been adopted by a number of creditor countries, although protection of the currency has not always been the only motive for such action. Strong precedents for government regulation of foreign issues may be found in pre-War France and Germany, where the object was to attach political conditions to loans to foreign governments.[28] The Johnson Act forbidding the raising of loans in the United States by governments which have defaulted on their war debts presents an example of a curious mingling of political and economic considerations. An embargo on foreign issues was implicit in the British exchange regulations of September 21, 1931. When restrictions on exchange dealings were removed, a warning was issued by the Chancellor of the Exchequer against any over-indulgence in foreign issues.[29] Shortly thereafter an embargo on all new capital issues in the United Kingdom was imposed, not primarily as an exchange control measure, but to insure the success of the first great War Loan conversion scheme by keeping competitive issues off the investment market. Early in 1933 this prohibition was removed except for issues on behalf of borrowers domiciled outside the Empire or issues "the proceeds of which would be remitted directly or indirectly to countries outside the Empire."[30] Gradually, however, loans came to be permitted to all countries in the sterling area and

---

[27] *The Times*, London, September 29, 1931.

[28] Cf. P. Einzig, *Exchange Control* (London, 1934), p. 181 and H. Feis, *Europe: The World's Banker, 1870–1914* (New Haven and London, 1930), *passim*.

[29] *The Times*, London, March 3, 1932 (editorial).

[30] *Ibid.*, January 14, 1933. The prohibition against "the optional replacement of existing issues by new issues if those new issues rank as trustee securities and involve either underwriting or an invitation to the public to subscribe new cash" was also retained.

to countries which would use "the proceeds of loans mainly in a manner directly beneficial to British industry." [31]

For the most part, mild exchange restrictions have served to help countries over the uncertain transitional period associated with depreciation or devaluation of the currency. In no case have they been designed to maintain the currency for a long period at an artificially high rate. The experience of the countries enforcing them has been very different from that of the nations of Central and Southeastern Europe which were determined to maintain their currencies at par. It has differed also from the experience of the Latin American countries which, while willing to permit their currencies to depreciate, nevertheless faced the problems common to all countries with large outstanding debts.

b. Severe systems. When we come to the countries which have introduced stringent exchange regulations, we find that almost all were debtor countries faced with difficult transfer problems after the onset of the depression and with the danger of a simultaneous flight both of domestic and of foreign capital after the monetary crisis of 1931. Transfer moratoria on foreign capital had eventually to be declared in many instances. Relatively mild measures to prevent the flight of domestic capital, such as those already described, had to be supplemented by a network of complicated devices designed to stop up the various loopholes through which capital might escape illegally. As already indicated, regulation of all foreign exchange dealings was usually placed in the hands of the central bank or of an exchange control commission. Frequently, the central bank was given a monopoly of all dealings in foreign exchange, while permits for exchange purchases were issued by an exchange control commission which had general jurisdiction over the working of the system. In many cases, certain specified

---

[31] Richardson, *British Economic Foreign Policy,* p. 74. Restrictions on foreign lending were tightened at the end of 1938. (*The New York Times,* December 21, 1938.)

banks were permitted to deal in exchange subject to close supervision by the central bank or the exchange control commission, or both. All such dealings were to be conducted at "official" rates fixed by the authorities. Exporters and others were required to sell all foreign exchange currently acquired to the control authorities at the official buying rate. This exchange would then be rationed out to importers and others having foreign remittances to make at the official selling rate according to certain predetermined rules of precedence.[32]

Lack of space prevents our considering in detail the regulations in every country, but we shall attempt to form some idea of the main types of measures adopted, confining our attention first to problems concerned with the commandeering of the supply of foreign exchange. In general, the discussion will relate to the situation prevailing in each country when exchange control was most stringent. The various measures taken in the direction of relaxation of exchange restrictions will be discussed in the next chapter, since the paths pursued differed considerably in different countries.

Measures to control the supply of foreign exchange: export receipts. First of all, every country with rigid exchange regulations required the surrender of foreign balances accruing from exports. In a number of countries, drafts for amounts below a certain minimum were exempted from the surrender provisions, though frequently this minimum was reduced or removed altogether as the exchange holdings of the central bank dwindled. Further, various means of preventing evasion of the regulations had to be devised. In the latter half of 1931 and the first half of 1932, many of these debtor countries found that, despite a substantial export surplus, the foreign exchange

---

[32] A small margin between the official buying and selling rates is, of course, to be expected, in order that the central bank or other banks dealing in exchange may cover expenses. Where the margin is wider than is required for this purpose, sales of exchange are restricted more than they otherwise would be, and banks dealing in exchange receive an abnormally large profit.

holdings of the central bank were rapidly diminishing. Austrian exports totalled 109 million schillings in December, 1931, and yet export drafts for only a little over nine millions were sold to the Austrian National Bank.[33] It was believed that exporters were selling largely on long-term credits. In addition, a fairly active "black" bourse evidently flourished in Vienna at that time.[34] Some indication of the extent of the discount on schillings in the free market is provided by the fact that early in February, 1932, when the official National Bank rate on London ranged from 24 to 24½ schillings to the pound, rates quoted in London were between 30 and 34 schillings to the pound.[35] German exporters, in the autumn of 1931, were not only leaving the proceeds of their exports abroad, but were repaying their foreign debts with foreign balances acquired from sales of exports.[36] As regulations were progressively tightened and penalties made more severe, new means of evasion were discovered. Exporters were found to be accepting, in payment for their goods, German securities held by foreigners who wanted to evade the regulations stipulating that the yield from sale of such securities must remain in Germany.[37]

A further explanation of the failure of exporters to turn over foreign drafts to the authorities was to be found in the fact that exchange restrictions abroad made it difficult for exporters to collect payment from their foreign debtors. Frozen commercial debts were piling up at an alarming rate during the latter half of 1931 and all through 1932 in the central banks of many countries in Central Europe and Latin America. We shall come back to this question in connection with our analysis of restrictions on the demand for foreign exchange. Hungary

[33] *The Times*, London, February 2, 1932.

[34] *Ibid.*, February 29, 1932. According to the article cited, "even relatively honest men" found themselves "engaged in uncongenial clandestine transactions in bars and back offices."

[35] *Ibid.*, February 4, 1932.

[36] *The Economist*, CXIII (1931), 659.

[37] *The Times*, London, December 30. 1931.

was reputedly hit especially hard by this particular difficulty.[38]
A survey issued by the National Bank after eight months of
exchange control showed that export drafts surrendered to the
Bank had amounted to less than ⅓ of total merchandise exports during this period.[39]

Among the measures adopted to combat this failure of control authorities to receive exchange from exporters, the most
common, introduced in a large number of countries with severe
exchange restrictions, was a provision that exporters were to
make a declaration containing full details as to the value of
shipments every time goods were exported. Prices at which
goods were invoiced were carefully checked by the authorities,
to make certain that exporters were not under-valuing their
shipments, in order to leave part of the proceeds abroad. Frequently, prior permits or licenses had to be obtained before
goods could be shipped.[40] Some countries, e.g., Argentina and
Austria, required that exports be made only against invoices in
foreign currencies.[41] Austrian exporters, for instance, had been
invoicing export bills in schillings, thereby avoiding the acquisition of foreign drafts which they would have been forced to
turn over to the National Bank at the official rate, while permitting the foreign importer to acquire schillings abroad at a
lower rate or to utilize balances held in Austria in payment for
the goods. The German Reichsbank exerted pressure on those
attempting to evade the exchange regulations by refusing
credit to any applicant firm which could be shown to have
engaged in illegal practices. Exporters in a number of countries were forbidden to grant credits to foreigners without per-

---

[38] *The Economist*, CXIII (1931), 1009–1010.

[39] Cited in *ibid.*, CXIV (1932), 738. In addition to the 100.2 million pengö
which the Bank acquired, however, 30 millions were utilized by exporters (with
permission of the Bank) to import raw materials under compensation schemes.
Cf. pp. 170–71 below.

[40] This was one of the principal features of the short-lived exchange control
regime in New Zealand in 1932. Cf. *The Times*, London, December 24, 1931.
(New Zealand reimposed control at the end of 1938.)

[41] Cf. *The Economist*, CXIV (1932), 119.

mission of the control authorities. Finally, heavy penalties were imposed for illicit dealings in exchange. Penalties have been made especially severe in the last few years in Italy and Germany, where a violation of the exchange regulations has come to be regarded as a major crime against the totalitarian state.[42]

Measures to control the supply of foreign exchange: other foreign assets. As a general rule, the countries which required sale of export drafts to the central bank insisted on the surrender also of foreign balances acquired through other current transactions.[43] Such action was usually necessary if the country was to make a determined effort to render the official rate of exchange effective for all dealings in its currency. It was much more difficult, however, to devise means for enforcing the sale of foreign drafts received for services than it was to force the sale of export drafts. Shipping and insurance companies conducting a foreign business could be required to render an account of their transactions, but it was difficult to check up on the dealings of private individuals. A few countries, from the beginning, required the surrender at the official rate of only a certain proportion of the value of foreign drafts.[44] In Ecuador, for example, banks and exporters were to turn over

[42] On December 1, 1936, the German Cabinet issued a decree against "Economic Sabotage," which ordered the death penalty for German citizens who "consciously, without scruple, for clearly egoistic reasons or other base purposes," transferred "property abroad against legal restrictions" or allowed "property to remain abroad subject to such restrictions." (*The New York Times*, December 2, 1936.)

[43] In most exchange-control countries, exports constitute by far the most important source of foreign exchange. Cf. League of Nations, *Report on Exchange Control*, p. 13. Capital imports are, of course, virtually out of the question, since nobody will invest funds in a country from which he will not be permitted to withdraw interest or principal payments. Receipts from most service items are likely to be small for most debtor countries. They were especially small in 1931 and 1932, when tourist expenditures and emigrants' remittances, which normally produce fairly substantial amounts of foreign exchange for a number of countries in Central and Southeastern Europe, fell off drastically.

[44] As exchange restrictions were gradually relaxed in a number of countries, such regulations became much more common. Cf. pp. 99–102 below.

80 per cent of all foreign drafts at the official rate.[45] Poland allowed exporters to retain sufficient foreign currency to pay transportation costs.[46] In Portugal, half of all acquisitions of foreign exchange had to be sold to the Bank of Portugal.[47]

In addition to requiring the sale to the control authorities of foreign balances currently acquired, most of the European countries with rigid restrictions required all holders of foreign currency or claims in foreign currency to register such holdings and offer them for sale to the central bank.[48] Such action was usually taken shortly after the introduction of exchange control and was frequently repeated periodically or spasmodically, especially if the exchange situation became more precarious. The central banks tended to exercise their option to purchase these holdings if and when they wished to replenish their foreign exchange reserves. This type of measure was less common in Latin America, where attempts to enforce official rates of exchange were less thoroughgoing, and "black" bourses were not seriously interfered with.[49]

Frequently, registration of holdings of foreign securities was

[45] Or the total amount, if the owner's need for the remaining 20 per cent was not warranted in the opinion of the central bank. (*Foreign Financial News: Special Circular*, No. 388 [February 20, 1933], p. 17.)

[46] *Ibid.*, No. 421 (April 1, 1937), p. 14.

[47] *Ibid.*, No. 388 (February 20, 1933), p. 23. The percentage was reduced by stages in a series of regulations dating from December, 1932.

[48] The National Bank of Czechoslovakia offered the following definitions of "foreign currency" and "claims in foreign currency":

"By foreign currency is meant, . . . , both currency, i.e., paper money (state notes, bank notes) and gold coins of foreign countries, and exchange, i.e., bills of exchange, cheques, letters of credit, money-orders, and all other kinds of remittances in foreign currency. By claims in foreign currency are meant: 1. call or/and time deposits in foreign currency on current accounts with foreign financial institutions and firms; 2. call or/and time deposits in foreign currency on current accounts at finance institutions and firms in this country . . . ; 3. deposits in foreign financial institutions and firms; 4. cash bonds issued by foreign financial institutions and short-term cash bonds of foreign states; 5. account claims in foreign currency on persons and firms both abroad and in this country." (Notice of the Minister of Finance, October 20, 1931, No. 164, National Bank of Czechoslovakia, *Bulletin*, Supplement to No. 59 (September, 1931), p. 17.)

[49] Cf. pp. 102–11 below.

also required, but attempts to force sale of such securities to the central bank met with considerable opposition and were usually undertaken only as a last resort. In Austria, compulsory surrender of all foreign means of payment, required by decree of October 9, 1931, did not yield the amounts anticipated. Rumors of a proposed decree to enable the National Bank to acquire all holdings of foreign securities brought forth energetic protests. It was pointed out that the public had suffered severe losses on purely Austrian shares, and that forced sale of foreign shares would deprive people of their last assets.[50] Germany required the sale only of short-term claims at first,[51] but later certain types of foreign securities had to be registered with the control authorities. A concerted drive to compel holders of foreign securities to turn over such property to the Reichsbank began late in 1936, but was not carried through with quite the degree of thoroughness that had been anticipated.[52] Czechoslovakia likewise gradually took over foreign

[50] *The Economist,* CXIII (1931), 908.

[51] A decree issued in July, 1931, placed upon all persons liable to the property tax the obligation to make a declaration to the Reichsbank of "foreign means of payment and claims expressed in foreign currencies," and the Reichsbank or any institution nominated by it was given the right to purchase these holdings for marks. Foreign securities and claims not repayable for more than three months were excepted, save such as had been acquired since July 12, 1931. All holdings under 20,000 marks were also exempted. The Reichsbank was not to exercise its right to purchase even short-term claims if it was proved that the holdings were required for legitimate purposes "in the interests of the national economy, or otherwise for genuine and useful business." (*The Times,* London, July 20, 1931.)

[52] Holders of certain foreign securities were required to deposit them with a foreign exchange bank (November 16, 1936), and the purchase and disposal of foreign securities admitted to trading on a German stock exchange were made subject to permit (February 27, 1937). See *Foreign Financial News: European Financial Notes,* No. 252 (October 24, 1937), p. 8. Although these measures were not followed by a general commandeering of foreign securities, as had been expected, the Reichsbank took over several hundred million reichsmarks of such securities which were sold abroad. It was during this period that Dr. Schacht was putting forth renewed efforts to build up a "secret" gold reserve. The first quarter of 1937 witnessed a net gold import exceeding 100 million reichsmarks, paid for mainly with exchange obtained from the sale abroad of foreign securities. (*The New York Times,* May 17, 1937.) On September 24, 1937, a decree was published requiring all individuals and corpora-

security holdings by a series of measures which commenced in October, 1931, and culminated at the end of 1936 with a campaign on the part of the central bank to bring about the sale of certain securities still owned by Czechoslovakians.[53]

Just as the first World War gave rise to attempts on the part of several countries, notably Great Britain, to mobilize foreign assets, so more recent wars have led to the taking over by the state of claims to foreign currencies. In May, 1935, Italy required that all foreign securities held by Italians be deposited with the Bank of Italy, which would collect interest and dividends, converting them into lire for the holders at official exchange rates; but in August, when the war with Ethiopia was well under way, it was decreed that all such securities, as well as all Italian private credits in foreign countries, were to be transferred to the government.[54] Similarly, among the emergency war measures passed by the Japanese Diet in a special five-day session held early in September, 1937, was a bill authorizing the Minister of Finance to require any Japanese subject to liquidate all his assets in foreign countries and transfer the proceeds to the Bank of Japan.[55] With the outbreak of war in 1939, Britain and France prepared to apply the lessons learned from 1914 to 1918 in liquidating foreign assets.

In general, the problem of acquiring control of the supply of foreign exchange has been most difficult (1) for countries which have attempted, over a period of several years, to maintain their currencies at a value considerably higher than that

tions to notify the Reichsbank of their holdings as of September 20. See *Foreign Financial News: European Financial Notes,* No. 252 (October 24, 1937), p. 8.

[53] Cf. *ibid.,* No. 179 (October 9, 1934), p. 6; No. 187 (February 9, 1935), pp. 5–6; No. 232 (December 24, 1936), p. 4; and No. 233 (January 9, 1937), p. 4.

[54] *Ibid.,* No. 195 (June 9, 1935), p. 10, and No. 205 (November 9, 1935), p. 10.

[55] *Foreign Financial News: Far Eastern Financial Notes,* No. 239 (October 4, 1937), p. 7.

which would have prevailed in an unrestricted market, and
(2) for countries which have become involved in wars or highly
developed programs of economic self-sufficiency.[56] Expectations
as to political stability sometimes play as important a part as
the more purely economic considerations. The countries which
in the years from 1931 on were free of political disturbances
and, in one way or another, reduced the values of their currencies, succeeded gradually in modifying their restrictions on
the disposal of foreign means of payment. The methods by
which this was accomplished will be considered at some length
in the next chapter.

Measures to control the demand for foreign exchange. Turning to measures to restrict the demand for foreign currencies,
one finds, as might be expected, that the most drastic restrictions have been characteristic of countries in which the supplies of exchange coming into the hands of the authorities have
been least adequate to take care of the demand. The universal
method of restricting purchases of foreign exchange has been
to require permits from the exchange control commission or central bank for all such purchases. Sometimes blanket permits
have been issued to authorized banks or importing firms allowing them to use certain specific amounts of exchange in
designated ways.

The first and most important aim of such a permit system,
of course, is to prevent purchases of foreign securities or exports of capital in any other form. We have already discussed
this problem in connection with mild exchange restrictions and
with the commandeering of the supply of foreign exchange.
There remain to be mentioned certain loopholes, in the form
of illegal purchases of foreign currencies, through which capital
might escape abroad. Measures restricting the amounts travelers might carry abroad, which have been very common, have
served the double purpose of restricting expenditures by nation-

---

[56] As the reader will readily recognize, certain countries belong in both of
these categories.

als touring in foreign countries and of forestalling attempts to carry capital out in person.[57] Applications for exchange to pay for imports have had to be accompanied by invoices, which have been carefully checked to prevent attempts to get capital out by over-valuing imports. Austria sought to check the smuggling of currency and checks out of the country through the mails by censoring all registered letters addressed to foreign countries,[58] and there is a widespread impression that the totalitarian states have gone in for thorough censorship of the mails. A number of countries found that the illegal export of notes could be discouraged by imposing an embargo on the import of notes.[59] Thus, notes which had been smuggled abroad for the purpose of purchasing foreign securities or in payment of debts would find a less ready market abroad if they could not be repatriated.

Space does not permit an exhaustive account of the innumerable complicated regulations which have been devised to prevent the escape of capital.[60] A special problem has arisen

[57] In Germany, the limit for a considerable period was 200 marks per month. (J. W. Thelwall, *Economic Conditions in Germany to September, 1932*, Great Britain, Department of Overseas Trade, Report No. 529 (London, 1932), p. 13.) This was reduced by degrees to 10 marks per month, while inhabitants of regions close to the border were permitted to take out only three marks per month. Cf. A. Piatier, *Le Contrôle des Devises dans l'Économie du IIIe Reich* (Paris, 1937), p. 77. Tourists' expenditures, like expenditures for imports, however, have become a popular subject of international bargaining.

[58] *The Times,* London, March 1, 1932.

[59] As early as February, 1932, a German decree provided that mark notes reaching German banks from abroad had to be credited to a "blocked account." (*The Times,* London, February 20, 1932.) A decree of December 6, 1935, forbade the importation of reichsmark notes from abroad, except by special permission or unless they were definitely sent from abroad to be deposited in the special reichsmark note and specie blocked accounts. See *Foreign Financial News: European Financial Notes*, No. 208 (December 24, 1935), p. 10. Italy and Czechoslovakia also restricted the import of notes. Cf. *ibid.*, No. 205 (November 9, 1935), p. 10, and No. 210 (January 24, 1936), p. 5.

[60] From time to time, accounts of apprehensions for the illegal export of capital by some original method have appeared in the press. One such account concerns an Austrian who purchased 10 steamship tickets to New York in Vienna, later canceling them for cash in Paris. *The Times,* London, January 8, 1932.

in connection with the capital of the German *émigrés,* who have been compelled by a network of restrictions to leave most of their property in Germany.[61]

Aside from stopping the drain of capital abroad, the main problem confronting the exchange authorities has been to make decisions concerning the allocation of their limited supplies of exchange among the various types of applicants. Usually, the broad outlines of the policy to be pursued are laid down by the legislature or by governmental decree, while the exchange control commission makes its own rulings with respect to the details involved in carrying out this policy. Frequently, the rulings of the commission are not made public, in which case it is difficult to determine precisely what considerations govern the allocation of exchange. Even when rulings are made public, it is difficult to discover to what extent discrimination enters into the decisions of the commission, especially with respect to the allocation of exchange for imports. Discrimination may take the form of favoring certain importing *firms* or imports

[61] According to a report in *Time: The Weekly News Magazine,* XXXII (September 26, 1938), 22, the German Government had received 313,000,000 marks ($125,200,000) in revenue since 1933 from a 25 per cent tax levied on the capital of all refugees "whose income during any single year since 1931 reached $8,000 or who have had a one-year property assessment of $20,000 in the same period." This does not mean, however, that Jewish émigrés were permitted to take out 75 per cent of their capital. A network of additional restrictions was imposed, with the net result that Jews considered themselves lucky if they could get across the border with 6 per cent to 8 per cent of their original possessions (*ibid.*). Only very small amounts of cash could be taken out, and funds left in Germany had to lie placed in special blocked accounts, which could be used only for highly restricted purposes *within* Germany. (See pp. 89–96 below, for discussion of blocked marks.) These emigrants' blocked marks formerly could, with special permission, be sold abroad, but at a discount of 80 per cent to 90 per cent. On June 4, 1938, German exchange offices were instructed to permit no transfers of emigrants' blocked accounts until further notice, except for accounts belonging to non-Jews, foreign citizens, or individual emigrants with total property not exceeding 5,000 marks. As a result, discounts on emigrants' blocked marks declined still farther. On November 30, 1938, Helmuth Mainz and Co. of Amsterdam were quoting the purchase price of the German Golddiskontbank for this category of marks at 7½ per cent of the value of free marks. See *Foreign Financial News: European Financial Notes,* No. 269 (July 9, 1938), p. 9, and No. 280 (December 24, 1938), p. 6.

from certain *countries*. Discrimination as among countries from which imports originate has, however, become overt in numerous cases and has been embodied in international agreements to an increasing extent.

In the early months of exchange control (1931), there was a tendency for permits to be issued for all foreign payments needed to meet genuine liabilities or to fulfill legitimate needs. Only exports of capital were discriminated against, while exchange requirements below a certain minimum amount were satisfied without permits.[62] If supplies of exchange coming into the hands of the authorities became inadequate, as they invariably did, only a certain percentage of the amount specified in each application was granted. This system was defended on the ground of impartiality, but it resulted in the rapid accumulation of frozen commercial debts, with disastrous effects on trade, for exporters in other countries could not continue to conduct business with large amounts of funds tied up abroad.

A few illustrations will indicate the seriousness of the situation which developed in the latter part of 1931 and the early months of 1932. In Chile, early in 1932, exchange for imports was being allotted at the rate of four per cent every 60 days.[63] In the latter part of 1932, Bulgarian importers were being supplied with exchange only after the expiration of three months from the date of the clearing of merchandise through the customs, and even then, the National Bank was frequently unable to supply more than 20 to 50 per cent of the amount required.[64] These are some of the more extreme examples, but

---

[62] In Czechoslovakia, this minimum amount was 20,000 crowns. (National Bank of Czechoslovakia, *Bulletin,* Supplement to No. 59, September, 1931, p. 27.) In Germany, exchange restrictions at first applied only to transactions amounting to more than 3,000 marks per month. Later, this amount was drastically reduced. (J. W. F. Thelwall, *Economic Conditions in Germany to September, 1932,* p. 13.)

[63] *The Times,* London, January 25, 1932.

[64] *Foreign Financial News: Special Circular,* No. 388 (February 20, 1933), pp. 10–11.

even in a country such as Argentina, where the situation was considerably less acute, almost 400 million pesos awaited remittance to foreign exporters on September 30, 1932.[65]

Special restrictions on certain types of transactions were early introduced to alleviate this situation. Limitations on the amounts tourists might take abroad have already been mentioned. Gradually, a whole scheme of preferences grew up, sometimes embodied in law or governmental decree, sometimes ascertainable only through a study of the rulings of the exchange control commission. Imports regarded as essential were given first preference by the majority of countries. The Chilean Exchange Control Law of April 20, 1932, specified that preference would be given to applications involving the importation of raw materials for Chilean industries, articles of prime necessity, drugs, and prepared medicines.[66] In Uruguay, a priority list was drawn up, with imports of necessities, raw materials, fuel, and certain other articles leading the list in the order specified.[67] Evidently a desire to keep up governmental revenues deriving from import duties played a part in such decisions, as well as the more obvious purpose of preventing a general breakdown of the economic system.[68]

Where interest on long-term foreign debts continued to be met in full, a primary task of the exchange control commission was to reserve sufficient foreign exchange for this purpose before making allocations for other foreign payments. If this meant sacrificing *essential* imports, the government generally resorted to a transfer moratorium on its foreign debts. The list of countries which declared transfer moratoria or defaulted on the service of foreign debts at some time during the de-

[65] *Ibid.*, p. 3. By the middle of 1933, there were blocked accounts, or accounts virtually blocked, in 22 countries. (League of Nations, *World Economic Survey, 1932–33*, p. 278.)

[66] *Foreign Financial News: Special Circular*, No. 377 (undated), p. 2.

[67] *Ibid.*

[68] Cf. the discussion of the Argentine case by G. E. Leguizamon in "An Argentine View of the Problem of Exchange Restrictions," *International Affairs: Journal of the Royal Institute of International Affairs*, XII (1933), 511.

pression, is very long. It includes a majority of the countries of South America and a large number of countries in Central Europe.[69] Where transfer moratoria were declared, the amounts due were paid into special blocked accounts at the central bank. The subsequent history of these and other types of blocked accounts will be taken up in the next chapter.[70]

Private foreign debts have frequently received considerably less favorable treatment than public foreign debts. Argentina, which scrupulously met the service charges on the foreign debts of the federal government throughout the depression, allocated exchange for financial remittances of public service companies and other private companies only after the amounts required by other applicants had been largely provided.[71] Germany, on the other hand, at first accorded certain foreign debts of both categories preferential treatment. It was provided on August 1, 1931, that interest and amortization payments on long-term foreign loans and payments within the framework of the stand-still agreements did not require written authorization. On July 1, 1933, a partial transfer moratorium was declared on all payments falling due on foreign debts, with the exception of interest and amortization payments on the Dawes Loan and

[69] Unfortunately, there exists no satisfactory compilation of information with respect to defaults and transfer moratoria following the financial crisis of 1931. Partial or complete transfer moratoria on long-term foreign debts were declared by Hungary (December, 1931), Bulgaria (April, 1932), Greece (April, 1932), Austria (June, 1932), Yugoslavia (November, 1932, and January, 1933), Rumania (January and August, 1933), and Germany (July, 1933, and June, 1934). Defaults by *central or local* governmental bodies took place during 1931 in Bolivia, Peru, Chile, Brazil, Uruguay, Argentina, the Dominican Republic, and Colombia. Later defaults occurred in Costa Rica (December, 1932), Cuba (March, 1933), and Paraguay (June, 1933). (League of Nations, *World Economic Survey, 1932–33,* pp. 276–79 and *World Economic Survey, 1933–34,* pp. 17–20, 354.) This list does not include defaults on war debts to the United States. For more recent information, see Institute of International Finance, *Bulletin,* No. 93 (July 6, 1937), p. 14; Corporation of Foreign Bondholders, London, *Annual Reports;* and Royal Institute of International Affairs, *The Problem of International Investment* (London and New York, 1937).

[70] Cf. pp. 88–98 below.

[71] Cf. Leguizamon, *op. cit.,* pp. 510–11. Financial remittances, of course, might include profits and dividends, as well as interest on bonds.

interest payments on the Young Loan.[72] This was followed, in
June, 1934, by a complete transfer moratorium, except for the
"standstill" debts. In both cases, however, subsequent negotiations with individual creditor countries led to arrangements for
substantial partial payments.[73]

Not only did payments for current imports of an essential
nature receive precedence over interest on governmental and
private long-term debts, but they were given preference, also,
over payments for past imports for which exchange had not
yet been granted. In other words, importers were issued exchange for current imports before any exchange was allocated
for the liquidation of frozen commercial debts.[74] Periodically,
the regulations would be revised as new foreign debts accumulated, but almost invariably the tendency was to give
precedence to payment for current imports. Here, again, the
desire to prevent a breakdown of the internal economy was apparently the dominant motive.

*Trend toward rigid control of imports through exchange re-
strictions.* As the system of allotting exchange more or less
impartially gave way to a highly preferential system, the
methods employed in distributing exchange among importers
grew more elaborate. Several aims were pursued simultaneously. In the first place, through requiring permits for exchange
to pay for imports to be secured well in advance of the actual
shipment of goods from abroad, an attempt was made to limit
the demand for foreign exchange to the available supply,

[72] *The Times,* London, July 1, 1933, and Harris, *Germany's Foreign Indebtedness,* pp. 51–52. The 25 Years' Sinking Fund Gold Loan of the Potash Syndi-
cate was also excepted.
[73] Cf. E. C. D. Rawlins, *Economic Conditions in Germany to March, 1936,*
Great Britain, Department of Overseas Trade, Report No. 641 (London, 1936),
p. 157. For further details, see pp. 90–92 below.
[74] When Greece left the gold standard on April 27, 1932, she inaugurated a
set of exchange restrictions which provided for the settlement of commercial
debts contracted in foreign countries prior to April 27, 1932, on an installment
basis over a period of years. *Foreign Financial News: Special Circular,* No. 388
(February 20, 1933), pp. 19–20.

thereby preventing the accumulation of frozen debts. Secondly, exchange control became more and more openly a weapon of protectionism, permits from a general import control board frequently being required before exchange could be issued for certain imports. The decisions of this import control board would be governed, not merely by the availability of exchange, but by more general economic considerations, and often, of course, by the demands of various economic pressure groups. Thirdly, as part of the attempt to equate the demand for foreign exchange with the available supply, efforts were made to balance the trade with individual countries by preferential allocations of exchange for imports from those countries with which the balance of trade was most "favorable," or which, in turn, granted preferential treatment to the first country.[75] Frequently, the preferential allotment extended to allocations of exchange for all purposes, not merely for imports. Thus, exchange control became a weapon of direct discrimination among countries, while the system of giving precedence to certain types of imports indirectly favored the countries which supplied such products.

This does not mean that every country sooner or later adopted a policy with respect to the allocation of exchange for imports which gave expression to all three of these aims. It means, simply, that these were the methods which, on the whole, came to be favored by countries with rigid exchange control systems. The preferential allocation of exchange for imports of raw materials and necessities was evident from the

[75] This is our first reference to the policy of "bilateral balancing," which has become so prominent in recent years. Countries have utilized not only exchange restrictions, but all other weapons of commercial policy, in their drives to equate imports and exports in the trade with every other country. This policy has been partly inevitable, in so far as exchange allocations have been concerned, for the very existence of a network of exchange restrictions and clearing or payments agreements has made it difficult, and in many instances impossible, to settle obligations in one country by remitting drafts on a second country. Exchange control authorities have, under certain circumstances, been obliged to permit payments to a given country only in so far as balances were available in *that* country. See Chapters VI and VII, below.

very beginning of exchange restrictions in certain countries, but it was only gradually that rules of preference became embodied in a systematic prior permit system.

Denmark was one of the first countries to adopt such a system. A law of January 29, 1932, provided that, before importing goods, importers would have to secure a certificate from the National Bank demonstrating that there was no objection to the importation for exchange reasons. Unconditional preference was to be granted to imports of raw materials and of auxiliary materials that were utilized in the manufacture of exports and hence "produced" foreign exchange.[76] Further, it soon became clear that, in the administration of the law, imports from Great Britain, which was the principal market for Danish goods, were favored. A statement issued by the Danish Legation in London in June, 1932, showed that, for the ensuing three months, permits to import British goods were being issued in sufficient amounts to bring about an increase of 15 per cent in imports from Great Britain over the corresponding period of the previous year. Meanwhile, total imports were being reduced by 30 to 40 per cent.[77]

In Argentina, all imports were, with a few exceptions, granted exchange on an equal basis until May 1, 1933, when the well-known Runciman-Roca Agreement was signed with Great Britain. This became the model for subsequent agreements with other countries and marked the beginning of a thorough-going application of the principle of discriminating in favor of Argentina's best customers.[78] Uruguay has worked out an elaborate system, whereby not less than 75 per cent of the foreign exchange derived from exports to any given country is allocated for payments to that country. From the exchange thus made available all transfers of funds to the country con-

[76] *The Times,* London, January, 30, 1932.
[77] *Ibid.,* June 9, 1932.
[78] The adoption of this principle was recommended by a Financial Advisory Commission in November, 1932. Cf. Leguizamon, *op. cit.,* pp. 512–13. For the provisions of the Runciman-Roca Agreement, see pp. 190–91 below.

cerned, whether for imports, debt service, or other requirements, must be paid. In the issuance of permits for imports, account is taken (a) of the amount of exchange which may be utilized for payments to a given country in the light of the 75 per cent minimum principle and (b) of the nature of the commodities involved.[79] Both Argentina and Uruguay, as well as a number of other Latin American countries which have adopted multiple exchange rate systems,[80] grant preferential treatment, in the allocation of official or controlled exchange, to countries with which the balance of trade is active or with which special agreements have been signed.

In Germany, where allotments of exchange to importers were for a considerable period made on an impartial basis,[81] exchange control gradually became an important part of a far-reaching drive for military power and economic self-sufficiency. An attempt to discriminate in favor of essential imports early in August, 1931, brought forth threats of reprisals from foreign governments.[82] Apparently in order to avoid such reprisals, Germany adhered for over three years to a system of distributing exchange for imports to each importing firm in proportion to its volume of business in the past.[83] This system worked reasonably well during the Bruening regime, primarily because it was combined with a policy of drastic internal deflation. The Von Papen and Schleicher Governments, and later, the Hitler Government, gradually abandoned Bruening's deflationary pol-

---

[79] U. S. Tariff Commission, *Extent of Equal Tariff Treatment in Foreign Countries*, p. 35.

[80] Cf. pp. 102–11 below.

[81] Apart from the operation of clearing agreements. See Ch. V.

[82] *The Times*, London, August 7, 1931.

[83] Every six months import houses obtained from foreign exchange offices in their districts quotas which permitted the purchase of a certain maximum amount of foreign exchange. These quotas were based on the amount of exchange required by the individual firms from July 1, 1930, to June 30, 1931. This basic amount was then reduced in accordance with the decline in the volume of trade and the fall in prices in the various commodity groups. Every month the Minister of Economics fixed a certain percentage of this adjusted figure as the amount of exchange which importers were permitted to buy. See *Foreign Financial News: Special Circular*, No. 388 (February 20, 1933), p. 18.

icy in favor of more and more inflationary measures.[84] The
resulting rise in the price level made it increasingly difficult
for German exporters to compete with foreign exporters, especially those in depreciated-currency countries. Further, since
raw material prices began to increase during the course of 1933
in relation to industrial prices, Germany experienced a "worsening" in her terms of trade, which had tended to improve from
1929 on.[85] For these and other reasons, Germany's active
balance of trade rapidly disappeared, and the year 1934 was
characterized by a substantial excess of imports.[86] The Reichsbank's foreign exchange reserves fell off at an alarming rate, and
the quota of exchange granted to importers was progressively
reduced between February and May, 1934, from 50 per cent to
five per cent of their basic allowances. During the summer of
1934, importers received a day-to-day allotment based on the
Reichsbank's intake of foreign exchange.[87]

This situation could not continue, for outstanding commercial debts were rapidly accumulating.[88] In September, 1934,
Dr. Schacht announced the "New Plan" for foreign trade control, whereby foreign exchange to pay for imports was to be
released only on presentation of official exchange certificates
(*"Devisenbescheinigung"*), which were to be procured by im-

---

[84] Cf. C. R. S. Harris, *op. cit.*; pp. 40 ff.

[85] Germany imports primarily raw materials but exports industrial goods.

[86] Cf. *ibid.*, pp. 47–49.

[87] Rawlins, *op. cit.*, p. 154.

[88] Importers continued to bring goods into the country to some extent,
even though they could not secure exchange to pay for them. Furthermore,
under the terms of special exchange agreements which Germany had concluded
with countries of Western and Northern Europe, payments for imports from the
countries concerned could be made into *Sonderkonten* (special accounts), set
up at the Reichsbank in favor of the central banks in the exporting countries
and available to pay for imports of German goods into these countries. Payments into *Sonderkonten* by German importers involved no purchases of foreign exchange and hence were not subject to exchange restrictions. Consequently, when allotments of exchange were drastically cut down in the spring
and summer of 1934, importers diverted their purchases to *Sonderkonten* countries, with the result that payments into these special Reichsbank accounts increased from 68 million RM in March, 1934, to 130 million RM in July. See
W. A. Fischer, *Devisenclearing* (Berlin, 1937), p. 24.

porters for each individual transaction before goods were brought into the country.[89] The power to issue these certificates was given to twenty-seven Import Control Boards (*Überwachungstellen*), each responsible for certain groups of goods, and each rendering its decisions in accordance with a comprehensive governmental scheme designed to discourage all imports except those considered essential for the German economy.[90] The Boards were to issue certificates only when the necessary foreign currency was actually in the possession of the Reichsbank or would be in its possession by the time payment was due.[91] In conjunction with the new scheme, the Reich Minister of Economy was given broad powers to regulate trade and distribution *within* Germany.[92]

It should be noted, at this stage, that, in the years since 1934, the major proportion of Germany's foreign trade has come to be carried on under the terms of clearing, payments, or compensation arrangements, leaving a relatively small fraction to be conducted on a free foreign exchange basis.[93] This fact does not diminish in any way the significance of the import control system, however, for imports coming under bilateral payments arrangements have been made subject to the supervision of the control boards.[94]

[89] Without such a certificate, an importer could still import the goods, but he had no assurance of receiving exchange with which to pay for them. Cf. "Von der Zahlungsüberwachen zur Einfuhrgenehmigung," *Die Wirtschaftskurve*, XIII (1934), 170.

[90] Rawlins, *op. cit.*, pp. 154–55.

[91] *Ibid.*

[92] See *The Economist*, CXIX (1934), 488. Import control boards for certain raw and semi-finished industrial materials had previously been set up by a law of March 22, 1934. (*Ibid.*) Imports of commodities coming under this law had not been affected by the drastic exchange-rationing measures of February–September, 1934. Cf. *ibid.*, CXVIII (1934), 1191.

[93] According to official statistics, only 15 per cent of German foreign trade at the end of 1937 was carried on by means of free foreign exchange, to which might be added a further five per cent to account for exchange which Germany was permitted to dispose of freely under the terms of payments agreements. See Reichs-Kredit-Gesellschaft, *Germany's Economic Situation at the Turn of 1937–38* (Berlin, 1938), p. 92. For further details, see p. 183 below.

[94] See pp. 152 ff. below.

Under the New Plan, exchange certificates have from the beginning been issued to importers in accordance with the following scheme of preference: (1) raw materials, (2) daily necessities, and (3) comforts and luxuries. As time went on, however, increasing emphasis was given to the rearmament program, especially after the appointment of General Goering as Commissioner of Foreign Exchange and Raw Materials and the inauguration of the second Four Year Plan in 1936. Allotment of exchange for imports became an important part of a scheme for promoting the production of armaments, synthetic materials, and foodstuffs which would make Germany self-sufficient in the event of war. Raw materials were to be rationed in accordance with the following schedule of needs: (a) rearmament, (b) safe-guarding of the nation's foodstuffs, (c) building up of home production of raw materials, (d) production of goods for exports, and (e) provision of improved dwelling places for the working population.[95] This policy provoked vigorous protests from manufacturers of export goods, who claimed that it would be impossible for them to secure enough raw materials to maintain a steady flow of production.[96] For a time there were indications that the government, alarmed over the decline in German exports, was becoming somewhat more attentive to this point of view.

Emphasis on autarky has, in the last few years, become the dominant characteristic of Italy's system of foreign exchange control, while, in Japan, the primary aim has been to satisfy the country's immediate need for materials to carry on the war in China. In both these countries, import permits tend to perform, to a considerable extent, the functions performed in certain other countries by exchange permits issued to importers. It is probable, however, that the distinction is more nominal than real, for in most countries the various regulatory

[95] Reichs-Kredit-Gesellschaft, *Germany's Economic Condition at the Turn of 1936–37* (Berlin, 1937), p. 4.
[96] *The New York Times,* February 24, 1937.

bodies work in close collaboration. We shall have more to say about the relations between exchange permits and import licenses in the next chapter.[97] In a number of countries, substitution of import permit or license requirements for exchange permit requirements constituted one of the ways in which exchange restrictions were relaxed in the years from 1933 on. We shall now turn to a consideration of the various paths which relaxation followed.

[97] See pp. 115–16 below.

CHAPTER V

Exchange Control: Measures of Relaxation

1. *Some General Considerations*

The recent epidemic of exchange control, as we have seen, had its origins primarily in a severe transfer crisis. Debtor countries throughout the world found themselves unable to meet their financial obligations in the face of a catastrophic decline in prices of their export products. Their difficulties were aggravated by the outbreak of a general financial panic, involving withdrawals of foreign and domestic capital. Relaxation of exchange restrictions, therefore, depended on the achievement of certain readjustments. In the first place, debtor countries would obviously benefit markedly from a rise in prices of their export products. Thus, when prices of raw materials and agricultural commodities began to recover in 1933, the majority of the exchange-control countries experienced an easing of the pressure on their balances of payments. In most cases, however, certain additional readjustments were required. Foreign financial obligations had to be scaled down to levels which debtor nations could reasonably be expected to meet. Countries which had clung to parity in 1931 found it necessary to devaluate, in order to bring their currencies once more into line with the leading world currencies. Confidence had to be restored if a further flight of capital was to be prevented, and this depended, not only on the achieving of the economic readjustments which have already been mentioned, but on the outlook for political as well as economic stability. Finally, many of the smaller countries could not relax exchange restrictions appreciably unless similar action was taken by countries which purchased large shares of their exports.[1]

By the middle of 1937, certain of these conditions had been satisfied in a number of countries, and, outside of Germany, Italy, and Japan, a substantial degree of relaxation of exchange control had been achieved. Since that time, the international situation has deteriorated, both politically and economically, and while some further progress toward relaxation has been made, a number of countries have been obliged to tighten their restrictions.[2] Because our interest is primarily in the *technique* of exchange control, we shall concentrate our attention, for the remainder of this chapter, on the *methods* by which relaxation was achieved.

2. *The Scaling Down of Foreign Indebtedness*

International indebtedness was reduced to a surprising extent during the nineteen-thirties. Long-term debts were cut down through repatriations or redemptions. A number of countries succeeded in liquidating external indebtedness through issuing internal securities for this purpose. Operations of this kind were carried through on a considerable scale by such countries as Argentina, Belgium, Finland, Canada, India, and South Africa.[3] Depreciation of the currencies of the chief creditor countries reduced the burden of indebtedness, although this constituted a net advantage only in the cases of debtor countries which had not themselves devaluated or which had retained former par values in effect for purposes of debt payments.[4] The service on foreign debts, moreover, was scaled

[1] Cf. League of Nations, *Report on Exchange Control,* p. 46.

[2] This tendency was, of course, accentuated after the outbreak of war in 1939.

[3] Bank for International Settlements, *Eighth Annual Report* (Basle, 1938), p. 69. Such operations have been facilitated by the existence of surpluses on current account in the balances of payments of these countries.

[4] Debtor countries, of course, benefited, also, if their own currencies did not depreciate by the same proportion as the currencies in which their debts were expressed.

down through conversion operations or through arrangements
with creditors. Thus the interest on Poland's foreign loans was
reduced from 7 per cent to 4½ per cent in 1937, after negotiations with American, British, and other creditors, while, in the
same year, a comprehensive agreement was reached between
Hungary and her creditors, involving a plan for future debt
payments on a basis of lower interest rates and prolonged ma-
turity.[5] The world-wide decline in interest rates facilitated
such arrangements.

Of less significance for our purpose is the decline in total
international short-term indebtedness, for a large proportion of
these debts consisted of obligations of one creditor country to
another. Exchange-control countries, however, succeeded in
paying off short-term debts to an appreciable extent. Most
of these debts, it will be recalled, were "blocked" in the debtor
countries after the introduction of exchange restrictions. A
blocked debt, or blocked account, may be defined as a sum,
deposited to the account of a foreigner in a bank or credit institution, the disposal of which is subject to certain restrictions
set forth in the exchange regulations.[6] Certain of these blocked
short-term debts were subject to so-called "standstill" agreements with creditors. In the early years of exchange control,
there was a tendency for the blocked debts of exchange-control
countries to increase, as a result of (a) the failure to transfer
interest and amortization payments on long-term debts under
the terms of transfer moratoria and (b) the failure to provide
foreign exchange in full to allow importers and others to meet
foreign obligations.[7] As time went on, however, much of this

[5] *Ibid.*, p. 70.
[6] Cf. Piatier, *op. cit.*, p. 55.
[7] According to estimates published by the Bank for International Settlements,
total international short-term indebtedness at the end of 1933 amounted to 32
billion Swiss francs, of which about 11.5 billion consisted of sums blocked
through currency regulations, standstill agreements, and similar measures.
(*Fourth Annual Report*, p. 27.)

blocked indebtedness was liquidated or converted into long-term indebtedness, while depreciation of the currencies of creditor countries was of assistance in some cases in reducing the total amount outstanding.

Solution of the problem of blocked accounts usually took one of the following forms: (*a*) creditors were paid off by installments; (*b*) blocked debts were funded by inducing creditors to accept interest-bearing bonds in exchange; and (*c*) permission was given for limited use of these accounts in payment for exports from, or tourist expenditures within, the debtor country.[8] The first two methods present no special problems. Repayment by the installment plan was carried through by Germany on a portion of her "standstill" debts and by a number of other countries, e.g., Greece and Bulgaria, on frozen commercial debts and back interest payments.[9] Argentina successfully funded the greater part of her blocked indebtedness, and Germany funded part of her blocked interest payments.[10] It is the third method of repayment, namely, the use of blocked accounts in payment for exports or tourist expenditures, which creates the most interesting issues in connection with the technique of exchange control. Perhaps the best means of unraveling the complexities of the subject is to examine in some detail the history of blocked accounts in Germany, where the existence of an unrivalled amount of foreign indebtedness gave rise to an involved network of regulations.

Blocked accounts in German reichsmarks were created at first as a result of measures restricting the withdrawal of

---

[8] Repayment was also made under the terms of clearing, payments, or special debt-transfer agreements. See Chs. VI and VII.

[9] To trace through the complicated history of the various compromises which Central European countries made with their creditors would carry us too far afield. Complete information can be found in the annual reports of the Corporation of Foreign Bondholders, London, and in the *Bulletin* of the Institute of International Finance, New York.

[10] See p. 92 below.

foreign capital from Germany. Short-term credits to banks
and municipalities were covered by the standstill agreements,[11]
while the disposal of other types of foreign credits came to be
regulated by a series of measures, adopted originally in the latter half of 1931 and the first half of 1932, and elaborated or revised in later years. After the transfer moratorium of July 1,
1933, interest and amortization payments on all debts subject
to the moratorium had to be made into a special conversion
fund (*Konversionskasse für deutsche Auslandsschulden*) at the
Reichsbank for the account of the creditor.[12] Finally, blocked
accounts arose in connection with clearing agreements (see
Chapters VI and VII).

Transfers of blocked marks (blocked accounts in reichsmarks) from one foreigner to another were not prohibited,
although special permission of the German authorities had to
be secured in connection with transfers of certain types of accounts. Thus a market for these restricted marks grew up
abroad, the original owners selling them at a discount to other
foreigners. The discount on the various classes of blocked
marks varied according to the restrictions on their use. In
1932 and the first part of 1933, certain types of blocked marks
could be used in partial payment for so-called "supplementary"
(*Zusatz*) exports, even if it was not the original owner who used
them. "Supplementary" exports were exports which could
profitably be made only if the exporter were paid, at least
partly, in depreciated marks. In other words, in order to make
himself eligible for partial payment in blocked marks, the exporter had to show that he could meet the prices quoted by his
foreign competitors only by selling at a loss unless the importer
were allowed to acquire part of the necessary means of payment at a discount. The maximum percentage of the price of an

[11] Cf. p. 36 above.

[12] J. W. F. Thelwall, *Economic Conditions in Germany, to June, 1933*, Great
Britain, Department of Overseas Trade, Report No. 553 (London, 1933), p. 9.
Payments continued to be made into the *Konversionskasse* after the second
moratorium of June, 1934.

export commodity which might be paid with funds from blocked accounts was fixed at 60 per cent.[18] The purpose of these stipulations was to prevent a falling off in accruing supplies of free foreign exchange, a result which would have followed from allowing any and all types of German exports to be paid for in blocked marks. Actually, despite these precautions, the system did have the effect of reducing the supply of free foreign exchange. In view of the necessity of competing with foreigners who were benefiting from depreciated currencies, it was not difficult for many German exporters to show that they would be obliged to sell at a loss unless they were paid partially in depreciated marks. Consequently, after the 1933 moratorium was declared, supervision of all dealings in blocked marks was centralized in the hands of the Conversion Office and the Gold Discount Bank. Export subsidization via the blocked mark method continued for a year on a strictly regularized basis, involving the utilization of the amounts blocked under the terms of the transfer moratorium, as well as the blocked accounts previously in existence.[14]

After the announcement of the second transfer moratorium on June 14, 1934, the stimulation of exports through the utilization of depreciated blocked marks was so narrowly restricted

---

[13] H. Heuser, "The German Method of Combined Debt Liquidation and Export Stimulation," *Review of Economic Studies*, I (1934), 213.

[14] Under the terms of the agreements made with creditors, interest and amortization payments were transferred *in part* after the moratorium of 1933. Foreign creditors received the remainder in the form of debt certificates or "scrip," which could be sold to foreign banks, according to an arrangement with the Gold Discount Bank, at a discount of 33%. The Gold Discount Bank then purchased the depreciated marks ("scrip") and sold them to German exporters, who were entitled to redeem them at their face value in marks at the *Konversionskasse*. As a result of this complicated process, German exporters received a profit, equal to the difference between the face value and the depreciated value of the marks. They were, however, permitted to purchase scrip only in amounts which would just compensate them for losses which they would otherwise have undergone on their export transactions. For a full and interesting exposition of this so-called "scrip" system, cf. *ibid*. Cf. also J. W. F. Thelwall, *Economic Conditions in Germany to June, 1934*, Great Britain, Department of Overseas Trade, Report No. 582 (London, 1934), pp. 36–37.

as to become of little practical importance.[15] Its place was taken by direct export subsidies and by special forms of indirect subsidization through clearing and compensation arrangements.[16]

The status of blocked marks as of the early part of 1939 can best be understood by examining the various uses to which they could be put. It is important to note that a sharp distinction was drawn between the *original owner* of blocked marks and the *secondary acquirer* of such credits. On the theory that the discount on blocked marks forced the original owner to undergo, when he sold his marks, a sacrifice which was not shared by the secondary acquirer, the restrictions imposed on the uses to which blocked marks could be put were less severe for the former than for the latter.[17] Since the application of this principle naturally resulted in an increase in the discount on blocked marks, the extent to which the original owner who wished to get his money out of Germany benefited was somewhat problematical.

In general, blocked marks could be used *by original owners*

[15] The announcement of June 14, 1934, offered to foreign creditors on Germany's medium and long-term obligations the following alternatives: (1) to receive interest payments in the form of three per cent ten-year funding bonds of the *Konversionskasse* in the same currency as the interest coupon, (2) to sell their coupons for *Devisen* to the Reichsbank at 40% of their face value, or (3) to retain all their rights under the coupons but receive no immediate payment. Subsequently, agreements were made with England, France, Switzerland, Sweden, the Netherlands, Belgium, Italy, and Finland, providing in all cases for payment in full of interest on the Dawes and Young loans. England was able to secure, for its nationals holding other loans, an offer of four per cent funding bonds (instead of three per cent), while agreements made with the other countries mentioned (except France) provided for the payment of full interest on Reich loans and of interest up to 4½ per cent on non-Reich loans. American creditors were unable to secure any special arrangement, partly because of the U. S. Government's unwillingness to enter into clearing agreements, partly because America's "favorable" balance of trade with Germany rendered difficult the conclusion of any sort of payment arrangement, and partly for other reasons. See Rawlins, *op. cit.*, pp. 22–24 and Harris, *Germany's Foreign Indebtedness,* pp. 57–58. On the relation between the balance of trade and the conclusion of clearing or payments agreements, see pp. 124–25, 193 below.

[16] See Chs. VI and VII.

[17] Cf. F. Rosenstiel, "Ausländische Sperrguthaben in Deutschland," *Die Wirtschaftskurve,* XIV (1936), 302.

for (*a*) purchases of German securities, (*b*) certain other long-term investments in Germany, (*c*) expenses of a non-business journey to Germany by the owner of the account, his family, and suite, up to a maximum of 2,000 marks per person per month, (*d*) gifts to relatives or charitable, religious, educational, and similar institutions in Germany, and (*e*) payment of 25 per cent of the invoice price of German goods purchased for the account of the original holder of the credit, provided the cost of foreign materials contained in the goods did not constitute more than 20 per cent of their total value.[18] With certain exceptions, special permission of the exchange control authorities was required in every case, and certain of the above transactions were forbidden to holders of some classes of blocked marks. In granting permission for investment of funds in Germany, the authorities saw to it that foreigners should not acquire the controlling interest in a German enterprise, that they should not receive more than a stipulated rate of interest, that their funds should be invested for a term of at least five years, and that, in general, their investments should be beneficial to the German economy.[19]

The outlets for "acquired" blocked marks were circumscribed by regulations which became progressively more rigid as time went on. After July 15, 1937, holders were permitted to utilize them only for such investments as "Four Year Plan" projects, the production of substitute (*"Ersatz"*) commodities, the exploitation of sub-marginal domestic raw materials, and other ventures of a risky or unprofitable nature.[20] This policy nat-

[18] Cf. *ibid.*, pp. 302–10, Rawlins, *op. cit.*, pp. 31–36, and *Foreign Financial News: Special Circular*, No. 407 (April 8, 1935) and No. 410 (August 19, 1935), pp. 6–8. Permission to use blocked marks in the purchase of German goods held only for new orders and did not apply to goods for export to certain countries which had concluded clearing or payments agreements with Germany.

[19] Cf. Piatier, *op. cit.*, p. 58. Although the purposes for which blocked marks could be used were outlined in the exchange control regulations, the exchange control offices could utilize a considerable amount of discretion in granting or refusing permission for transactions. Cf. *Foreign Financial News: European Financial Notes*, No. 262 (March 24, 1938), p. 8.

[20] *Ibid.*

urally discouraged the acquiring of blocked marks and led to a sharp decline in their market value, which was already low. (See Table IV.)

Registered marks belong in a special category. They arose under a clause of the third standstill agreement (signed in February, 1933), which provided that repayments of standstill credits should be made into special accounts at the Reichsbank in favor of the registered titleholders. The purposes for which these accounts could be used were governed by the provisions of the third and subsequent standstill agreements. The regulations were somewhat more liberal than in the case of other blocked marks, and in addition to being used for certain types of investments in Germany, they could be sold, through foreign bank creditors or other authorized institutions, to foreign travelers going to Germany. A relatively steady demand for these marks on the part of foreign tourists (who naturally preferred purchasing blocked marks at a discount to paying the full price for "official" marks) tended to maintain their price at a higher level than that of other blocked marks with more restricted outlets.

Still later, the purchase of registered marks for "benevolent remittances," in limited amounts, to persons living in Germany was permitted. In fact, under the provisions of the more recent standstill agreements, registered marks destined to be sold for this and certain other purposes were split off from the main body of registered marks and given new names. Thus arose the "travel" mark (*Reisemark*), sold exclusively to foreign tourists, and the "assistance" mark (*Register-Geschenkmark* or *Unterstutzüngsmark*), sold exclusively for benevolent remittances. These new categories of registered marks, being in greater demand than those destined merely for investment within Germany, were quoted at smaller discounts than registered marks proper. They were subject, however, to a special license fee, to be paid by the purchaser, which tended to reduce their attractiveness. After December 1, 1938, this fee amounted to $3.75 per hundred RM, whereas "travel" marks formerly bore a tax of $2.50 per hundred RM and "assistance" marks no tax at all.[21]

TABLE IV

Quotations for Certain Important Classes of Blocked Marks,
December 16, 1938 [a]

(In per cent of free marks)

Credit blocked marks	11⅞ to 12¼
Security blocked marks	10⅝ to 11
Emigrants' blocked marks	6½ [b]
Assistance marks	60⅜ to 61¾
Registered marks	43⅜ to 44¾

[a] Source: *Foreign Financial News: European Financial Notes*, Vol. I (NS), No. 1 (January 9, 1939), p. 6.
[b] Purchase price of German Golddiskontbank.

Thus, while blocked reichsmarks ceased to be of any importance as a means of stimulating German exports, they continued to play a significant rôle in connection with the German tourist trade. The purchase of registered marks at depreciated rates by foreign tourists was made possible by the fact that foreign creditors chose to sell their blocked reichsmarks at a discount rather than to gamble on the prospect of being repaid in full at some vague future date.

Before we leave the subject of blocked debts and export stimulation in Germany, we should mention a closely allied practice, also arising out of the exchange restrictions, whereby Germany succeeded for a period in simultaneously reducing her *long-term* foreign indebtedness and subsidizing her exports. Although purchases of securities in foreign markets by German nationals were naturally forbidden under the exchange regulations, a series of measures, promulgated in 1932, allowed ex-

[21] See *The Economist*, CXXXIII (1938), 487, and the New York *Staats-Zeitung und Herald*, November 22, 1938. In accordance with the terms of the seventh standstill agreement (1937), the proceeds of the license fee imposed on travel marks under the agreement were to be placed in a special foreign exchange fund, to be held in trust by the Reichsbank and to be used for repayment in foreign exchange of cash advances and similar obligations to standstill creditors. (*Foreign Financial News: European Financial Notes*, No. 239 [April 9, 1937], p. 6.)

porters to retain a certain proportion of the foreign exchange accruing from their exports for the purchase abroad of German bonds issued in foreign currencies. Special permission was required for each transaction, and the exports involved had to be "additional," in the sense in which this term has been used in connection with blocked accounts. Since, as a result of the exchange restrictions, prices quoted for German bonds in foreign markets were much lower than those prevailing in German markets, exporters could make substantial profits by reselling these bonds in Germany, thereby compensating themselves for losses on exports. Operations of this kind were for several years carried on under the auspices of the Gold Discount Bank and were responsible for the liquidation of a significant fraction of Germany's long-term foreign debt, but, officially at least, they were later forbidden.[22]

By the early part of 1938 Germany's foreign debt amounted to only about 37 per cent, in terms of reichsmarks, of the total outstanding in the middle of 1930. As the following table shows, the larger proportion of the reduction took place in short-term debts, but long-term indebtedness declined by more than half.

Germany is not the only country which permitted foreigners' blocked accounts to be utilized to some extent to stimulate exports or foreign tourists' expenditures. A number of other countries in Central and Southeastern Europe, such as Austria, Hungary, Rumania, and Yugoslavia, adopted similar measures in 1932 and later years, especially in connection with tourists' expenditures. In general, their regulations with respect to blocked accounts were somewhat more liberal than those of Germany. Since currency values were eventually adjusted

---

[22] Cf. Piatier, *op. cit.*, p. 139. Transactions of this kind, if permitted freely, tended to defeat their own purpose in the long run, for, as German bonds were purchased abroad, their prices in foreign markets rose and approached the prices prevailing within Germany. Cf. *Commerce Reports*, October 29, 1932, p. 73. For further discussion of this device, see E. Wolfgang and E. Cahnmann, "Schuldentilgung durch Anleiherückkäufe," *Die Wirtschaftskurve*, XII (1933), 43–53.

TABLE V

GERMANY'S FOREIGN DEBT, 1930–1938 [a]

(In billions of RM)

DATE		LONG-TERM DEBT	SHORT-TERM DEBT		GRAND TOTAL
			Total	Standstill	
Middle of					
	1930	—	—	—	26.8
	1931	10.7	13.1	6.3	23.8
February					
	1933	10.3	8.7	4.1	19.0
	1934	7.2	6.7	2.6	13.9
	1935	6.4	6.7	2.1	13.1
	1936	6.1	6.3	1.7	12.4
	1937	5.4	5.4	1.2	10.8
	1938	5.0	5.0	0.9	10.0

[a] Source: Reichs-Kredit-Gesellschaft, *Germany's Economic Situation at the Turn of 1937–38*, p. 84, and *Germany's Economic Development during the First Half of the Year 1938* (Berlin, 1938), p. 74.   About six billion RM of the reduction between 1930 and 1937 resulted from devaluations of foreign currencies. The figure for total indebtedness in the middle of 1931 is smaller than that cited on p. 29, above, and is evidently based on the Wiggin Committee figure.

downward by one means or another in all these countries,[23] there was less need for elaborate precautions to protect "official" exchange rates. As exchange restrictions were gradually relaxed in Austria, the direct transfer at market exchange rates of more and more categories of blocked schillings was permitted, and by 1936 a substantial proportion of Austria's blocked indebtedness had been paid off.[24] Foreign holders of blocked lei accounts in Rumania were, in July, 1937, granted permission to dispose freely of such accounts, subject, however, to the approval of the Rumanian National Bank.[25]

[23] See pp. 100–102, 111–14 below.

[24] For a more complete account of the history of blocked accounts in Austria and Hungary, the reader is referred to H. S. Ellis, "Exchange Control in Austria and Hungary," a special supplement to the *Quarterly Journal of Economics*, LIV (November, 1939, Part II), *passim*.

[25] See *Foreign Financial News: European Financial Notes*, No. 248 (August 24, 1937), p. 9.

So long as blocked currencies remain within the debtor country, they tend to form a basis for credit expansion. Certain types of blocked accounts, especially frozen commercial debts or blocked interest and amortization payments, represent a net increment to investible funds in the debtor country and are likely to provide the foundation for an extension of bank credit. If deposited in the central bank, their potentialities in this direction may, of course, be greatly enhanced. In certain countries, foreigners' blocked accounts have formed a basis for government borrowing.[26] The use of this expedient to tide over a temporary budgetary crisis may very well prove beneficial to the country's creditors in the long run. It is clear, however, that credit expansion in any form, whether based on blocked accounts or not, tends to enhance the need for an eventual devaluation of the currency.

3. The Readjustment of Currency Values

a. A discussion of various methods. The great majority of exchange-control countries eventually resorted to some form of currency devaluation, partial or complete, in the years from

---

[26] On November 30, 1938, the German *Konversionskasse* had the following assets, in thousands of RM:

Claims against the Reichsbank		82,665
Other Claims		21,675
Investments		648,478
	Total	752,818

(*Foreign Financial News: European Financial Notes,* Vol. I (NS), No. 1 [January 9, 1939], p. 7).

Although no breakdown of these figures is published, it has long been believed that a substantial proportion of the *Konversionskasse's* funds has gone into government employment bills. Cf. *ibid.,* No. 198 (July 24, 1935), p. 6.

The Financial Committee of the League of Nations, recognizing the acute budgetary difficulties of the Hungarian government, reported, early in 1933, that it would not be contrary to the interests of foreign creditors if, out of the blocked pengö accounts, an amount not exceeding 50 million pengö were utilized, against an issue of Treasury bonds, to cover the budgetary deficit for the current fiscal year. Report cited in *The Times,* London, January 26, 1933.

1932 on. The liquidation of blocked accounts at a discount represents a partial depreciation of the currency, even though the official exchange rate remains effective for most transactions. This is not the only form of partial depreciation or devaluation which exchange control countries permitted, however. Many countries passed through a period during which a number of different exchange rates ruled for various types of transactions, and in certain countries this situation still prevailed in the summer of 1939.

The manner in which a downward adjustment of the value of the currency has been achieved has differed greatly among the various exchange control countries. In general, the following methods may be distinguished:

    (*a*) Straightforward devaluation while maintaining control;
    (*b*) Permission to exporters to sell an increasing proportion of their foreign exchange freely on the domestic market;
    (*c*) Enforcement, for certain types of transactions, of governmentally fixed exchange rates higher than the "official" rate;
    (*d*) Payment of premia on exports and imposition of surcharges on imports as a means of compensating for the difference between the official exchange rate and the rate which would prevail in the absence of restrictions;
    (*e*) Employment in clearing agreements or compensation transactions of a rate of exchange intended to approximate that which would prevail in the absence of restrictions. (This method has been utilized to some extent in most exchange control countries and will be discussed in Chapters VI and VII.) [27]

The first method, devaluation, calls for no special comment, except to point out that, where rigid exchange restrictions have been enforced for a considerable period prior to devaluation, it is sometimes difficult to determine what the new exchange rate should be. Czechoslovakia reduced the value of her currency by approximately 16 per cent in 1934, but was forced to lower its value again at the time of the gold *bloc* devalua-

[27] Cf. League of Nations, *Report on Exchange Control*, pp. 46–47.

tions.[28] The rate in force from 1934 to 1936 had proved difficult to enforce. Italy represents another case of an important exchange-control country which carried through a straightforward devaluation. The fact that the Italian exchange restrictions were not relaxed to any appreciable extent after the devaluation was effected in the autumn of 1936 is not necessarily an indication that the value of the currency was not lowered sufficiently at that time, since the exchange control regime shortly thereafter became bound up with an intensified drive for autarky. In this connection, it may be well to point out that the success of devaluation, whether in an exchange-control country or a free-exchange country, will depend, not only on estimating with reasonable accuracy the proper limits of devaluation in the first place, but also on subsequently pursuing a monetary and economic policy designed to maintain the currency at its new level.[29]

The second method, gradual official recognition of the free exchange market, as noted in the League of Nations *Report on Exchange Control*,[30] has the "great merit that it permits the real rate of exchange to be gauged." The prototype of the countries which pursued this path to relaxation of exchange control was Austria.[31] Early in 1932, the Austrian National Bank began to grant permission to exporters to sell foreign exchange directly to authorized Austrian importers.[32] Such transactions, since they involved the direct offsetting of imports against exports, were called "private clearings" and were conducted on the basis of the free "international" exchange rate for

[28] See Table II.
[29] Even where, as in the case of France, the value of the currency after devaluation is not fixed but is allowed to seek its own level between an upper and lower limit, subsequent devaluation may prove necessary. (See pp. 39 ff. above.)
[30] P. 47.
[31] Others were Portugal, Bulgaria, and Latvia. Cf. *ibid.*, and League of Nations, *Money and Banking, 1937–38*, I, 31–32.
[32] Only a brief review of the Austrian experience, based primarily on the League of Nations quarterly reports on the *Financial Position of Austria*, will be given here. For a complete account, see Ellis, *op. cit.*

the schilling, i.e., the rate at which transactions in schillings were being conducted in important foreign markets such as Zurich and London. At first, permission for dealings of this kind was granted only exceptionally, in connection with "additional" exports and certain essential imports, but by the end of 1932, the National Bank had ceased to allocate "official" foreign exchange for commercial purposes, and Austria's foreign trade was being conducted on the basis of officially supervised private clearings, handled through the *Wiener Giro und Kassenverein,* or on the basis of dealings in unofficial markets.[33] Gradually, the market rate of exchange was made effective for transactions in connection with invisible items in the balance of payments as well as for trade transactions.[34] By the middle of 1933, this market rate had settled at a point which represented a depreciation of 21–22 per cent on the basis of the former gold value of the schilling, and from that time on it showed only minor fluctuations.[35] As the system became regularized, the rate was established daily by the National Bank, on the basis of the volume of exchange offerings and bids as reported by the Austrian banks.[36] Exchange control was not abandoned, but the restrictions which were enforced were of an extremely mild sort. While a permit had to be secured from the National Bank for all purchases of exchange, no difficulty was encountered in securing such a permit for legitimate transactions with free-exchange countries. The situation, of course, has changed vastly since March, 1938, for the absorption of Austria into the German Reich was followed by a series of measures whereby Austrian foreign exchange transactions were

[33] Trade with some countries was regulated by clearing agreements, and "private compensation" transactions were permitted under certain conditions. See Chapters VI and VII.

[34] On April 6, 1933, all persons, whether foreign or native, were freed from the obligation of surrendering exchange to the National Bank. See League of Nations, *Financial Position of Austria in the First Quarter of 1933* (Geneva, 1933), p. 9.

[35] See League of Nations, *Money and Banking, 1937–38,* I., 108.

[36] *Foreign Financial News: Special Circular,* No. 416 (April 25, 1936), p. 2.

to be carried on in terms of reichsmarks and were to be subject to the provisions of the German exchange regulations.[37]

Austria was fortunate in securing, in August, 1933, an international loan, as a result of a provision of the Lausanne Agreement of July, 1932, but it was only through careful management that the Austrian government succeeded in relaxing exchange restrictions so smoothly and quickly. Other countries, which pursued an essentially similar path toward relaxation of exchange control, adopted regulations differing somewhat from those of Austria and, in general, proceeded more slowly.[38]

Latin American countries, like Austria, pursued a policy which involved gradually official recognition of the "black bourse" rate, but, in a number of cases, they also set up controlled rates which were intermediate between the "official" rate and the "black bourse" rate. Hence, they combined methods (*b*) and (*c*) [39] and in the process evolved a type of exchange control which was more or less peculiar to Latin America and may be characterized as a "multiple exchange rate" system. Since the regulations have tended to be somewhat complicated in nature, we shall describe the system in some detail.

b. Multiple exchange rates in Latin America. We have already noted that the spirit of exchange regulations in Latin America, from the very beginning, differed from that in Europe. No attempt was made to maintain currency values at their former levels. In fixing official exchange rates, the authorities recognized substantial degrees of depreciation, and, as time went on, official rates were frequently revised, in order to take account of further depreciation. Black bourses were not seriously interfered with, and the exchange regulations had the

---

[37] See *Foreign Financial News: European Financial Notes,* Nos. 262–80 (March–December, 1938).

[38] In Portugal, exporters, even in 1932, had to sell only 50 per cent of their exchange to the central bank, and this percentage was gradually reduced until October, 1937, when exchange restrictions were completely abolished. See *Foreign Financial News: Special Circular,* No. 388 (February 20, 1933), p. 23, and League of Nations, *Money and Banking, 1937–38,* I, 33.

[39] See p. 99 above.

effect, on the whole, merely of permitting exchange for essential imports and governmental payments abroad to be secured at preferential rates.

In 1931 and 1932, most of the Latin American countries, largely as a result of currency depreciation, experienced increases in their active balances of trade which tended to relieve the pressure on the exchanges. This made possible, and in some cases was encouraged by, a relaxation of the regulations requiring exporters to sell their exchange at official rates. Official rates continued to be enforced for certain types of transactions, while black bourse rates received official recognition for other types of transactions. In addition, semi-official intermediate rates came into being. The operation of this system can be made clear by a few concrete examples.

In Chile, during the first ten months of exchange control, official exchange, at a rate of approximately 40 pesos to the pound sterling, was available only for limited purchases of raw materials and essentials from abroad. Meanwhile, foreign currencies could be purchased on the black bourse at a rate which was equivalent to approximately 96 pesos per pound sterling. Exporters were in theory required to sell their exchange to the Banco Central at the official rate, but the strict enforcement of this principle would have limited seriously their ability to compete in foreign markets. "Hence, in practice and from the outset, exporters exercised the right to compensate exports with imports authorized by the Control Committee, importing merchandise of an equal value, or ceding their rights to third parties." [40] The rate of exchange at which these operations were effected was the so-called *export rate,* which was determined by demand and supply conditions. It tended to fluctuate slightly below the black bourse rate but well above the official rate.

In April, 1932, this system was regularized by a new exchange control decree, which reduced the official exchange

---

[40] Banco Central de Chile, *Monthly Report on Credit and Business Conditions,* August, 1934, p. 3.

value of the peso to 80 per pound sterling. A decree of September, 1932, provided that exporters were required to sell to the Banco Central at the *official rate* only certain fixed percentages of the value of their exports. These percentages ranged from a maximum of 20 per cent for a few articles, such as wool and skins, to a minimum of one per cent. As a result of these regulations, the following situation prevailed:

(1) The Banco Central purchased at the *official rate* certain small percentages of the foreign exchange received by exporters, which it in turn sold (*a*) to the national government for any foreign expenditures it might make,[41] (*b*) to importers for the payment of customs duties, and (*c*) to importers of a few raw materials and necessaries.

(2) Exporters were permitted to sell the remainder of their exchange at the *export rate* to importers who held permits from the Banco Central. The majority of imports were financed in this way, the central bank seeing to it that permits were granted only for amounts equivalent to the value of exchange being delivered by exporters at this rate.

(3) Foreign balances coming into the possession of Chilean residents as a result of transactions other than exports could be sold at the *unofficial* (black bourse) *rate*. Importers unable to secure permits to purchase official or export exchange were allowed to purchase unofficial exchange.

(4) In addition, *compensation rates* of exchange were fixed for transactions coming under clearing or compensation agreements. (See Chapter VII.) [42]

The Chilean authorities have attempted to "peg" the unofficial or free market rate by setting a maximum rate above which banks were not permitted to sell free exchange. The

[41] Chile had defaulted on the service of its foreign debts, however. Cf. p. 77 n. above.

[42] Banco Central de Chile, *Monthly Report on Credit and Business Conditions*, August, 1934, p. 3. Foreign exchange, derived from gold produced in Chile, has in recent years been available at the *gold exchange rate* for imports of certain luxury and dispensable articles. Dealings at this rate have not, however, been especially important, and no very consistent policy has been pursued by the government with respect to them. See *Foreign Financial News: Latin American Financial Notes, seriatim.*

result has been the existence, at most times, of a "legalized free" rate (somewhat below the true curb rate), which was of little practical importance, since the banks did not, in fact, sell exchange at this rate. Late in 1938, Chilean banks were given unofficial authorization by the Exchange Control Commission to deal in curb exchange at market rates.[43]

The net result of this apparently complicated system has been that the bulk of Chile's foreign trade has been conducted on the basis of a peso considerably lower in value than the official peso. This has permitted the exchange authorities to follow, on the whole, a relatively liberal policy with respect to allotments of exchange for imports, and, in consequence, Chile's exports and imports have been brought into a kind of equilibrium through the quasi-automatic working of the foreign exchanges rather than through stringent restrictions on the demand for foreign currencies. Meanwhile, the government has been in a position to earmark certain of the exchange profits for its rearmament program.[44]

The course of events in Argentina differed from that in Chile, in that a vigorous attempt was made to enforce the official rate for all exchange transactions throughout the first two years of exchange control. The official paper peso was equivalent to 25.8¢ in terms of the United States currency, which represented a depreciation of approximately 39 per cent from the previous par value. No exceptions to the regulation requiring exporters to turn over their foreign means of payment at this rate were allowed, aside from the fact that amounts below a certain minimum might be retained. Supplies of exchange coming into the hands of the Banco Nacional were, however, inadequate to pay for all imports *in toto,* and a sizable amount of blocked balances to the credit of foreigners accumulated.[45] Beginning with the Runciman-Roca Agreement of May 1, 1933, with

[43] *Ibid.,* No. 254 (October 29, 1938), p. 4.
[44] *Ibid.,* No. 251 (September 14, 1938), p. 5.
[45] Cf. p. 76 above.

the United Kingdom, a series of agreements with foreign countries provided for the funding of these blocked balances. As a
result, the Argentine authorities felt free to modify the exchange restrictions.

The first series of modifications was made in November,
1933. In the first place, the official exchange value of the peso
was reduced by 16.6 per cent. Secondly, foreign exchange was
to be sold to importers by tender, allotments going to the highest bidder. Only importers securing advance permits were
to be permitted to make bids, and the distribution of these advance permits would depend on the available supply of exchange. Importers failing to secure permits were allowed to
have recourse to the black bourse which was thereby officially
recognized as a free market. Thirdly, exporters were to continue to sell exchange at the official rate; *but,* producers of certain important export commodities, i.e., wheat, maize, and linseed, were to be subsidized out of the profits which the government expected to make on its exchange operations.[46] Further, it
was expected that the profits could also be applied to re-
imbursing the government for the additional cost of meeting
the foreign debt service resulting from the devaluation of the
peso.

A month later, it was decreed that exchange derived from
exports of goods not regularly exported in the past could be
freely negotiated in the open market. This measure was intended to encourage the export of wine, grapes, and other
products that could not be profitably exported at the official
rate.

---

[46] A Grain Board was to be created with authority to purchase these commodities on government account from growers, at prices that exceeded world
prices, and resell to shippers at world prices. Other similar boards were later
set up. The power of the Grain Board to purchase wheat and linseed at fixed
minimum prices was revoked in December, 1936, but revived in November,
1938. Cf. *Foreign Financial News: Latin American Financial Notes,* No. 257
(December 14, 1938), p. 1, and V. L. Phelps, *The International Economic Position of Argentina* (Philadelphia, 1938), pp. 71–73.

As a result of these and other minor changes in the system, three exchange rates emerged:

(a) The *official buying rate,* at which exporters, in general, were required to sell their holdings of foreign means of payment. After January, 1934, this rate was pegged to the pound sterling, at 15 pesos to the pound.

(b) The *official selling rate,* at which exchange was sold to holders of advance permits for remittances in connection with imports or financial services. A fixed selling rate of 17 pesos to the pound sterling was eventually substituted for the tender system.

(c) The *free market rate.* Exchange on this market derived from non-goods transactions and from two types of exports, (a) exports of goods not regularly exported in the past and (b) exports to certain neighboring countries. It could be purchased by non-holders of advance permits for imports or financial remittances.[47]

Essentially, then, there have been two markets for foreign exchange in Argentina, the official market and the legalized free market. In the official market, a relatively wide margin has been maintained between the selling rate and the buying rate. The differentiation of exchange rates has made possible for the Argentine authorities the accomplishment of four principal objectives. In the first place, the margin between the official buying and selling rates has permitted the accumulation of exchange profits, which have been utilized mainly (a) for export subsidies, (b) to meet exchange losses on the service of the national debt, and (c) to set up an Exchange Equalization

[47] For a time there also was an *official rate for private remittances,* fixed at 10 per cent above the average accepted tender rate for imports and financial services. This rate disappeared on August 1, 1934, after which private remitters were permitted to purchase exchange on the free market. On all this, see S. G. Irving, *Economic Conditions in the Argentine Republic, March, 1935,* Great Britain, Department of Overseas Trade, Report No. 608 (London, 1935), pp. 42–45; *The Economist,* CXVII (1933), 1120; *Foreign Financial News: Special Circular,* No. 397 (April 1, 1934), pp. 2–3, and *Foreign Financial News: Latin American Financial Notes,* No. 240 (March 29, 1938), pp. 1–5. For statistics on exchange rates, see Banco Central de la Republica Argentina, *Annual Report,* 1936, p. 12.

Fund. The profits have, on the whole, been larger than was anticipated; and, as a result of the rise in world prices for cereals between 1933 and 1936, only a small proportion of these profits had to be utilized to reimburse the Grain Board for its losses.[48]

Secondly, the differentiation of exchange rates has permitted Argentina to grant preferential rates for remittances to countries with which her balance of trade has been active or with which she has signed special agreements modeled on the Runciman-Roca Agreement with Great Britain.[49] In general, the policy pursued has been to issue advance permits for remittances of "official" exchange to individual countries up to the amount of the country's purchases of Argentine products. Importers and others failing to secure such permits have been obliged to have recourse to the free market.[50] In 1934 and the early part of 1935, the advantage of securing advance permits threatened to disappear, for the free market rate was showing a tendency to approach the official selling rate. Accordingly, in April, 1935, it was provided that all imports not covered by prior permits, with certain unimportant exceptions, were to be subject to a surcharge in foreign currency, which, when added to the difference between the official selling and the free market rates, would represent a margin of 20 per cent above the former.[51] In January, 1938, the prescribed margin was reduced to 10 per cent, but the depreciation of the free rate

---

[48] The great profitableness of the exchange operations for 1934 facilitated the formation, early in the following year, of a central bank, which took over the handling of the exchange. (Irving, *op. cit.*, pp. 43–44.)

[49] Cf. pp. 190–91 below.

[50] Argentina's policy of exchange allocations has been somewhat flexible, in that advance exchange permits have been granted for importations of certain necessities, even if the balance of trade with the country supplying them was passive. See *Foreign Financial News: Special Circular,* No. 409 (August 1, 1935), p. 1. At the end of 1937, the Central Bank reported that 83 per cent of the country's imports were paid for through purchases of official exchange. (Banco Central de la Republica Argentina, *Annual Report,* 1937, p. 4.)

[51] S. G. Irving, *Economic Conditions in the Argentine Republic, April, 1936,* Great Britain, Department of Overseas Trade, Report No. 639 (London, 1936), p. 7.

which occurred at about the same time rendered the reduction ineffective in practice.[52]

A third objective accomplished by the multiple rate system has been the stimulation of certain types of exports which Argentina has not regularly sold abroad in the past, through permitting exporters of the commodities concerned to sell their exchange at the higher rates prevailing in the free market. These exports, which are somewhat analogous to the "additional" or "supplementary" exports already mentioned in connection with the exchange regulations of certain European countries,[53] do not, however, occupy a position of much importance in Argentina's foreign trade. About 90 per cent of the export exchange is sold in the official market, and, of that sold in the free market, the major portion is derived from exports to certain neighboring countries.[54] In a number of other Latin American Republics, where only a fraction of export exchange must be sold in the official market, certain dominant exports, such as Brazilian coffee or Bolivian tin, have been relied on to provide the bulk of official exchange. Even in the case of these commodities, however, only a certain percentage of the export proceeds need be surrendered at the official rate.[55]

Finally, in the view of the Argentine authorities, a fourth objective has been achieved as a result of the differentiation of exchange rates. Substantial amounts of capital, to a large extent in the form of short-term funds, tend to flow into Argentina during periods of prosperity and out again during periods of depression.[56] To a considerable degree, these capital

[52] Cf. League of Nations, *Money and Banking, 1937–38,* I, 35–36.

[53] See pp. 90 ff. above.

[54] See Banco Central de la Republica Argentina, *Annual Report,* 1937, pp. 4, 5.

[55] The regulations have been subject to frequent alteration. In November, 1937, Brazil abolished the requirement that 35 per cent of the exchange proceeds of coffee exports had to be surrendered at the official rate. (League of Nations, *Money and Banking, 1937–38,* I, 35.) It would be interesting, though statistically very difficult, to determine the comparative advantage of any one of a number of Latin American countries with respect to its various exports, and then to study the results in the light of existing exchange regulations.

[56] Cf. Bank for International Settlements, *Eighth Annual Report,* pp. 66–67.

movements are speculative in nature, being motivated partly
by anticipations of changes in exchange rates. Under the present set-up, they are handled entirely through the free market
and have no direct effect on the fixed rates in the official
market. Thus, the free market, which absorbs the effects of
unstable international monetary developments, is regarded as
a sort of safety valve for the official market.[57] Because most
of Argentina's foreign trade is handled through the stable official market, export, and import prices, and through them the
internal economy, tend (it is argued) to be insulated from the
effects of fluctuations in the exchange rates. Meanwhile, the
rate in the free market is controlled, to some extent, by means of
official intervention on the part of the Central Bank through
its Exchange Equalization Fund.[58]

It is clear, however, that any marked tendency for the value
of the currency to depreciate in the free market would eventually have repercussions on the official market, for there would
be a tendency for sales of exchange to be diverted, legally or
illegally, to the free market, while purchasers of exchange
would seek to buy at the relatively favorable rate in the official market. Thus we find that the *official selling rate*, which
had been lowered to 16 pesos to the pound sterling in December, 1936, during a period of prosperity in the export industries, was raised to 17 pesos in November, 1938, at a time when
unfavorable developments in the export market were resulting
in a substantial rise in the free exchange rate. In addition,
a decree of November 7, 1938, inaugurated a requirement of
advance permits for all imports, including those handled
through the free market.[59]

[57] Banco Central de la Republica Argentina, *Annual Report,* 1937, p. 5.
[58] *Ibid.,* pp. 5–14. The whole system represents a rather unusual type of
"managed currency standard." It is interesting to compare this attempt to
insulate the internal price-structure from the effects of unstable capital
movements with the former system of gold "sterilization" in the United
States.
[59] *Foreign Financial News: Latin American Financial Notes,* No. 255 (November 14, 1938), p. 1.

Other South American countries developed, for the most part, multiple exchange rate systems more closely resembling that of Chile than that of Argentina. In the last few years there has been some tendency for the distinction between official and free rates to disappear, generally in consequence of the abolition of the former official rates and the legalization of the free rate for all transactions.[60] This development has usually been followed, however, by the appearance of new curb or "black bourse" rates, which may eventually be officially recognized in their turn. Exchange developments in Latin American countries tend to follow very closely the fluctuations in prices of dominant export commodities, and the immediate future of exchange control in this region will depend to a considerable extent on what happens to prices of raw materials and agricultural products. It is improbable, however, that the multiple exchange rate technique will be altogether abandoned in the near future, for it has clearly been made to serve a multitude of purposes.

c. The premium and surcharge method of currency adjustment. Several of the Danubian countries which have not officially reduced the values of their currencies have secured the benefits of a *de facto* devaluation through the inauguration of a premium and surcharge system. The central bank buys foreign exchange at a premium over the official parity, while importers and others purchasing exchange must pay a surcharge. Through the adoption of this device, Hungary, Rumania, and Yugoslavia attempted to bring their currencies into line with the important "free" currencies of the world without relinquishing nominal adherence to former gold parities. Although the manner in which the system evolved differed somewhat in the three countries, essentially the same result was secured. A brief examination of the measures adopted by Hungary will therefore give us an adequate picture of the nature of this method of currency alignment.

[60] Cf. League of Nations, *Money and Banking, 1937–38,* I, 34–35.

In December, 1932, Hungary adopted a limited system of official premia and surcharges for the purpose of promoting agricultural exports and securing essential supplies of raw materials from abroad.[61] Exporters of certain agricultural commodities were paid a premium over the official purchasing rate for foreign exchange surrendered to the National Bank, in cases where prices abroad were so low as to render export of their products difficult or impossible without such assistance. The funds required for payment of these premiums were raised by imposing a surcharge on importers who were allotted foreign exchange for the purchase abroad of certain important raw materials. The foreign balances accruing from exports made possible in this manner were allocated to a separate fund, handled by the "Hungarian Agricultural and Foreign Trading Compensation Office," and, except for a certain percentage retained by the National Bank, were utilized to pay for imports of raw materials coming under the scheme. Premium and surcharge rates were variable, no more being granted to exporters than was necessary to permit them to market their products at a reasonable profit. Since an attempt was being made to avoid any rise in internal prices, the authorities were anxious to limit the size of premiums and surcharges as much as possible. At first, premiums received by exporters ranged from 3 to 20 per cent, while importers paid a surcharge of 13.5 to 17 per cent.[62] Later, the rates showed a tendency to increase, and in the first eleven months of 1935 average monthly premiums for exports ranged from 21.7 to 24.8 per cent and, for imports, from 21.6 to 28.5 per cent.[63]

---

[61] Cf. *Devisenbewirtschaftung in Ungarn* (Budapest: Verlagsabteilung der Sparkassen und Banken, 8th ed., April 20, 1937), p. 31.

[62] League of Nations, *Financial Position of Hungary in the First Quarter of 1933* (Geneva, 1933), p. 11.

[63] League of Nations, *Financial Position of Hungary in the Fourth Quarter of 1935* (Geneva, 1936), p. 8. The procedure was not at first applicable to countries with which Hungary had clearing agreements, but during the course of 1933 most of the clearing agreements were revised to permit extension of the scheme to trade coming under the agreements. Premiums and surcharges tended

During the course of 1933 and the two following years, a few minor modifications were made in the exchange regulations to provide for the payment of premia or surcharges in connection with certain of the invisible items in Hungary's balance of payments.[64] The system of variable *agios*, however, was not conducive to stability. No marked expansion of Hungarian trade could take place as long as exporters and importers could not be certain in advance what the premium or surcharge rate would be for any given transaction. By the end of 1935, various factors, including a gradual rise of internal prices and a tendency toward greater stability in the discount on pengö in foreign markets, rendered desirable the introduction of a system of generalized and uniform *agios*. Consequently, a new set of regulations was adopted in December, 1935. In the case of transactions with countries with which Hungary had no clearing agreements, a uniform premium of 50 per cent was to be paid on all foreign exchange surrendered to the National Bank, while a surcharge of 53 per cent was to be exacted on all exchange released by the Bank.[65] The new rates were to apply to non-goods as well as to goods transactions. By agreement with the countries concerned, generalized premia and surcharges

---

to be relatively low for trade with clearing-agreement countries (see p. 114 below), a fact which must be borne in mind in interpreting the averages cited in the text. Thus, while premia applied in the case of clearing countries averaged about 23 per cent toward the end of 1935, rates for non-clearing countries averaged about 38 per cent. (*Ibid.*, p. 10.)

[64] From April, 1933, on, for example, the payment of a 20 per cent surcharge was required in the case of purchases of exchange for foreign travel. See *The Economist*, CXVI (1933), 911.

[65] See League of Nations, *Financial Position of Hungary in the Fourth Quarter of 1935*, pp. 8–10, and *Foreign Financial News: European Financial Notes*, No. 210 (January 24, 1936), p. 13. The surcharge of 53 per cent corresponded to the premium which the Hungarian authorities were paying for gold. Meanwhile, however, blocked pengö were being sold at varying discounts which in many cases greatly exceeded 53 per cent. Cf. *ibid.*, No. 211 (February 8, 1936), p. 16. Hungary's trade with non-clearing countries, however, is relatively unimportant. The major portion is conducted on a clearing or compensation basis. Moreover, in practice, the premia and surcharges actually set by the administrative authorities are not altogether uniform. (Cf. Ellis, *op. cit.*, p. 99 n.)

were also to apply to transactions with clearing countries, but
the rates varied for different countries and were originally lower
in all cases than for non-clearing countries. Furthermore, they
have since been modified from time to time to take account of
changes in currency conditions in certain of these countries, e.g.,
the devaluation of the Swiss and French francs and of the
Italian lira. The Hungarian authorities have apparently attempted in each case to arrive at something like the exchange
ratio which would prevail between the two currencies concerned
in the absence of exchange control. Where the former mint
parity between the pengö and the other currency concerned still
constituted the nominal basis of currency conversion in the
clearing agreement, the premia and surcharges tended to be
relatively low. Thus the agreement with Germany, from March
20, 1936, on, called for an export premium of 18 per cent and
an import surcharge of 19½ per cent.[66]

Essentially similar, though differing somewhat in detail, was
the evolution of the premium system in Rumania. It is interesting to note that the adoption of a uniform *agio* of 38 per cent
on all "strong" currencies took place in December, 1935, the
very month in which Hungary generalized her premia.[67] Yugoslavia, on the other hand, arrived at a uniform *agio* of 28½ per
cent as early as 1933 and later relaxed her exchange restrictions
in other respects to a considerably greater extent than either
Hungary or Rumania. Thus, the percentage of foreign exchange which exporters had to surrender to the National
Bank was gradually reduced from 80 per cent in 1931 to 25 per
cent in January, 1938.[68]

---

[66] See *Devisenbewirtschaftung in Ungarn,* p. 35. The fixing of relatively low
premia and surcharges for Germany implied official recognition by the two governments concerned that the German reichsmark, on the basis of its official valuation, was out of line with other currencies. On the other hand, the fact that
premia and surcharges were paid at all implied that the purchasing power of
the pengö was actually lower, in terms of its former par value, than that of the
mark.

[67] In general, "strong" currencies are those of countries with no official exchange control.

[68] See League of Nations, *Money and Banking, 1937–38,* I, 32.

4. *Other Measures of Relaxation*

In the main, apart from currency readjustment and special devices with respect to blocked indebtedness, measures of relaxation of exchange control during the thirties consisted simply in the gradual removal of various restrictions on the purchase or sale of foreign exchange or in the more lenient administration of existing regulations. Most of these changes call for no special comment, except to point out that the problem of currency readjustment cannot be considered as separate from the problem of liberation of restrictions, for, every time a restriction is removed, a step is taken toward subjecting the exchange rate to the operation of the free forces of demand and supply.

One aspect of the movement toward relaxation deserves special attention. As indicated at the end of the preceding chapter, a number of countries which removed exchange restrictions on imports substituted for them an import licensing or quota system. In what way did this alter the situation?

Much depended on the manner in which the exchange restrictions were administered. While import quota or licensing systems restrict the quantities or values of individual commodities which may be imported, exchange restrictions limit the amount of foreign exchange which an importer may acquire. The former type of regulation is directed primarily at protecting the home market from foreign competition, and decisions are usually based on a study of the quantities of individual commodities which are required or can be absorbed by the domestic market. Exchange control authorities, on the other hand, are concerned, in the first instance, with the supply of foreign exchange available, and their problem is one of rationing this supply. Furthermore, where scarcity of foreign exchange is an acute problem, the importation of all commodities other than certain essentials is rendered difficult or impossible by the lack of foreign means of payment.[69] Import quotas or licenses, how-

[69] Except in so far as importers succeed in acquiring means of payment on the illicit market.

ever, usually restrict the importation only of specified commodities, while all other imports are admitted without limitation.

It is clear that these distinctions hold only in a very general
way and that they may become practically meaningless where
both types of control operate in the same country. We have
noted in Chapter IV, that while exchange control authorities
began, in 1931, by restricting the allotments of exchange for
imports in an unselective fashion, the regulations tended to
become more and more selective and discriminatory as time
went on. The needs of the country were carefully studied to
determine what imports, and in what quantities, were most
needed, while purchases were diverted to countries with which
the balance of trade was "favorable." Hence, the decisions of
exchange control commissions came to be guided by considerations which would be given most weight by an import licensing
authority, although the scarcity of exchange always operated
in the background as the basic limiting factor. In fact, a number of exchange-control countries, such as Greece, Hungary,
Poland and Rumania, set up import permit systems in the
relatively early stages of exchange control. Frequently, importers of certain commodities had to secure, first, the permission of an import control board and, secondly, the permission
of the exchange control commission before bringing in their
goods. In Germany, the Import Control Boards were granted
the power to issue exchange permits on the basis of quotas of
exchange allotted to them periodically, but their decisions were
based on a careful study of the needs of the domestic market.

In general, one may say that, as the scarcity of exchange
became less acute, it gradually assumed less importance as a
factor restricting imports. Some countries, like Denmark and
Czechoslovakia, found themselves in a position to place more
and more commodities on a free list, consisting of goods which
could be imported without a permit of any kind. Others, like
Argentina, found that a larger proportion of the applications

for exchange could be granted. This development tended to be facilitated wherever currency values were adjusted downward.

In the meantime, the tendency to plan imports in the light of the needs of the national economy was becoming more and more widespread, both in countries which did, and in countries which did not, practice exchange control. Countries which were relaxing exchange restrictions found themselves reluctant to relinquish the power to direct imports. Hence, powers were transferred from exchange control commissions to import control boards. Importers found that their freedom to bring in certain types of commodities, which had formerly been excluded purely on grounds of exchange scarcity, was enhanced, but that rigid limitations governed the import of commodities which competed with domestic products or which were subject to internal price regulation schemes or other forms of governmental control. Further discussion of the nature of import control must be reserved, however, for our chapter on import restrictions.

5. *Conclusions*

Exchange restrictions were introduced, as we have seen, largely as emergency measures. From the point of view of the individual countries concerned, the resort to exchange control was practically unavoidable; but the effect on world trade of the multiplication of restrictions in country after country was disastrous. Moreover, the exchange restrictions, by their very nature, not only operated to prevent the adjustments required to bring the internal and external values of currencies into line, but actually tended to intensify the maladjustment in many cases, through their effects on internal prices.

The countries which first took steps to readjust the values of their currencies achieved, in general, the most rapid recovery and found themselves in a position to relax restrictions at a relatively early date. It is probable that a number of other countries, especially those in Central and Eastern Europe, would have been less reluctant to devaluate in the early years of exchange control had they been in a position to foresee the consequences of their attempts to cling to former par values. In any event, the conclusion of a general international agreement on the question of debts and currency values at the time of the World Economic Conference of 1933, or even earlier, might have meant the avoidance of many later difficulties. As time went on, however, the chaotic state of international relations played an increasingly important rôle in preventing abandonment of exchange control in countries which had succeeded in substantially liberalizing their regulations.

Furthermore, while exchange restrictions were introduced as emergency measures, they came to be utilized as convenient weapons of commercial policy. Arbitrary exchange allocations which favored the products of certain countries constituted an indirect means of evading the most-favored-nation clause but could be defended on grounds of protection of the national currency. Through the differentiation of exchange rates, the government could be assured of securing foreign currencies at favorable rates for its own purposes without jeopardizing the country's export markets. In these and numerous other ways, countries attempted to manipulate exchange restrictions to their own advantage. Whether their trade really benefited from such manipulation or not is a question which we shall not attempt to answer here.

Our picture of exchange control, however, will not be complete until we have studied the nature of clearing agreements and the other special payments arrangements which grew out of exchange regulations and became an integral part of the exchange control systems of many countries in Europe and Latin America.

CHAPTER VI

CLEARING AGREEMENTS

1. *The Resort to Special Payment Arrangements*

It has already been made clear that the network of exchange restrictions introduced in the latter half of 1931 threatened to bring international trade, especially in certain parts of the world, to a virtual standstill. The flow of means of payment among the various countries of the Danubian region dwindled to a mere trickle, and the situation in South America was very nearly as bad. Exporters were accumulating frozen credits abroad at such a disturbing rate that they began to stop further shipments.

It was an intolerable situation; and it was not long before business men and governments sought methods of making possible the carrying on of trade in spite of the restrictions. The means which were devised to meet this impasse form the subject matter of the next two chapters. Although there were great variations in detail, these measures all aimed either at elimination of bilateral payments between pairs of countries through the offsetting of equivalent obligations, or at control of bilateral payments to prevent the accumulation of a net balance owed by one country to the other.

The simplest of the new devices was merely a modern adaptation of the age-old principle of barter. If country A's wheat were to be exchanged for country B's pig iron, no payments would have to be made between the two countries provided the total value of wheat involved in the transaction equalled the total value of pig iron. Arrangements could be made whereby the importer in country A might settle his obligation by direct payment to the exporter in country A, and similarly for country B. Sometimes governments have been involved in such barter or compensation transactions, and the arrangement has been described as a *compensation agreement*. More often, however, the negotiations have been conducted by private individuals or firms, in which case the term *private compensation* has been used to describe the transaction.

The other methods evolved to avoid payments over the foreign exchanges depended, not on the balancing of individual import and export transactions, but rather on the offsetting of streams of bilateral payments between pairs of countries, through intergovernmental agreements designed to achieve this end. The two main forms of bilateral agreements of this nature in force at the present time are *clearing agreements* and *payments agreements*.

The nature of a clearing agreement can best be made clear by a concrete example. The first of these agreements which, at least in essentials, apparently formed a model for later agreements, was concluded between Switzerland and Austria in November, 1931.[1] Austrians were to meet obligations incurred as a result of purchases in Switzerland by making payment *in schillings* into a clearing account at the National Bank of Austria. Swiss importers of Austrian goods were to make payment *in Swiss francs* into a similar account at the National Bank of Switzerland. Austrians who had exported goods to Switzerland would then be paid by the Austrian National Bank, while Swiss exporters who had credits due them in Austria would be paid by the Swiss National Bank.[2]

---

[1] For the text of the agreement, see *Recueil Officiel des Lois et Ordonnances de la Confédération suisse*, XLVII (1931), 789–92. Switzerland signed an agreement with Austria on November 12, and one with Hungary on November 14. The latter is frequently referred to as the first clearing agreement, since it was the first to become effective.

[2] Technically, the clearing account at the Austrian National Bank was to be held in the name of the Swiss National Bank, while the clearing account at the latter institution was to be in the name of the Austrian National Bank; but

The Swiss-Austrian agreement contained an additional feature which is found in many, but by no means all, clearing agreements. Since Switzerland's balance of trade with Austria was passive, it was expected that the amounts paid into the Swiss central bank would exceed the amounts paid into the Austrian central bank. Consequently, it was arranged that a certain percentage of the funds received by the Swiss National Bank would be reserved for the service of the Austrian debt in Switzerland. Thus, a portion of the proceeds of Austria's exports to Switzerland was "ear-marked" for payment to Swiss holders of Austrian securities. Obviously, the success of the agreement depended on the maintenance of an appropriate trade ratio between the two countries. Clearing agreements which make provision for payments on commercial or financial debts in arrears are sometimes referred to as *clearing and payments agreements*.

Unlike clearing agreements, *payments agreements* do not interfere with the normal method of payment over the foreign exchanges. In the typical case, where one of the partners to the agreement is an exchange-control country and the other partner has not introduced exchange control, the exchange-control country agrees to allocate the foreign exchange derived from its exports to the other country in certain specified ways.[3] Generally, a certain percentage of this foreign exchange is to be utilized for imports from the free-exchange country, an additional percentage is to be set aside for payments in connection with debts owed to that country, while a residual percentage is placed at the free disposal of the exchange-control country. Thus the agreement guarantees that, in the trade between the two countries, the exchange-control country shall

---

this feature did not interfere with the primary purpose of the agreement, to eliminate commercial payments between the two countries.

[3] Such an undertaking would not be possible, of course, if the exchange-control country did not require the surrender to the central bank of foreign exchange derived from exports.

have an excess of exports. In fact, it provides specifically for
a given trade ratio, except in so far as a measure of flexibility is
permitted through placing at the free disposal of the exchange-
control country a certain proportion of the funds derived from
its exports. This is perhaps the most essential point of difference between a payments agreement and a clearing agreement,
which does not call for a fixed trade ratio unless special provisions are inserted. Payments agreements are sometimes concluded between two exchange-control countries, in which case
no new principle is involved, but the details of operation are
somewhat different.

We have used the term *compensation agreement* to describe
a single barter transaction in which at least one government is
involved.[4] The term is sometimes used in a considerably
broader sense, to cover various types of agreements which aim
directly at bilateral balancing of all *or part* of the trade between the two countries concerned. This end may be achieved
in a number of different ways: (*a*) through a provision whereby
all trade between the two countries shall be conducted on a
private compensation basis; (*b*) through a provision equating
the total amount of imports (in value terms) which each country shall admit from the other in a given period; or (*c*) through
an undertaking on the part of each country to admit specified
amounts of certain commodities from the other in a given
period. Such agreements do not, on the whole, introduce any
new method of payment. Their terms vary, some agreements
calling for payment through clearing accounts, others for the
settlement of obligations directly between importers and exporters in the same country, while still others provide for
normal payments over the foreign exchanges. In fact, what we
actually have, in most of these cases, is a clearing agreement,
or an ordinary commercial agreement, with a *compensation
clause,* the object of which is to balance the trade between the
two countries so that no actual transfer of funds from one

[4] See p. 120 above.

country to the other will be required.[5] I propose, therefore, to regard agreements involving such trade-balancing clauses as special forms of clearing or commercial agreements and to use the term *compensation agreement* only in the narrow sense in which it has been employed above.

Compensation clauses sometimes aim, not at an equating of bilateral trade, but at the achievement of a balance in "favor" of one of the countries. Thus we may distinguish between agreements which call for a 1:1 trade ratio and those which call for some other ratio, say 2:1. A further alternative is a provision that the exports of one country shall exceed those of the other by a definite *amount* in terms of one of the two currencies. Such inequalities in bilateral trade relationships are permitted when one country must transfer to the other a net balance arising out of one or more invisible items in the balance of payments (interest payments, insurance or freight charges, etc.).

Bilateral payment arrangements which do not fit precisely into any of the categories we have mentioned have been concluded from time to time in the years since 1931. Furthermore, many agreements are hybrid in nature, involving the use of various combinations of methods here considered. To describe all these variations would carry us into too much unnecessary detail, and would involve discussion of certain devices which are of no practical importance at the present time.

This chapter will be devoted to a study of clearing agreements, while other payment arrangements will be taken up in the following chapter. We shall have occasion, in the latter part of the book, to refer to commercial agreements with compensation features.

---

[5] There is no need for separate compensation clauses in most payments agreements, since the provisions governing the allocation of exchange by the exchange-control country determine the trade ratio, within limits. See, however, p. 196, below, on the French payments agreements.

2. *The Origin and Spread of Clearing Agreements*

Clearing agreements were first suggested as a means of meeting the impasse created in the autumn of 1931 by the multiplication of exchange restrictions in the Danubian area. The countries in this area depended on each other's markets to a very considerable extent and, in addition, had important trade connections with the creditor nations of Western Europe, to which they were at this time, as we have seen, heavily indebted. Thus the creation of a network of rigid exchange restrictions and the accumulation of frozen commercial debts in the Danubian countries were matters of mutual concern both to these countries themselves and to the Western European countries.

At a conference of the Danubian countries, held in Prague in November, 1931, under the auspices of the Bank for International Settlements to consider exchange problems, representatives of the Austrian government suggested the possibility of clearing agreements.[6] Largely in response to this suggestion, several agreements were concluded in the closing months of 1931. Many more were signed in 1932 and later years. Most of the earlier agreements involved (*a*) two exchange-control countries in Central and Southeastern Europe or (*b*) an exchange-control country in this area and a free-exchange, creditor country in Western Europe.

Where two exchange-control countries were involved, the chief object was to permit the carrying on of trade which involved no payments over the foreign exchanges and hence no drain on dwindling foreign exchange reserves. Agreements between exchange-control and creditor (generally free-exchange) countries arose, on the other hand, at the instigation of creditor countries. Not only were exporters in the creditor countries of Western Europe accumulating frozen commercial

[6] League of Nations, *Financial Position of Austria in the Last Quarter of 1931* (Geneva, 1932), p. 10.

credits abroad, but foreign investors in those countries were suffering from the various transfer moratoria which had been invoked by debtor nations. Yet in many such cases, the creditor country had a heavy excess of imports in its trade with the debtor country. In other words, creditor countries were remitting funds to debtor countries which, because of leakages of one kind or another,[7] did not get into the hands of the debtor country's central bank, or, to the extent that they did, were not allocated for payments on debts. Under these circumstances, it is not surprising that creditors in the countries of Western Europe began to exert pressure on their governments to devise means of commandeering such payments to exchange-control countries for the benefit of the countries that remitted them.

This pressure resulted in the adoption of a more or less uniform type of procedure in a number of creditor countries. Outward commercial payments to exchange-control countries were temporarily blocked in order to bring those countries to terms. Usually, the threat of such action induced exchange-control countries to enter into negotiations for clearing agreements; and, in fact, the conclusion of many of the early clearing agreements followed closely upon the enactment by creditor countries of legislation providing for the blocking of transfers to countries with exchange restrictions. A decree of February 15, 1932, in France required importers of goods from certain countries (to be designated in later decrees) to make payment into a compensation office which was to be set up at the Paris Chamber of Commerce.[8] Similarly, a Swedish law which went into effect June 17, 1932, provided that, in case another country restricted the rights of a Swedish subject to dispose freely of his credits, the Swedish government might establish by decree a unilateral clearing arrangement whereby Swedish subjects indebted to citizens of such a country would have to meet their

[7] Cf. pp. 65–66 above.
[8] *Journal Officiel de la République française*, LXIX (1932), 1994.

obligations by making payment to the Swedish Riksbank. If no clearing agreement had been signed with the foreign government concerned, the payments which had been made into the Riksbank would be held until transfer was authorized by the Swedish government.[9] Other countries to enact similar legislation or promulgate corresponding decrees in 1931 and 1932 were Switzerland, the Netherlands, and Belgium. In 1934 and 1935, Norway, the United Kingdom, and Austria followed suit.

Where provision for the service of financial debts or the payment of commercial debts in arrears was included in a clearing agreement, it was usually arranged that a designated proportion of the funds paid into the clearing account in the creditor country would be utilized to pay for current exports, the remainder being given over to the settlement of debts. Since the creditor country ordinarily had a passive balance of trade with the debtor country, the funds paid in by importers of the former country were expected to be sufficient to take care of both types of creditors, so long as the terms of the agreement provided for only a *gradual* repayment of frozen debts.

It appears, then, that the early clearing agreements were concluded for three main purposes: to make possible a continuation of trade in spite of exchange restrictions, to secure repayment of commercial debts in arrears, and to safeguard the repayment of, or service on, financial debts. An overwhelming majority of the replies submitted by the various governments to a questionnaire sent out by the League of Nations Joint Committee for the Study of Clearing Agreements emphasize one or more of these factors.[10] A few of the exchange-control countries, however, emphasized the further fact that they entered into clearing agreements in order to protect the reserves against their currencies, or, what amounts to the same

[9] *Foreign Financial News: European Financial Notes,* No. 165 (March 10, 1934), p. 15.

[10] League of Nations, *Enquiry into Clearing Agreements* (Geneva, 1935), pp. 55–61.

thing, to relieve pressure on the foreign exchanges.[11] The Netherlands mentioned a desire to "retaliate against unilateral action on the part of certain countries in the matter of foreign exchange." Finally, the reply of Greece gave as one of her two purposes in entering into clearing agreements that of attaining "balanced imports and exports" with each of the countries with which trading was rendered difficult by a "shortage of foreign exchange." [12] A similar motive undoubtedly influenced decisions of other countries with respect to the early agreements, though perhaps to a less important degree; and there is no doubt that this motive has taken on increasing significance as a factor affecting the spread of the clearing system as time has gone on. As the scarcity of exchange in many of the exchange-control countries became less acute, the factors which led to the signing of the earlier agreements began to disappear from the situation; but, in the meantime, clearing agreements had become an integral part of a widespread system of balanced bilateral trade, which was being encouraged by all the weapons of commercial policy that governments could bring to their command. This fact will become clear as we examine in detail the development of the clearing system.

Clearing agreements were negotiated in great numbers from the beginning of 1932 on. The system spread rapidly throughout Europe, until a substantial proportion of the trade among the countries of Continental Europe was conducted on a clearing basis. For the most part, however, the rest of the world remained outside the system. Certain countries in Latin America, especially Chile, concluded clearing agreements with European nations, but very few agreements have been signed by pairs of countries *within* Latin America. Great Britain remained aloof from the clearing system for several years, but the difficulty of realizing on frozen debts and service items in

[11] Cf. the replies of Latvia and Yugoslavia. *Ibid.*, pp. 57–58.
[12] *Ibid.*, p. 59.

certain European countries finally induced her to enter into a limited number of clearing agreements in 1935 and 1936. On the whole, the United Kingdom has been inclined to favor payments agreements, modeled after the Anglo-German Agreement of November 1, 1934.[13] The United States has remained altogether outside the system, partly because it is incompatible with the spirit of the Reciprocal Trade Agreements program, which is based on thoroughgoing adherence to the most-favored-nation principle.[14] On the whole, strong inducement to enter into clearing agreements has been lacking for countries whose trade or financial relations with European exchange-control countries have not been especially important. This has been the case, for the most part, with the British Dominions, which have not been involved in clearing agreements to any significant extent.

From the end of 1935 on, the number of new clearing agreements negotiated was relatively small, although those already in force were usually renewed on expiration. There has been some tendency in recent years for clearing agreements to be replaced by payments agreements. Most of the payments agreements in force in the summer of 1939, however, were between free-exchange countries of Western Europe, on the one hand, and exchange-control countries in Central and Southeastern Europe or Latin America, on the other. Unless they assume a very specialized form,[15] which does not differ substantially from bilateral clearing in practice, they are not adapted for use by pairs of exchange-control countries. The major proportion of

[13] See pp. 191–92 below.

[14] On the relation between clearing agreements and the most-favored-nation clause, see p. 377 below. Clearing agreements, as a means of enforcing debt payments, were virtually out of the question for the United States, in any event, in view of her active trade balance with many of the debtor countries of Europe and Latin America. Furthermore, the American government refrains, as a matter of established policy, from taking as active a part in negotiating for collection of private foreign claims as do many European governments. Cf. H. G. White, Jr., "Blocked Commercial Balances in American Foreign Policy," *American Economic Review*, XXIX (1939), 74–91.

[15] See p. 197 below.

trade *between* pairs of European exchange-control countries
is subject to clearing agreements.

The geographical distribution of clearing and payments
agreements is indicated in Table VI, which is based on the
results of surveys published in 1936 and 1939 by the International Chamber of Commerce. Agreements are classified in
accordance with definitions worked out by that body, as
follows:

"A. *Clearing Agreements*

I. The two contracting parties enter into an agreement with
regard to the settlement of their commercial transactions as a whole
(transactions prior and subsequent to the conclusion of the agreement). Importers have to pay their debts in national currency and
exporters collect their debts also in national currency. Transfer of
foreign exchange for settlement of trade debts is thus suppressed.

II. In each of the contracting countries, a special body is in-
structed: (*a*) to receive in national currency the sums paid in by
importers; (*b*) to pay exporters on the fund thus constituted in so
far as permitted by the available assets, provided that in the other
country the importers have remitted to their executive organization the amounts which they owe.

III. The exchange rate of the currencies of the contracting
countries is fixed for transactions carried out under the agreement
(gold-parity, official rate or agreed rate).

IV. The sums paid into the different accounts do not bear
interest.

B. *Clearing and Payments Agreements*

In addition to the above clauses (I, II, III and IV), this type of
agreement contains one of the two following provisions:

Va). In the country which has not introduced foreign exchange
control, a certain percentage of the sums remitted by the importers
is placed at the free disposal of the Central Bank of the other
contracting country, for the payment of trade debts contracted
prior to the conclusion of the agreement, and/or for the amortization of debts other than trade debts (public debts or private debts
of a financial nature), or for any other purpose. The balance alone
is reserved for the payment of exports subsequent to the conclusion
of the agreement.

TABLE VI

CLEARING AND PAYMENTS AGREEMENTS IN FORCE, BY COUNTRIES: INTERNATIONAL CHAMBER OF COMMERCE COMPILATION, 1936 AND 1939

COUNTRIES	1936 (JUNE 1)[a]			1939 (JANUARY 1)[b]		
	Clearing	Clearing and Payments	Payments	Clearing	Clearing and Payments	Payments
Argentina	—	—	4	1	1	8
Austria	2	4	1	—	—	5
Belgium and Luxemburg	1	9	3	1	7	—
Brazil	—	1	—	2	—	—
Bulgaria	4	9	—	7	10	1
Canada	—	—	—	—	—	—
Chile	1	8	—	2	7	—
Colombia	—	—	—	1	—	1
Czechoslovakia	7	3	—	4	5	1
Denmark	1	—	—	2	1	—
Danzig[b]	1	—	—	—	—	—
Eire	—	—	1	—	1	2
Estonia	5	2	—	5	1	1
Finland	—	2	—	6	—	—
France	3	7	—	1	4	7
Germany	15	13	4	21	7	7
Greece	4	9	—	10	7	2
Hungary	4	8	1	7	6	4
Iceland	—	—	—	2	—	—
Iran	1	—	—	1	—	—
Italy	12	4	1	19	4	2
Japan	—	—	—	—	—	1
Latvia	4	—	1	10	—	1

	[a]			[b]		
Lithuania	—	—	—	6	—	—
Manchoukuo	1	—	—	—	1	1
Netherlands	1	5	1	1	5	1
New Zealand	—	1	—	—	1	—
Norway	3	—	—	4	1	1
Poland	2	1	—	7	1	—
Portugal	1	14	—	2	10	2
Rumania	3	—	—	4	—	—
South Africa	1	6	—	—	8	—
Spain	3	2	—	3	2	2
Sweden	4	9	1	5	8	2
Switzerland	—	—	—	2	—	1
Syria and Lebanon	—	—	—	—	9	2
Turkey	9	9	—	12	1	—
U. S. S. R.	2	1	—	4	3	5
United Kingdom	2	2	3	1	2	3
Uruguay	1	2	1	—	6	3
Yugoslavia	4	7	—	5	6	3
Total [c]	51	69	11	79	59	33
Total Clearing and Clearing and Payments Agreements	120			138		
Grand Total	131			171		

131

[a] Source: International Chamber of Commerce, *Accords de Compensation* (Paris, 1936), p. 38. The definitions used in this publication are identical with those used in *Clearing and Payments Agreements*, except for slight differences in wording.

[b] Source: *World Trade*, XI (February, 1939), 11. Certain agreements included in this list were not included in the 1936 list although they were in force at that time. Further, the incorporation of Austria into the German Reich reduced the number of agreements in force, since the clearing accounts of the Austrian National Bank were taken over by the German *Verrechnungskasse*, and Germany's clearing and payments agreements were revised to include Austria. Similarly, the Free City of Danzig no longer has any separate agreements but is included in the Polish agreements. Thus, the two lists are not altogether comparable.

[c] The reader should note that, in order to arrive at the true total for each column, the arithmetical total must be divided by two, since each agreement appears twice, being listed beside the name of each of the two countries concerned.

Vb). In countries with foreign exchange control, the payment of trade debts contracted prior to the conclusion of the agreement is assured by the free transfer of exchange placed at the disposal of importers.

C. *Payments Agreements*

Under a payments agreement, a country with foreign exchange control (*A*) undertakes in respect of a country without such control (*B*) to authorize its importers to transfer freely to the account of exporters in (*B*) a certain percentage, fixed in the agreement, of the total amount of foreign exchange previously transferred by (*B*) for the payment of its current trade debts to (*A*). The transfer of exchange between the two countries for payment of trade debts therefore takes place within the scope of the agreement.

(*A*) further undertakes to reserve a certain percentage of the total amount of foreign exchange transferred by (*B*) for the amortization of one of the following categories of debts which it has contracted with (*B*):

(*a*) trade debts, prior to the conclusion of the agreement; or

(*b*) debts other than trade debts (public debts or private debts of a financial nature); or

(*c*) debts mentioned under (*a*) and (*b*) together." [16]

Table VII indicates the proportions of the trade of individual countries and of world trade affected by clearing agreements in 1937.[17] It should be noted that the figures do *not* include trade coming under payments agreements or compensation transactions lying outside the scope of clearing agreements.

3. *The Meaning of Bilateral Clearing*

It is important to note, at this stage, that the concept of clearing in international trade is not new. In fact, the working

[16] International Chamber of Commerce, *Clearing and Payments Agreements* (Stuttgart and Basel, 1938), Introduction.

[17] Trade statistics based on gold value are of doubtful significance in a world in which currencies have depreciated by varying amounts in relation to gold. It is difficult, moreover, to calculate gold values for countries with multiple exchange rate systems or differential rates of exchange depreciation. Hence, the percentages in Columns 2 and 4 of Table VII should be interpreted as being only roughly indicative of the actual situation.

TABLE VII

TRADE BY CLEARING IN 1937 [a]

The following table shows to what extent the trade of individual countries (columns 1 and 3) and the trade of the world (columns 2 and 4) was conducted in 1937 through the machinery of clearing.

COUNTRY	TRADE BY CLEARING			
	IMPORTS BY CLEARING		EXPORTS BY CLEARING	
	As percentage of country's total imports (national currencies) —1—	As percentage of total world imports (gold value) —2—	As percentage of country's total exports (national currencies) —3—	As percentage of total world exports (gold value) —4—
Argentina . . .	11.10	0.20	7.00	0.20
Belgium-Luxemburg .	3.90	0.13	3.70	0.12
Brazil	24.10	0.29	17.30	0.23
Bulgaria . . .	87.60	0.19	70.20	0.17
Chile	33.60	0.10	27.60	0.21
Colombia . . .	13.40	0.05	12.40	0.05
Czechoslovakia .	28.70	0.40	30.30	0.48
Denmark . . .	25.00	0.33	19.30	0.25
Estonia	36.10	0.04	36.90	0.04
Finland	20.80	0.15	15.00	0.12
France	2.20	0.14	2.40	0.09
Germany . . .	52.60	4.21	57.10	5.22
Greece	56.00	0.28	53.20	0.18
Hungary . . .	60.10	0.31	55.70	0.37
Iran	22.30	0.06	6.50	0.04
Italy	45.60	1.21	40.70	0.86
Latvia	37.20	0.06	41.40	0.08
Lithuania . . .	24.00	0.03	18.40	0.03
Netherlands . .	23.40	0.73	17.40	0.42
Norway . . .	18.50	0.21	16.70	0.13
Poland-Danzig .	20.70	0.18	23.00	0.20
Portugal . . .	17.20	0.07	14.80	0.03
Rumania . . .	74.90	0.38	66.70	0.59
Spain	32.00	0.19	59.40	0.29
Sweden	24.20	0.47	17.30	0.34
Switzerland-Liechtenstein .	36.00	0.54	28.40	0.32
Turkey	72.10	0.24	74.30	0.31
United Kingdom	2.10	0.36	2.10	0.21
Uruguay . . .	11.80	0.03	13.30	0.04
U. S. S. R. . . .	17.90	0.17	9.20	0.12
Yugoslavia . .	61.00	0.26	49.00	0.27
Total		12.01		12.01

[a] Adapted from *World Trade*, XI (February, 1939), 10.

of the normal foreign exchange mechanism is based entirely on a clearing principle. It is the business of banks dealing in foreign exchange to balance credits due from foreign countries against debts owed to those countries. Their dealings involve, basically, purchases and sales of balances in foreign banks. No actual international movement of funds takes place unless the bankers in a given country find that current receipts of foreign exchange (claims to balances in foreign banks) are insufficient to take care of the current demand for foreign exchange. This will happen, under normal circumstances, only if a country is a net debtor in its current transactions with the outside world *as a whole,* for a scarcity of balances in one country can usually be made up by sales of excess balances in some other country. Thus, clearing in the foreign exchange market operates on an *international,* not on a *bilateral,* basis.

A clearing agreement, on the other hand, segregates the reciprocal payments of the two countries concerned from the main stream of dealings in the foreign exchanges.[18] Country A's balances in Country B may be used *only* for payments in Country B. They cannot be sold to settle a claim in Country C. It is clear that the proper working of such agreements requires that where invisible items in the balance of payments between the two countries are unimportant, reciprocal merchandise trade shall approximately balance, while in cases where debts of one kind or another are provided for in the clearing agreement, the creditor country shall have an excess of imports of the proper amount. Only under such conditions can the accumulation of an unsettled balance in one or the other of the two clearing accounts be avoided.

The working of the normal foreign exchange mechanism, on the other hand, does not require that the trade of each country with every other country must balance. A debit balance with one country may be offset by a credit balance with another country. The United States may accumulate sterling credits in

[18] In so far as they are covered by the agreement.

London, as a result of an active balance of trade with the United Kingdom, and these credits can be used to settle a debit balance in America's trade with Brazil. Under normal conditions, the mechanism of the foreign exchange market is excellently adapted to take care of such so-called triangular trade. Further, if Germany is indebted to France as a result of loans floated in Paris, it is not necessary for her to have an active balance in her trade with France exactly equivalent to the service on her debt. She may find that belga credits arising from an excess of exports in her trade with Belgium can be utilized to meet part of the service on the franc loan. All that a debtor country requires is that its trade as a whole produce an active balance sufficiently large to take care of the service on its total foreign indebtedness. In fact, it need not rely entirely on its merchandise trade to produce such an active balance if it can accumulate credits abroad through selling shipping services to foreigners or attracting foreign tourists on a large scale. Further, and this is a circumstance which introduces complications into the working of clearing agreements, the trade balances between individual pairs of countries may fluctuate markedly from year to year, as a result of changes in harvest conditions, shifts in demand, and numerous other factors.

Whether it has in fact been possible to reconcile the highly unstable conditions of international trade with the more or less rigid requirements of clearing agreements is one of the questions which we shall have in mind in our study of the clearing system.

4. *The Administration and Duration of Clearing Agreements*

Clearing agreements are usually administered by central banks. Sometimes a special clearing office (such as the German *Verrechnungskasse*) is set up to manage the accounts, but the clearing funds are almost invariably kept on deposit at the central bank. The French Compensation (clearing) Office is

located at the Paris Chamber of Commerce.[19] Italy has set up
a special commission to supervise the working of clearing
agreements.[20]

The fact that balances of trade between pairs of countries
tend to be highly unstable means that clearing agreements must
be frequently adjusted to take care of changing conditions.
Their duration is usually relatively short, from three months
to a year, but the provision is ordinarily made that the agreement will be automatically renewed unless one or the other of
the two countries signifies a desire to terminate or revise it.
Most of the agreements, once signed, have been renewed from
year to year, but revisions are frequently made at the time of
renewal.

The necessity for frequent adjustment of the agreements has
meant that certain officials are almost constantly employed in
watching the working of the agreements to which their country
is a party, while negotiations with officials in countries with
which agreements have been concluded are often required.
France and Germany met this problem by setting up a permanent commission to meet once a month and discuss problems
arising in connection with the Franco-German clearing agreement.[21] The Belgo-German Agreement of September, 1934,
and numerous other agreements have likewise provided for the
setting up of an intergovernmental commission.[22]

5. *The Items Covered by Clearing Agreements*

There is no reason why all payments between two countries,
arising from every item in the balance of payments, might not
be made subject to the provisions of clearing agreements.

[19] It should be noted that the French word for clearing is *compensation.*
[20] *Foreign Financial News: European Financial Notes,* No. 182 (November
24, 1934), p. 13.
[21] P. Jolly, *Traité des Opérations de Compensation* (Paris, 1935), pp. 217–18.
[22] *Foreign Financial News: European Financial Notes,* No. 179 (October 9,
1934), p. 2.

Actually, the majority of agreements are not so comprehensive. Most of the earlier agreements covered all payments for current merchandise trade, while special provisions for the liquidation of blocked commercial debts were common. Where financial debts entered into the balance of payments between the two countries, the agreement usually took account of the service on these debts, for, as we have seen, many clearing agreements were concluded with the object of protecting the interests of creditors. It is interesting to note, however, that in the cases of some agreements between creditor and debtor countries, commercial payments alone were covered in the clearing agreement, financial debts being made the subject of a separate so-called "debt" agreement. The Greek agreements "are in principle confined to the field of operations that come within the [commodity] trade balance, since it is the other active elements of the Greek balance of payments on which Greece has to rely for meeting all her obligations to foreign countries other than those arising out of the import of goods." [23] Thus we find Greece signing a separate debt agreement with France, October 18, 1932, providing for the transfer by installments of French commercial credits blocked in Greece on somewhat more favorable terms than were accorded to other countries not benefiting from a similar agreement. Provision for the settlement of Hungarian financial debts was likewise left in some cases to separate agreements.[24]

A number of clearing agreements cover expenses incidental to merchandise trade, such as shipping expenses and insurance premiums.[25] Tourist expenditures, diplomatic expenditures, fees for licenses and patents and other similar payments are frequently included. As officials have gained experience in handling clearing agreements, there has been a growing tendency to

[23] Greek reply to the League of Nations Committee. (*Enquiry into Clearing Agreements*, p. 64. Matter in brackets mine.)
[24] *Ibid.*
[25] *Ibid.*, pp. 29–30 and 61–66.

make provision for service items of this kind in agreements.[26]

At the opposite extreme from agreements which take account of many invisible items in the balance of payments are certain limited clearing agreements which subject only a part of the merchandise trade between the countries concerned to the clearing mechanism. As Einzig has pointed out,[27] perhaps the simplest form of agreement is that exemplified by an Italo-Bulgarian arrangement which came into force January 1, 1933. It applied only to purchases of Bulgarian tobacco by the Italian tobacco monopoly and to certain sums owed by Bulgarians to Italian industrial undertakings, payments for these purposes to be made into a clearing account in each country, as under agreements of wider scope. A number of similar agreements were signed in the early years of the clearing system. Frequently, however, the agreement may apply to a *group* of designated commodities, payments for all other commodities being made in the normal manner. The reply of Czechoslovakia to the League Committee pointed out that certain of that country's agreements were of this character.[28] An example of another type of partial clearing arrangement is the agreement between France and Ecuador of July 27, 1933, which provided that only 50 per cent of debts incurred by French importers of goods from Ecuador had to be paid through the clearing system, the remainder to be paid directly to exporters by importers in the customary manner.[29] Further, some clearing agreements provide that payments in connection with private compensation transactions need not be made through the clearing accounts, although permission of the clearing authorities is generally required for such transactions.[30]

Particularly difficult to handle has been the question of whether or not transit trade should be included in the clearing system. The usual answer has been to confine the clearing to

[26] Cf. P. Einzig, *The Exchange Clearing System* (London, 1935), p. 79.
[27] *Ibid.*, p. 75.
[28] *Enquiry into Clearing Agreements*, p. 63.
[29] Cf. *Journal Officiel de la République française,* LXV (1933), 8287.
[30] *Enquiry into Clearing Agreements,* pp. 68–74.

goods originating in the contracting countries on the ground that the inclusion of transit trade would encourage traders in third countries, not parties to the agreement, to seek certain of the benefits of clearing.[31] Where transit trade is permitted to come under the clearing system, it is usually defined in such a way as to prevent abuses.[32]

Clearing agreements differ with respect to the inclusion or non-inclusion of colonial territories. None of the great colonial powers participating in clearing agreements seems to follow a very consistent policy in this respect.[33]

6. *The Allocation of Clearing Funds Among Various Groups of Creditors*

It is chiefly in cases where clearing agreements are expected to provide for debt repayments out of the export surplus of the debtor country in its trade with the creditor country that

[31] Transit trade was included in the first Swiss-German agreement (as in some of the other Swiss agreements), with the result that exporters in third countries, prevented from securing payment for goods shipped to Germany by the operation of German exchange restrictions, attempted to send merchandise into Germany through Switzerland, thereby becoming entitled to payment from the clearing account at the Swiss National Bank. This encouraged the accumulation of a debit balance on the German side of the clearing account and resulted in the exclusion of transit trade from the Additional Agreement of December 8, 1934. (Cf. *ibid.*, p. 29.)

[32] The Netherlands-Rumanian agreement of February 10, 1935, provided for the inclusion under the clearing system of imports into Rumania from the Netherlands of goods of non-European origin which had regularly entered into previous commercial transactions between the two countries and which were imported into Rumania through an established firm in the Netherlands which had engaged in such trade prior to the entering into effect of the agreement. (*Foreign Financial News: European Financial Notes*, No. 190 [March 24, 1935], p. 14.) More common, however, is a provision that specific costs arising in the territory of one of the contracting parties in connection with transit traffic to or from the other country may be settled through the clearing accounts, while the balance of the payments for these goods must be made in foreign exchange. The Netherlands-German agreement of September 21, 1934, covered the payment of costs in connection with transit traffic through Holland from Germany and through Germany from Holland. (*Ibid.*, No. 180 [October 24, 1934], p. 12.) The handling of the finishing trade is similar.

[33] For further information, see *Enquiry into Clearing Agreements*, pp. 106–107, and International Chamber of Commerce, *Clearing and Payments Agreements, passim.*

the question of the allocation of funds among groups of creditors becomes an important issue. The debtor country usually seeks an arrangement providing for a slow repayment of debts, on the ground that a larger proportion of its balances in the creditor country will thereby be made available for current imports.[34] The creditor country, in trying to resolve the conflict between commercial and financial creditors, is often tempted to accord somewhat more favorable treatment to the former than to the latter,[35] since the maintenance of the export trade is considered vital to the national interest.[36] No two solutions are alike, for the various factors which have to be taken into consideration differ in every case. What the percentage allocations specified in the agreements really determine is the rates of repayment, e.g., whether a given exporter will wait six or nine months before he receives payment on a back debt. Sometimes, financial creditors agree to accept interest rate reductions.

Usually 50 per cent or more of the funds paid into the clearing office in the creditor country goes to pay for current exports to the debtor country, while specified fractions of the remainder go to various creditor groups. A typical arrangement appears in the Italo-Rumania agreement of August 27, 1934, which provides that, of the sums paid into the clearing account at the Bank of Italy by Italian importers of Rumanian goods, 50 per cent shall be used for current Italian exports to Rumania, 20 per cent for the payment of Rumanian commercial debts in arrears, and 30 per cent for the payment of financial debts and other Rumanian obligations in Italy.[37] Some agreements pro-

---

[34] See the account of negotiations in connection with the French-Italian agreement of August 11, 1936, in *Foreign Financial News: European Financial Notes*, No. 225 (September 9, 1936), p. 9.

[35] Cf. *Enquiry into Clearing Agreements*, p. 30.

[36] In the case of the British clearing and payments agreements, however, as H. J. Tasca has clearly demonstrated, collection of debts, whether of a commercial or financial nature, is given definite priority over the interests of the current export trade. (*World Trading Systems* [Paris, 1939], pp. 85, 89, 94–95, 122.)

[37] *Bolletino di Informazioni Commerciali*, VIII (1934), 687.

vide that all amounts up to a certain minimum shall be allocated for current exports, while sums paid into the clearing office in excess of that minimum shall be utilized primarily for the settlement of past obligations, commercial and financial.[38]

A creditor country which has no exchange restrictions in force frequently places part of the funds available in its clearing account at the free disposal of the debtor country, often at the insistence of the latter.[39] These funds are not always transferable, however, *"although,"* as the League Committee points out, *"this is not to be gathered from the terms of the treaty."* [40] That they should be expended in the creditor country is considered to be in keeping with the spirit of clearing agreements. Actually, many agreements have designated certain specific purposes within the creditor country for which the sums left at the "free" disposal of the debtor country are to be used, e.g., the Austrian agreements and the Spanish-Uruguayan agreement which went into effect, January 10, 1935.[41] The "freedom of disposal" in such cases extends only to the detailed administration of payments, not to the purposes for which payments shall be made. These cases, however, are the exception rather than the rule; usually, no *obvious* "strings" are attached in the terms of the agreement itself. Nevertheless, there is a clear understanding that the funds in question are to be spent in the creditor country. The amounts involved in free disposal provisions vary from small fractions to well over half of the funds paid into the clearing office of the creditor country. Their size will obviously depend to a large extent on the nature of the balance of payments between the two countries. Some agreements, notably certain of those to which Greece is a party, go

[38] See the provisions of the Swiss-German agreement of April 17, 1935, in *Recueil Officiel des Lois et Ordonnances de la Confédération suisse*, LI (1935), 712–16.

[39] Cf. reply of Bulgaria to League Committee, *Enquiry into Clearing Agreements*, pp. 91–92.

[40] *Ibid.*, p. 31. (Italics in original.)

[41] International Chamber of Commerce, *Accords de Compensation*, pp. 15, 21.

so far as to provide, at least nominally, for the transfer of certain amounts in free exchange.[42]

Sometimes, definite priority is given to certain types of payments, e.g., tourist expenditures in a number of Austrian agreements, no funds being allocated for other purposes until these payments have been met. In other cases, specific obligations are balanced against one another. There is the well-known provision, which appeared in the early Swiss-German agreements, whereby funds paid in by Swiss importers of German coal were set apart to finance German tourist expenditures in Switzerland. In certain agreements between two countries, each of which is indebted to the other, provision is made for debt payments to be set off against one another, any balance to be transferred in free exchange, e.g., the Czechoslovak-Greek agreement.[43] More interesting are the numerous cases in which proceeds from the export of a specific commodity are subject to special allocation provisions.[44] In the Chilean agreements with European creditor countries, funds accruing from European imports of Chilean products other than nitrate are utilized to pay for current European exports to Chile, whereas funds originating from nitrate imports are in part (15 to 30 per cent) allocated for the liquidation of Chilean frozen debts and in part placed at the free disposal of the Bank of Chile (thereby facilitating the repayment of debts in England and America). The reasons for these provisions are incomprehensible unless one takes into account (1) the existence of stringent European restrictions on imports of Chilean nitrate, (2) the nature of the Chilean exchange control scheme, and (3) the fact that Chile has a large comparative advantage in the production of natural nitrates. European countries were evidently willing to import increased amounts of Chilean nitrate provided part of the funds accruing to Chile therefrom would be used to liquidate debts.

[42] *Ibid., passim.*

[43] *Ibid.,* p. 27.

[44] Apparently, a number of European agreements have contained secret clauses providing for arrangements of this sort.

Further, the prospects of success for such a scheme were enhanced by the willingness of the Saltpetre Sales Corporation of Chile to convert the required amount of foreign exchange at the official rate, thereby making possible a provision that debtors could meet their obligations by making the necessary deposits in the Bank of Chile on the basis of this low rate.[45] Nitrate exports could take place profitably, even though part of the proceeds were converted at the official rate, because of Chile's substantial comparative advantage with respect to this commodity. Similar clauses appear in many of the Rumanian clearing agreements, which provide that debt repayments (and in some cases expenditures of Rumanian tourists or of the Rumanian government abroad) shall be met in large part from the proceeds of Rumanian oil exports.[46] Furthermore, Rumania has been able to demand, because of its extremely favorable position as an exporter of oil to Central European countries, that the proceeds of oil exports be transferred, in some cases, in free foreign exchange.

The desire of creditor countries, in certain instances, to control or limit imports which are offset, not by exports, but by debt repayments is illustrated by provisions of the Franco-Hungarian agreement of July 18, 1935, and of the Franco-Turkish agreement of August 6, 1935, which allocated sums paid in by French importers of commodities subject to quotas to the repayment of back debts, whereas funds accruing from imports of commodities not subject to quotas were to be used to pay for current exports.[47]

Finally, mention should be made of the fact that several agreements provide for an increased rate of debt liquidation

[45] See replies of Chile to League Committee, *Enquiry into Clearing Agreements*, pp. 58–59, 62, 75, and 78; Banco Central de Chile, *Monthly Report on Credit and Business Conditions* (August, 1934), pp. 2–4; and cf. also, for description of Chilean exchange control system, pp. 103–105 above.

[46] *Accords de Compensation, passim.*

[47] *Journal Officiel de la République française*, LXVII (1935), 7867–68 and 8995.

or the allocation of certain additional sums for the purpose of debt liquidation, if the creditors will agree to reductions in interest rates.[48]

7. *Technical and Procedural Matters*

Under clearing agreements, exporters may arrange whatever terms of payment they like with their foreign clients, provided these terms do not conflict with the procedure outlined in the agreement. There is nothing to prevent an exporter from drawing on an importer in his (the exporter's) own currency, making the bill payable in, say, three months' time.[49] He may even arrange to have the bill discounted by a bank, just as he would under ordinary circumstances.[50] When the bill falls due, however, the importer must make payment to his clearing office in his own currency.

The exporter will be paid by his clearing office in his national currency, but under no circumstances will he receive payment until his debtor has deposited the amount due in the foreign clearing office.[51] Even then, he may be obliged to wait, often for a considerable period, for his clearing office can meet his claim against it only if it has sufficient funds on hand. Funds in the clearing account in Country A will be insufficient to meet all claims if a net balance is accumulating in its favor in Country B's clearing account. This will happen, obviously, if Country A's balance of trade (or balance of those payments which come under the clearing agreement) with Country B is

[48] See provisions of Franco-Hungarian, and Belgo-Luxemburg-Hungarian agreements in *Accords de Compensation,* pp. 23 and 29.

[49] Exporters in free-exchange countries often insist on cash payment for goods exported to countries with stringent exchange restrictions. If a clearing agreement is in force with such a country, however, they may be more willing to grant the usual credit terms. Cf. Einzig, *The Exchange Clearing System,* p. 98.

[50] The existence of a clearing agreement sometimes enhances the willingness of banks to discount exporters' bills.

[51] The two clearing offices notify each other of payments received.

active. The general rule is that all creditors are paid in chronological order of payments by their debtors, whether it is a question of current debts or debts in arrears.[52]

Of some importance is the question as to whether payment into a clearing office constitutes a discharge of liability for a debtor. If it does, the exporter is exposed to an exchange risk, owing to the fact that the exchange rates may change between the date of payment by the debtor and the date on which the exporter's claim is actually settled in his own currency.[53] Many of the earlier agreements were silent on this point, while others provided that payment into the clearing office constituted a discharge of the debtor's liability. In some cases, however, it was stipulated that the debtor remained liable until the creditor was finally paid the full amount of his claim, and, on the whole, there has been a growing tendency to include this provision in later agreements. Apparently, it is felt that when the creditor stipulates payment in his own currency or in any currency other than that of the debtor, he is entitled to the exact amount designated, or its equivalent, in the currency specified.

The exporter or importer who is carrying on business subject to the terms of a clearing agreement must go through certain formalities. The requirements seek to prevent both the evasion of the clearing system and its illegitimate employment by persons not entitled to make payment through it. In a number of countries, the importation of goods from clearing countries is made subject to the presentation at the customs office of an invoice, a customs declaration, and a declaration to the effect that the importer will make payment to the clearing account.[54]

---

[52] In France, whenever funds are insufficient to pay exporters, they are sent a document called a *récépissé*, on which is recorded the amount of the claim on the clearing office. This document may be pledged as security for a loan, or the creditor may cede the rights to which it entitles him to a third party, provided the proper legal formalities are gone through. (Jolly, *op. cit.*, pp. 53–69.)

[53] Cf. *Enquiry into Clearing Agreements*, p. 27.

[54] *Ibid.*, pp. 86–91.

In order to prevent the illegitimate inclusion of goods from third countries in the clearing system, certificates of origin are frequently required.

Imports from clearing countries, furthermore, are not exempt from import quotas, nor are they, in a number of countries, exempt from the exchange permit requirements of the foreign exchange authorities. It is easy to see why they are subject to import quotas, the object of which is to limit the imports of a given commodity rather than to protect the supply of exchange. The reason for the requirement of foreign exchange permits is less obvious, since payment through the clearing system involves no drain on the foreign exchange reserves. What happens, however, when imports from clearing countries are exempted from exchange restrictions, is that purchases are diverted to clearing countries and large debit balances accumulate on the clearing accounts. This problem is rendered the more serious because of the fact that the commodities imported from clearing countries are frequently of a nonessential nature and/or are purchased at abnormally high prices. We shall come back to this question in connection with the effects of clearing agreements on trade balances.

8. *The Rate of Conversion*

Clearing agreements lay down regulations governing the rate at which one currency is to be converted into another. If an importer is paying for goods from a country with which a clearing agreement is in force, he must meet his obligation by making a remittance to his clearing office in his own currency, even though that obligation may be expressed in the seller's or some other currency. He determines the amount due the clearing office on the basis of the rate of conversion specified in the clearing agreement. The clearing office in the seller's country is then notified, and the amount due the seller is calculated by converting the buyer's remittance into the seller's national currency, again on the basis of the rate laid down in the agreement.

In the early agreements, the rate chosen was generally the official rate or the legal gold parity. Some agreements, however, specified a conventional rate, either fixed once and for all or altered from time to time by agreement between representatives of both countries. In yet other cases, the market rate was selected as the basis of conversion.

However the rate is defined, the important question is whether it calls for conversion in terms of the so-called "real" value of the currency (the rate which would prevail in the absence of exchange restrictions), or of some artificial value.[55] A conventional rate might conceivably be so defined as to approximate the real value quite closely, especially if provision were made for its alteration from time to time. The rate in a given market or on a given bourse, on the other hand, might be an artificial rate if the currency were as strictly controlled as, say, the German mark.

Wherever a clearing agreement calls for an artificial rate of conversion, imports into the country with the over-valued currency are stimulated and exports discouraged. Accordingly, the balance of trade tends to move in a direction "unfavorable" to this country. Exporters, further, will be induced to evade the agreement or to enter into private compensation transactions, which are generally conducted on the basis of an uncontrolled exchange rate.[56] The situation in the other country will be just the opposite.

It was soon recognized that the tendency for the balance of trade to turn in favor of the free-exchange countries after the

---

[55] Actually, a grave question arises as to whether one can conceive of a "real" or "equilibrium" rate of exchange in the usual sense between the currencies of two countries conducting reciprocal trade under the terms of a clearing agreement. For some discussion of this point, see Tasca, *World Trading Systems,* pp. 124–25.

[56] Cf. Jolly, *op. cit.,* pp. 93–94 on the working of the Franco-Austrian agreement of April 16, 1932.

conclusion of clearing agreements was in part attributable to conversion on the basis of gold parity or an official rate close to gold parity. The adoption of rates more nearly expressing the true value of the currency in clearing agreements, however, has largely depended on the attitude assumed toward exchange control in general. A country like Chile, which as early as April, 1932, was officially conducting much of her foreign trade on the basis of a depreciated exchange rate, found no difficulty in writing equivalent rates into her clearing agreements.[57] Most of Austria's early agreements were scrapped because the depreciation of her currency made them unworkable, subsequent agreements providing usually for conversion on the basis of a stable third currency or a "current exchange rate."[58] Yugoslavia and Hungary eventually applied their premium systems to clearing transactions as well as to foreign exchange transactions.[59] Italy devised a special premium system to apply to clearing agreements concluded from July 15, 1936, on, but this expedient was given up after the official devaluation of the lira in October of the same year.[60] Germany, on the other hand, adhered for a considerable period to the official value of the mark in her agreements.[61] It is important to recognize the fact, however, that if two exchange-control countries both adhere to the official values of their currencies in clearing transactions with each other, the exchange-ratio is exactly the same as if both altered the values of their currencies by equal amounts; and, if, further, the maladjustment between the internal and external value of the currency is similar in amount and direction in the two countries, the exchange-ratio will not operate to the advantage or disadvantage of either country.

[57] Except in so far as debt repayments were involved. Cf. pp. 103–104 above.
[58] See *Enquiry into Clearing Agreements*, p. 77.
[59] Cf. *ibid.*, pp. 80 and 82, and *Foreign Financial News: European Financial Notes*, No. 210 (January 24, 1936), p. 13. See also pp. 113–14 above.
[60] *Foreign Financial News: European Financial Notes*, No. 228 (October 24, 1936), p. 13.
[61] See, however, pp. 161–62, below, on Germany's attitude toward this matter in recent negotiations with countries of Southeastern Europe.

Thus, German exporters suffered from no currency disadvantage in selling on the basis of official exchange rates to Central and Eastern European countries whose currencies were over-valued about as much as the German mark.[62]

9. *The Liquidation of Credit Balances*

Clearing agreements may make provision for the liquidation of credit balances of two types: (1) any balance remaining in favor of one of the countries at the end of a short period, say, one month, and (2) any balance owed by one country to the other on the expiration of the agreement. Special provision for credit balances of the former type is relatively rare, unless we include here the clauses which place certain sums at the free disposal of the central bank in the exchange-control country. A credit balance of given dimensions (proportionally, at least) is in such cases anticipated. Occasionally, provision is made that any *additional* balance in favor of the exchange-control country shall likewise be placed at the free disposal of that country's central bank.[63] The German-Rumanian agreement of May 1, 1933, on the other hand, provided that any balance existing at the end of each month should be settled by a delivery of goods from the debtor country to the creditor country or by some other means determined upon by the two central banks.[64] Frequently, credit balances are to be applied

---

[62] The relatively low premia and surcharges called for in Hungary's agreements with certain countries in Central and Eastern Europe are of interest in this connection. (See p. 114 above.)

[63] The German-Norwegian agreement of September 6, 1934, for example, placed 15 per cent of the sums remitted by Norwegian importers of German goods at the free disposal of the *Deutsche Verrechnungskasse* (German Clearing Office). An additional portion was likewise to be placed at the "free" disposal of the same body, though its amount and the purpose for which it was to be used were to be settled later by the two governments. Finally, any balance in excess of 500,000 crowns in favor of the *Deutsche Verrechnungskasse* at the end of each bi-monthly period was to be transferred to that institution. (*Accords de Compensation*, p. 9, and *Enquiry into Clearing Agreements*, pp. 94–95.)

[64] Cf. *ibid.*, p. 95.

to debt liquidation. In some cases, provisions for the periodic disposal of unused balances are elaborate, covering various invisible items in the balance of payments.[65] As experience with the operation of clearing agreements has accumulated, there has been a tendency to provide for frequent meetings of representatives of the two governments concerned, the purpose being, among other things, to devise means of forestalling the accumulation of a credit balance on either side.[66]

Balances remaining at the expiration of a clearing agreement are almost invariably liquidated through continued remittances to the clearing office by importers of the country to which the balance is due, until sufficient funds have accumulated to pay off the exporters who hold claims on the clearing office. This is usually true whether the agreement definitely calls for this particular method of settlement, or whether the matter is left to be handled when the agreement actually expires. A transfer of funds in foreign exchange is usually considered out of keeping with the spirit of a clearing agreement,[67] and, in fact, exchange-control countries often insist, before concluding an agreement, that they are not under any condition to be called on to make such transfers. Occasionally a country which has accumulated a favorable balance may be willing to encourage increased imports from the debtor country by relaxing import restrictions on that country's goods, in order to liquidate a balance. Since clearing agreements have generally been renewed in revised form on expiration, provision for liquidating this balance is in practice customarily included in the revised

---

[65] The Italo-German agreement of September 26, 1934, provides that unused balances at the end of any calendar month may be set aside to meet future trade and tourist requirements; or they will be credited, wholly or in part, to special accounts maintained for the settlement of shipping expenses, balances due in connection with communications or railway services, or payments not otherwise specified. Should conditions underlying the agreement change radically, either party may request a re-opening of discussions, with a view to modifying the provisions of the agreement. (*Foreign Financial News: European Financial Notes*, No. 181 [November 5, 1934], p. 10.)

[66] Cf. p. 136 above.

[67] Cf. *Enquiry into Clearing Agreements*, p. 34.

agreement. Before discussing in detail the manner in which the problem has been met, we shall examine the actual experience with credit balances.

10. *Clearing Agreements and Bilateral Trade Balances*

One of the most serious difficulties encountered by countries concluding clearing agreements is that the balance of trade tends to turn against the country with relatively severe exchange restrictions. This is particularly likely to happen in the case of an agreement between an exchange-control country and a free-exchange country.

The reasons for this phenomenon have already been indicated. The first has to do with the choice of a conventional or official rate of conversion which places an artificially high value on one of the currencies. This problem frequently arises in the case of agreements between exchange-control countries and free-exchange countries, in which the rate of conversion ordinarily chosen involves, or at least did involve in the earlier agreements, an over-valuation of the controlled currency. Imports into the exchange-control country from the free-exchange country are then stimulated and exports discouraged. An analogous situation may develop between two exchange-control countries, however, if the rate of conversion chosen differs substantially from the rate which would prevail in the absence of restrictions.

The harmful effects of an artificial rate of conversion on the working of the clearing agreement make themselves felt not only through changes in the actual volume of trade carried on, but also through evasion of the clearing system. Exporters in the exchange-control country and importers in the free-exchange country find it profitable to seek means of carrying on trade at the black bourse rate, or at some rate more advantageous than the official rate. Their methods of evasion are identical with those of traders seeking to "get around" foreign exchange restrictions. Goods are sold indirectly through firms in third countries, fictitiously low values are assigned to the goods in order that the importer may deposit part of the purchase price in a bank in his own country for the benefit of the exporter, or goods are sold in the importing country through a branch office of the exporter which does not transfer the proceeds to the exporting country.[68] Occasionally, the purchaser is granted a very long term for payment, in the hope that in the meantime the clearing agreement may be abolished and the exchange situation improved.[69]

Alternatively, the choice of an artificial rate of conversion may stimulate private compensation transactions. These will have no harmful effects on the working of the agreement, if its success calls for an equalized balance of trade between the two countries. If, however, as is generally the case with agreements between free-exchange countries and exchange-control countries, the proper working of the agreement requires that the free-exchange country have a passive balance of trade, the conducting of an abnormally large volume of trade by the private compensation method may very well interfere with debt liquidation under the agreement.

A second reason for the change in the balance of trade is the fact that imports into exchange-control countries from clearing countries involve no drain on precious foreign exchange reserves. Hence, at least in the early years of clearing agreements, such imports were generally exempt from foreign exchange restrictions which applied to imports from non-clearing countries. Importers accordingly diverted their foreign purchases to clearing countries, even though those countries were more expensive sources of supply for some of the commodities wanted. Frequently, moreover, articles were purchased from clearing countries which were not really needed by the importing country or which, under normal circumstances, would

[68] Cf. pp. 65–68 above, and *Enquiry into Clearing Agreements*, pp. 37–38.
[69] Cf. *ibid.*, p. 37.

not have been imported at all. The result was that certain exchange-control countries piled up huge deficits on clearing accounts. These very countries were usually the ones which had been expected to repay large frozen debts through the clearing accounts.

A third factor which was of considerable importance in causing shifts in trade balances was the tightening of import restrictions in free-exchange countries from 1931 on.[70] The new trade barriers were not aimed exclusively at clearing countries, but they had the effect of cutting down imports from these countries substantially.[71]

The countries which accumulated credit balances objected to this feature of clearing agreements, because it meant that exporters had to wait long periods before being paid. Furthermore, the fact that balances frequently had to be liquidated by increased imports seemed undesirable at a time when protection of the home market was being stressed to an unprecedented degree.

The history of clearing agreements since about the middle of 1933 has been largely a history of the development of methods for liquidating balances and for preventing the accumulation of further balances. On July 28, 1933, Switzerland agreed to liquidate a balance in her favor which had accumulated in the National Bank of Hungary under the first Swiss-Hungarian agreement by purchasing 500,000 quintals of Hungarian grain.[72] Increased imports by the creditor country have not always constituted the sole means relied on to eliminate a credit balance, however. One of the purposes of a Czechoslovakian loan to Rumania in July, 1936, was to

---

[70] See pp. 243–52 below.

[71] See the replies of Chile and France to the League Committee, *Enquiry into Clearing Agreements*, pp. 56, 58–59, 112–13, 119–20, 122 and 123–24. See also Jolly, *op. cit.*, pp. 174, 186.

[72] *Recueil Officiel des Lois et Ordonnances de la Confédération suisse*, XLIX (1933), 760–61. In the earlier agreements, Switzerland had agreed to stimulate imports from Hungary.

liquidate a clearing balance in favor of the former country.[73] French exporters who had experienced delays in collecting claims from the Hungarian clearing account were, in the latter part of 1935, given the opportunity to sell their claims at a discount not exceeding 30 per cent if they so chose.[74]

Measures designed to prevent the accumulation of further balances helped also to facilitate the repayment of old balances, and it is not always possible to draw a sharp distinction between the two types of measures. Exchange-control countries brought their imports from clearing countries under more strict control, often as a result of pressure exerted on them by creditor countries. Whether they at first subjected imports from clearing countries to the requirement of foreign exchange permits or not, many of them later introduced such provisions. Czechoslovakia and Denmark required the presentation of an import permit issued by the foreign exchange office in the case of all goods ordinarily subject to such a permit, while Latvia and Hungary also required the approval of the foreign exchange authorities.[75] Chilean imports from clearing countries were to take, for the most part, the form of private compensation transactions. The importer applied for a private compensation permit, the granting of which would not in any case be subject to the limitations imposed by the supply of exchange since no net outward payment was involved. When compensation transactions were not involved, the importer had to apply for an import license, which was freely granted only when funds were available for this purpose in clearing accounts abroad.[76]

[73] The loan, extended by private interests, was approved and guaranteed by the Czechoslovakian government. That part of the proceeds destined for liquidation of the clearing balance would, of course, be paid over to Czechoslovakian exporters. See *Foreign Financial News: European Financial Notes,* No. 224 (August 24, 1936), p. 2.

[74] *Ibid.,* No. 206 (November 24, 1935), p. 7.

[75] See *Enquiry into Clearing Agreements,* pp. 87 and 89–90.

[76] *Ibid.,* pp. 78, 86–87, and Banco Central de Chile, *Monthly Report on Credit and Business Conditions,* August, 1934, p. 4.

Countries which accumulated clearing balances abroad sometimes took action on their side to prevent further immobiliza-
tion of credits. Not only did they occasionally encourage imports by relaxing restrictions, as already indicated, but the
limiting of exports was by no means uncommon. Under the
Swiss-German agreement of April 16, 1935, Swiss exports to
Germany were limited to 13 million francs.[77] Yugoslavia, early
in 1937, decided to limit exports to Germany to 90 per cent
of imports from Germany, the remaining 10 per cent of import
proceeds to be applied to the liquidation of a portion of the
clearing balance.[78] Toward the end of 1937, Austria was reported to be planning a temporary restriction of exports to
Germany.[79]

Frequently, the terms of clearing agreements themselves or
of accompanying commercial agreements have called for restriction of imports by the exchange-control country. Italy
has, in a number of her agreements, undertaken to limit her
imports of the other country's products to a specified percentage of the quantities imported in 1934.[80] A more usual
arrangement is one which provides for a fixed relationship between the imports of the two countries. Whenever the terms
of an agreement call for such a fixed trade ratio, the agreement may be said to contain a *compensation clause*.[81] The inclusion of compensation clauses of one kind or another in

[77] Holders of German bonds and of short-term credits in Germany were
also forced to accept interest-rate reductions. (*Foreign Financial News: European Financial Notes*, No. 194 [May 19, 1935], p. 7.)
[78] *Ibid.*, No. 240 (April 24, 1937), p. 16. See p. 165 below.
[79] *Ibid.*, No. 255 (December 9, 1937), p. 1.
[80] Thus imports from Sweden were restricted to 80 per cent of verified quantities imported during 1934 by the terms of a commercial agreement which
accompanied a clearing agreement signed June 24, 1935. (*Commerce Reports*,
August 31, 1935, pp. 161–62.) Similar agreements have been concluded with
other countries, but the percentages have varied from country to country.
Special quotas, not subject to the general percentage restriction, have usually
been granted for certain commodities. Cf. W. G. Welk, "League Sanctions and
Foreign Trade Restrictions in Italy," *American Economic Review*, XXVII
(1937), 100.
[81] Cf. pp. 122–23 above.

clearing agreements or in accompanying trade agreements has become more and more common. In fact, cases in which the trade between two clearing countries is not subject to some sort of compensation arrangement probably constitute the exception rather than the rule.

Compensation clauses may, as already indicated, assume a number of forms. In some cases, countries which have accumulated clearing debts have undertaken to issue permits for imports only as funds became available in the clearing office of the other country. The Franco-Hungarian clearing agreement of March 30, 1934, contained a provision which was included in substantially the same form in several later French agreements and which was similar to a provision of the Swiss-Hungarian agreement of February 7, 1934.[82] The Franco-Hungarian clearing office at the Chamber of Commerce in Paris was to notify the National Bank of Hungary, at the beginning of each month, as to the total value of French imports from Hungary declared to it in the preceding month. The National Bank of Hungary would then take steps to restrict payments in pengös by Hungarian importers of French goods to the amounts available in Paris for payments to French exporters.[83] The German-Polish agreement of November 4, 1935, provided that the German authorities must submit payments for imports of Polish goods to the usual exchange certificate system, authorizations to be made only in accordance with the funds available in the Polish clearing office.[84]

A number of clearing agreements define precisely the ratio

[82] See Jolly, *op. cit.*, p. 279. For text of Swiss-Hungarian agreement, see *Recueil Officiel des Lois et Ordonnances de la Confédération suisse*, L (1934), 201–203.

[83] Hungarian importers of French products were issued visas entitling them to make payment through the clearing system. These visas were made available only within the limits of the funds paid into the Paris office, after account had been taken of the amounts which had to be set aside to liquidate frozen debts.

[84] League of Nations, *Chronology of International Treaties and Legislative Matters*, VII (1935–36), 24.

which is to be maintained in the trade between the two countries. One of the earliest of these was the agreement of July, 1933 between Czechoslovakia and Denmark, which provided that Denmark's imports under the agreement should be one and one-half times those of Czechoslovakia, control to be achieved through the issuance of foreign exchange permits. In addition the agreement fixed the minimum amounts of imports on each side for the last five months of 1933, calling for Danish imports from Czechoslovakia totalling at least 4.5 million Danish crowns and for Czechoslovakian imports from Denmark of at least 3.0 million Danish crowns.[85] The agreement of September 7, 1934, between the Belgo-Luxemburg Economic Union and Germany called for a trade ratio of 100:62½ "in favor of" Germany.[86] If Germany's favorable balance showed an increase at the end of any quarter, import restrictions could be established by the Economic Union, unless Germany permitted increased imports. Furthermore, if the Belgian credits at the Reichsbank tended to exceed three million marks for a reasonable period, the German foreign-currency office could cause a reduction in imports to 50 per cent of the base allotments.[87]

The provisions for a definite trade ratio have frequently been included, not in the clearing agreement itself, but in an accompanying trade agreement. A Hungarian-Turkish commercial agreement which went into effect May 1, 1934, in conjunction with an extension of the clearing agreement between the two countries, called for a 1:1 trade ratio and fixed the maximum total value of exports from each country to the other for the ensuing six months.[88] A number of other clearing agree-

[85] Moreover, 50 per cent of Czechoslovakia's imports of Danish goods were to consist of agricultural products. (*Foreign Financial News: European Financial Notes,* No. 154 [September 20, 1933], pp. 4–5.)

[86] *Ibid.,* No. 179 (October 9, 1934), p. 2.

[87] *Ibid.*

[88] *Ibid.,* No. 176 (August 23, 1934), p. 13. The agreement also provided that if the elimination of a net balance was not achieved during the first six months, the period could be extended until the "compensation" had been effected.

ments are related to commercial agreements of one sort or another. Where a definite trade ratio is called for, one or both countries agree, usually, to coöperate in achieving the desired balance through their import control systems. Thus, in her commercial agreement of May 24, 1934, with Spain, containing clearing provisions, Turkey agreed to admit unrestricted amounts of certain Spanish goods and fixed quotas of other specified Spanish goods until a balance of trade between the two countries was attained.[89] It is obvious that such provisions are possible only if at least one of the countries involved exercises some degree of quantitative control over its imports.

Provisions calling for compulsory private compensation in the trade between the two countries concerned are occasionally found in clearing agreements or in accompanying commercial agreements. This means that every import transaction must be compensated by an export transaction to which it is linked. A definite trade ratio is thereby automatically established. The ratio need not be a 1:1 ratio, if provision is made that in every compensation transaction the exports of one country must exceed the exports of the other country. Bulgaria, Hungary, and Turkey have been parties to clearing agreements calling for compulsory compensation of transactions.[90] Imports into Chile from clearing countries have largely taken place, as already noted, on a compensation basis, and import licenses for uncompensated imports have been issued only when funds have been available to pay the foreign exporter in clearing accounts abroad. Thus the effect on the balance of trade has been identical with that of all-round compulsory compensation. In Bulgaria, too, the resort to private compensation, where not compulsory, has been common, because of official encourage-

---

[89] *Commerce Reports,* September 1, 1934, pp. 143–44.
[90] See *Accords de Compensation,* p. 17, for provisions of Bulgaria's agreements with Hungary and Turkey.

ment through the granting of import permits on more lenient terms when imports were to be compensated.[91]

In summary, although the success of clearing agreements depends on the maintenance of a prescribed ratio in the trade between the two countries concerned, there is nothing in the clearing mechanism itself to ensure the achievement of the desired ratio. In fact, clearing agreements may, for reasons already indicated, result in an undesired shift in trade balances. Consequently, the proper working of the agreements depends on the manipulation of import and export restrictions by the trade authorities of the two countries. It is primarily for this reason that the attitude toward clearing agreements has undergone a marked change since they were first inaugurated. They have, on the whole, gained in popularity with certain countries, such as Germany and Italy, which have aimed at balanced bilateral trade with all other countries through rigid control by the trade authorities. They have lost favor with other countries, like France and Belgium, whose exporters were constantly experiencing lengthy delays in collecting sums due them through the clearing system. These latter countries have tended to turn to payments agreements, under which the desired trade ratio can be achieved without the necessity of constant adjustments in import and export restrictions.

There has been considerable discussion in the press, especially in the last few years, concerning Germany's manipulation of her clearing agreements with the countries of Southeastern Europe in order to gain certain trade advantages for herself. While our survey of clearing agreements would not be complete without some reference to this interesting subject, it is important to note that Germany's methods are in no sense typical of the methods of clearing countries in general. The trade relations of the Reich with the Danubian and Balkan

[91] See *Foreign Financial News: European Financial Notes*, No. 167 (April 10, 1934), p. 2.

countries are affected by a number of special factors the nature of which will become clear as we proceed.

Germany first negotiated clearing agreements with the countries of Southeastern Europe in 1932, in an effort to secure liquidation of her frozen commercial claims in this region. Later, in 1933 and 1934, when the Reichsbank was experiencing a serious drain on its foreign exchange reserves, Germany began to divert purchases to countries with which she had concluded clearing agreements, thereby avoiding payment in foreign exchange.[92] As important sources of supply for agricultural products and raw materials, the countries of Southeastern Europe found their sales to Germany increasing rapidly.[93] As time went on, Germany stimulated purchases from these countries, not merely in order to secure imports in spite of a scarcity of foreign exchange, but as a means of carrying out a policy of encouraging the growth of economic interdependence throughout a vast area, which would comprise the Reich and the entire Danubian and Balkan region, stretching eastward to the Russian Ukraine.

Germany has always been an important market for the Southeastern European countries, which have in turn proved natural outlets for German manufactured products. From this adjacent area, Germany can secure various raw commodities of which she has need—petroleum, tobacco, ores, fibers, fruit, eggs, and a number of other products. Hence the

---

[92] Cf. J. C. de Wilde, "German Trade Drive in Southeastern Europe," *Foreign Policy Reports*, XII (1936–37), 215–16.

[93] The countries of Western Europe were affected by this diversion of purchases to clearing countries, also, and Germany's clearing debts mounted rapidly, reaching a total of 500 million RM in August, 1934. (Fischer, *Devisenclearing*, pp. 23–24.) After the introduction of the "New Plan" in September, 1934, however, clearing debts to Western European countries ceased, on the whole, to grow. New clearing agreements, providing for repayment of frozen commercial debts, were negotiated to replace the less rigid "Swedish clause" agreements which had previously been in force with countries of Western and Northern Europe. The new agreements contained, in most cases, clauses designed to prevent the accumulation of further frozen balances in Berlin. For a description of the "Swedish clause," cf. *ibid.*, pp. 20 ff.

Nazi emphasis on the development of a *"Grossraumwirtschaft"* (resembling, in some respects, the pre-War *"Drang nach Osten"* policy) is based on the theory that an economic union between the Reich and the area to the southeast would mean the emergence of a balanced, more or less self-sustaining, agricultural and industrial economy.

Using the clearing agreements as a framework, Germany has developed various techniques for encouraging trade with the Danubian and Balkan countries. From the beginning, the most important of these devices has been the practice of stimulating purchases of primary products from this area through her import control system. Thus, Yugoslavia, Rumania, and the other countries affected have found themselves accumulating large clearing credits in Berlin, which could be liquidated only through increased purchases from the Reich, whether they had a real need for additional German products or not. Furthermore, with her over-valued mark, Germany could pay prices which, translated into Rumanian lei or Yugoslav dinars, were higher than world market prices. This development proved popular with the agricultural producers of Southeastern Europe for a time, but their enthusiasm waned somewhat when they found that Germany's activities were threatening to destroy the world market for their products. Not only were their prices becoming unattractive to third countries, but Germany was actually discovered to be dumping their goods on world markets at prices well below those which she had paid for them.[94] Recently, Germany has made matters even more difficult for some of the Danubian and Balkan countries by deliberately attempting to keep their currencies under-valued in terms of the reichsmark but over-valued in terms of sterling and other free currencies.[95] Since the exchange rate at which clearing transactions are conducted is fixed by the terms of the clearing agreement concerned, Ger-

[94] Cf. *The Economist*, CXXXIII (1938), 262–63.
[95] *Ibid.*, CXXXIV (1939), 82.

many seeks to carry out her intentions in this respect whenever a clearing agreement comes up for renewal. A policy of
depressing the values of Southeastern European currencies in
relation to the reichsmark would seem, at first sight, to be undesirable for Germany's export industries; but, actually, if it
has the effect of diverting the exports of, say, Yugoslavia, to
Germany, Yugoslavia will be forced to import more German
goods in order to liquidate her clearing accounts.

The accumulation of large clearing balances in Berlin has
been a source of great inconvenience to the countries of Southeastern Europe. It has meant, of course, that clearing funds
in the central banks of these countries have been inadequate
to pay exporters, who have, in many cases, been the recipients
of government or central bank advances.[96] Moreover, clearing
funds in Berlin have reputedly had to be liquidated through
the purchase of nonessential German goods at relatively high
prices, while imports of needed raw materials from third countries have had to be foregone, owing to the inadequacy of
foreign exchange reserves in free currencies. In fact, Germany
has been charged with selling to these countries only stocks
of goods which were not wanted by free-exchange countries.[97]
There are indications, however, that some of these charges
have been exaggerated and that prices of German goods sold
to Balkan countries have ordinarily been competitive.

In some cases, Germany has stimulated exports to the Danubian and Balkan countries, not through the pressure of in-

[96] Early in 1936, it was announced that the Bank of Greece would cease
paying exporters in full as soon as German purchasers of Greek goods had
deposited payment in reichsmarks in Berlin. Thereafter, the responsibility for
collections and exchange losses was to be borne by exporters, who would, however, receive as loans without interest from the Bank of Greece 60 per cent
of the amounts of their invoices. This plan was promptly abandoned, however, owing to the protests of exporters, who continued to receive payment
in full. The government purchased from the Bank of Greece its 22 million RM
credit with the Reichsbank, borrowing the necessary funds from the Bank at
3 per cent. See *Foreign Financial News: European Financial Notes*, No. 220
(June 24, 1936), pp. 13–14.

[97] *The Economist*, CXXXIII (1938), 262–63.

creased imports, but through the sale of goods on a long-term credit basis. If the clearing agreement called for the compensation of sales and purchases, as many of the later agreements have, such exports gave Germany the right to import goods from these countries immediately. Meanwhile, however, how were Rumanian or Greek exporters who had supplied Germany with goods to be reimbursed, when their fellow-countrymen who had purchased German products on a long-term credit basis would not make payment into the clearing account in the Rumanian or Greek central bank for, perhaps, ten years? [98] Here again, the Danubian and Balkan central banks were called upon to make advances to exporters.

This does not exhaust the list of special sales-promotion techniques developed by Germany, but enough has been said to indicate the manner in which the clearing agreements have been manipulated to serve Germany's purposes.[99] Export subsidies, which could be utilized with or without clearing agreements have also played a part.[100] Nazi policy has recently been directed toward organizing the economies of the Danubian and Balkan countries to complement that of Germany through (a) encouraging their output of primary products, and (b) promoting industrialization and improvement of their communications in order to create a demand for German manufactured goods.[101]

The more dependent the Southeastern European countries become on their trade with Germany, the more they have to lose by attempting to thwart German policies. Partly as a result of the German trade drive and partly as a result of the incorporation of new territories into the Reich, they have come

[98] Cf. *ibid.*

[99] See P. Einzig, *Bloodless Invasion: German Economic Penetration into the Danubian States and the Balkans* (London, 1938), pp. 17–56, for an account of other devices utilized by Germany.

[100] See pp. 326–28 below.

[101] *The Economist*, CXXXIII (1938), 266. See pp. 425–26, below, on the German-Rumanian Agreement of March, 1939.

to be, on the whole, considerably more dependent on trade with Germany than they were in 1929. Table VIII compares the position in 1938 with that in 1929. It must be recognized, moreover, that, as Germany's political power is enhanced, these countries cannot afford, from a strategic point of view, to resist German pressure in the economic sphere.

TABLE VIII [a]

A. PERCENTAGE OF TOTAL EXPORTS OF CERTAIN COUNTRIES TO GERMANY, AUSTRIA, AND CZECHOSLOVAKIA

COUNTRIES	EXPORTS TO GERMANY [b] %		EXPORTS TO GERMANY, AUSTRIA, AND CZECHOSLOVAKIA %
	1929	1938	1938
Bulgaria	30	59 [c]	63.5
Greece	23	38.5	43
Yugoslavia	8.5	36	50
Turkey	13	43	47.5
Hungary [d]	12	28	50
Rumania	28	26.5 [c]	36

B. PERCENTAGE OF TOTAL IMPORTS OF CERTAIN COUNTRIES FROM GERMANY, AUSTRIA, AND CZECHOSLOVAKIA

COUNTRIES	IMPORTS FROM GERMANY [b] %		IMPORTS FROM GERMANY, AUSTRIA, AND CZECHOSLOVAKIA %
	1929	1938	1938
Bulgaria	22	52 [c]	58
Greece	9	29	32
Yugoslavia	16	32.5	50
Turkey	15	47	51
Hungary [d]	20	30	48
Rumania	24	37 [c]	50

[a] Source: League of Nations, *World Economic Survey, 1938–39*, p. 202.
[b] Excluding Austria and Sudetenland.
[c] Including trade with Austria.
[d] Excluding free ports.

Germany has not by any means had things entirely her own way, however. Before the signing of the Munich Agreement, and even to some extent since, the countries of Southeastern Europe have taken definite steps to prevent the growth of further clearing balances in Berlin. We shall mention here only a few of these measures, to illustrate the manner in which resistance has been shown. It has already been noted, in another connection, that Yugoslavia, early in 1937, ruled that exports to Germany should be restricted to 90 per cent of imports to Germany. The remaining 10 per cent of the import funds paid into the Bank of Yugoslavia were to serve to liquidate the clearing balance in Berlin, until it should be reduced to 10,000 RM. Furthermore, not more than 55 per cent of Yugoslavia's exports to Germany were to consist of agricultural products and livestock.[102] At the end of 1938, Yugoslavia expressed her independence by lowering the value of her currency in terms of the pound sterling and fixing rates for imports from all non-clearing countries accordingly.[103] It is interesting to note, also, that the new regulations provided for a system of multiple exchange rates, much like that in vogue in Latin American countries. Similarly, Rumania, in August, 1938, adopted a provision designed to stimulate trade with free-exchange countries. Exporters of cereals and certain other products were to be required to surrender only 70 per cent of their foreign exchange proceeds to the National Bank at the official rate. The remaining 30 per cent might be sold through authorized banks for certain types of payments to free-exchange countries, i.e., specified types of financial remittances and payments for imports, whether or not the importer had been allotted a quota.[104]

---

[102] *Foreign Financial News: European Financial Notes*, No. 240 (April 24, 1937), p. 16.

[103] *The Economist*, CXXXIV (1939), 82, and *Foreign Financial News: European Financial Notes*, I (NS), No. 2 (January 24, 1939), pp. 24–25.

[104] *Ibid.*, No. 275 (October 9, 1938), pp. 12–13. See also *ibid.*, No. 279 (December 9, 1938), p. 10, and No. 280 (December 24, 1938), p. 10.

11. *Conclusions*

Clearing agreements were at first concluded to permit the carrying on of trade or the transfer of debt payments in spite of exchange restrictions. There is little doubt that some of the early agreements made possible certain transfers which could not have taken place over the foreign exchanges. Bilateral clearing has long since ceased to be an emergency mechanism, however, and has become an integral part of the exchange control regime in many European countries. Very few clearing agreements have been scrapped, although some have been replaced by payments agreements. There was every indication in September, 1939, that the clearing agreements then in force would continue to be renewed as they expired, at least as long as exchange control persisted in Central and Eastern Europe and in certain Latin American countries.

Many of the difficulties associated with the earlier agreements have disappeared as the countries concerned have adopted conversion rates more nearly conforming to the exchange rates which would prevail in the absence of restrictions. There are still cases, however, in which the exchange rates enforced in clearing agreements are out of line with other rates. In a few instances, artificial rates are deliberately adopted for clearing transactions, in order to force the currents of trade into certain channels, desired for special economic or political reasons.

Clearing agreements, as we have seen, operate successfully, only if a given ratio is maintained in the trade between the two countries concerned. Accordingly, import and, in some cases, export control has been adopted in order to achieve the desired ratio. Trade is thus forced into bilateral channels, and triangular trade is largely excluded.[105] Since import and ex-

---

[105] Trilateral clearing has been attempted, in a few cases, notably in certain of the earlier Greek agreements, but it has never made much headway. The Turkish-Greek agreement has carried a provision whereby sums paid in

port restrictions inevitably have repercussions on internal price structures, the new trade channels tend to become permanent, and forces are set in motion tending to perpetuate the clearing system. Cyclical or secular fluctuations, on the other hand, may work havoc with trade ratios and lead to the necessity for major adjustments of import or export restrictions in order to liquidate the inconveniently large credit balances which accumulate on one side or the other. Accordingly, viewed as an instrument of commercial policy, bilateral clearing commends itself only to those countries which are anxious to develop their trade along bilateral lines and are willing to subject their foreign trade to constant direction and rigorous control.

Ultimately, the future of bilateral clearing is probably bound up with the future of exchange control. If the obstacles to the removal of exchange restrictions could be overcome, clearing accounts could be liquidated without great difficulty. It is possible that certain countries might cling to clearing agreements in order to carry out bilateral balancing policies. There is reason to believe, however, that most countries would prefer to aim at bilateral balancing through trade restrictions rather than through bilateral clearing. Objections are constantly being raised, even in countries which make the most widespread use of clearing agreements, to the fact that exports to a clearing country give rise to blocked balances which *must* be spent in that country. On the other hand, certain strategic advantages of clearing agreements must not be overlooked. Under some conditions, a country's ability to contract short-

---

by Greek importers of lignite could be utilized by the Turkish Central Bank for payments to a central bank or compensation office of another country with which Turkey had concluded a clearing agreement and whose balance of trade in respect of Turkey was active. (International Chamber of Commerce, *Clearing and Payments Agreements,* p. GR. TR [analysis of agreement between Greece and Turkey].) There have been a few other examples of triangular arrangements. For the most part, in so far as triangular trade is possible under clearing agreements, it is rendered so by clauses placing funds at the free disposal of one of the countries or permitting transfers in free foreign exchange.

term indebtedness by running up adverse clearing balances may prove a convenient method of tiding over temporary difficulties. Furthermore, certain types of discriminatory commercial policies can be most easily carried out through the manipulation of the clearing system. Clearing agreements are not, however, magic devices for reaping advantages at the expense of other countries. No policy can succeed for long without the acquiescence of the other party to the agreement. In this respect, clearing agreements are no different from other instruments of commercial policy.

CHAPTER VII

Other Payments Arrangements

1. *Private Compensation Transactions*

The object of private compensation transactions, like that of clearing agreements, is to eliminate the need for remittances of means of payment across international boundaries. Although the process in some ways resembles barter, the amounts of goods to be exchanged are determined on the basis of the price mechanism, and monetary payments take place within the boundaries of the countries concerned. In some cases, payments are actually made in foreign exchange, but since the obligation of country A equals that of country B, no *net* transfer of funds needs to take place.

Let us assume that Brazilian coffee is to be exchanged for German machinery on a private compensation basis. Four parties ordinarily will be concerned: the German importer, the German exporter, the Brazilian importer, and the Brazilian exporter. If the terms of the transaction can be arranged in such a way that the value of machinery involved will equal the value of coffee involved, an agreement can be reached whereby the German importer will make payment to the German exporter, while the Brazilian importer will settle with the Brazilian exporter. Thus no international payments will be required.

Most of the early transactions of this kind took place between two exchange-control countries or between an exchange-control country and a free-exchange country. It was possible in this way, not only to bring about the import into exchange-control countries of commodities for which payments through the ordinary channels would not have been permitted, but also to effect exports from such countries which could not have taken place at the official exchange rates. In fact, exporters in exchange-control countries were often induced to enter into such transactions because the terms arranged tended to compensate them for losses which they would have incurred on exports made at the official rate. Frequently, it was the prices of the commodities which were adjusted to take care of this discrepancy rather than the basis of currency conversion. However the adjustment was made, the importer in the country with the relatively over-valued currency was forced to pay to the exporter in his country a premium over and above the amount he would have had to pay for the goods had he purchased official exchange and settled his debt in the normal manner. The importer could afford to pay a premium if he had purchased a foreign commodity affected by import or exchange restrictions in his own country, since the internal price of such a commodity would tend to be higher than the world price.[1]

Clearly all this required the sanction of the exchange control authorities. To be sure, no demand for foreign exchange was involved; but, as we have seen, wherever exchange restrictions were severe, a permit was required for every import and export transaction, in order to prevent evasion of the regulations. Permission was generally granted for compensation transactions in the early years of exchange control, on the ground that trade could thus be carried on without any drain on the foreign exchange reserves. Further, no objection was ordinarily raised to the payment of a premium by the importer to the exporter, since no purchase of foreign exchange was involved. Governments tended to show considerable leniency, in particular, in permitting large firms to meet necessary payments abroad, especially for raw materials, out of foreign balances acquired

[1] Cf. pp. 232–43 below, on the theory of import quotas.

through exports, thereby waiving in such cases the requirement that all foreign exchange accruing from exports be surrendered to the central bank.[2] Later, it was found necessary
to subject all private compensation dealings to rigid official control. Before we trace the evolution of governmental policy
with respect to barter trade, however, let us examine certain
of the difficulties which were encountered in attempting to
conclude such transactions.

It was no simple matter to find partners to deals which involved the equating of values of imports from a given country
and exports to the same country. Imports of certain foodstuffs
and raw materials into industrial countries, moreover, tended
to be particularly heavy at certain seasons of the year, whereas
exports of manufactured goods from such countries did not
usually show marked seasonal variations. Attempts to arrange
barter deals between agricultural and industrial countries were
obviously greatly complicated by this factor. Finally, it was
frequently difficult to secure an agreement on prices. Whereas
normally only two parties need agree on the terms of a contract, these private compensation transactions required the
consent of four parties. In the case of commodities with well-
organized international markets, the world price in terms of
some uncontrolled currency could serve as a guide, but such
commodities constitute a minority. The *agios* being paid for
uncontrolled currencies on black bourses constituted an index
of sorts to the premiums which exporters in exchange-control
countries might expect to receive, but dealings on black bourses
were often influenced by speculative factors and the extent to
which prices in exchange-control countries were out of line
with world prices varied for different commodities.

None of these difficulties constituted insuperable obstacles.

---

[2] Thus, in Hungary, even during the first few months of foreign exchange
control, the National Bank permitted certain of the larger firms to use their
export foreign exchange to cover requirements connected with the continuation
of their business. See Bank for International Settlements, *Foreign Exchange
Regulations in the Different Countries* (Basle, 1931–38), XIV, C.

Where large transactions were involved, powerful firms could afford to enter into lengthy and complicated negotiations. Smaller firms have suffered from a handicap in attempting to conclude barter deals. To some extent, however, they have been able to employ the services of middlemen who made it their business to get into contact with all potential partners to private compensation transactions and to balance, if necessary, a whole series of possible imports against a corresponding series of possible exports. A number of firms were organized for just this purpose in 1932 and later years, while the services of chambers of commerce were also utilized to arrange contacts between importers and exporters. The Polish Company for Compensation Trade, which began operations in November, 1932, was one of the more important of these organizations. Although not strictly a governmental agency, its activities were closely controlled by the Polish Government.[3] The Hamburg Chamber of Commerce established a clearing information bureau for barter transactions in 1932.[4] Similar organizations were set up in other German cities. Five importing firms in Copenhagen organized in 1934 the Association for Commodity Exchange to arrange private compensation transactions with foreign firms.[5] A number of companies have been formed for the purpose of specializing in promoting barter trade between particular pairs of countries.[6]

As it became clear that exchange restrictions and quantitative import controls were likely to persist for some time, the whole process of private compensation began to be regularized under

[3] See *Foreign Financial News: European Financial Notes,* No. 150 (July 25, 1933), p. 6, and No. 155 (October 9, 1933), p. 9.

[4] *Ibid.,* No. 135 (December, 1932), p. 6.

[5] *Ibid.,* No. 186 (January 19, 1935), p. 5.

[6] Thus, a private organization, known as Compensation Brokers, Ltd., was set up in London late in 1936 to facilitate barter transactions primarily between the British Empire and Germany. (*Ibid.,* No. 233 [January 9, 1937], p. 9.) In March, 1937, the Continental Export and Import Corporation was formed in Germany, with the support of the German Government, to promote trade with the United States, much of which has been on a barter basis in recent years. (*Ibid.,* No. 241 [May 9, 1937], p. 8.)

governmental provisions setting up the conditions under which such transactions could be effected. In some cases, the pairing of individual export and import transactions was rendered unnecessary by partial relaxation of the exchange restrictions to permit, as a regular process, the sale of foreign exchange at a premium to importers wishing to purchase foreign goods on a compensation basis.[7] Here, the barter feature lay simply in the requirement that imports be compensated by exports of equivalent value, while payments took place through purchases of foreign exchange rather than through transfers within countries. In addition, the conditions under which quota or exchange restrictions on imports could be waived for private compensation transactions were laid down in systematic governmental regulations. The German Government went so far as to create a special type of blocked mark for the barter trade.[8]

Government encouragement of private compensation transactions in exchange-control countries has proceeded on the assumption that it was desirable to facilitate a type of trade which created no drain on foreign exchange reserves. In this way commodities could be imported for which no official exchange was available, and exports could take place in spite of the handicaps of an unfavorable exchange rate and, in some cases, of trade restrictions abroad. The promotion of the barter trade, moreover, was regarded as one means of equalizing the balance of trade with individual countries. Triangular

[7] It was essentially this process which was involved in the "private clearing" transactions, through which the Austrian foreign exchange restrictions were relaxed. (Cf. pp. 100–102 above.) In Bulgaria, exporters of certain types of goods have been permitted, subject to the approval of the National Bank, to sell at a premium a portion of the foreign exchange received from their exports to importers of specified commodities. (*Foreign Financial News: European Financial Notes,* No. 212 [February 24, 1936], pp. 2–3.) In Chile, a special "export" rate of exchange for compensation transactions was early recognized. (Cf. pp. 103–105 above.) The premium system in Hungary first developed in connection with the "compensating" of certain types of imports by certain types of exports, the offsetting being performed by a governmental agency rather than by private firms. (Cf. p. 112 above.)

[8] See pp. 178–85 below.

compensation transactions have not, as a rule, been encouraged.[9]

The granting of unlimited freedom to effect bilateral compensation transactions has been found, however, to carry with
it numerous disadvantages, and most governments have imposed rigid limitations on this type of trade as time has gone
on. The most common complaint has been that such transactions tended to interfere with the accumulation of "free" exchange, since the proceeds of exports on a barter basis were
utilized to pay for imports which had already taken place or
were earmarked for purchases from a given country. The
tendency for exports to be diverted into barter channels was
strong if there was a wide deviation between the official exchange rate and the rate at which compensation transactions
were conducted. Furthermore, the fact that high prices were
frequently paid for imports brought into the country on a
compensation basis interfered with official attempts to prevent
prices from rising, while the importation of nonessentials
through these channels seemed undesirable at a time when
supplies of official exchange were by no means adequate to
take care of the more urgent requirements for imported commodities.

The nature of these difficulties immediately suggests the
form which government regulation of compensation transactions
took. There has been a tendency (as in the case of blocked account regulations, and for the same reasons) to permit exports
on a compensation basis only if it was a question of "supplementary" or "additional" exports (those which could not take
place profitably at official exchange rates).[10] Lists of commodities which might be exported in barter deals were drawn
up, or exporters were required to submit evidence that their
goods could not be sold abroad profitably through the official

[9] In Bulgaria, private compensation deals were not required to be bilateral.
See *Foreign Financial News: European Financial Notes*, No. 213 (March 9,
1936), p. 4, and p. 178 below.
[10] Cf. pp. 90 ff. above.

channels. In some cases, it was provided that the value of the exports in any compensation transaction should exceed the value of the imports by a given percentage, while the surplus in free foreign exchange accruing to the exporter was to be turned over to the central bank.

Secondly, an attempt was made to see that imports which took place on a compensation basis were related to the needs of the country. While these imports were generally exempted from ordinary exchange or import permit requirements, they were frequently confined to commodities appearing on a published list. Permission has in some cases been required for each individual transaction.

Compensation transactions were sometimes prohibited with countries with which the balance of trade was active or rendered compulsory for countries with which the balance was passive.[11] Where exchange or import restrictions discriminated heavily against countries of the latter category, additional imports on a compensation basis were sometimes permitted. Imports of specified nonessentials have, in some countries, been subjected to compulsory compensation. Certain bilateral agreements have called for compulsory compensation between the two countries concerned. Furthermore, one may state in general that private compensation transactions have been permitted with clearing countries, if, and only if, they have not tended to interfere with the objectives of the agreement.[12]

Finally, there has been some tendency, as time has gone on, to control the exchange rates or prices at which compensation transactions might be conducted. Not only has some measure of control seemed desirable from the point of view of the country imposing the regulations, but it has sometimes been introduced partly in response to the enforcement, or threat of

---

[11] Among countries which have pursued a policy of requiring that imports from countries with which the trade balance was passive be compensated by exports to those countries are Greece, Turkey, and Colombia. Rumania also attempted to enforce this requirement for a time.

[12] Cf. p. 152 above.

enforcement, of penalty import duties by other countries which felt that they were being subjected to a special form of "exchange dumping."

Very little systematic information is available concerning the extent or relative importance of compensation transactions. They played a substantial part in the trade of many exchange-control countries in 1934 and 1935, by which time the procedure had been more or less systematized but exchange restrictions were still, on the whole, relatively severe. Payment for nearly half the imports (in value terms) admitted into Bulgaria in the first nine months of 1935 was made on a compensation basis.[13] Toward the end of 1934, the German exchange authorities were apparently issuing certificates for the import of only one commodity from the United States, cotton linters, while payment for all other imports had to take place through compensation channels, or not at all.[14] As exchange restrictions were relaxed, there was, in general, less inducement to enter into compensation transactions. Meanwhile, governments, more and more impressed with the disadvantages of this type of trade, were surrounding it by increasingly severe restrictions. During 1938, however, as we have seen, many of the exchange-control countries had to face, once more, a problem of more or less acute scarcity of foreign exchange. It was not surprising that, under these circumstances, certain governments which had been discouraging compensation transactions reversed their attitude.[15]

A brief examination of some of the concrete regulations adopted by certain representative countries will throw further

[13] *Foreign Financial News: European Financial Notes*, No. 212 (February 24, 1936), pp. 2–3.

[14] *Ibid.*, No. 188 (February 25, 1935), p. 8.

[15] Rumania is a case in point. Compensation transactions had been drastically limited early in 1937 but, toward the end of that year, a more lenient attitude was adopted, and in the latter part of 1938, new regulations were introduced which provided considerably increased scope for compensation trade. Cf. *ibid.*, No. 273 (September 9, 1938), p. 10, and *Commerce Reports*, January 15, 1938, p. 62.

light on the part played by compensation transactions in practice.

The Greek government has, since the worst years of the depression, pursued, on the whole, a policy of attempting to balance the trade with each individual foreign country. Accordingly, in 1933 and 1934, unilateral regulations were adopted requiring that trade with certain countries, with which Greece tended to have an excess of imports, be conducted on a bilateral private compensation basis. Permission for all transactions covered by these regulations had to be secured from the Bank of Greece. Countries affected in 1933 and 1934 were Japan, Denmark, Norway, Russia, Rumania, Iceland, Brazil, Argentina, Portugal, Spain, Belgium, and Finland.[16] In 1935, Latvia and the French possessions and mandated territories in Northern Africa and Asia Minor were added to the list.[17] Certain of these countries later concluded clearing agreements with Greece. Meanwhile, imports of certain nonessentials had been made subject to compulsory compensation, regardless of geographical origin, while in the cases of certain other commodities, extra-quota imports were permitted on a compensation basis.[18] In 1935, the entire import quota system was revised and elaborated. Imports were classified into eight groups, largely in accordance with their importance to the Greek economy, and each group was to receive different treatment. Thus, List A was composed of commodities which could be imported without any quantitative restriction, regardless of country of origin. List B included commodities which might be imported only in full or partial exchange for exports of Greek products or from countries with which Greece had a favorable balance of

[16] *Foreign Financial News: European Financial Notes*, No. 153 (September 11, 1933), p. 8; No. 160 (December 28, 1933), p. 9; and No. 189 (March 9, 1935), p. 9. Imports of wheat from Russia were exempted from this requirement.

[17] *Ibid.*, No. 196 (June 24, 1935), p. 11.

[18] *Commerce Reports*, February 4, 1933, p. 78; June 9, 1934, p. 363; and August 25, 1934, p. 126.

trade, and so on.[19] This development represents a rather good illustration of a tendency, commented on in an earlier chapter, for exchange or import restrictions, originally adopted primarily to "improve" the balance of trade, to be refined in accordance with a more or less elaborate study of the needs of the national economy. After the beginning of 1937, the Greek authorities responsible for the administration of exchange and quota restrictions were unofficially reported to be discouraging private compensation transactions.

In Bulgaria, permission was granted for extra-quota imports of certain commodities, provided they were offset by compensating exports of specified goods.[20] Offers of available foreign exchange were posted by holders, and agreements for disposing of such exchange to importers were registered with compensation offices. All transactions had to be approved by the National Bank, which retained a portion of the exporters' exchange. From May, 1936, on, premia paid by buyers of foreign exchange to sellers were not permitted to exceed certain maxima established by the government. The maximum premium for purchases of "free exchange," i.e., currencies of countries with no exchange restrictions, was fixed at 35 per cent, close to the prevailing rate.[21] An interesting and rather unusual feature of the Bulgarian regulations was the fact that compensating exports did not necessarily have to be consigned to countries from which imports were derived.

2. *The German Askimark System*

Germany's regulation of compensation transactions presents certain unique features, for a special type of blocked currency was developed for use in the compensation trade. This new currency made its appearance in October, 1934, the month

[19] *Ibid.*, February 2, 1935, p. 77. See also pp. 274–76 below.
[20] *The Economist*, CXIX (1934), 587, and *Foreign Financial News: European Financial Notes*, No. 167 (April 10, 1934), p. 2.
[21] *Ibid.*, No. 220 (June 24, 1936), p. 4.

following the adoption of the "New Plan." Since the latter part of 1931, German firms had been entering into compensation transactions to some extent, but the restrictions were severe and the conclusion of the necessary arrangements had proved a cumbersome process.[22] The new currency was designed to simplify the procedure.

It was arranged that foreign banks, in countries of Central and South America or other non-European countries not having clearing agreements with Germany, could open with German banks special accounts, called *Ausländer Sonderkonten für Inlandszahlungen*.[23] Germans importing foreign goods, for which the necessary permits had been secured from an Import Control Board, could deposit their payments, in reichsmarks, in these accounts to the credit of the foreign seller. Marks deposited in such accounts, which came to be known as "askimarks," could be used for one purpose only, the purchase of German goods for export abroad.[24] Let us assume that an American exporter was selling goods to Germany under this procedure. The German importer would make payment, to the credit of the American seller, into an aski account in a German bank, held in the name of a New York bank. The American exporter could then arrange, through the New York bank, to sell his "askimarks" to an American importer wishing to purchase German goods. The German exporter would be paid by the German bank in which the aski account was held, on the instructions of the New York bank.[25]

Obviously, this arrangement eliminated the necessity for pairing of individual import and export transactions, since foreign banks handling dealings in askimarks could arrange to

---

[22] For early German compensation regulations, see *Commerce Reports*, April 1, 1933, pp. 202, 208, and H. Bachfeld, "Die Kompensationsgeschäft in der Praxis," *Die Wirtschaftskurve*, XIII (1934), 213–23.

[23] Originally, foreign exporters in any country were permitted to open such accounts, but the system was modified in December, 1934.

[24] See *Commerce Reports*, December 8, 1934, p. 362.

[25] For a more detailed description of this procedure, see *Foreign Financial News: Special Circular*, No. 411 (September 24, 1935).

sell them to importers in large amounts or in driblets, as the occasion demanded. Any given foreign bank, however, had to confine its activities to acting as intermediary between importers and exporters; it could not transfer the funds on its account, say, to another bank, by check or other similar instruments. Furthermore, trade conducted on the basis of askimarks had to be strictly bilateral in nature, since German goods exported on an aski basis had to be shipped to the country of origin of the imports which had given rise to the account. Maximum limits were set on the amounts which could be paid into aski accounts in any one month.[26]

Imports of certain dispensable types of goods could take place on an aski basis only if the transaction yielded a surplus of free foreign exchange to the Reichsbank. German imports were divided into three classes: (1) essential raw materials, (2) commodities the lack of which would entail some hardship but which were not absolutely essential to industrial operations, and (3) goods the lack of which would not cause hardship or for which German products, even if inferior, could be substituted. German goods exported in exchange for imports of the first group could be paid for entirely in askimarks (a 1:1 trade ratio). Goods in the second group had to be imported on a 1.3:1 ratio; that is, the value of the exports involved had to exceed that of the imports by 30 per cent, the surplus to be paid in free exchange and delivered to the Reichsbank. In the case of the third group of imports, the trade ratio had to be *at least* 2:1.[27] As in the case of all German compensation transactions, exports were to be "additional."

Although the German regulations prohibited the payment of any bonus or rebate by one partner in a compensation transaction to the other, the German authorities could not prevent

[26] *Foreign Financial News: European Financial Notes*, No. 187 (February 9, 1935), p. 11.

[27] *Ibid.*, No. 183 (December 5, 1934), pp. 9–10. The exact ratio would depend on the urgency of the need for the imports and the percentage of foreign raw materials used in the compensating exports.

the sale of askimarks at a discount, since the transactions took place outside of Germany. Actually, dealings in askimarks have been conducted at a discount from the beginning, for foreign importers could not, in many instances, be induced to buy German goods at the prices prevailing in Germany unless they could purchase marks at a more favorable rate than the artificial official rate. Foreign exporters, in order to compensate themselves for the losses involved in selling their askimarks at a discount, quoted relatively high prices to German importers. Not only did the rate paid for askimarks, therefore, tend to approach, subject to the limitations involved in the restrictions on dealings in these blocked marks, the rate which would have been paid for ordinary marks in a free market, but the fluctuations in quotations on askimarks tended to act as an equilibrating factor in Germany's bilateral trade with the countries involved. If German imports from, say, Brazil increased markedly, Brazilian banks found themselves with excessive supplies of askimarks, which they could sell only by lowering the rates quoted. This tended to reduce the prices of German goods for Brazilian importers, thereby leading to an increase in German exports to Brazil.

While German trade tended to expand as a result of the introduction of askimarks, the German authorities were not altogether pleased with the results. It was very difficult to enforce the use of askimarks only for "additional" exports, since exports of all types tended to be diverted into the more profitable aski channels on a large scale. In some cases, apparently, these exports failed to yield a surplus in foreign exchange, because the imports for which they were traded were not properly classified as nonessentials. Moreover, the fact that goods were imported into Germany at high prices tended to interfere with official efforts to keep the German price level from rising.[28]

As a result, the employment of aski marks was made subject to more and more restrictions as time went on. The restrictions

[28] *Ibid.*, No. 211 (February 8, 1936), pp. 10–12. See also pp. 264–67 below.

applied also to ordinary compensation transactions not concluded on the basis of askimarks. A prohibition was placed
on the export, through compensation transactions, of specified
commodities, including certain raw and semi-finished materials needed by German industry, goods in which Germany
had a monopoly or strong competitive position in world
markets, and goods manufactured from imported materials of
which there was a shortage in Germany. Some of these prohibitions did not apply to countries with which Germany had
clearing agreements or to South and Central America, China,
and Manchuria.[29] Larger surpluses of free exchange were required in connection with compensation transactions involving
imports of nonessentials. The Control Boards were made responsible for preventing the importation and domestic sale of
foreign goods at excessive prices.[30] Furthermore, barter and
askimark transactions were altogether prohibited in the trade
with Egypt and certain Asiatic regions.[31] They were also prohibited in trade with the United States, although limited use,
for certain commodities, of a special type of "inland" account
was permitted.[32] Finally, compensation transactions in which

[29] *Ibid.*, No. 196 (June 24, 1935), p. 8; No. 209 (January 9, 1936), p. 6;
No. 211 (February 8, 1936), pp. 10–12; and *Commerce Reports,* November 16,
1935, p. 356.

[30] A price was considered excessive when, apart from transportation expenses,
etc., it exceeded the export price in the seller's market for an article of equal
grade, or, failing export price quotations, when it exceeded the price that would
be paid in official exchange. Cf. *Foreign Financial News: European Financial
Notes,* No. 211 (February 8, 1936), pp. 10–12.

[31] The prohibition affected the Philippine Islands, China, Siam, Egypt, Sudan,
British India, Ceylon, Burma, and the Straits Settlements. (*Ibid.,* No. 237
[March 9, 1937], p. 7.)

[32] In June, 1936, the U. S. Treasury Department, after investigating the
nature of askimark transactions, imposed countervailing duties on certain imports from Germany under Section 303 of the Tariff Act of 1930. The German
Government replied, on August 3, 1936, with a prohibition on aski and barter
transactions in trade with the United States. Several months later the U. S.
Treasury sanctioned the use of certain types of special procedures in connection
with imports from Germany. (1) Controlled mark credits might be employed
if the German goods were purchased for "the actual account of the original
and continuous owner" of such credits; (2) payment might be made out of
the proceeds of the sale in Germany of merchandise exported from the United

the value of exports involved did not equal at least 50,000 RM were forbidden.[33]

The net result of all these restrictions was that compensation transactions came to play a relatively insignificant rôle, except in the trade with Central and South America. At the end of 1937, compensation transactions accounted for not quite 20 per cent of the total value of German imports, as compared with approximately 65 per cent covered by clearing or payments agreements.[34] The German authorities were evidently willing to impose fewer limitations on compensation deals with Latin American countries partly because exchange restrictions in these countries prevented payment for German goods in free foreign exchange and partly because, for political reasons, Germany was anxious to stimulate trade with these countries through the employment of depreciated askimarks. Trade with certain of the Latin American countries (Brazil, Chile, and Uruguay) was governed by clearing agreements of a specialized type, administered by specified banks, and calling either for payments in askimarks or for the employment of clearing marks

States, provided such proceeds had been continuously owned by the person for whose actual account the American merchandise was sold in Germany and the German goods were purchased in that country; (3) combinations of the foregoing two procedures might be employed; and (4) merchandise might be exchanged between single German and American parties without any monetary transaction actually taking place. (*Foreign Financial News: Special Circular*, No. 426 [July 15, 1938], pp. 1–2.) Following this release, the German Government authorized transactions involving the importation into Germany of American cotton, cotton linters, and cotton waste, and the exportation to the United States of certain specified German products. A few months later, regulations were issued governing the establishment of inland accounts (*Inlandskonten*) to be utilized in connection with these cotton barter transactions. (*Ibid.*) For further comment on these developments, see Tasca, *World Trading Systems*, pp. 39–42.

[33] This step was taken to suppress large numbers of small transactions which had been carried on by small firms not regularly engaged in foreign trade and which had tended to depress the price levels of German products in foreign markets. (*Foreign Financial News: European Financial Notes*, No. 230 [November 24, 1936], p. 9.)

[34] Clearing agreements accounted for something like 50 per cent and payments agreements for about 15 per cent. (Reichs-Kredit-Gesellschaft, *Germany's Economic Situation at the Turn of 1937–38*, p. 92.)

(*Verrechnungsmark*) with variable quotations.[35] In other cases, provision was made for askimark transactions through commercial agreements or unofficial agreements of an informal nature between German commercial firms on the one hand and Latin American banks on the other. In addition, Germany undertook to import given quotas of specified commodities in trade agreements with a number of these countries, in return for similar concessions for her exports.

In her trade relations with Latin America, Germany has been charged with manipulations similar to those employed in connection with Southeastern Europe. Space prevents an extended discussion of this question here, but it is interesting to note that, in one respect at least, the askimark constitutes a more flexible device for manipulation than does the ordinary clearing agreement which provides for a fixed exchange rate. Let us assume that the German government wished to make a concentrated drive against British or American competition in a given Latin American country, say, Venezuela. The Import Control Boards would attempt to divert German purchases of petroleum from other countries to Venezuela. Venezuelan banks would be forced to lower their quotations for askimarks, since they would find themselves with excessive supplies on their hands. As a result, German exports to Venezuela would enjoy the benefits of a sudden exchange depreciation. If this mechanism did not suffice, by itself, to secure the desired objective, export subsidies might be brought into play.

Germany succeeded in expanding her trade with a number of the Latin American countries, but her methods met with resistance here as well as in Southeastern Europe. Exports to Germany were subjected to restrictions, and dealings in

---

[35] The agreements with Brazil and Uruguay have not been published, but the text of the agreement with Chile may be found in *Reichsgesetzblatt*, 1935, II, No. 3, pp. 30 ff. Payments in connection with current trade debts between Chile and Germany were made in variable clearing marks, but payments on Chilean debts in arrears were made on the basis of a fixed rate. Cf. pp. 142–43 above, on Chile's clearing agreements.

askimarks were, in a number of cases, taken over by Latin American central banks (Brazil, Colombia, Costa Rica) or subjected to governmental control. On several occasions, the Bank of Brazil temporarily suspended purchases of aski-marks.[36] There was a tendency, on the other hand, for Latin American countries to encourage compensation transactions when raw material prices were low and exports to free-exchange countries depressed.

It is interesting to note that Italy has shown some tendency in recent years to utilize methods similar to those of Germany in her trade relations with Latin America. In February, 1937, the Bank of Brazil and the *Istituto Nazionale per i Cambi con l'Estero* entered into an agreement which resembled strongly the Brazilian-German clearing agreement.[37] Later that year, a proposed compensation arrangement between Germany and Italy, on the one hand, and Chile, on the other, was reported.[38] Like Germany, however, Italy has imposed drastic restrictions on compensation transactions in general.

3. *Compensation Agreements*

Whenever one or more governments are involved in an individual compensation transaction, the arrangement may, as we have seen, be classified as a compensation agreement. Transactions of this nature do not call for extended comment, since they have not played an important rôle in international trade. Outside of countries like Russia, where foreign trade is a government monopoly, and the totalitarian states, most governments do not, in peacetime, participate in international trade sufficiently to conclude arrangements of this kind. At

---

[36] See *The New York Times,* December 1, 1938.

[37] *Foreign Financial News: Latin American Financial Notes,* No. 217 (April 14, 1937), p. 4.

[38] *Ibid.,* No. 225 (August 14, 1937), p. 5, and No. 229 (October 14, 1937), p. 10. Chile, however, was to be required to make payment partially in free exchange.

the bottom of the "great" depression, when countries were desperately striving to dispose of unwanted surpluses of such commodities as wheat, governments which ordinarily leave the initiative in foreign trade to private individuals occasionally entered into compensation agreements. At least one exchange-control country was usually involved, and, as in the case of private compensation transactions, official exchange rates were ignored in determining the basis on which one commodity was to be exchanged for the other.

There were some cases in which negotiations were conducted by governmental agencies engaged in purchasing or selling commodities. Thus, the U. S. Federal Farm Board was reported, in the summer of 1932, to be negotiating with Chile for the exchange of about two million bushels of wheat for at least 40 thousand tons of nitrate.[39] Even in 1931 and 1932, however, the only *government* which entered into compensation agreements with any degree of frequency was the Russian government.[40]

In more recent years, most of the compensation agreements reported have involved either the German or Italian Government. Of a rather special nature was an arrangement concluded in 1935 between the Czech Bata Company and the Italian Government, for the purchase of 300,000 pairs of military boots for the latter. Half of the sum of 30 million crowns owed by the Italian Government was to be paid to the Bata Company by the Prague office of an Italian insurance company, which owed money to the head office in Italy for insurance premiums collected in Czechoslovakia. The Italian Government would, of course, make payment to the head office of the insurance company. The remaining 15 million crowns

---

[39] *The Times,* London, August 24, 1932. The nitrate was to be acquired by the War Department and held as a military reserve.

[40] Russia, in the second half of 1931, entered into such arrangements with Chile, Canada, Japan, and certain Central European countries. (J. Bataille, *Les Offices de Compensation et leur Rôle dans la Restauration du Commerce Extérieur* [Paris, 1934], p. 40.)

were to be paid through a similar financial arrangement or by the shipment of Italian goods to Czechoslovakia.[41] Here we have an example of the utilization of the compensation principle to make possible a financial transfer impeded by exchange restrictions. Such cases have been relatively frequent in connection with private compensation transactions, as well as with governmental agreements. Actually, such an arrangement does not differ from the liquidation of blocked accounts through the export of goods.

Many of the recent German and Italian compensation agreements have been with Latin American countries. In most cases, these have been bilateral in nature, but there are a few interesting examples of triangular deals. The arrangement for a joint sale of German and Italian airplanes to Chile was mentioned at the end of the preceding section. Another interesting case, occurring in the middle of 1938, involved an exchange by Germany of about 60,000 head of cattle, which had been purchased through a barter arrangement with Argentina, for Dutch horticultural and dairy products and straw. The Netherlands Government required the cattle to carry out a plan of distributing meat to the unemployed.[42] On the whole, however, triangular compensation agreements have been rather rare.

Representing an interesting departure from the traditional policy of both countries was the Anglo-American compensation agreement of June 23, 1939. The transaction involved the exchange of 600,000 bales of American raw cotton (valued at about 30 million dollars) for British rubber of equivalent value. Since the intention of the two governments was to acquire wartime reserves of needed war materials and to avoid depressing current market prices, the agreement included a joint undertaking not to dispose of the stocks acquired, except

[41] *Foreign Financial News: European Financial Notes,* No. 205 (November 9, 1935), p. 4.

[42] *Foreign Financial News: Latin American Financial Notes,* No. 246 (June 29, 1938), pp. 2–3.

in the case of a major war emergency, for a period of seven years.[43]

A special type of compensation agreement involves the granting of a credit by one country to another on the understanding that the debtor country shall make repayment in goods. Of this nature have been recent German credits to Turkey and Poland. The Turkish credit, arranged in October, 1938, was to have a duration of 10 years and was to be used for armaments, military aviation, electrification, and other similar purposes in Turkey.[44] Since Turkey was to purchase many of the materials needed in connection with this program from Germany, the arrangement meant, in large part, an exchange of goods for goods. The Polish credit, also arranged in October, 1938, was granted for the purchase of German machinery and other industrial equipment, repayment to be made through exports of Polish agricultural products.[45] Differing somewhat in detail, but similar in certain essentials, was an arrangement, concluded between the British and Turkish governments in May, 1938, whereby the British Export Credits Guarantee Department would guarantee £10,000,000 of purchases by Turkey in the United Kingdom prior to December 31, 1940. The agreement provided for the formation of a company, to be known as Anglo-Turkish Commodities, Ltd., which would be organized in London for the sale in the British Empire and certain foreign countries of Turkish products. The proceeds from these sales were to be used to meet the financial requirements of the credits.[46] Here we have an example of an arrangement which is far more flexible than the usual compensation agreement and which cannot, in fact, be strictly classified as relating to a single transaction.

[43] *The New York Times,* June 24, 1939.

[44] *Foreign Financial News: European Financial Notes,* No. 276 (October 24, 1938), p. 7.

[45] *Ibid.,* No. 277 (November 9, 1938), p. 9, and *The New York Times,* October 19, 1938.

[46] *Foreign Financial News: European Financial Notes,* No. 267 (June 9, 1938), p. 9. For an interesting discussion of the implications of this arrangement, see Tasca, *World Trading Systems,* pp. 130–31.

In view of the complicated negotiations involved, it is rather unlikely that, at least in peacetime, the compensation agreement in its simple form will assume much more importance in the future than it has in the recent past, even though the present trend toward increased governmental control of foreign trade continues. The Russian Government, with its foreign trade monopoly, has, in recent years, tended to favor the type of bilateral agreement under which Russia's exports to the country concerned must represent a specified proportion of its imports from that country over the course of a year or more.[47] It is quite possible, however, that credit agreements, particularly of the flexible Anglo-Turkish type, may become more common if exchange restrictions continue. They represent one method whereby international capital movements can be revived on a limited scale in spite of the existence of economic and psychological barriers.

4. *Payments Agreements*

Payments agreements have been defined in the preceding chapter.[48] For the most part they have been concluded between an exchange-control country, on the one hand, and a free-exchange country, on the other. The exchange-control country, which usually has debt payments to meet in the free-exchange country, agrees to allocate the foreign exchange derived from its exports to that country in certain specified ways. Usually, a substantial proportion of this exchange is reserved for imports from the free-exchange country, while a further share goes to meet debt payments in that country. In addition, a given amount may or may not be placed at the free disposal of the exchange-control country.

The first creditor country to make use of payments agreements in its relations with debtor countries was the United Kingdom. The Anglo-German Agreement of November 1,

[47] See p. 414 below. Some of these agreements include provisions for credits to Russia.
[48] Pp. 121–22.

1934, is generally regarded as the model for subsequent payments agreements. Actually, the British Government first employed the payments principle in the Runciman-Roca Agreement of May 1, 1933, with Argentina. Article 2 of that agreement provided that:

> "Whenever any system of exchange control is in operation in Argentina, the conditions under which foreign currency shall be made available in any year shall be such as to secure that there shall be available, for the purpose of meeting applications for current remittances from Argentina to the United Kingdom, the full amount of the sterling exchange arising from the sale of Argentine products in the United Kingdom after deduction of a reasonable sum annually towards the payment of the service of the Argentine public external debts (national, provincial and municipal) payable in countries other than the United Kingdom." [49]

The size of the "reasonable sum" and the exact order in which exchange was to be made available to the various classes of applicants for remittance to the United Kingdom were determined in a supplementary agreement. It was decided that the sum to be reserved for remittances to other countries should not exceed £3,000,000. The order of priority in which the available exchange was to be distributed was as follows:

(*a*) Public debt
(*b*) Import of goods
(*c*) Freights
(*d*) Interest on debentures and other loans
(*e*) Private British remittances
(*f*) Payment of dividends on preferred and ordinary shares of British companies operating in Argentina.[50]

[49] Great Britain, *Treaty Series*, No. 2 (1934), Cmd. 4492, p. 4. Argentina further agreed to apply 12 million paper pesos out of the sterling exchange becoming available in 1933 to the paying off of frozen British peso balances, and to issue sterling bonds in exchange for the remainder of these blocked balances. In addition, she promised Great Britain most-favored-nation treatment in the allotment of exchange, "whether in respect of peso balances or of current transactions."

[50] *The Economist*, CXXIII (1936), 364.

It is to be noted that, once the Argentine Government inaugurated its multiple exchange rate system in November, 1933,[51] it was obliged, under the terms of this agreement, not only to allocate to Great Britain the bulk of the exchange arising from exports to that country, but to make such exchange available at the favorable "official selling" rate. This result automatically ensued from the fact that the Argentine Government had agreed that applications for exchange for remittance to the United Kingdom should receive most-favored-nation treatment.[52]

In the Anglo-German Payments Agreement of November 1, 1934, the exact manner in which the exchange received from exports to the United Kingdom should be apportioned was more precisely defined. The German Government agreed that 55 per cent of the value of German exports to the United Kingdom should be definitely earmarked for the payment of German imports from the United Kingdom.[53] This involved a continuation of approximately the ratio which had previously prevailed in the trade between the two countries, and the German Government agreed to issue foreign exchange permits for the import of British goods without restriction, at the outset, although it reserved the right to restrict their issue temporarily after consultation with the British Government.[54] Germany further undertook to allocate, out of the foreign

---

[51] See pp. 105–11 above.

[52] Similar benefits accrued to the countries which later concluded payments agreements with Argentina.

[53] More specifically, it was arranged that the Reichsbank would "out of the foreign exchange received from German exports to the United Kingdom earmark each month for the payment of United Kingdom exports to Germany an amount equal to 55 per cent of the average between the value of exports from Germany to the United Kingdom during the last month but one as shown by the German statistics, on the one hand, and the value of imports into the United Kingdom from Germany during the same month as shown by the United Kingdom statistics, on the other hand." (Great Britain, *Treaty Series*, No. 26 [1935], Cmd. 4963, p. 2.) The Reichsbank was permitted to make certain minor deductions from this amount for specified purposes.

[54] *Ibid.*

exchange received from German exports to the United Kingdom, amounts sufficient to ensure, within a period of 12 months
from the date of signing of the agreement, the liquidation of
outstanding commercial debts owed to that country.[55] In addition, Germany was to continue to provide sterling for the
service of the Dawes and Young loans in Great Britain.[56] The
agreement also included provisions with respect to the issue
of foreign exchange certificates by the German authorities for
the payment of freight expenses in sterling.[57]

Clearly, a payments agreement, like a clearing agreement,
segregates remittances between the two countries concerned
from the main stream of dealings in the foreign exchanges and
sets them off against one another. It differs from a clearing
agreement (a) in permitting payments to take place over the
foreign exchanges and (b) in eliminating, in the free-exchange
country, the necessity for centralization of transactions with
the exchange-control country. In fact, the free-exchange country need exercise no control whatsoever over payments to and
from the exchange-control country, apart from keeping an eye
on the working of the agreement. The responsibility for carrying out the provisions of the agreement rests entirely with the
exchange-control country.

A payments agreement depends for its success, as does a
clearing agreement, on the maintenance of a given ratio in the
trade between the two countries and, in fact, implicitly calls

[55] The amount allocated for this purpose was provisionally fixed at 10 per
cent of the value of German exports to the United Kingdom but was to be increased if necessary to ensure the complete liquidation of the outstanding debts
in the time allotted. On the signature of the agreement, furthermore, the
Reichsbank was to provide a sum of not less than £400,000 towards the liquidation of outstanding commercial debts. (Ibid., pp. 8, 10.)

[56] British creditors on other German medium and long-term obligations were
to be offered by the German Government, in respect of interest, dividends, etc.,
Funding Bonds bearing interest at 4 per cent. (Ibid., pp. 10, 12.) Cf. p. 92 n.
above.

[57] Ibid., p. 6. A new Anglo-German Payments Agreement, involving certain
revisions, was signed in July, 1938. See The Economist, CXXXII (1938),
70–71.

for such a ratio, except in so far as it may place certain funds at the free disposal of the exchange-control country. A creditor country is in no position to conclude a payments agreement with a debtor country unless its balance of trade with that country is passive. Otherwise, if it wished the agreement to provide for both current trade and debt payments, it would be obliged either to submit to a reduction in its exports to the exchange-control country or attempt to increase its purchases from that country by removing import barriers. Neither of these alternatives is popular with creditor countries.

As already indicated, payments agreements are favored by certain free-exchange countries, not only because the responsibility for seeing that their provisions are carried out rests with the exchange-control country, but also because they eliminate many of the frictions associated with clearing agreements. Exporters are paid promptly by the normal methods, there is no accumulation of arrears in either country, and import and export restrictions do not need to be adjusted constantly to take care of fluctuations in the bilateral trade balance. It should be recognized, however, that while payments agreements, at least in the ordinary case, exercise no control over the *absolute amount* of trade between the two countries concerned, they tend to rigidify the bilateral trade *ratio*. Thus if England's imports from Germany were to contract as the result of, say, a slump in British internal trade conditions, her exports to Germany would decline by a corresponding proportion. Clearly, this is not necessarily the way things would work out in the absence of a payments agreement. Moreover, triangular trade is largely excluded, exactly as in the case of clearing agreements, unless a substantial amount of funds is placed at the free disposal of the exchange-control country.

Payments agreements are by no means so numerous as clearing agreements.[58] There was a definite tendency, from about

[58] See Table VI.

the end of 1934 on, for clearing agreements to be replaced by payments agreements, but this movement later became less pronounced. The majority of payments agreements have involved free-exchange countries in Western Europe, on the one hand, and exchange-control countries in Central or Eastern Europe and Latin America on the other. A few payments agreements were concluded between pairs of exchange-control countries, and Germany signed agreements with certain British Dominions and Asiatic countries.

Although the major responsibility for seeing that the provisions of the agreement are carried out is, as we have seen, left to the exchange-control country,[59] many of the agreements provide for the setting up of a mixed commission, composed of representatives of the two countries concerned, to supervise the working of the agreement and to make recommendations for changes in the event of unsatisfactory developments. Article 6 of the French-Yugoslavian Agreement of December 14, 1937, provided for the establishment of such a commission to see to the satisfactory execution of the agreement and to seek opportunities of intensifying commercial relations between the two countries without interfering with the trade ratio set up in the agreement.[60] The two governments concerned sometimes agree, moreover, to coöperate in preventing evasion of the exchange-control country's regulations requiring the surrender of export exchange to the proper authorities. Thus, the Anglo-Argentine Agreement of May, 1933, provided that the British Government should coöperate with the Argentine Government

---

[59] Where two exchange-control countries are involved, the detailed administration of the provisions of the agreement frequently rests with the country with relatively severe restrictions. Thus the agreement between Denmark and Rumania, signed June 23, 1937, provided that the National Bank of Rumania should allocate to Rumanian importers of Danish goods 50 per cent of the foreign exchange received in payment for Rumanian exports to Denmark. (International Chamber of Commerce, *Clearing and Payments Agreements,* p. DK–R.) Rumania's exchange restrictions are more rigid than Denmark's. Cf., also, p. 197 below.

[60] *Journal Officiel de la République française,* LXX (1938), 138.

to see that the amount of sterling exchange realized in Argentina from Argentine products exported to the United Kingdom should correspond as closely as possible with the value realized for such products in the United Kingdom, due allowance being made for transportation expenses.[61]

Since payments agreements call for purchases of foreign exchange in the normal fashion, there is not the same need for special provisions with respect to the exchange rate to be used as there is in the case of clearing agreements. In exchange-control countries, transactions coming under payments agreements are usually subject to the ordinary foreign exchange regulations, in so far as the exchange rate requirements are concerned. If the official rate applies to normal exchange transactions, it applies to dealings with payments-agreement countries, while any special provisions for the payment of premia and surcharges or the relaxation of exchange-surrender requirements in the case of specified commodities usually apply, also, to dealings with payments-agreement countries. Clauses specifying the exchange rate which is to prevail are included in some, but by no means all, agreements.

Provisions governing the allocation of exchange by the exchange-control country may be very simple or very complicated, depending on the importance of various types of service or capital items in the balance of payments between the two countries. Certain of the British agreements, particularly that with Hungary, contain very elaborate arrangements in this respect, though they are hardly more elaborate than the corresponding provisions of certain clearing agreements governing the disposal of funds in clearing accounts.[62] In some cases, the exchange-control country is granted a considerable amount of discretion in the allocation of exchange, while there are instances in which the funds placed at the free disposal of the

---

[61] *The Times*, London, May 3, 1933.

[62] For major provisions of British payments agreements, see International Chamber of Commerce, *Clearing and Payments Agreements*.

exchange-control country amount to as much as 50 per cent of the value of its exports to the free-exchange country.[63]

The French Government insisted on the inclusion of a compensation clause in some of its later agreements. Thus, in the French-Yugoslavian Agreement of December 14, 1937, Yugoslavia undertook to grant the necessary permits for the importation of, and payment for, French products without delay or restriction *as long as* the commercial balance between the two countries was satisfactory. Article 3 of the agreement provided that the balance would be considered satisfactory as long as the total of French sales to Yugoslavia did not exceed 80 per cent of the total of Yugoslavian sales to France.[64] Here a certain flexibility was permitted in that French sales to Yugoslavia might, presumably, amount to less than 80 per cent of Yugoslavian exports to France. In the Franco-Polish Agreement of December 29, 1937, however, the value of French exports to Poland was *fixed* at 80 per cent of the value of Polish exports to France.[65] Still another variation is found in the Franco-Rumanian Agreement of March, 1938, in which Rumania undertook, not only to reserve for payment for French exports an amount of exchange equal to 50 per cent of the F.O.B. value of Rumanian exports to France and Algeria, but also to admit imports equal to 50 per cent of the F.O.B. value of Rumanian exports to the same two areas.[66] The latter clause might seem to be superfluous in view of the former, but there was the possibility that the exchange earmarked by the Rumanian National Bank for payments for French goods might not have been utilized for that purpose, owing to the failure of the Rumanian import control authorities to issue the necessary import permits.[67]

---

[63] The agreement of March 8, 1938, between France and Rumania is a case in point. (*Journal Officiel de la République française*, LXX (1938), 2915.)

[64] *Ibid.*, p. 138.

[65] *Ibid.*, p. 139.

[66] *Ibid.*, p. 2915.

[67] Rumania has, in addition to exchange control, an import permit system.

In payments agreements between two exchange-control countries, considerable variation is found in clauses governing the allocation of exchange by each of the countries concerned. The Argentine-Hungarian commercial treaty of December 24, 1937, contained an exchange clause in which Argentina undertook to permit the transfer of funds to Hungary up to the F.O.B. value of regular exports of Argentine products to Hungary, after having deducted a reasonable annual sum for the purpose of the Argentine foreign debt service in third countries, while Hungary merely agreed to permit the transfer of funds to the Argentine Republic without difficulties.[68] A protocol to the commercial convention between Argentina and Chile, signed February 18, 1938, on the other hand, contained the following exchange clause:

> "Article VII—Both Governments obligate themselves to give all possible facilities in order that the available exchange arising from the commercial interchange between the two countries shall be used without any restriction in payment of the merchandise acquired from the other contracting party." [69]

Obviously the precise form which such clauses will take is likely to depend on the nature of the balance of trade between the two countries.

Payments agreements, like clearing agreements, are sometimes concluded in conjunction with commercial agreements in which one or both of the two countries undertake to admit designated quotas of specified commodities from the other. Occasionally, clauses to this effect are included in payments agreements themselves. The Canadian-German Payments Agreement of October 22, 1936, in which Germany undertook to issue exchange certificates for German purchases in Canada equal in value to Canadian purchases in Germany, included

[68] *Foreign Financial News: Latin American Financial Notes*, No. 235 (January 14, 1938), p. 1. Both Governments agreed to authorize transfers at an exchange rate no less favorable than that applied to or realized by any third country.

[69] *Ibid.*, No. 239 (March 14, 1938), p. 3.

provisions whereby, of the total exchange available in Germany for imports from Canada, specified percentages were to be allocated for the import of 22 listed commodities, each commodity being given its own percentage. The amount of exchange so earmarked equalled 63.1 per cent of the total.[70] In a commercial agreement which accompanied the Argentine-Spanish Agreement of December 29, 1934, Spain granted Argentina annual import quotas for specified Argentine products and reserved for Argentina substantial percentages of its annual import quotas of corn and wheat.[71] On the whole, however, as we have indicated, payments agreements tend to entail less control over the flow of trade than do clearing agreements.

A few payments agreements have a clause authorizing private compensation transactions by joint permission of the proper authorities in the two countries, but most agreements make no provision for such transactions, and some definitely exclude them. Here, as in the case of clearing agreements, much depends on whether or not the resort to private compensation is likely to interfere with the working of the agreement.

On the whole, payments agreements have given rise to many fewer complaints than have clearing agreements.[72] A country which is suffering from a scarcity of foreign exchange cannot acquire imports without effecting any transfer of foreign exchange under payments agreements as it can under clearing agreements. Hence, the tendency for bilateral trade balances to move in a direction unfavorable to exchange-control countries is less marked in the case of payments agreements. Moreover, it should be borne in mind that most payments agreements were concluded after exchange-control countries

[70] *Commerce Reports,* November 7, 1936, p. 898.

[71] *Ibid.,* March 16, 1935, p. 175. The agreement also included certain additional concessions, similar to those mentioned, on the part of Spain.

[72] On January 26, 1937, the Chancellor of the Exchequer made a statement in Parliament which expressed the satisfaction of the British Government with the manner in which the Anglo-German Payments Agreement had worked out. (*Foreign Financial News: European Financial Notes,* No. 236 [February 24, 1937], p. 8.)

had begun to adjust the values of their currencies downward, whereas the earlier clearing agreements were concluded in 1931 and 1932, before many steps had been taken in this direction. Thus the exchange rates which have been in effect for transactions coming under payments agreements have, on the whole, been much closer to the rates which would prevail in the absence of exchange control than were the artificial rates of conversion which were written into the early clearing agreements. Finally, payments agreements, by their very nature, tend to guarantee the maintenance of a bilateral trade balance which conforms with the objectives sought by the two countries concluding the agreement.

5. *Concluding Remarks on the Control of International Payments*

The currency problems of the exchange-control countries have been solved almost exclusively through unilateral or bilateral action. Most of these countries have resorted to devaluation, officially or unofficially. In some cases, readjustment of the value of the currency was delayed for several years, partly for fear of revaluing too soon or too high, partly, perhaps, in the hope that world prices would recover to some extent. Meanwhile, however, the very existence of exchange control, through interfering with the flow of funds out of the country concerned, tended to prevent deflation and to render more difficult the type of adjustment necessary to maintain the currency at or near its former value. The outcome has been currency readjustment in all but a few countries. Germany and Poland remained at the outbreak of war in 1939 the outstanding examples of countries which had avoided devaluation, but in the case of Germany, considerable foreign trade was conducted on the basis of a depreciated mark.

With currency readjustment came, usually, a relaxation of exchange restrictions. Other factors, such as the rise in the world price level between 1933 and 1937 played a part here also. Few countries actually abandoned control of their currencies, however, and in most cases the restrictions which remained in force were by no means merely nominal.

Meanwhile, a network of bilateral agreements grew up, regulating payments between pairs of exchange-control countries and between exchange-control countries, on the one hand, and free-exchange countries, on the other. These agreements were based on the theory that foreign balances arising from goods, and perhaps services, supplied to any given country, should be utilized exclusively, or almost exclusively, for payments to that country—in other words, that countries should strive to balance bilateral trade or bilateral payments. The application of this principle leads to results quite different from those which ensue when international payments are permitted to follow their natural course. Importers are no longer free to purchase their goods in the cheapest market—frequently they are obliged to pay non-competitive prices in order to make purchases in countries with which their country happens to have an active trade balance. Bilateral balancing is sought, not only through clearing and payments agreements, but through the operation of unilateral exchange regulations. In so far as trade is thereby diverted into abnormal channels, it ceases to follow the lines of comparative advantage.

This system, obviously, is not without its repercussions on countries which wish to remain aloof from the principle of bilateral balancing. The effects are not invariably harmful, however. Such countries may find their exports receiving preferential treatment in certain markets and discriminatorily unfavorable treatment in other markets, depending on the state of their balance of trade with the countries concerned. Moreover, and this result is perhaps less obvious, they are likely to find themselves in a superior bargaining position with respect to countries with which their bilateral trade balance is passive and in an inferior bargaining position with respect to countries with which their trade balance is active. Thus, the United States, which has avoided the conclusion of clearing or payments agreements has, *on the whole,* found its exports receiving relatively favorable treatment in Greece and Turkey, countries in which its purchases tend to exceed its sales, and relatively unfavorable treatment in Germany and Argentina, countries in which its sales normally exceed its purchases.[73] In its relations with the two latter countries, moreover, it has found itself in a definitely inferior bargaining position in comparison with, for example, Great Britain, which, with its large excess of imports, has been able to demand favorable treatment for both its exporters and its financial creditors.[74]

Clearly, a country like the United States, which does not subscribe to the principle of bilateral balancing, is likely, none the less, to find its trade with many individual countries approaching an even balance, merely as a result of the policies of the countries concerned. In so far as this development tends to weaken the arguments for remaining aloof from the system, it may conceivably have the effect of encouraging the spread of bilateral balancing to ever-widening areas. We shall have more to say on this point in later chapters.

It would be a mistake to assume that the widespread application of the theory of bilateral balancing to international payments is merely an indication of a crude mercantilistic mentality. In part, it is an inevitable consequence of the failure to secure a multilateral solution to the problem of currency stabilization which would apply to exchange-control, as well

[73] This statement is subject to certain reservations. The United States had a passive balance of trade with Argentina in 1935, 1936, and 1937, and in those years received more favorable treatment under the Argentine exchange permit system than before or since. Similarly, the treatment which its exports have received in Turkey has tended to fluctuate somewhat in response to variations in the state of its trade balance.

[74] Cf. *The Economist,* CXXXII (1938), pp. 70–71, on the revised Anglo-German Payments Agreement, signed in July, 1938.

America's unfavorable bargaining position with respect to Argentina must be attributed, in part, to the failure of the U. S. Senate to ratify the 1935 sanitary convention between the two countries. Cf. p. 466 below.

as to free-exchange countries. International lending, on either
a short-term or a long-term basis, cannot revive to any appreciable extent so long as many of the borrowing countries of
the world retain exchange restrictions. Since exchange-control
countries have little, if any, access to foreign credit, they can
avoid depreciation only by restricting their purchases of foreign exchange to the available supply. It is but a step from the
recognition of this necessity to acceptance of the idea that payments to each individual country must be restricted to the
amounts of foreign exchange made available by exports to that
country. The taking of this step is rendered especially likely
by certain additional considerations. The currency instability
of the last eight years has very definitely impaired the power of
London, or any other great financial market, to act as a clearing center for the foreign exchange operations of countries all
over the world. The fact that London performed this function before the War of 1914–18, and, to a lesser extent, after
the War, was a very important factor in permitting triangular
trade to develop as it did.[75] Furthermore, the huge passive
trade balance of the United Kingdom was an extremely vital
link in the complicated system of triangular trade which existed
prior to 1931.[76] Britain has been not *altogether* unwilling to
maintain her passive trade balance, in general, but has taken advantage of her passive balance in relation to individual countries
to enforce the transfer of funds to the United Kingdom out of
the proceeds of British purchases from the countries concerned.
Other creditor countries have pursued the same policy. The
result has been the "earmarking" of the foreign balances of
exchange-control countries to such a marked degree that there
remains little scope for them to seek to encourage triangular
trade with the free balances which remain to them. They themselves, out of what evidently seemed to them dire necessity at

[75] New York and Paris shared this function with London to some extent
during the nineteen-twenties.

[76] Cf. F. Hilgerdt, "The Approach to Bilateralism—A Change in the Structure of World Trade," Svenska Handelsbanken, *Index*, August, 1935.

the time, encouraged this development through negotiating clearing agreements with one another.

It must be emphasized, at this stage, however, even at the risk of some repetitiousness, that in the summer of 1939 exchange control was largely confined to Latin America, to Central and Eastern Europe, and to certain Oriental countries, and that clearing, payments, and compensation arrangements were confined to transactions which involved exchange-control countries. As we shall see in the next chapter, much of world trade continued to be conducted on the basis which generally prevailed before 1931.

PART III

CONTROL OF THE INTERNATIONAL
MOVEMENT OF GOODS

PART III

CONTROL OF THE INTERNATIONAL
MOVEMENT OF GOODS

CHAPTER VIII

TARIFF POLICY AFTER 1931

1. *Direction of Tariff Changes*

Over the course of the years since 1931, tariff changes have been, on the whole, distinctly upward. The wave of duty increases which characterized the early depression years acquired momentum after the financial crisis of 1931, and the upward tendency continued until about the autumn of 1936, though with reduced intensity as trade began to recover from the depression. Following the conclusion of the Tripartite Monetary Agreement in the autumn of 1936,[1] efforts to bring about a relaxation of the barriers to international trade were intensified, and, for a period of about a year, during which world trade, especially in primary products, was more prosperous than at any time since 1929, some progress was made toward lowering the general level of customs duties. Just as we found, however, that exchange restrictions were tightened during the course of 1938, in response to a decline in world trade and a fall in the prices of primary products, so we find that the movement toward relaxation of tariff barriers received, on the whole, a setback in that year.[2]

How much significance can be attached to generalizations about the direction of tariff changes, in a world in which direct restrictions on imports have reputedly so dominated the scene? One frequently hears the view expressed that tariffs have ceased

[1] Cf. pp. 42–43 above.
[2] Cf. H. Chalmers, "Foreign Tariffs and Commercial Policies during 1938," *Commerce Reports*, February 4, 1939, pp. 91–92.

to have much influence on the movements of international trade. It is certainly true that in most of the countries of Continental Europe, direct control of imports through exchange regulations, import quotas and monopolies, and other similar restrictions has been developed to such a point that tariff changes are of relatively minor importance. Outside of Europe, however, such thoroughgoing reliance on direct trade restrictions was much less common up to the outbreak of war in 1939. Imports into the United States, the United Kingdom, and the British Dominions were still regulated *mainly* by tariffs. With the relaxation of exchange restrictions in Latin America from 1933 on, tariffs assumed a fairly important rôle in determining imports into the countries in that region. A report issued by the United States Tariff Commission at the end of 1936 pointed out that the major part of world trade remained unrestricted or restricted only by tariffs.[3] In the following two years, exchange restrictions were introduced or tightened in China, New Zealand, and Afghanistan, while Japan greatly intensified her exchange restrictions and introduced an elaborate system of import control. Nevertheless, it was still undoubtedly true in the summer of 1939 that close to half of the world's trade was restricted by tariffs alone.[4] An examination of the major developments in the field of tariffs since 1931 must, therefore, form a part of our inquiry into recent commercial policy, although in the course of our discussion it will become apparent

---

[3] *Extent of Equal Tariff Treatment in Foreign Countries*, p. 1. "Countries having substantially no restrictions except tariffs" accounted "for about half of the trade of the world, and the nontariff restrictions in the other countries" were "by no means always applicable to the whole of the trade." (*Ibid.*, p. 1 n.)

[4] A more recent survey by U. S. Government officials, based on 1937 statistics, indicated that over 70 per cent (in value) of total world trade was still carried on by countries whose trade was *not predominantly controlled*. Countries whose trade was predominantly controlled included Japan, China, Germany, Italy, Russia, and certain countries of lesser importance. (Chalmers, "Foreign Tariffs and Commercial Policies during 1938," p. 93.) This is a rather different classification from that utilized in the earlier study by the Tariff Commission. Obviously, there are countries whose trade is not predominantly controlled but is subject, nevertheless, to *some* restrictions other than tariffs.

that it is impossible to survey tariff trends without constant reference to other forms of restriction and to treaty negotiations.

As already noted, one of the first reactions to the depression in many countries was to increase tariffs, in order either to protect the home market against cheap imports or to increase revenue. The widespread tariff increases which took place toward the end of 1929 and throughout 1930 have been discussed in an earlier chapter.[5] As the depression deepened and the effects of the financial crisis of 1931 began to be felt all over the world, protection of individual industries receded in importance as a motive for tariff increases. Faced with budgetary and exchange crises, countries resorted to higher tariffs, more and more for the purpose of increasing revenues and improving foreign trade balances.[6] Duty increases tended to be non-selective in nature. Special surtaxes or percentage increases, affecting all imports, were imposed as emergency measures, to be removed as soon as the crisis had passed. In some cases, commodities of a luxury or "dispensable" nature were subjected to more drastically increased duties than other commodities. Governments were granted power to alter tariffs by decree, since the slow process of parliamentary action proved too cumbersome for dealing with the rapidly changing economic situation.

Customs duties were increased during the course of 1931 in Austria, Argentina, Australia, Belgium, Brazil, Bulgaria, Denmark, France, India, Italy, Latvia, Lithuania, the Netherlands, Poland, South Africa, and Switzerland, while new duties were imposed on a wide range of commodities by the United Kingdom in November of that year.[7] Early in 1932, a Chilean tax measure provided for surtaxes amounting to 10 per cent of

---

[5] See pp. 31–35 above.

[6] Cf. H. Chalmers, "Foreign Tariff and Trade-Control Developments during 1931," *Commerce Reports*, February 22, 1932, p. 403.

[7] Cf. League of Nations, *World Economic Survey, 1931–32*, p. 288. See pp. 216–22 below, for further details on the British tariff.

existing import duties on articles of a luxury nature, the proceeds to be used to provide funds for unemployment relief.[8] In June of the same year, Estonian customs duties, chiefly on imports regarded as nonessential, were increased to levels amounting to 1½ to 5 times the former duties.[9] The French surtax of 2 per cent, levied on nearly all imports, was increased to 4 per cent for semi-manufactured goods and to 6 per cent for manufactured goods in March, 1932.[10] The Netherlands, traditionally a free-trade country, having increased its import duties by 25 per cent as an emergency fiscal measure at the beginning of 1932, imposed a surtax, amounting to 30 per cent of existing duties, on certain commodities of a kind not produced in the Netherlands and increased certain other duties in December of the same year.[11] The measures cited serve to illustrate the type of action which was taken as the depression deepened.

There was widespread hope that the World Economic Conference to be held in London in the summer of 1933 would put a stop to this wave of tariff increases, which, along with quantitative trade restrictions, was serving merely to cut down drastically the volume of world trade without improving the trade balances of individual countries. A brief cessation in the upward movement of rates resulted from the adherence of nearly all countries of any importance in world trade to a customs truce, proposed by the United States in the spring of 1933 to provide a stable basis for the Conference.[12] As everyone knows, the Conference failed completely, primarily as a

[8] *Commerce Reports,* May 23, 1932, p. 486.

[9] *Ibid.,* July 25, 1932, p. 186.

[10] *Ibid.,* May 9, 1932, p. 359. A series of bilateral agreements later provided for the removal of these additional surtaxes from semi-manufactured and manufactured products originating in the countries concerned. The conclusion of such an agreement was occasionally preceded by the imposition of retaliatory duties on French products.

[11] *Ibid.,* January 7, 1933, p. 12.

[12] See H. Chalmers, "Foreign Tariffs and Commercial Policies during 1933," *Commerce Reports,* February 24, 1934, p. 115. See also p. 428, below.

result of the unreadiness of certain countries to agree to currency stabilization, which was regarded as an essential preliminary to the removal of trade barriers.[13] The natural reaction to this failure was an intensification of measures of trade restriction. On the Continent of Europe, tariff increases had tended, even before the Conference, to become less numerous, as more and more reliance was placed on other restrictive devices; and this trend now continued. In Latin America, exchange restrictions and, in some cases, sheer scarcity of exchange available for foreign purchases, continued to dominate the picture, although there were a few rather important instances of tariff reductions in commercial treaties.[14]

With the improvement in prices of primary products which got under way toward the end of 1933 and continued in 1934, the economic position of the areas producing these commodities began to improve. In Latin America, the value of exports increased, relieving the scarcity of foreign exchange and permitting, as we have seen, some relaxation in exchange restrictions. Tariffs began once more to assume a position of some significance in determining the amount of trade. A number of tariff revisions took place, involving both increases and reductions in rates. On the whole, the tendency observable in this area during the nineteen-twenties, toward stimulating industrial development through increased protection for young and growing industries and lowered duties on raw materials and industrial equipment, continued to dominate the scene.[15] Tariff reductions in treaties, concluded mainly with overseas countries, were quite numerous in 1934. Definite impetus toward a movement for freer trade had resulted from the Pan American Con-

---

[13] Cf. pp. 429–30 below.

[14] Brazil concluded treaties with Argentina and Uruguay providing for substantial tariff reductions on certain commodities. The Runciman-Roca Agreement between Argentina and the United Kingdom, already discussed in connection with exchange control and payments agreements ((pp. 190–91 above), also provided for the reduction of many Argentine duties. Cf. H. Chalmers, "Foreign Tariffs and Commercial Policies during 1933," p. 116.

[15] Cf. pp. 21–22 above.

ference held at Montevideo in December, 1933.[16] Not only were Latin American countries stimulated to negotiate for tariff reductions, but the resolutions passed at the conference had some influence in bringing about the passage by the United States Government of the Reciprocal Trade Agreements Act in June, 1934.[17] Only one treaty, that with Cuba, was concluded under this program in 1934, but in 1935 eight agreements were signed, some with European countries and some with countries on the American Continent.[18] These agreements, together with those which have followed in later years, have constituted an important force in the direction of modification of tariff levels.

Meanwhile, the beginnings of economic recovery had influenced European countries to seek to expand their exports through the negotiation of trade treaties, and many bilateral agreements, generally of a short-run nature, were concluded. On the whole, however, these agreements did not provide for tariff reductions to any appreciable extent, nor did they bring about an appreciable expansion of trade. Their effect in most instances was simply to divert purchases from one country to another through quota concessions or special payments arrangements. As we have already noted, the principle of bilateral trade balancing was gaining in popularity, and it exerted a very definite influence on commercial agreements, as well as on the clearing and payments agreements which we have previously examined. Latin American countries, dependent as they were on European outlets for many of their exports, were occasionally drawn into commercial agreements which were trade-diverting rather than trade-enlarging in nature.

Throughout 1935 and the greater part of 1936, no clear tendency in the direction either of higher or lower tariffs emerged. Certain countries were making a definite effort to

[16] Cf. pp. 464–65 below.
[17] See pp. 392–408 below.
[18] Cf. pp. 394–95 below.

bring about duty reductions, while others continued in effect more or less drastic import restrictions which rendered tariffs of little importance. It began to be increasingly clear that very little progress could be made toward any widespread relaxation of trade barriers until certain countries had re-aligned their currencies. The conclusion of the Tripartite Monetary Agreement, followed as it was by the devaluation of the French, Dutch, Swiss, Italian, and other lesser currencies, appeared to provide at least a partial solution to this difficulty. Prompt action was taken to lower tariffs and relax quotas, at least to a moderate degree, in the countries which had devalued.[19] Meanwhile, France and England urged the modification of trade barriers, and especially the relaxation of exchange restrictions, before the Assembly of the League of Nations.[20] The conviction was apparently strongly held that further tariff reductions could come only after the relaxation of other types of restrictions.

The progress which has been made since the autumn of 1936 has been, on the whole, disappointing, in view of the hopes which were entertained at that time. During the course of 1937, tariff reductions were more frequent than increases in many countries, the modifications having been effected primarily, though not exclusively, through the conclusion of reciprocal

[19] By a decree of October 3, 1936, French import duties were reduced by 20 per cent on raw materials, 17 per cent on semi-manufactured goods, and 15 per cent on manufactured products. The reductions did not apply to commodities the importation of which was restricted or prohibited, but license taxes imposed on importers of goods subject to quotas were reduced by corresponding percentages. In addition, special duty reductions were made in the case of a few commodities, the exchange depreciation surtax (see pp. 225–26 below) was abolished, a commission was established to revise the French tariff, and a special committee was appointed to recommend duty and license tax reductions and quota modifications. (*Commerce Reports,* October 10, 1936, p. 821.) On October 5, 1936, Italy abolished her import surtax of 15 per cent ad valorem and revised the duties on a long list of articles, some upward, some downward. (*Ibid.,* October 17, 1936, p. 838, and November 7, 1936, p. 899.) Switzerland relaxed the operation of her quota system, while the Netherlands and other countries which had devalued also effected modifications in import duties or restrictions.

[20] *The New York Times,* October 5 and 6, 1936.

agreements.[21] The weakness of the franc, however, brought about a restoration of French tariff rates in July, 1937, to very nearly the levels which had prevailed before the reductions of the preceding autumn.[22] As a result of further increases later imposed, French tariffs eventually exceeded these levels.[23] The other members of the former gold *bloc* made little, if any, further progress in the direction of lower tariffs or less rigid import restrictions after the autumn of 1936. The Netherlands, indeed, at the end of 1938, amended its Tariff Empowering Act to permit the Government to alter import tariffs for purposes of protection, while Switzerland was one of a large group of European countries to effect tariff increases during the course of 1938.[24]

On the whole, in fact, tariff changes were mostly upward during 1938, in spite of the numerous reductions embodied in certain commercial agreements, of which that concluded between the United States and the United Kingdom was by far the most important.[25] A number of European countries, which had reduced import duties on grain and fodder to help meet the situation created by temporary crop shortages in 1937, withdrew the reductions in 1938 in response to greatly improved harvests.[26] The year 1938, indeed, was one of enhanced agricultural protectionism, while tariff increases on industrial prod-

[21] Cf. H. Chalmers, "Foreign Tariffs and Commercial Policies during 1937," *Commerce Reports,* January 29, 1938, p. 95.

[22] *Commerce Reports,* July 17, 1937, p. 571.

[23] In January, 1938, all import duties which had not already been increased to the level in effect prior to the reductions of October, 1936, were increased to that level. (*Ibid.,* March 5, 1938, p. 230.) This measure was followed by numerous further increases in the early months of 1938 and by the announcement in May of a proposed general revision of the French tariff, primarily for the purpose of obtaining increased revenues. (*Ibid.,* May 14, 1938, p. 444.)

[24] *Ibid.,* January 7, 1939, p. 22, and Chalmers, "Foreign Tariffs and Commercial Policies during 1938," p. 92.

[25] Other agreements of importance were those concluded by the United States with Czechoslovakia, Canada, and Turkey, and the Anglo-Irish agreement of April, 1938, which brought to an end a tariff war of several years' standing between the two countries. (*Ibid.,* pp. 91–92.)

[26] *Ibid.,* p. 92.

ucts were relatively numerous, although a number of young industrial countries, such as Finland, Uruguay, and Turkey reduced duties on certain types of industrial equipment.

In summary, it would seem that such progress as has been made in the direction of relaxation of tariff barriers since 1931 has been, on the whole, disappointing in extent. Where reductions have been effected, they have come about very largely through the medium of bilateral agreements. Autonomous tariff reductions have been undertaken, to some extent, by young industrial countries on imports of raw materials and industrial equipment, but these reductions have been in large part balanced by duty increases, on the part of the same countries, affecting products of infant industries. More detailed discussion of the content of bilateral commercial agreements must be reserved for later chapters. Two points are worth mentioning, however, at this stage. Tariff reductions embodied in such agreements have been, for the most part, extended to all countries entitled to most-favored-nation treatment. There has been some tendency in the direction of regional or intra-imperial preference in tariff bargaining, but few tariff favors of an exclusive nature have been granted. The second point to be noted is that tariff bargaining has taken on an increasingly political flavor in the last few years. Among the countries in which tariffs still played a dominant rôle as an instrument of commercial policy in the summer of 1939 were to be found a number of the leading democracies. It would be impossible to measure the extent to which tariff reductions effected in bilateral treaties between these countries were motivated by a desire to strengthen the bonds between democratic governments and promote international solidarity, but it is certain that this consideration played a significant part.

2. *British Protectionism*

England's conversion to protectionism has been the outstanding single development in the tariff history of recent years and, as such, merits separate attention. The repercussions of this historic reversal of Britain's trade policy on other countries have been of profound importance, not only because the British market forms an exceedingly important outlet for exports from all parts of the world but also because the United Kingdom has become one of the leading participants in tariff bargaining.

At the outbreak of the World War in 1914, the great bulk of British imports entered the country free of duty regardless of their origin. A few commodities were subject to tariffs, but for revenue purposes only. The free trade policy was not without its dissenters, who regarded it as highly unfortunate that Britain's attempt to win other countries over to a similar outlook had proved abortive. Of these, the most influential was Mr. Joseph Chamberlain, whose tariff reform scheme, launched in 1903, laid special emphasis on imperial preference.[27] His program was, however, twice rejected at the polls, primarily because of widespread opposition to tariffs on food, which were included in the proposal.

The wartime McKenna Duties, introduced in 1915, marked the first move in the direction of protectionism.[28] A tariff of 33⅓ per cent ad valorem was imposed on a few commodities regarded as luxuries.[29] The British industries affected experienced considerable growth during the War and successfully opposed the removal of the duties after the return of peace.

The effect of the War on free trade opinion in Great Britain has been indicated in an earlier chapter.[30] Not only was Eng-

---

[27] Cf. Richardson, *British Economic Foreign Policy*, pp. 85–87.

[28] See p. 10 n. above.

[29] Richardson, *op. cit.*, p. 87. The commodities were private motorcars, clocks, watches, cinematograph films, and musical instruments.

[30] See pp. 17–18 above.

land's dependence on foreign countries for certain commodities of vital importance in wartime regarded as undesirable, but the War, in addition, served to demonstrate the great value of close economic and political ties with the Empire, so that public opinion became more receptive than formerly to a policy of imperial preference. Consequently, one of the earliest post-War measures provided for the granting of a rebate of one-sixth of existing revenue duties on imports of commodities produced in Empire countries. There followed the Safeguarding of Industries Act of 1921, which provided for protection to "key" industries and for anti-dumping duties.[31] Because of the rather rigid criteria which were later set up to determine whether or not an industry was entitled to protection under this act, the duties were actually applied to a relatively small number of commodities, although the law was enforced more vigorously by Conservative governments than by Labor governments. In practice, Britain was still predominantly free trade in 1930. Out of £1,030 millions of imports in that year, £138 millions paid revenue duties, while only £13 millions were subject to McKenna or Safeguarding duties.[32]

If the wartime experience weakened the faith of the British public in free trade, however, the economic developments of the post-War years did much to shatter completely the traditional aversion to tariffs. England did not share in the worldwide boom of the late nineteen-twenties to any appreciable extent. For a number of reasons, of which the failure of sterling costs to adjust themselves to the external value of the pound from 1925 on was one of the most important, British exports never regained the position of preëminence which they had enjoyed before the War.[33] Once the depression got under

---

[31] See p. 18 above. Empire products were not subjected to "key" industry duties or anti-dumping duties.

[32] These figures are based on calculations published in *The Economist*, CXIV (1932), 1009.

[33] For fuller discussions of the depressed conditions of Britain's export industries in the post-War period, see Committee on Finance and Industry, *Report,*

way, growing concern began to be felt in England over the susceptibility of her free trade market to a "flood" of cheap imports from abroad. In view of the hopelessness of the prospect for export expansion, it was argued that the only way to "improve" the "worsening" balance of trade was to restrict imports by raising tariffs.[34] This argument gained potency as it became clear that foreign governments were bent on meeting the depression by raising tariffs and, more especially, after the attempt to secure a multilateral tariff truce in 1930 met with failure.[35] The events of the summer of 1931 served to lend new weight to the proposal for a tariff to improve the balance of trade, while the general recognition of the need for a balanced budget tended to reconcile the British public to further taxes on imports for revenue purposes. The depreciation of the pound following the abandonment of the gold standard in September was expected to reduce the excess of imports, but this argument was given little weight by the preponderant Conservative element in the new National Government, which was bent on seizing the opportunity to introduce tariffs, not merely for short-run corrective purposes, but as a long-run measure of protection and as a fore-runner to imperial preference.

The first action taken, however, was of an emergency nature. Under the Abnormal Importations Act of November, 1931, the Board of Trade was given power for a period of six months to impose duties up to 100 per cent ad valorem on imports from non-Empire countries of a long list of manufactured or mainly

---

pp. 46–55, and Alexander Loveday, *Britain and World Trade* (London, 1931), *passim.*

[34] The proposal for a general tariff to reduce the excess of imports received the support of a group of British economists, led by J. M. Keynes. Their arguments, to the effect that a restriction of foreign purchases would divert spending to domestic products and hence reduce unemployment, were presented in a series of articles in *The New Statesman and The Nation* in March and April, 1931, and in various letters to the press. The opposite point of view was defended by another group of economists in W. H. Beveridge and others, *Tariffs: The Case Examined* (New York and London, 1931).

[35] See pp. 32–33 above.

manufactured goods.[36] Orders were immediately issued for duties of 50 per cent ad valorem, in addition to any existing duties, on a substantial list of articles.[37] Agricultural products of a nonessential nature were next affected by the Horticultural Products Act, which granted the Minister of Agriculture similar powers with respect to certain fresh fruits, flowers, and vegetables imported from non-Empire countries.[38]

Meanwhile, the Government busied itself with the preparation of a permanent tariff measure, which was introduced into the House of Commons early in 1932. Although the need for revenue, the precarious position of the pound, and the desirability of a tariff for bargaining purposes were stressed by Mr. Neville Chamberlain in putting the proposal before the House, it was clear that the measure provided the basis for substantial protection to British industry and for preferences within the Empire.[39] In its final form, the Import Duties Act of March, 1932, provided for a general tariff of 10 per cent ad valorem on all imports into the United Kingdom, with the exception of goods already subject to duty and a few basic foods and raw materials.[40] The duties were not to apply to goods originating in the British colonies, while imports from the Dominions were exempted until after the forthcoming Imperial Conference at Ottawa in July. In addition to this general levy, the Act provided for the imposition of duties higher than 10 per cent, by Treasury Order, on articles of luxury or on articles being produced or likely to be produced within a reasonable time in the United Kingdom in substantial quantities in relation to British consumption.[41] An Import Duties Advisory Committee was set

[36] *Commerce Reports,* November 30, 1931, p. 525.

[37] *Ibid.*

[38] *Ibid.,* December 7, 1931, p. 577, and January 11, 1932, p. 102.

[39] Cf. *The Economist,* CXIV (1932), 283.

[40] *Commerce Reports,* February 15, 1932, p. 388. The chief articles of food exempted from the new duties were meat, tea, wheat, and animals, while the raw materials exempted included raw cotton, raw wool, hides and skins, iron ore, scrap iron and steel, and a few others of similar importance.

[41] *Board of Trade Journal,* CXXVIII (1932), 322.

up to recommend such additional duties.[42] It was this provision of the Act, obviously, which opened the door to the possibility of greatly increased protectionism.

For tariff bargaining purposes, a provision was included in the Act authorizing the Treasury on the recommendation of the Board of Trade to permit entry of goods from specified foreign countries duty free or at duties less than the regular rate.[43] Power was also granted to impose duties up to 100 per cent ad valorem, in addition to existing duties, on imports from countries discriminating against British goods. Thus, the Act set up a multiple-column tariff system. Actually, tariff concessions granted in bilateral agreements with non-Empire countries have been extended to *all* such countries, and penalty duties have been applied only for short periods and under unusual circumstances. Consequently, since the Ottawa Conference, the United Kingdom has maintained in practice a double-column tariff, the higher rates applying to foreign countries, and the lower rates applying to products of the British Empire.[44]

As a result of recommendations made by the Import Duties Advisory Committee, numerous changes in rates, mostly upward, have been made since the passage of the Tariff Act of 1932. The schedule of duties has become considerably more selective and decidedly more protectionist in effect in consequence of these alterations. The first extensive series of changes took place on April 26, 1932, when the 10 per cent duties on most classes of manufactured goods, some semi-finished goods, and a few foodstuffs were increased by varying amounts.[45] The new rates ranged from 15 to 33⅓ per cent ad valorem, a duty

[42] The criteria set up in the Act for entitling an industry to protection were less rigid than those applied in connection with the Safeguarding of Industries Act. Cf. Richardson, *op. cit.*, p. 95.

[43] *Ibid.*

[44] Cf. U. S. Tariff Commission, *Extent of Equal Tariff Treatment in Foreign Countries*, p. 57. In most cases, the preference granted to Empire products consists of free entry into the British market. (*Ibid.*, p. 60.)

[45] *Commerce Reports*, May 2, 1932, p. 299, and *Board of Trade Journal*, CXXVIII (1932), 603–606.

of 20 per cent being applied to the majority of manufactured articles, while higher rates were imposed on certain luxury or semi-luxury articles and certain chemicals.[46] With a few exceptions, products originating in the British Empire were again unaffected by the changes.[47] This continued to be true even after the conclusion in August, 1932, of the Ottawa Agreements, which will be discussed in a later chapter; [48] for Britain's main concession in each of these agreements consisted of a promise to continue exemption of Empire products from the Import Duties Act of 1932, while maintaining duties of at least 10 per cent on specified foreign products.[49] She also undertook to impose new or increased duties on imports from foreign countries of certain commodities, chiefly foodstuffs and raw materials, in which the Dominions were especially interested.[50] It was estimated (on the basis of 1930 trade statistics) that the changes would have the effect of reducing the percentage of imports *from foreign countries* which could enter duty-free to 25.2 per cent, as compared with 30.2 per cent just previous to the Ottawa Conference and 83.0 per cent in 1930.[51]

Since 1932, duties have from time to time been increased when such action has been deemed necessary to protect the British manufacturer, while reductions have taken place on certain raw materials or on commodities which could not be produced economically in the United Kingdom.[52] Tariff reductions have also been granted in a number of bilateral agreements with foreign countries. Only a very slight modification of the British tariff level has resulted from the conclusion of these commercial agreements, for Britain has, on the whole, been rather sparing of her concessions in negotiations with the

[46] Cf. *ibid.*, and Richardson, *op. cit.*, p. 96.
[47] The exceptions were silk hosiery and rubber tires. (*Commerce Reports*, May 2, 1932, p. 299.)
[48] See pp. 458–63 below.
[49] Cf. Richardson, *op. cit.*, p. 140.
[50] *Ibid.*
[51] Calculated from figures published in *The Economist*, CXV (1932), 588. Cf., also, Richardson, *op. cit.*, p. 128.

many countries with which she has an unfavorable balance of trade. Such countries have in a number of cases been obliged to agree to admit greatly enlarged quantities of British goods in order to prevent their exports to the British market from being materially restricted.[53]

3. Increased Resort to Unequal Tariff Treatment

The years since 1931 have been characterized, not only by a general rise in tariff levels, but also by an increase in the number of countries employing multiple-column tariff systems and by a more widespread application of penalty duties of one kind or another. The need for adoption of protection against the various forms of ordinary dumping, "exchange" dumping, or so-called "social" dumping has been regarded as particularly urgent. In a world, moreover, in which successful multilateral action to reduce tariffs has been conspicuously absent from the scene, tariff systems which will lend themselves to bilateral bargaining have commended themselves to governments.

Multiple-column tariff systems have long been the rule on the Continent of Europe, while single-column tariffs have been applied, in practice, in most of the rest of the world. Since 1931, however, a number of the smaller countries of Latin America have adopted multiple-column systems. Colombia, Cuba, Ecuador, Guatemala, Haiti, El Salvador, and Uruguay have enacted definite statutory changes in this direction, while certain other Latin American countries have tended to apply differential tariff treatment to an increased extent in practice. A number of the new laws, unlike the older laws in force in most European countries, provide for the application of tariffs differentiated in accordance with the state of the trade balance with each country from which goods are imported.[54] A good

[52] Ibid., p. 98.

[53] Cf. pp. 408–15 below.

[54] This is true of the laws at present in force in Cuba, El Salvador, Guatemala, Ecuador, and Haiti, while there is some tendency to apply multiple-column

illustration of this type of system may be found in Cuba, where a law, enacted March 16, 1935, provided for the setting up of a three-column tariff schedule. Maximum rates (100 per cent higher than minimum rates) were to be applied to countries whose purchases from Cuba amounted to less than one-quarter of the value of their sales to Cuba (as recorded in Cuban foreign trade statistics). Intermediate rates (25 per cent higher than minimum rates) would apply to countries whose purchases from Cuba amounted to more than one-quarter but less than one-half of their sales to Cuba. The minimum rates were to apply to countries whose imports from Cuba represented at least half of the value of their exports to Cuba.[55] Certain raw materials and other articles of prime necessity were to be subject to minimum duties, regardless of origin.[56] Periodically, the Cuban Government publishes lists of countries classified in accordance with the type of tariff treatment to which they are entitled.

Throughout the British Empire, preference margins in favor of other members of the Empire have been widened as a result of the Ottawa Agreements.[57] In addition, South Africa and

---

tariffs in such a way as to promote bilateral balancing in Colombia as well. For a thorough survey of this subject, see U. S. Tariff Commission, *Extent of Equal Tariff Treatment in Foreign Countries, passim.*

While laws of this kind represent one aspect of the widespread trend in the direction of bilateral balancing, a special factor in influencing the countries of Latin America to adopt them in recent years has been the astonishingly rapid expansion of Japanese exports to this region. The new laws have been designed, in part, to induce Japan to increase her purchases from the countries concerned as she increases her sales to them.

[55] By virtue of their most-favored-nation agreements with Cuba, France and Spain were to be entitled to minimum rates, regardless of the state of their bilateral trade balances, while products of the United States were entitled to special preferential rates, lower than the minimum rates, in accordance with the Trade Agreement of August 24, 1934. (*Commerce Reports,* March 30, 1935, p. 211.)

[56] Surcharges were authorized, early in 1936, on raw materials and articles of prime necessity imported from countries with which the trade balance was notably unfavorable to Cuba, but they were never put into effect.

[57] The whole subject of imperial preference and of other preferential arrangements will be discussed in a later chapter.

Australia have altered their tariff systems to provide greater freedom for bargaining, mainly with non-Empire countries.[58] The new South African tariff schedule, which went into effect on May 10, 1935, provides for three columns of rates. Products of foreign countries are, for the most part, entitled to intermediate rates, which are higher than the minimum rates accorded in agreements with British countries.[59] The maximum schedule is to be applied to imports from specified countries, by special proclamation only. It is intended for penalty and bargaining purposes, particularly in connection with countries with which South Africa's balance of trade is passive.[60]

Although no marked alterations in European tariff systems took place during the period under survey, measures which had the effect of increasing the margins between maximum and minimum rates through raising the duties applicable to imports from nontreaty countries were adopted in a number of instances during the worst years of the depression. The most drastic change of this kind was introduced by Greece in 1931, when duties on goods from nontreaty countries were increased tenfold.[61] Special exemption from the new rates was later granted in particular cases, and, on May 26, 1934, the law was modified to permit the application of the previous maximum rates to imports admitted on a compensation basis. Since most Greek imports from nontreaty countries were subject to a

[58] The tariff system of the United Kingdom has also been altered in this direction, but in practice, as we have seen, uniform rates are generally applied to all countries outside the Empire. (Cf. p. 220 above.)

[59] British countries are granted preferential or minimum rates, under the South African tariff, *only* in so far as such rates have been established in separate negotiations with each country. The law allows for extension of minimum rates to non-British countries, also, as concessions in trade agreements.

[60] See *Commerce Reports*, August 3, 1935, p. 87 and U. S. Tariff Commission, *Extent of Equal Tariff Treatment in Foreign Countries*, pp. 41–42. Maximum rates were applied, shortly after the law became effective, to a small number of products imported from the United States and several other countries. (*Commerce Reports*, August 3, 1935, p. 87.)

[61] *Commerce Reports*, December 7, 1931, p. 574.

compulsory compensation regime,[62] the 1931 rates came to have but a limited application.[63] Surtaxes on goods from nontreaty countries were imposed by Lithuania in 1931 and by Italy in 1933.[64] Finland achieved a similar result by different means in 1933, when she increased duties on a number of imports, affecting mostly products of nontreaty countries.[65]

Numerous governments have granted powers to their executive branches to impose penalty rates of one kind or another under special conditions, while anti-dumping and other similar legislation already in effect has been enforced, on the whole, with increased vigilance. Activity in this direction was particularly marked during the bottom of the depression but tended to become less noticeable as prices rose and exchange rates became more stable.

Among the most common of these penalty measures have been surtaxes levied, as in the period of currency instability following the War,[66] on imports from countries with depreciated currencies. Authority to impose such surtaxes is granted in the general customs laws or in the anti-dumping laws of many countries (a number of these laws dating from the early nineteen-twenties), and widespread use was made of this power from the autumn of 1931 on, especially by countries which were attempting to cling to the gold standard or to protect the par values of their currencies. Prominent among duties of this kind were those levied by France, which applied surtaxes to imports from a large number of countries with depreciated currencies through a series of decrees commencing in November, 1931. The rates varied for different countries and were altered from time to time.[67] At the end of 1933, provision was

[62] Cf. pp. 177–78 above.
[63] Cf. U. S. Tariff Commission, *Extent of Equal Tariff Treatment in Foreign Countries,* p. 100.
[64] *Commerce Reports,* February 29, 1932, p. 513 and June 3, 1933, p. 350.
[65] *Ibid.,* March 11, 1933, p. 157.
[66] Cf. p. 17 above.
[67] Thus the first decree, published November 14, 1931, established ad valorem surtaxes on imports from specified countries, as follows: British India, 7 per

made for the revocation of surtaxes in cases of countries which had achieved *de facto* stabilization, and all remaining exchange surtaxes were removed after the conclusion of the Tripartite Monetary Agreement in the autumn of 1936.[68] Among other countries to impose similar duties at one time or another during the depression were South Africa, Germany, Italy, Egypt, and Canada. The country most frequently affected by such measures was Japan, whose currency fell to approximately 40 per cent of its former par value.[69]

In order to protect their exports from discriminatory or restrictive treatment abroad, a number of countries accorded wide powers to the executive branches of their governments to retaliate against such action through penalty duties or other appropriate devices. Authority of this kind was granted in Finland, Germany, Italy, and Japan. New anti-dumping legislation was enacted in Argentina and the Netherlands in 1931, while elsewhere, as we have seen, existing anti-dumping laws were enforced with enhanced vigor. Special mention should be made of Canada's system of arbitrary import valuations, which proved an effective instrument for keeping out undesirably

---

cent; Norway, 8 per cent; Argentina and Uruguay, 10 per cent; Australia, Denmark, Mexico, Sweden, and the United Kingdom, 15 per cent. (*Commerce Reports,* November 23, 1931, p. 466 and December 21, 1931, p. 695.) A month later, additional countries were affected and adjusted surtaxes applied to imports from certain countries mentioned in the first decree, as follows: Canada, 11 per cent; Egypt, Finland, and Irish Free State, 15 per cent; British India, Norway, Argentina, and Uruguay, 15 per cent. (*Ibid.,* December 21, 1931, p. 695.) Later decrees effected further additions and changes.

[68] Cf. *ibid.,* January 20, 1934, pp. 45–46 and p. 213 n. above. Surtaxes on Swedish and Finnish goods had been removed in March, 1933, in return for reciprocal concessions granted to France. (*Ibid.,* March 25, 1933, p. 190.)

[69] The currencies of certain other countries, especially in Latin America, fell even farther than that of Japan, but these countries were chiefly exporters of primary products, the import of which, early in the depression, was restricted in a number of industrial countries by measures other than tariffs (Cf. pp. 243–52 below.) Japan had the distinction of achieving a notable expansion of exports in certain highly competitive manufactured lines as early as 1932, when similar exports from other countries were still falling off. This is not to say, however, that Japanese exports were not affected by quantitative restrictions in a number of instances.

"cheap" imports. Under a provision of the Canadian customs act, the Governor General in Council may authorize the Minister of National Revenue to fix the value of any class or kind of goods, if it can be shown that such goods are being imported into Canada under conditions which "prejudicially or injuriously affect the interests of Canadian producers or manufacturers." [70] Under this authority, ad valorem duties were assessed on the basis of official valuations substantially higher than the invoiced values of imported goods. In addition, special anti-dumping duties, equal to the difference between the official value and the invoice value, were collected.[71]

This brief survey has covered by no means all of the recent regulations providing for unequal tariff treatment of the products of different countries, but the extent to which such discrimination actually affects the course of world trade at the present time should not be exaggerated. Although the governments of most countries possess, under existing laws, the power to impose penalty duties under a wide variety of circumstances, considerable restraint is actually exercised in practice in the enforcement of these laws. During the worst years of the depression, abnormal measures seemed to be called for, but even then governments did not always make extensive use of the powers granted to them, and the inflicting of penalty rates tended to slacken off as trade recovered. Exchange depreciation surtaxes, as one might expect, were abolished as currency conditions became more stable. Under ordinary circumstances, governments hesitate to discriminate for fear of retaliation. Unequal tariff treatment, furthermore, can be undertaken only if marks-of-origin requirements are introduced and carefully enforced. This is an expensive and complicated process.

Just as the existence of laws permitting the infliction of penalty rates does not necessarily mean that such laws are

[70] *Commerce Reports*, November 5, 1932, p. 92.

[71] Imports from the United States, which had been adversely affected by this practice, have been treated more liberally since the conclusion of the first trade agreement with Canada on November 15, 1935. Cf. p. 406 below.

228 INTERNATIONAL MOVEMENT OF GOODS

frequently invoked, so the widespread existence of multiple-column tariff systems does not necessarily imply a thorough-going application of unequal tariff treatment in practice. Many countries having general-conventional tariffs in theory actually extend their conventional rates to all countries whether entitled to most-favored-nation treatment or not, thus enforcing a single-column tariff in practice.[72] Where maximum-minimum systems are enforced, the rates in both columns are frequently identical for many types of goods. After a careful survey of this whole question, the United States Tariff Commission concluded at the end of 1936, in a report previously mentioned, that "the major part of world trade" was conducted "on the basis of the lowest tariff rates of the respective importing countries."[73] One might add that, while the most-favored-nation clause has received a considerable setback in the years since 1931, the decline in its importance has come about only to a minor extent in connection with tariffs. The trend toward discriminatory methods in commercial policy has been associated primarily with other types of trade restrictions.

[72] Thus far in our discussion, it has been unnecessary to refer to the distinction between general-conventional and maximum-minimum tariff systems. Under the general-conventional system, the general or higher rates are statutory, while the conventional or lower rates are determined by negotiation with other countries and incorporated in treaties. The conventional rates may be "bound" or "consolidated," as a result of an undertaking in a treaty with another country not to increase them for the duration of the treaty. Under the maximum-minimum system, both the higher and lower rates are statutory, and concessions to other countries consist in granting to them the application of the minimum rates on all or part of their exports to the first country. The minimum rates are subject to change at any time by legislative action and hence can never be "bound" in treaties. Thus countries entitled to the minimum rates are not entitled to any particular rates, but merely to the lowest rates in force at any given time. In practice, the distinction between the two systems is blurred, and certain countries like France, which have maximum-minimum systems, have actually consolidated rates in treaties on a considerable scale. Cf. p. 245 below.

[73] *Extent of Equal Tariff Treatment in Foreign Countries*, p. 6.

CHAPTER IX

Import Quotas

1. *The Nature of Import Quotas*

When a government, or group of individuals, wishes to exercise control over the production, marketing, or consumption of a commodity, quotas, or quantitative restrictions, are frequently employed as instruments of control. They have also proved convenient weapons for regulating the flow of imports and exports. An import quota involves a limitation on the quantity or value of imports of a specified commodity which may be admitted into a country within a given period of time. In practice, limitations on the *value* of imports occur most frequently in conjunction with exchange control regimes. We shall be concerned in this chapter *primarily* with restrictions on the *quantity* of imports, for it is this type of limitation which one ordinarily has in mind when one speaks of an import quota. The United States might decide, for example, to limit imports of coffee to 50 million pounds a year. Once this amount had been admitted no further coffee could be brought in until the next year.

Import quotas may be administered with or without the help of a licensing system. When no licenses are issued to importers, the quota for the quarter or year, or whatever the period may be, is announced, and a scramble takes place to get goods into the country before the quota is filled. In order to avoid the confusion resulting from this system, most countries have found it necessary to require that importers secure licenses before bringing in commodities subject to quota restrictions.

229

The license may specify the total amount which the importer is permitted to bring in during the entire quota-period, or, alternatively, importers may be required to secure licenses for each individual transaction. In the latter case, the government sometimes makes no announcement as to the total amount of the commodity to be admitted in any given period.[1] Whether such an announcement is made or not, the purpose of the licensing system, like that of a straight quota system, is almost invariably to restrict the quantity of imports to an amount less than that which would enter the country in the absence of control.[2] Therefore, from an economic point of view, there is no fundamental distinction between a quota system and a licensing system. The latter may be regarded as a more or less essential adjunct of the former.

Clearly, when importers of a given commodity must obtain a license for every individual import transaction, what we actually have is an import prohibition, subject to the granting of exceptions by special permission. In fact, the import licensing systems of the World War period were frequently referred to as import prohibition systems. The economic effects of such a system will obviously depend on the extent to which exceptions are permitted. The limiting case would be that of an outright prohibition, no exceptions whatsoever being permitted.

[1] In fact, this system of requiring licenses for each import transaction commends itself to governments because of the secrecy which it makes possible. Cf. K. Häfner, "Die Politik der mengenmässigen Einfuhrregulierung," *Weltwirtschaftliches Archiv*, XL (1934), 45–47. Where importers are issued licenses permitting them to import a given quantity during the quota-period, a government may refrain from making any announcement as to the size of the quota as a whole, but it would clearly be a simple matter for firms engaged in the trade to estimate this amount.

[2] Licenses are sometimes required to see that imports of a given commodity meet certain qualitative specifications. In such a case, presumably, there would be no question of quantitative restriction of imports which meet the standards. For purposes of economic analysis, this type of control might best be considered as an outright import prohibition on all specimens of the commodity not meeting the quality specifications. In practice, licensing systems of this type are relatively rare in connection with imports but have become increasingly common in connection with exports. Cf. pp. 352–53 below.

Absolute prohibitions of this sort are usually imposed on non-economic grounds, when a commodity is considered undesirable from the point of view of the public health, morals, or welfare. In recent years, however, they have occasionally been introduced for economic reasons, chiefly in the case of nonessential imports which have been excluded to "improve" the balance of trade. In addition, exchange restrictions, as we have seen, have frequently had the *effect* of excluding imports of luxury articles altogether. We shall return to a more detailed consideration of import prohibitions at a later stage.

A distinction should be drawn between the ordinary quota and the tariff, or customs, quota. Once the ordinary quota is filled, no further imports of the commodity may be admitted, unless the administering body is permitted to make exceptions in special cases. The tariff quota, on the other hand, permits imports in excess of a limited quantity provided a higher duty is paid. Thus, in the example used above, the United States might allow 50 million pounds of coffee to be admitted duty-free, all further imports to be subject to a duty of 25 per cent ad valorem; or, 50 million pounds might be admitted at a duty of 10 per cent, the remainder to be subject to the 25 per cent rate. In the case of a tariff quota, imports at the lower of the two rates may be made subject to license. This type of measure is not to be confused with the case of an ordinary quota accompanied by a tariff. The import of a commodity is frequently subject to both a quota and a tariff. This is quite natural in view of the fact that quotas are frequently introduced to limit the import of commodities which are already subject to tariffs.

Special types of measures which must be considered in connection with quotas are mixing or linked-utilization regulations, which have played a rather prominent part in recent European commercial policy, especially in connection with agrarian protectionism. These measures, which aim indirectly at restricting imports of a commodity to a certain percentage of domestic consumption, will be considered at some length in the next chapter.

Finally, quotas may be determined autonomously or by agreement with another country. Both types have played an important part in commercial policy in recent years, and the introduction of an autonomous system of quotas generally leads to bargaining with the countries whose exports are effected. Tariff quotas are frequently found in commercial agreements, sometimes in connection with preferential arrangements whereby the treaty partner is granted a preferentially low duty on a limited quantity of imports of a specified commodity.

2. *Theoretical Analysis of the Effects of an Import Quota*

Although we have thus far in this study given little attention to theoretical issues, many of the problems which have arisen in the administration of import quotas cannot be properly understood without some preliminary consideration of the theoretical effects of quantitative import restrictions. Furthermore, a theoretical analysis of quotas throws much light on the working of a number of other types of trade restrictions.

The simplest case is that of an import quota unaccompanied by a tariff.[3] Let us make the further assumption that the quota is restrictive in nature, that is, that less of the commodity may be imported than would come in under free trade conditions.[4]

---

[3] For a full theoretical discussion of import quotas, see K. Häfner, "Zur Theorie der mengenmässigen Einfuhrregulierung," *Weltwirtschaftliches Archiv*, XLI (1935). I take this opportunity to acknowledge my indebtedness to Mr. Häfner for much, though not all, of the analysis which follows in the text. Briefer discussions of the theory of quotas may be found in Haberler, *The Theory of International Trade*, pp. 346–49, and *Liberale und Planwirtschaftliche Handelspolitik*, pp. 83–97, and in H. Heuser, *Control of International Trade* (London, 1939), pp. 149–67. See also F. A. Haight, *French Import Quotas* (London, 1935), pp. 14–19, and J. N. Reedman, "Some Notes on the Theoretical Aspects of Import Quotas," *South African Journal of Economics*, IV (1936).

[4] It is conceivable that the quota might be sufficiently large to permit importation of a quantity equal to that which would come in under free trade conditions, but this case is hardly likely to occur in practice. It is obvious, of course, that, whatever the size of the quota, imports will not exceed the quantity which would come in under free trade conditions.

If this is the case, a price-differential between home and for-eign markets, over and above transportation costs, will tend to appear. The size of this differential cannot be predicted in advance, unless the government is assumed to have complete knowledge of demand and supply conditions. The case is illustrated in Diagram I, in which the analysis is confined to

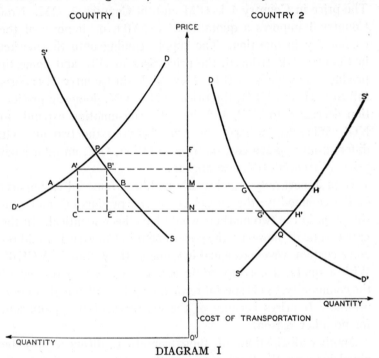

DIAGRAM I

ᵃ This diagram is based, with minor modifications, on the one which Mr. Häfner uses on p. 193 of the article cited above. The reader will note its re-semblance to the diagrams used by Haberler in the analysis of the effects of a tariff. Cf. *The Theory of International Trade*, pp. 171–72, 229, and 258.

two trading countries, Country 1 representing the importing country and Country 2 the exporting country. It is assumed that perfectly competitive conditions prevail in both markets and that the commodity in question is produced under condi-tions of increasing cost. DD' represents the demand curve and

SS', the supply curve, in each country. In the case of Country 1, the traditional direction of the X axis has been reversed. Under free trade conditions, Country 1 will import AB from Country 2, GH (=AB) representing Country 2's exports. Country 1 consumes AM, of which BM is produced at home. Country 2 produces MH, of which MG is consumed at home. The price in Country 1 is O'M and, in Country 2, OM. Now Country 1 imposes a quota, A'B' (<AB), on imports of the commodity in question. The supply coming onto the market in Country 1 is reduced, the price rises to O'L, and domestic production expands to B'L. Meanwhile, in Country 2, exports fall to G'H' (=A'B'), the price falls to ON, domestic production decreases to NH', and domestic consumption expands to NG'. Whereas formerly the price between the two markets differed only by the cost of transportation, OO', an additional price differential, LN, now appears.

If an import duty equal to LN had been imposed on imports of the commodity, the effects on prices, production, and consumption in the two markets would have been identical. In the case of a tariff, however, the government in Country 1 would receive customs revenues equal in value to the rectangle A'CEB'. With a quota, a corresponding amount accrues to traders of the commodity. This special reward may be designated "quota-profits." It arises because of the existence of the quota and for no other reason.

Another distinction, of fundamental significance, may be noted between the tariff case and the quota case. The tariff, provided it is not prohibitive, does not interfere with the working of the normal price-mechanism, except in so far as it sets up a price-differential between the home and foreign markets. If a shift in the demand or supply schedule in Country 1 were to set up forces tending toward an increase in price for the commodity in question, further imports would result, the price in Country 2 would increase, and the price in Country 1 would rise less than would have been the case in the absence of foreign competition. A new equilibrium would be reached involving a larger volume of trade in the commodity concerned between the two countries and a somewhat higher price in both markets, although the price-differential between the two markets would still equal LN (the amount of the duty). Similar results would ensue from a fall in price in Country 2, the new equilibrium being reached in this case at a lower price in both countries. A rise in price in Country 2, on the contrary, would lead to a reduced volume of trade and higher prices, while a fall in price in Country 1 would result in a smaller volume of trade and lower prices in the two markets. In this way, as every student of international trade knows, price changes in one country are transmitted to other countries.

A quota, on the other hand, interferes with the spreading of price changes from one market to another. A rise in price in Country 1, induced by a change in domestic conditions of demand or supply, could have no effect on the volume of imports of the commodity concerned, nor could it affect the price in Country 2. A permanently higher price in Country 1 and an altered volume of domestic production and consumption [5] would result. Similarly, a fall in price in Country 2 could not bring about an enhanced volume of imports into Country 1, nor could it affect the price in Country 1. In either case, the price-differential between the two markets would increase, thereby enhancing the profits of traders. A price-decline in Country 1, again, would not affect the price in Country 2 or the volume of imports from Country 2, *unless* the price were to fall sufficiently so that even under free trade conditions no more would be imported than the quota (in which case A′B′ and G′H′ would lie on the same horizontal line). Beyond this point, any further decline in price in Country 1 would be reflected in a reduced volume of imports and a fall in price in Country 2.

---

[5] Whether production and consumption would increase or decrease would depend on whether the rise in price resulted from a shift in the demand curve or in the supply curve.

The quota would not be fully utilized. Similarly, a rise in price in Country 2 would have no effect on Country 1 up to the point at which less than the quota would be imported. In either of these cases, the quota-profits would be reduced and, when free trade conditions were reached, would disappear altogether.

It is very easy to see what qualifications must be introduced into the argument when the import of the commodity into Country 1 is subject to a tariff as well as a quota. If the tariff is set at LN and the quota at A'B', the existence of the tariff simply means that quota-profits are wiped out and the treasury gets receipts represented by the area A'CEB'. A price-rise in Country 1 would not effect the volume of imports but would increase the price-differential between the two markets and create some quota-profits. A price-decline in Country 2 would have similar effects. Were the price to fall in Country 1, the case would be rather different. With the existing tariff, a volume of imports as large as A'B' could not be maintained. The quota would not be fully utilized, and its existence would cease to make any difference. The resulting changes would be identical with those which would take place if the import of the commodity were restricted by a tariff alone. The price-decline would be reflected in Country 2, and a new equilibrium would be reached with a lower volume of trade in the commodity between the two countries and lower prices in both markets, the price-differential remaining at LN. A rise in prices in Country 2 would lead to a reduced volume of trade and higher prices in the two markets.

Now assume the tariff to be less than LN, the quota being A'B' as before. Since the price-differential is now greater than the tariff, the traders get some quota-profits, and the quota is the effective instrument of restriction. In order for the tariff to become effective, the price would have to fall in Country 1 or rise in Country 2 to the point at which the price-differential equalled the tariff. If the tariff is greater than LN, assuming again the quota to be A'B', the quota is ineffective, and the price-mechanism operates as though no quota existed. The volume of imports would, of course, be less than A′B′, and the price-differential would equal the height of the tariff.[6] The quota would become effective only if appropriate changes in market conditions either in Country 1 or Country 2 were to take place.

Thus far we have assumed that Country 1 derives all its imports of the restricted commodity from Country 2. Actually, of course, its imports are likely to be drawn from a number of exporting countries, and the extent to which the imposition of a quota by Country 1 will affect the world price will depend on the importance of Country 1 as an import market for the commodity concerned. Furthermore, the shares of the various exporting countries in the markets of Country 1 will depend on the nature of their demand and supply curves and on such factors as relative costs of transportation.[7] If licenses are not issued to importers in Country 1, the factor of geographical proximity may assume an undue importance in determining the sources of Country 1's imports, as we shall see when we take up the problem of administering import quotas. Furthermore, it is obvious that, if the country imposing the quota specifies the amounts to be admitted from each exporting country, a further factor alien to the price-mechanism is introduced, in that exporting countries may receive a larger or smaller share of the market than would fall to their lot under free trade or simple tariff conditions.

Whether or not licenses are issued to importers is an immaterial factor in the effects of a quota on the price in the importing country, so long as we assume that competitive conditions prevail. Our analysis makes it clear that the price-increase which is likely to take place after the introduction of

---

[6] Plus, of course, the cost of transport. We avoid constant reiteration of this minor qualification, which should be read into the text at appropriate points.

[7] For further discussion of this point see Häfner, "Zur Theorie der mengen-mässigen Einfuhrregulierung," pp. 199–205.

a quota is a result of the restriction of imports, not of the issue of licenses. It is obvious, of course, that the holder of a license occupies a peculiarly favorable position with respect to the sharing of whatever quota-profits arise, since his goods are assured entry into a sheltered market.

At this stage, let us relax our assumption of pure competition and take account of the possibility that the commodity may be imported under monopolistic conditions. It is evident that, where licenses are issued to importers, the formation of a combination or monopoly may be facilitated. If license-holders enter into an agreement for the control of imports, they are assured that the securing of their objectives will not be jeopardized by the entry of new importers into the field. Indeed, under certain conditions, it might be possible for an importer or group of importers to purchase all outstanding licenses.[8] Under given demand and supply conditions, a monopoly or combination *may* find it profitable to restrict imports of the commodity to an amount less than the quota, thereby creating an additional price-differential between home and foreign markets, and securing for itself monopoly-profits *in addition to* the quota-profits created by the governmental import restriction. Such further restriction of imports would not, however, prove profitable for a monopoly which had been in existence prior to the introduction of the quota.[9]

Now let us turn to the situation in the exporting country, or countries. Thus far, we have assumed that the commodity is exported under competitive conditions. So long as this is the case, and so long as licenses are issued to importers in the

[8] On the transferability of licenses, see pp. 259–60 below.

[9] For a full analysis of this case, with diagrammatic illustrations, see Heuser, *Control of International Trade,* pp. 151–52. Essentially, the argument runs as follows: The monopolist importer would have arrived at his position of optimum profitability, involving a given volume of profits, prior to the introduction of the quota. Since the quota would presumably restrict imports below this (for him) optimum amount, it would reduce his profits. Any move on his part to limit imports further would simply lower his profits still more, since it would move him even farther from his optimum position.

country imposing the restriction, there is little likelihood that exporters will share in any quota-profits which arise. The importers of the commodity are, if they hold licenses, in a strategic position to secure not only all the quota-profits, but, under certain conditions, monopoly-profits as well. Any tendency toward combination among the exporters, however, will interfere with this result, and may lead to the securing of all or part of the quota-profits, and perhaps of additional monopoly-profits, by the exporters. The formation of an effective monopoly among exporters is, of course, in the normal case, a difficult matter, since it involves an agreement which will bring in all or most of the exporters in every important exporting country. In the case of certain types of finished goods, however, where geographical specialization has been carried to considerable lengths, or where there are only a few large producers, it may be a relatively simple matter for exporters to form a monopolistic selling organization. Furthermore, in a number of instances, licenses to import are issued, by countries imposing import restrictions, to associations of foreign exporters rather than to domestic importers.[10] When this is the case, the formation of an export monopoly is facilitated.[11] Even if exporters continue to sell competitively, they have, as license-holders, an excellent chance of acquiring all the quota-profits. Where monopolistic tendencies exist among both importers and exporters, it is impossible to determine, on *a priori grounds*, how the quota-profits will be divided.

Now let us turn to the case of a tariff quota.[12] Whether the

[10] Cf. pp. 277–81 below.

[11] As Heuser points out, in *Control of International Trade*, pp. 152–54, restriction of exports to the country imposing the import limitation to an amount less than the quota will not be profitable in a case in which exports were monopolized even before the introduction of the quota, but *may* be profitable where the export monopoly or selling organization was formed *after* the introduction of the quota. This conclusion is based on an analysis similar to that which applies in the case of an import monopoly.

[12] For a complete analysis of this case, cf. *ibid.*, pp. 161–62. The tariff quota, it will be recalled, permits imports in excess of a limited quantity provided a higher duty is paid. Cf. p. 231 above.

effects of this type of quota resemble more closely those of a straight tariff or those of an ordinary quota depends on whether or not the rate of duty on goods admitted in excess of the quota is prohibitive. This upper duty will be prohibitive if it equals or exceeds the price-differential between home and foreign markets created by the quota. In other words, referring again to Diagram I, an upper duty equal to or exceeding LN will be prohibitive, if the quota is fixed at A'B'; for, in order to bring in additional imports profitably, importers must receive a price at least as high as O'L (export price + transportation costs + tariff), but the home market is not capable of absorbing further imports at this price. In this case, therefore, the tariff quota would not differ from an ordinary quota, at least in its initial effects. If, however, a price-decline in the foreign market or a price-increase in the home market were to create a price-differential greater than the height of the tariff, additional imports would once more become possible. Hence, with an upper duty equal to or greater than LN, the price-link between home and foreign markets is destroyed for the time being but may reappear (in limited form) if the domestic price rises or the foreign price falls by an appropriate amount.

Now assume that the upper duty is less than LN. In this case, importers will find it profitable to import amounts in excess of the quota. These further imports will lead to a decline in the domestic price and a rise in the foreign price, until the price-differential between home and foreign markets equals the height of the upper duty. In this case, the price-link between domestic and foreign markets remains intact, and, regardless of the size of either the lower duty or the quota, it is the upper duty which determines the differential between the domestic price and the foreign price.[13] Importers will reap a special

---

[13] It should be recognized that, even in this case, the price-link between home and foreign markets may be destroyed if the price falls in the domestic or rises in the foreign market sufficiently to render the tariff prohibitive, i.e., to reduce the price-differential to a point at which it is equal to, or lower than, the upper duty.

profit, equal to the difference between the upper duty and the lower duty, on imports coming in under the quota, but the existence of the lower duty will be of no benefit to consumers, who will, of course, pay the same price for all units of the commodity purchased. It must be recognized, however, that these conclusions relate to the equilibrium position which would theoretically be reached once the economy had adjusted itself to the new tariff quota. Actually, of course, the transition from the old to the new position may take place in anything but a frictionless fashion, especially, though this is in practice unusual, if no license requirements are set up for that portion of the amount imported which is subject to the quota.[14]

What happens if an import quota is defined in terms of value rather than in terms of quantity? It is this type of quota, essentially, which is involved when importers are required to secure exchange permits under an exchange control regime, for the effect of such a limitation on outlay is to restrict the value of imports of each commodity covered by the regulations. If the exchange permits allotted to importers permit the bringing in of a smaller quantity of any given commodity than would be imported, at the same exchange rates, in the absence of any restrictions on the importation of that commodity, a price-differential between home and foreign markets will appear, exactly as in the case of a restriction on the quantity of imports. The home market will, however, not necessarily be isolated from foreign markets to the same extent as under an ordinary quota. Let us assume that the world price of the commodity in question falls. With their existing exchange allotments, importers can now bring in more of the commodity than formerly,

---

[14] Cf. *ibid.*, p. 162. Tariff quotas are usually contractual rather than autonomous; that is, they usually originate under the terms of commercial agreements. Switzerland employed them rather extensively on an autonomous basis for a time, but other countries did not follow her example to any appreciable extent. Accordingly, no separate section on the employment of tariff quotas in practice has been included in the present chapter, but the reader will find frequent references to tariff quotas in Chapters XII and XIII, which are concerned with bilateral agreements.

as long as the exchange authorities do not decide to reduce the amount of exchange granted. But suppose that, though exchange or import permits are issued in terms of value, the authorities keep a close eye on the exact quantity of the commodity which, in their view, is required in the light of internal needs, or suppose that their primary aim is an approach to national self-sufficiency with respect to the commodity concerned. It is not unlikely that, in such a case, the total value of exchange permits issued would be reduced if there were a fall in prices abroad, in order to maintain the volume of imports at a constant or declining level. Obviously, one cannot carry an analysis of this type of quota very far without some knowledge of the objectives of the control system, unless one is content with purely abstract considerations which have no relation to what goes on in practice. It is for this reason that the statement was made at the end of Chapter V that it is impossible, for practical purposes, to draw sharp distinctions between exchange permits and import quotas as alternative means of controlling imports.[15]

Thus far we have confined our analysis to the case of an import quota applied to a single commodity. Clearly, a country which introduces quotas on a wide scale is likely, other things being equal, to find its prices rising in comparison with prices abroad. This will have a discouraging effect on its exports. Accordingly, an attempt to "improve" the balance of trade through a resort to import quotas is likely to prove futile, at least over any considerable period. Secondly, a widespread adoption of quotas by any one country will tend to render its price structure insensitive to price changes in the rest of the world. Adjustments in its balance of payments will not take place automatically but will have to be guided by extensive governmental intervention, if the full force of the adjustment is not to fall on the prices of those few commodities which remain free of quota restrictions. In fact, if quotas are

---

[15] Cf. pp. 115–17 above.

retained as permanent instruments of commercial policy, control of internal prices and production tends to become a necessary adjunct. On the other hand, internal control schemes frequently lead to the introduction of quantitative restrictions on imports in order to facilitate the enforcement of such schemes. Many actual examples can be found to illustrate both these tendencies, as we shall see.

Finally, when many countries adopt import quotas on a wide scale, the forces which determine the flow of commodities in international trade tend to become quite different from those which prevail under a less controlled system. The relative position of prices in different countries still plays some part, but a highly restricted one, since the movements of trade do not react to price changes, except within very wide limits. The factor of intergovernmental bargaining becomes all important, purely economic considerations frequently being subjected to political or strategic considerations. But we shall be in a better position to discuss this broad problem at a later stage in our study.

3. *The Spread of the Quota System from 1931 On*

The quota is by no means a new instrument of commercial policy. It played a considerable rôle during the mercantilist period and continued to be employed to some extent through the early part of the nineteenth century. Except for occasional instances of tariff quotas in commercial treaties,[16] however, the quota very largely disappeared during the latter half of the last century. The abnormal conditions of the World War led, as we have seen,[17] to a thoroughgoing adoption of quotas in Europe, mainly in the form of licensing systems. These restrictions were retained, in Central and Eastern Europe, for

[16] Cf. W. Greiff, *Die Neuen Methoden der Handelspolitik* (Berlin, 1934), p. 21, and G. de Leener, "Les Systèmes de Contingentement douanier," Banque Nationale de Belgique, *Bulletin d'Information et de Documentation*, VII (1932), 65.

[17] Pp. 9–10 above.

a number of years after the war but had, for the most part, been abandoned by 1930.

There were, on the other hand, two types of quotas which were tending, if anything, to become more popular during the late nineteen-twenties. In the first place, nongovernmental import and export quotas were being utilized more and more by international cartels or combines to effect division of markets, generally along national lines. Secondly, tariff quotas were being employed to an increasing extent by European countries, especially in connection with the growing movement toward agricultural protectionism.[18] They were introduced autonomously in order to admit limited amounts of commodities duty-free or at relatively low duties, sometimes during periods of crop shortages; or they were incorporated into commercial agreements, as a form of tariff concession limited to a specified quantity of the article in question. In Germany, a tariff quota on imports of meat was in force from 1925 to 1930,[19] and an agreement with Finland in 1930 included a clause providing for the importation of a fixed quantity of butter at a rate below the minimum duty applicable to countries enjoying most-favored-nation treatment.[20]

By the middle of 1931, prices had fallen substantially and alarm was being felt in many countries over growing trade deficits. The financial crisis which had broken out in Vienna in May had given rise to widespread fears of enhanced instability and a continued decline of prices. The hope that the downward spiral of deflation would soon come to an end and that forces of recovery would be generated spontaneously by the economic system was growing dim, and governments were turning more and more to decisive emergency measures cal-

---

[18] Cf. de Leener, *op. cit.*, p. 66, and Häfner, "Die Politik der mengenmässigen Einfuhrregulierung," pp. 35–36.

[19] For an illuminating analysis of the effects of this measure, see Häfner, "Zur Theorie der mengenmässigen Einfuhrregulierung," pp. 208–18.

[20] The reduction was extended to other most-favored-nation countries by permitting them to ship the same quantity as Finland at the reduced rate. Cf. p. 270 n. below.

culated to resist deflation and perhaps stimulate a revival.

The first important country to adopt import quotas *on a large scale* as one means of combatting the depression was France. Although, as a country with a large invisible income from foreign tourists' expenditures and past foreign investments, France normally has a sizable excess of merchandise imports, the rapid "worsening" of the balance of trade in the early years of the depression was the occasion of considerable alarm within the country. The tendency for rapidly falling prices of agricultural products in world markets to lead to increased imports of foodstuffs into France was especially resented,[21] for support of domestic agriculture had long been a policy of the French Government, and the early years of the depression were characterized by strenuous efforts to maintain or raise prices of food products through substantial tariff increases and other measures.

In attempting to keep out foreign imports by tariff increases, the freedom of action of the French government was restricted, more specially with respect to manufactured products, by the fact that many duties were "bound" against increases in commercial treaties signed from 1927 on,[22] and the application of these consolidated rates had been extended to all countries enjoying most-favored-nation privileges. In 1931, 72 per cent of French tariffs were subject to such provisions.[23] But even where rates could be raised, it was felt that, with prices falling rapidly abroad, tariffs could not be adjusted quickly enough to meet changing situations without raising them to prohibitive levels. Whereas the effect of an increase in duty on the quantity of imports of a given commodity could not be precisely measured in advance, the use of a quota would permit the entry of precisely the quantity specified by the authorities.[24]

[21] See Haight, *op. cit.*, pp. 5–13, 42–55.
[22] See p. 25 above.
[23] Cf. E. B. Dietrich, "French Import Quotas," *American Economic Review,* XXIII (1933), p. 663.
[24] It is frequently argued that specific duties become more effective in periods

In addition, the quota would render the country immune from further price-declines abroad. Another argument was advanced, which, as our theoretical analysis has indicated, had no scientific validity. It was maintained that quotas would result in smaller price-increases than would tariffs.[25]

Beginning in May, 1931, the French Government issued a long series of decrees restricting imports into France of a variety of commodities. In most cases, a fixed quota, applicable to a specified period, was announced, although a few of the very earliest decrees simply set up license requirements without fixing any announced quota. By July, 1932, "the quota system had been extended to 1133 items of the tariff code" or about one-seventh of the tariff schedule.[26] The decrees of late 1931 had applied mainly to agricultural commodities, but in the early months of 1932 imports of many manufactured products were affected. Gradual additions were made to the list of quotas during the remainder of 1932 and throughout 1933. An important extension of the system took place on January 1, 1934, when import restrictions were imposed on 600 new tariff items.[27] After that time, further items were added to the list from time to time and other items were removed, but the number of commodities affected was not substantially increased. From 1934 on, the total number of tariff items subject to restriction ranged around 3,000.[28]

---

of falling prices. It is worth noting, however, that when a country with a relatively rigid price structure is confronted with rapidly falling prices abroad, a specific duty may become less effective because of the increasing price-differential between home and foreign prices. Cf. Häfner, "Die Politik der mengenmässigen Einfuhrregulierung," p. 25.

[25] Cf. Dietrich, op. cit. See also the statements of M. Duchemin, president of the Confédération générale de la production française and of M. Maspétiol, as quoted in Häfner, "Zur Theorie der mengenmässigen Einfuhrregulierung," p. 197 n.

[26] Dietrich, op. cit., p. 664.

[27] Haight, op. cit., pp. 13–14.

[28] This statement, together with much subsequent information contained in the present chapter, is based on unpublished material supplied the writer by the U. S. Department of Commerce from its files.

The example of France in restricting imports was soon followed by a number of other European countries. By the end of 1932, eleven European nations had full-fledged quota or license systems, and the popularity of this form of import restriction continued to spread in later years. It remained, at the beginning of 1939, primarily a European method of trade control. (See Table VIII.) Only two Latin American countries made any extensive use of it, while the United States and most of the British Dominions maintained quotas on a very small number of commodities.[29] In the Far East, however, quotas played a rôle that was by no means negligible, for Japan had recently gone in for this type of trade control in thoroughgoing fashion, Iran maintained a governmental monopoly of foreign trade which operated by means of an import licensing system, and the Asiatic possessions of Britain and the Netherlands employed quotas rather extensively. It remained true, nevertheless, that the major portion of world trade was not affected by quantitative import restrictions.[30]

One is not surprised to discover that the countries which relied most heavily on import quotas during the depression and the early part of the recovery period were among the members of the former gold *bloc*. In common with France, these countries were all concerned over their growing trade deficits and yet, in view of their financial resources, were not forced to resort to exchange restrictions. By the end of 1932, Belgium, Poland, Switzerland, and the Netherlands were relying heavily on import license systems to "improve" their trade balances. Like France, however, they instituted quotas which were designed, not *merely* to reduce the excess of imports, but also to afford protection to particular industries which were especially

[29] For a full discussion of American import quotas, see C. R. Whittlesey, "Import Quotas in the United States," *Quarterly Journal of Economics*, LII (November, 1937). Australia introduced import license requirements for a rather extensive list of commodities in May, 1936, but abolished them between December, 1937, and May, 1938.

[30] Cf. pp. 207–208 above.

TABLE VIII

IMPORT QUOTA OR LICENSE SYSTEMS IN FORCE, JANUARY 1, 1939 [a]

A. *European Countries*

COUNTRY	DATE OF EFFECTIVENESS [b]
Belgium	March, 1931 (agricultural products)
	March, 1932 (general)
Bulgaria	January, 1933
Czechoslovakia	In effect since World War; expanded 1931 and 1932
Eire	July, 1932
France [c]	May and July, 1931
Germany (in commercial treaties)	1932 and later dates
Greece	May, 1932
Hungary	In effect since World War; expanded 1931 and 1932
Italy [d]	February, 1935
Latvia	May, 1934
Lithuania (in commercial treaties)	Various dates
Netherlands	February, 1932
Poland	January, 1932
Rumania	November, 1932
Spain	December, 1931
Switzerland	February, 1932
Turkey	November, 1931
United Kingdom (mainly agricultural commodities)	1932
Yugoslavia	June, 1936

[a] Source: *Commerce Reports* and unpublished material supplied by U. S. Department of Commerce. The countries listed had quotas or license requirements applying to a substantial number of commodities. In addition, a few commodities (in some cases, only one) were affected by import restrictions in a number of other countries, including Albania, Estonia, Norway, Australia, Brazil, Cuba, Peru, Portugal, El Salvador, South Africa, Sweden, and the United States. Furthermore, there were certain countries, not included in the list, which had committed themselves, in a few cases, to admit specified quotas of certain commodities in agreements with other countries or which employed tariff quotas to a very limited extent. Several countries applied some quantitative restrictions to imports from countries with discriminatory trade policies.

[b] In most cases, the date given in the table refers to the inauguration of the quota system. No attempt is made to include dates at which new commodities were added to, or subtracted from, the list of those affected by restrictions.

[c] Quotas were introduced at later dates in certain of the French colonies.

[d] The import of a limited number of commodities was restricted by Italy previous to the date which appears in the table.

TABLE VIII — *Continued*

B. *Non-European Countries*

COUNTRY	DATE OF EFFECTIVENESS
Afghanistan	June, 1938
British colonies	1934 and later dates
Chile	June, 1932
Iran (Persia)	February, 1931
Japan [d]	October, 1937
Manchukuo [d]	October, 1937
Netherlands India	1933
New Zealand	December, 1938
Uruguay	November, 1934

[d] The import of a limited number of commodities was restricted by Japan and Manchukuo previous to the date which appears in the table.

affected by foreign competition. Had the sole motive been improvement of the trade balance, luxury goods would presumably have been hardest hit by the new restrictions. As it was, many of the earlier quotas affected staple agricultural commodities, and, in general, in the choice of imports to be restricted, there was clear evidence of a desire to protect individual industries.

Import license systems were also adopted by many of the European exchange-control countries in 1931 and succeeding years. In a few cases, licensing systems already in existence were extended and made more stringent. In these exchange-control countries, import permit requirements supplemented exchange restrictions. Frequently, as we have noted in Chapter V,[31] importers wishing to bring in a given consignment of goods were forced to secure both an import permit and an exchange permit. The exchange-control authorities sometimes turned down applications for exchange to pay for imports for which import licenses had already been granted, since it was the available supply of foreign exchange which ultimately de-

[31] Pp. 116–17.

termined whether or not the goods could be admitted. On the whole, where such dual control schemes existed, as we have already indicated,[32] the import permit requirements tended to serve the purpose of making possible a more careful selection of imports in the light of the internal economy's need for protection than was secured through the exchange restrictions. It is obvious, however, that import control schemes were not really necessary where the effect of the exchange restrictions was to bring about a highly selective limitation of imports. As the scarcity of exchange became less acute, and it was possible to relax exchange restrictions to some extent, import permit systems began to assume greater relative importance in determining the volume of imports into these exchange-control countries; and, as we have seen, import permit requirements were frequently extended as exchange restrictions were relaxed. An excellent case in point is Czechoslovakia, which, for a considerable period after 1931, maintained both exchange permit and import permit requirements. For the importation of some commodities, permits had to be secured from the exchange control authorities, while imports of other commodities were subject to permits issued by an import control board. There was still a third class of articles for which both types of permits had to be secured. As time went on, however, the exchange permit requirement was abandoned for more and more commodities, until, finally, after the second devaluation of the Czech crown in October, 1936, the exchange permit system was abolished altogether. Meanwhile, many commodities formerly subject to exchange permits were made subject to import permits, and the cessation of the exchange permit system was accompanied by the transfer of a substantial number of commodities to the import permit list. Exchange restrictions were again tightened in the autumn of 1938.[33]

Like exchange restrictions, import quota systems were highly

[32] Cf. pp. 115–16 above.
[33] Cf. p. 87 above.

contagious. Not only did France's action have an important influence in leading other countries to adopt quotas, but countries which felt their exports were being injured or discriminated
against by quantitative import restrictions abroad passed laws
giving their governments power to retaliate against countries
imposing quotas or discriminating in any way against the exports of the first country. Under the authority of such a law,
the Italian Government established import quotas, in July,
1932, on certain imports from France and Algeria,[34] although
Italy did not go over to a general import quota regime until
1935. Likewise Germany, in January, 1934, inaugurated license
requirements for imports of various French products, under
the authority of a law passed late in 1933, which had given the
German Government power to impose prohibitions or quotas
on imports from countries which discriminated against German
imports in a way incompatible with existing commercial treaties.[35] Similar powers were granted to the governments of
Hungary (January, 1932), Japan (March, 1934), Spain (December, 1931), and Venezuela (April, 1938).[36] Such powers
have not, however, been extensively utilized, even by governments which have thoroughgoing quota systems. Nevertheless, the importance of commercial bargaining considerations
in influencing, (a) the decision to adopt an import quota system, (b) the retention and expansion of that system, once
adopted, and (c) the manner in which quotas have been administered cannot be overemphasized. With the help of quotas,
bilateral commercial bargaining has, in recent years, been developed into an exact science. Reciprocal concessions can be
balanced with a precision that is impossible in connection with

[34] *Commerce Reports,* August 22, 1932, p. 336. Algeria is covered by the
French import quotas.
[35] *Ibid.,* September 30, 1933, p. 219, and February 10, 1934, p. 89.
[36] Cf. H. C. A. Carpenter, *Economic Conditions in Hungary, 1930–32,* Great
Britain, Department of Overseas Trade, Report No. 540 (London, 1933), p. 26,
and *Commerce Reports,* April 14, 1934, p. 235; January 4, 1932, p. 54; and
April 23, 1938, pp. 373–74.

tariffs, and the recognition of this fact by governments has had a profound effect on the evolution of quota systems.

In summary, quotas have been adopted to accomplish three main objectives: (1) to "improve" the trade balance, (2) to protect domestic industries, and (3) to facilitate bilateral commercial bargaining.[37] The relative importance of the latter two objectives has tended to increase somewhat since the bottom of the depression, especially in influencing countries to retain or expand quota systems; but at every stage, all three motives have played some part. It should be noted, in this connection, that import quotas, through removing the possibility of further imports regardless of price developments abroad, tend to guarantee the domestic producer a relatively secure position in the home market.[38] Consequently, the removal of a quota, once established, is likely to be firmly resisted by the protected industry; and, in fact, in so far as quotas lead to expansion of domestic production, they may give rise to new vested interests, which owe their existence entirely to the presence of the quantitative restrictions on imports. In addition, quotas, through insulating the domestic market from the effects of price changes abroad, prove to be virtually indispensable adjuncts of internal price-control or marketing schemes. It is primarily for this purpose that Great Britain has made use of them.

4. Inclusiveness of Quota Systems and Selection of Commodities to Be Affected

As we have seen, the United States has applied quotas to only a few scattered commodities, while up to September, 1939, Great Britain employed them primarily in conjunction with agricultural marketing schemes. On the Continent of Europe, quota systems tended during the nineteen-thirties to cover a

[37] Cf. Heuser, *Control of International Trade*, pp. 3–5, 17.
[38] Cf. E. B. Dietrich, *World Trade* (New York, 1939), pp. 105–106.

wide range of commodities, affecting, in some cases, the major portion of the country's imports. Table IX shows the proportion of imports affected by quotas in 1937 in European countries not employing exchange control. Among exchange-control countries, Poland and Italy applied quantitative restrictions

TABLE IX

APPROXIMATE PERCENTAGE OF TOTAL VALUE OF IMPORTS IN 1937 SUBJECT TO LICENSE OR QUOTA RESTRICTIONS [a]

France	58%	Ireland	17%
Switzerland	52%	Norway	12%
The Netherlands	26%	United Kingdom	8%
Belgium	24%	Sweden	3%

[a] *World Economic Survey, 1938–1939*, p. 189.

to all imports with a few minor exceptions.[39] Austria's import permit system at first covered only about one-fifth of the total value of Austrian imports, but by 1936 it had been extended to include more than half.[40] Greece and Czechoslovakia employed import permits extensively, while the comprehensive exchange permit requirements in Bulgaria and Germany were scarcely to be distinguished from import permit systems.

As we have had occasion to note, many of the earlier quotas, introduced in 1931 and 1932, affected agricultural commodities, at least in the European agricultural-importing countries. There were a number of reasons for this. Agricultural prices were falling more rapidly than industrial prices; yet production costs in agriculture are notoriously rigid. The specific tariffs which were employed all over the Continent became less and less effective as instruments of protection, as world prices of staple agricultural commodities continued to decline.[41] Further-

[39] The Polish import permit system was extended in 1936, at the time of the introduction of exchange control, to cover practically all imports. (*Commerce Reports*, May 23, 1936, p. 409.) In Italy, the only commodities free of import restrictions were manuscripts, newspapers, printed books, and the like. (Welk, *op. cit.*, p. 105.)

[40] Cf. Heuser, *Control of International Trade*, pp. 134–35.

[41] Cf. p. 245 n. above. Ad valorem duties would have declined in effectiveness at an even more rapid rate.

more, quotas, which assured domestic producers of a more or less definite place in the home market, were especially well adapted to carrying out European programs for encouraging the maintenance of the peasantry. There is a further point, of a theoretical nature, which can be comprehended at a glance if one refers to Diagram I. It is obvious that, if we are dealing with a commodity for which both demand and supply are relatively inelastic—and this is generally believed to be the case with certain staple agricultural commodities—a very high tariff must be imposed to bring about a material contraction of imports. In practice, it would be difficult to determine the exact height of the tariff which would be required in order to effect the desired reduction. By introducing a quota, however, imports can be immediately restricted to the desired level. The effect on the price in the domestic market will be identical with that of a tariff of the appropriate height, but the general public does not ordinarily realize this. Quotas have accordingly been introduced in a number of cases where a high tariff on food would have been politically out of the question.

In some countries, there has been a tendency, as in the case of exchange restrictions, though to a lesser extent, to limit imports of luxury articles more drastically than imports of essentials. This has been particularly true, of course, where improvement of the trade balance has been the dominant consideration. As time has gone on, however, quotas have tended to be utilized more and more, as we have seen, for protectionist ends. The choice of imports to be restricted has, as one might expect, frequently been determined very largely by the relative strength of various economic pressure groups. Furthermore, if imports of a given commodity show a sudden tendency to increase, this is almost invariably used as an argument for subjecting them to a new or more stringent quota.

In the last three or four years, the choice of commodities to be affected by quotas has been influenced to an increasing degree by the exigencies of armament programs and campaigns for military preparedness. In general, one may say that systems of import restriction, whether in the form of exchange permit requirements or import quotas, have been most stringent in the totalitarian states, where self-sufficiency has been a primary objective.

Where it is desired to discriminate against certain countries in the administration of the quota system, this can sometimes be accomplished indirectly through the choice of commodities to be restricted. It frequently happens in international trade that imports of a given commodity into a specified country originate primarily from a small number of countries, say two or three; and it is sometimes the case that one country is by far the most important source of supply. It can be easily seen, then, that the chief supplier or suppliers can be injured by restrictions on the imports of such a commodity, while other countries remain relatively unaffected. Meanwhile, imports of a similar and easily substituted commodity can be admitted from elsewhere. In other cases, not all imports of a commodity, but only those from certain countries, are subject to restrictions. Turkey has made wide use of this principle, but of this we shall have more to say when we take up the distribution of imports by countries.

5. *Administrative Details*

The fixing of quotas or the administration of licensing systems must be left, obviously, to the executive branches of the government. If the drawing up of a modern tariff schedule seems too complex and technical a problem for the rather cumbersome process of parliamentary action, it is obvious that the determination of appropriate quotas for a large number of commodities must be handled by administrative bodies. Ordinarily, a law is passed granting to the government authority to fix quotas or require licenses for imports. A special import control board may be established, or the responsibility for fixing quotas may be given to the Minister of Agriculture or the Minister of Commerce, depending on the type of commodity involved. Sometimes an interdepartmental committee, composed of representatives of various departments, is set up. Although the objectives of the quota system are usually set forth in the law, the choice of commodities to be affected is sometimes left altogether to the administrative bodies. There have been cases of governments, authorized to introduce quotas in retaliation against countries pursuing discriminatory trade policies, which have not actually utilized this authority.[42]

The length of the quota period usually varies from three months to a year, although there are instances of longer and shorter periods. Much depends on the nature of the commodity and the purpose for which the quota is being used. Annual quotas are sometimes broken into sub-quotas, which may be distributed unevenly over the year to take account of seasonal variations.

Quotas are constantly being altered in response to changing economic conditions. Since the detailed administration is left to governmental departments or committees, this can usually be accomplished without any parliamentary action. Where quotas have been granted to individual countries in commercial agreements, of course, no changes can be made until the agreement expires, but there is a strong tendency to limit the duration of commercial agreements to six months or a year when quotas are involved.

6. *Distribution of Imports among Importing Firms*

When imports can be brought in freely or are restricted only by tariffs, the amount imported tends to be adjusted to market conditions. Total imports of any given commodity will, apart from temporary frictions or maladjustments, tend to equal the

[42] Portugal is apparently a case in point.

amount which can be sold on the domestic market at a normal profit. A quota has the effect, ordinarily, of limiting imports to an amount less than that which can be sold at a normal profit. Accordingly, there is an inducement for importers to bring in an amount in excess of the quota—in fact, the inducement is especially great because of the existence of quota-profits arising out of the restriction. If no license requirements are set up, the natural result is a general scramble to get goods to the ports of entry before the quota is filled. There is likely to be an unusually large addition to the supply coming onto the domestic market in the early part of the quota period, followed perhaps by a scarcity toward the end of the period. Marked fluctuations in price are the inevitable result, while the importers whose goods arrive too late suffer the inconvenience and financial loss involved in shipping their goods elsewhere or holding them in storage until the next quota period begins. It is largely in order to avoid these disturbances that licensing systems are adopted.

Unless the issue of licenses is to take place on a basis of secrecy and favoritism, clearly some principle must be adopted for determining the distribution of licenses among the various importing firms. Usually, the volume of business conducted by the importer in some previous period (often a single year), is the criterion selected. Each importer is required to submit documents indicating the amount of his imports in the base period, and the license which he receives entitles him, under the regulations in force in a number of countries, to import a certain percentage of this basic amount.

This system generally gives rise to several complaints. In the first place, only those fortunate firms or individuals who happen to be importing in the base period can obtain licenses. The unfairness of this feature of the system has been to some extent corrected in a few countries as time has gone on by provisions which make allowance for the entry of new firms into the field. After several years of experience with licensing systems, the Swiss Government began to reserve a certain percentage of its quotas (varying up to 20 per cent) for allotment to new firms or to old firms which could, for some reason, claim special treatment.[43] A similar system was gradually developed in France.[44] Greece adopted a more flexible system whereby some account was taken of such factors as the capital value of the firm as well as of its imports in former years; while Rumania gave some weight to the turnover taxes paid by each firm.[45] On the whole, however, the regulations in force in most countries tend to favor established firms. Furthermore, it is clear that the dominant position of large firms tends to be perpetuated through their ability to secure the lion's share of the quota.

It has also been maintained that the system works to the advantage of firms which, for some reason, may have happened to import an unusually large amount in the base period.[46] This defect is sometimes, though by no means always, corrected by basing the allotments to firms on the average of their imports for several years, rather than using a single year as the criterion. When new quotas are introduced, a very recent year (in many cases, the previous year) is generally chosen as the basis for distribution of licenses among firms, even though an earlier year may be employed in the case of older quotas. This tends to prevent the granting of an unfair advantage, at least with respect to newly restricted imports, to firms which occupied a dominant position in the past. Frequently the base years formerly employed for the older quotas are dropped and more

---

[43] H. L. Setchell, *Economic Conditions in Switzerland, March, 1936*, Great Britain, Department of Overseas Trade, Report No. 640 (London, 1936), p. 23. After the devaluation of the Swiss franc in the autumn of 1936, the Swiss quota system was liberalized in a number of ways, and importers were no longer required to submit proof of previous importation in order to secure a license. (*Commerce Reports*, October 10, 1936, p. 819.)

[44] See *Commerce Reports*, February 3, 1934, p. 77, and Heuser, *Control of International Trade*, p. 105.

[45] *Ibid.*, p. 104, and *Commerce Reports*, March 25, 1933, p. 191.

[46] See, for example, an article on the Swiss quota system in the *Neue Zürcher Zeitung* for July 13, 1934.

recent years substituted. This type of modification, of course, is not very significant, for, if the new base year is 1934 and the former base was 1931, the relative amounts which the various firms were permitted to import in 1934 would have depended on their imports in 1931. Its chief value would be to effect a reallocation in the not infrequent cases in which firms had dropped out of the picture or had been applying for licenses which they had not fully utilized.

Since the privilege of importing under a license system depends on the obtaining of a license, and since the license-holder is generally in a position to secure quota-profits, it is not surprising that there has been a tendency for a trade in licenses to spring up, wherever this has been at all possible under the regulations in force. Clearly, the maximum price which a purchaser would be willing to pay for a license would equal the total quota-profits which he could secure by importing the amount specified in the license.[47] Subject to this limitation, prices paid for licenses may vary, and dealings may be, to some extent, speculative in nature. The consumer is, of course, not affected by this traffic in licenses, unless it leads to the development of a monopolistic situation. In most of the quota countries, licenses are not legally transferable, but this restriction proves exceedingly difficult to enforce in practice. Recognition of this fact influenced the Dutch Government, in 1934, to legalize the transfer of import licenses, all transfers to be supervised by the Crisis Import and Export Bureau.[48]

[47] With, perhaps, some allowance for risk and with the anticipated quota-profits discounted back to the date of purchase of the license. We assume, for the sake of simplicity, that importers receive a normal rate of profit which is about on a par with profit rates in other fields of enterprise. Under these circumstances, they would presumably invest their money elsewhere rather than eat into their normal profits by paying for a license a sum greater than the quota-profits.

[48] Cf. *Commerce Reports*, March 24, 1934, p. 188, and April 14, 1934, p. 235. Cf., also, Heuser, *Control of International Trade*, pp. 233–36, for further details on the action of the Dutch Government and on the attitude of other governments toward the traffic in licenses.

In Italy, certain types of imports were not subject to license but were re-

Similar action was taken in 1937 by the Danish Government, with respect to the transfer of import licenses issued in conjunction with its exchange regulations.[49]

It has frequently been alleged that the issue of licenses is fraught with favoritism and corruption. This complaint was apparently made in connection with wartime license systems as well as those of more recent years.[50] Clearly, the opportunities for favoritism are especially great if a separate license is issued for each individual import transaction and administrative bodies are not required to follow any definite, publicized principles in allocating the licenses among individual firms. This was the case in Poland and Czechoslovakia. It is where such a system prevails that complaints about discrimination or corruption tend to be heard with the greatest frequency.

In order to avoid the disadvantages of the methods of license-distribution now prevalent, governments might try selling licenses to the highest bidder.[51] This system would remove the rigidities connected with distribution on the basis of imports made by firms in some previous period. Furthermore, there would be a tendency for the government to receive all the quota-profits which now go to traders, for competition among importers would presumably drive the price of licenses up to an amount roughly equal to the quota-profits anticipated. The writer knows of no case in which this has been done in connection with import quotas, although the Argentine Government adopted, for a time, a system which involved a similar principle in connection with the issue of foreign exchange for imports.[52]

----

stricted to a specified percentage of imports of the commodity in a previous period. Importers were granted individual quotas based on their imports in the period designated, as indicated by customs receipts which they were required to present to the authorities. There was considerable opportunity for speculative dealing in such customs receipts, which were not made out to a particular firm. (Welk, *op. cit.*, p. 102.)

[49] *Commerce Reports*, April 24, 1937, p. 340.
[50] Cf. Haight, *op. cit.*, p. 25, on the wartime experience of France.
[51] Cf. Haberler, *The Theory of International Trade*, p. 348.
[52] Cf. pp. 106–107 above.

An alternative method of appropriating quota-profits, which does not remove the rigidities connected with prevalent methods of distributing licenses among firms, is for the government to inaugurate a suitable schedule of fees to be paid by importers wishing to obtain licenses. Fees would, of course, vary for every commodity, being made equal, for each unit of the commodity, to the difference between the domestic price and the foreign (export) price, in so far as such difference was not attributable to transportation costs or tariffs. It would, in practice, ordinarily be impossible to fix the size of the fee until the quota had been in operation for a long enough period to work out its effects on prices. Even then, the fee would have to be adjusted to compensate for any subsequent alterations in the domestic or world price.

In no case, so far as the writer is aware, has a government set out to appropriate all quota-profits by means of license fees.[53] The levying of license fees has been common, but in many cases the intention has been merely to cover the costs of administering the license system. A flat rate, consisting of a fixed percentage of the value of the imports (generally not more than 2 per cent, at the most), is charged for all commodities, no attempt being made to vary the rate in accordance with the price-differentials between home and foreign markets. A few governments, however, have imposed license fees which are clearly intended to tax away substantial proportions of importers' quota-profits, although one finds evidence of considerable confusion as to the exact nature of these levies, even, in some cases, on the part of the government officials responsible for them.

The French Government has been collecting sizable license fees since early in 1933, when the Government was given the power to impose taxes on holders of import licenses, the exact

[53] The Dutch Government, however, has enforced, since 1933, a schedule of fees intended to wipe out all importers' profits resulting from its control of agricultural imports. The control scheme is not strictly a quota system but involves rather the issue of import permits by semi-governmental import monopolies. For further details, see Ch. X, pp. 309–11.

height of the tax to be determined in each case by the appropriate ministry.[54] In defending the proposed levy before the Chamber of Deputies, the Minister of the Budget stated that the quota regime had had the effect of creating for the benefit of importers a "veritable monopoly," through which they had realized considerable profits. He therefore regarded it as perfectly legitimate for the Government to tax "a part" of these profits and indicated that the fees were not expected to bring about a rise in the cost of living.[55] It would require an intricate statistical study to determine the extent to which special profits which might have gone to importers as a result of price differences between French and foreign markets have actually gone to the government. The fees have been subject to frequent alterations in response to fluctuations in French or foreign prices. Whatever the intention of the officials responsible for the taxes, there have apparently been some cases in which, at least for temporary periods, the license fees on certain commodities were so high as to restrict imports to an amount less than the quota.[56] On the whole, however, there is little evidence that the Government has intended the fees to be protective in effect.[57]

[54] See *Journal Officiel, Débats Parlementaires,* Chambre des Députés, 15° Legislature, Session Ordinaire de 1933, I, 669.

[55] *Ibid.,* p. 672.

[56] This evidently happened on at least one occasion in connection with the quotas on imports of apples and pears from the United States, whereupon, in response to protests from the American Government, the license fees in question were reduced. (These statements are based on material contained in the files of the U. S. Department of Commerce. Detailed information on the license fees levied in connection with imports of apples and pears can also be found in *Commerce Reports, seriatim.*)

[57] Examples of some of the earliest fees were:

Coffee in the bean	100 francs per 100 kilos
Roasted or ground coffee	130 francs per 100 kilos
Coal	20 francs per 100 kilos
Eggs	fees varied in accordance with quality—highest grade subject to tax of 4 francs per kilo

Belgium has also attempted to tax the special profits accruing to importers as a result of the effects on prices of certain of its quotas.[58] In Rumania, the proceeds of import license fees have been devoted to export premiums.[59] The Spanish Government was authorized, early in 1935, to establish license fees, but these were not to be applicable to goods originating in countries which levied no import taxes or fees other than the regular customs duties[60] Thus, it is apparent that license fees have been levied for a variety of purposes.

Clearly, a third method of appropriating quota-profits would be to exact, in the case of all imports subject to quotas, the payment of customs duties which would equal the price-differentials between home and foreign markets (abstracting from transportation costs). This system would, however, accomplish nothing that could not be accomplished by a license fee system and would have the disadvantage of involving frequent administrative alterations of tariffs, which would undoubtedly give rise to political opposition at home and would be likely to work havoc with commercial relations with foreign countries.

The responsibility for the administration of quotas has in some cases been placed in the hands of importers' associations, some of which were formed for the purpose. This system has been adopted in Switzerland in connection with the importation of sugar, coal, certain types of mineral oils, and other commodities.[61] It was also utilized extensively in Czechoslovakia. The government laid down the general rules and regulations in regard to the issue of permits but made use of the facilities of the association in examining into the status of the various ap-

[58] Cf. Heuser, *Control of International Trade,* p. 237.

[59] *Commerce Reports,* June 23, 1934, pp. 399–400. This system is not to be confused with the premium and surcharge system applied to purchases and sales of foreign exchange. (Cf. pp. 111–14 above.)

[60] *Ibid.,* March 23, 1935, p. 193.

[61] For further details, see *Board of Trade Journal,* CXXIX (1932), 66, 436, and 863.

plicants for licenses. This system serves the purpose of facilitating the negotiation of private compensation transactions or of agreements with foreign governments, but it may, of course, encourage the resort to monopolistic practices on the part of the importers concerned.

7. *Import Quotas and Price-fixing*

A rising price-level has been regarded as undesirable in many European countries in recent years, both because of its internal repercussions in a period of labor unrest and severe unemployment and because of its deleterious effects on exports. Consequently, the price-increasing propensities of quotas have been viewed with alarm,[62] especially as many of the original proponents of quotas had argued that quantitative limitations on imports would not tend to raise prices as much as increased duties. Price-increases have been especially resented whenever it was suspected that they resulted from monopolistic collusion among importers, but the failure to distinguish between genuine monopolistic activity and the inevitable effects on prices of the quotas themselves has been responsible for many misguided and futile attempts to prevent price increases.

The French Government was given the power, in February, 1933, to fix by decree the maximum sale price of goods affected by license or quota restrictions.[63] Since this measure was passed in conjunction with the inauguration of license fees which were intended to tax quota-profits,[64] it is obvious that the object was not to prevent the appearance of any price-differential whatever between French and foreign markets as a result of the quota. Numerous modifications have since been made in the price-control legislation from time to time. The attempt

---

[62] This alarm, obviously, is not shared by the domestic producers of commodities subject to quotas.

[63] Cf. Haight, *op. cit.*, pp. 71–72, and *Journal Officiel, Débats Parlementaires,* Chambre des Députés, 15° Legislature, Session Ordinaire de 1933, I, 669.

[64] Cf. p. 261 above.

to prevent certain types of price increases has been recognized as futile, but permission of a price control board eventually had to be secured before prices of various categories of staple consumers' goods could be raised.[65] Switzerland has also attempted to regulate price increases through a price control board, but the cases in which the Government has actually interfered to prevent or nullify price increases have been relatively few and have evidently involved monopolistic activities on the part of dealers.[66]

The country which has developed the most elaborate system of price control and has made the most determined effort to enforce it is Germany. As we have seen, Germany has controlled imports, not through import licenses proper, but through the issue of exchange certificates. Many of the problems involved in connection with the two alternative systems of control, however, are identical and have been solved by identical methods. Thus exchange-control countries frequently allocate exchange permits among importers in accordance with the volume of trade conducted by these dealers in some previous period. Similarly, the price-control measures introduced by exchange-control countries have been much like those introduced by quota countries.

It is clear that any attempt to keep a quota from working out its effects on the domestic price of the commodity concerned will result in a maladjustment of demand and supply. If the price is prevented from rising to its new equilibrium point, demand will exceed supply, and the price-fixing authorities will have difficulty in enforcing the legal maximum price unless some system of rationing of demand is introduced. This, of course, is the familiar type of problem which is raised in connection with any attempt at official price regulation. The nature of the difficulties encountered will vary depending on

---

[65] *Commerce Reports*, December 4, 1937, p. 959.

[66] At one stage, the Federal Department of Public Economy warned that any illegal price increases would be followed by reprisals in the form of *reduced* import quotas.

whether the restricted commodity is a consumers' good or a producers' good. In either case, the rationing of demand will involve a greater degree of interference with economic life than is found in most countries outside of the totalitarian states. Up to September, 1939, Germany, Japan, and, to a somewhat lesser extent, Italy, were the only countries which had made any extensive use of it. In all three countries, the problem was similar—to impose drastic restrictions on most classes of imports in order to utilize available foreign exchange reserves for imports needed in connection with armament or preparedness programs, and yet, at the same time, to keep prices down in order (a) to prevent an unpopular rise in the cost of living, and (b) to maintain exports.

Actual rationing, of course, can be avoided to some extent by encouraging the consumption of domestic substitutes. If consumers can be induced to accept substitutes for patriotic motives, what the government is actually doing is bringing about a shift in demand motivated, at least in part, by non-economic forces. The employment of this policy in Germany and Italy is too familiar to require elaboration. It is obvious, however, that such methods do not prevent a decline in real incomes (assuming no increase in money incomes); the decline takes the form of directly restricted consumption, the use of inferior (and frequently more expensive) substitutes, and an increase in the prices of goods toward which expenditures are diverted.

On the whole, one may say that the tendency for import quotas to lead to extensive internal control of the economic system has been strongest where the effects of quotas on prices have not been allowed to work themselves out naturally. The complications involved in the administration of a licensing system, however, together with the fact that the issue of licenses encourages the formation of dealers' monopolies, may play a part in influencing the government to consider the adoption of official import monopolies, a more drastic form of control than quotas. But of this we shall have more to say in the next chapter.

8. *Distribution of Imports According to Country of Origin*

When tariffs constitute the only barrier to international trade, the sources of supply of imports are ordinarily determined by competitive forces, provided, of course, that the tariff system involves no discrimination among countries.[67] A quota system introduces a whole new set of problems. The simplest type of quota is the *global quota,* which involves no attempt to allocate imports among the exporting countries. If this type of quota is operated without a license system, goods are allowed to enter the country freely until the quota is exhausted, at which time further imports are refused admittance. Most of the early French quotas were of this type, but it soon appeared that the method gave an unfair advantage to exporters in neighboring countries, who could rush their goods to the ports of entry at the beginning of the quota period.[68] Thus, although global quotas seemed at first to offer the most reasonable way of avoiding discrimination, they were found, in practice, to discriminate against countries relatively distant from France. But the system involved further difficulties. We have already noted that, where no licenses are issued, abrupt fluctuations in market prices must be expected. Furthermore, the French authorities found that the quota was frequently exceeded, since a considerable delay was involved

---

[67] This statement does not hold true when markets are arbitrarily divided by international cartels or restriction schemes.

[68] Exporters in more distant countries might attempt to get around this difficulty by shipping goods sufficiently early for them to arrive at the port of entry at the beginning of the period, but this would frequently have to be done before the quota was announced, and, in any case, the uncertainty involved would be a deterrent. If the country imposing the quota permitted the admittance of goods which happened to be *en route* at the time of exhaustion of the quota, it is easy to see that the restriction would fail to achieve its purpose. Cf. Haight, *op. cit.*, p. 22. Where such imports are permitted, as in France, they are applied against the quota for the succeeding quota period.

in getting reports to and from the various customs houses as to how much was admitted each day.[69] Although France retains a few global quotas, the method early fell into disfavor, and other countries have made relatively little use of it.

Probably the best way of avoiding discrimination would be to combine the global quota with a license system. Each importer, in other words, would be issued a license specifying the amount he might bring in during the quota period but leaving him absolutely free to determine the geographical sources of his imports. If this were done, there would be every reason to expect that importers would purchase in the most favorable markets, just as they do when imports are subject merely to tariffs. Yet the confusion and violent market fluctuations associated with the simple global quota would be avoided. Actually, very few countries have left license-holders free to decide upon the sources of their imports. In the early years of quotas, Greece and Turkey followed this procedure, on the whole.[70] In more recent years, however, Greece has shown a tendency to discriminate in favor of countries with which her trade balance has been "favorable," while Turkey has come to utilize import restrictions *only* in connection with imports from certain countries with which she has had no clearing agreements or with which her trade balance has been "unfavorable." [71]

Once a nation decides to regulate the distribution of imports

---

[69] Cf. *ibid.*, p. 21. The excess can be subtracted from the quota for the succeeding period, although this sometimes means that the frontier is closed to imports of the commodity for several months. It has become a rather common practice, also, to specify the amount to be admitted through each customs house.

[70] Cf. Häfner, "Die Politik der mengenmässigen Einfuhrregulierung," p. 46.

[71] In the provisional commercial agreement between the United States and Greece, signed November 15, 1938, the allocation of global quotas into national contingents is left optional with the country imposing the quota. (U. S. Department of State, *Provisional Commercial Agreement between the United States of America and Greece*, Executive Agreement Series, No. 137, Article II.) For further discussion of this whole problem, see Tasca, *World Trading Systems*, Ch. II. Cf., also, pp. 401–403, below.

by countries, the question arises as to what method of allocation to adopt. It is in the handling of this matter that the greatest variation can be found among quota systems in operation at the present time. Some countries have made a real effort to pursue a general policy of fair treatment; others have frankly utilized the quota as a weapon of discrimination. The whole question is complicated by the fact that the most-favored-nation clause was developed in connection with tariffs and was never intended to deal with quotas. In 1931, when European countries began to resort to quotas on a wide scale, the most-favored-nation clauses in the majority of commercial treaties made no reference to quantitative restrictions in spite of the War and post-War experience with license systems.[72] Consequently, the way was left open for nations to seize on quotas as a means of evading their most-favored-nation obligations.

There is no way of rendering quotas completely compatible with the most-favored-nation clause. The best method, as already indicated, would be to issue licenses to importers but leave them free to determine the sources of their imports. The chief defect of this system, from the point of view of exporting countries trying to enforce their most-favored-nation rights, is that it would be very easy for the authorities in the importing country to exert secret pressure on importers to make their purchases in certain countries. Importers failing to comply might find it impossible to secure licenses for the next quota period. In any event, this method has not been employed in practice to any appreciable extent. A second possibility is to allot an equal share of the quota to each country entitled to most-favored-nation treatment. Clearly, this policy would bring about a distribution of trade totally unlike that which would result from the operation of competitive forces. Ordinarily, imports are derived chiefly from relatively few exporting coun-

[72] Some of the commercial treaties concluded during the nineteen-twenties did specify, as we have seen in Chapter II, that the most-favored-nation clause applied to import restriction schemes as well as to tariffs.

tries, while the share of other nations is comparatively insignificant. Hence an equal apportionment would work to the disadvantage of the countries which would normally be the chief suppliers. This system has occasionally been used in connection with the extension to third countries of quotas granted in bilateral commercial agreements, but the writer knows of no country which has adopted it in the administration of its autonomous quotas.[73]

On the whole, the usual practice among nations which have made any pretense of adhering to the spirit of the most-favored-nation clause in the administration of quantitative import restrictions has been to allot quotas to the various exporting countries on the basis of their proportional shares in the market of the country introducing the restriction in some previous period. The chief advantage of this method, from the point of view of exporting countries, is that it provides a recognizable formula for fair treatment, but it has several defects which in practice may prove important. In the first place, it tends to rigidify the channels of trade, no allowance being made for the effects of temporary fluctuations or permanent shifts in demand and supply conditions. Even a cursory study of trade statistics indicates that the currents of trade are constantly shifting and that the relative importance of various countries as sources of supply for any given commodity may change markedly in either the short or the long run. While the allocation of quotas in accordance with trade statistics for previous years prevents importers from purchasing goods in

[73] The case of the German tariff quota on butter has already been mentioned in another connection. In an agreement with Finland, concluded in 1930, Germany agreed to admit a fixed quota of Finnish butter at a reduced tariff rate, all additional imports to be admitted at the regular rate. The privilege of exporting the same quantity of butter to Germany at the reduced rate was extended to all countries having most-favored-nation agreements with Germany. Since Finland had been a relatively unimportant supplier of the German market, the arrangement was extremely disadvantageous to Denmark and other countries which had been exporting large quantities of butter to Germany. Cf. Röpke, *German Commercial Policy,* pp. 61–62.

countries which have not supplied them in the past, it cannot force them to continue buying from countries in which price increases have rendered purchases unprofitable. The occasional non-utilization of a quota for a given country bears witness to this fact.

The second serious defect of the method of allocating quotas in accordance with past experience is that a subtle form of discrimination may be involved in the choice of the base period. If the base consists of a single year, it may work to the disadvantage of a country which happened to have a bad harvest, a strike, or some other disturbing experience in that year; while, even if average imports over a period of several years are selected, the results may vary greatly, depending on whether a relatively remote period or the period just previous to the introduction of the quota is selected. Obviously, a country like Japan, whose exports showed a spectacular increase from 1932 on, could be materially injured if importing countries were to choose the period 1929–31, for example, as a basis for allocating import quotas.[74] In practice, one finds that a single country may select periods which vary widely for dif-

[74] In fact, Japanese exports have suffered considerably in certain markets for this very reason. In May, 1934, for example, the British Government announced that quotas had been imposed on imports of cotton and rayon piece goods from foreign (non-British) countries into the non-self-governing colonies and protectorates of the British Empire. Imports were to be restricted to an amount equivalent to average annual imports from each foreign country during the period 1927–31. Certain exceptions were made in the case of a few colonies. (*Commerce Reports,* May 19, 1934, p. 314.) The self-governing colonies followed with measures of their own instituting similar quotas. Japanese exports of cotton and rayon piece-goods to the British colonies had been increasing markedly in 1932 and 1933, at the expense of British exports. The new quotas had the effect of wiping out Japan's advance and permitting the Lancashire cotton industry (which was unaffected by the new quota) to recapture the dominant position in these markets which it had occupied previous to 1932.

An interesting instance of Japanese cleverness in evading similar restrictions in the Netherlands East Indies has been reported. Evidently, cotton shirts with tails three yards long were being sent from Japan to certain Dutch colonies. Since there was no quota on cotton clothing, the shirts were admitted without restriction, whereupon the tails were cut off and sold as cotton piece goods.

ferent commodities as bases for the apportionment of its quotas. This is the case, for example, with the Dutch and French quota systems. The only way in which an exporting country can protect its interests is through bargaining for the selection of base periods which will not be disadvantageous to its exports.

Few countries have adhered consistently to any one policy in determining the geographical sources of imports subject to quota or licensing system, and great variations in detail are to be found between systems which resemble each other in broad outlines. It is possible, however, to distinguish several divergent methods which have been followed in practice in the handling of this crucial problem.

First, let us consider the extent to which quotas have been allocated among exporting countries in accordance with their shares in the markets of the importing country in some previous period. The United Kingdom has adhered more or less consistently to this policy except in so far as it has granted favorable treatment to British, as opposed to non-British, countries. France and the Netherlands also followed this practice for a time, but, late in 1933, both these countries revised their methods of apportionment to render their quota systems more adaptable to commercial bargaining. France decided to apportion only 25 per cent of each quota to the various exporting countries in accordance with their relative shares in French imports of the commodity concerned in some previous period. The remaining 75 per cent was to be reserved for bargaining purposes and was to be apportioned among the various exporting countries according to their willingness to grant concessions to French exports.[75] In November, 1933, the Dutch quota law was amended in similar fashion. A provision of the new law authorized the Government to grant supplementary quotas to countries to be specified. The object, ap-

[75] Cf. Haight, *op. cit.*, p. 104. France has also granted certain countries supplementary quotas. Cf. pp. 403–404, below.

parently, was to reserve these supplementary quotas for concessions to countries which granted satisfactory counterconcessions to the Netherlands,[76] the basic quotas meanwhile being somewhat reduced.[77]

Thus, France and the Netherlands have, in general, abolished a policy designed to accord equitable treatment in favor of one which regards import quotas as instruments for securing export expansion. It is significant that this change took place at a time when recovery from the "great" depression was just getting under way and the outlook for export expansion seemed not altogether hopeless. Switzerland, on the other hand, had shown a tendency to regard its quotas as instruments of commercial bargaining from the beginning. The basis on which quotas were allocated among the various exporting countries was not made public, but favorable treatment was granted to countries which would offer corresponding advantages to Swiss exports.

In earlier chapters, we have had occasion to note the growing tendency, especially among European countries, to regard the balancing of bilateral trade with every individual trading country as a major aim of commercial policy. The influence of this attitude has been hardly less important in connection with import quotas than in connection with exchange control or clearing agreements. In fact, we have already indicated the extent to which clearing countries make use of import quotas in attempting to arrive at given ratios in their trade with other clearing countries. In view of this prevalence of "bilateral balancing," one is not surprised to find that the majority of European exchange-control countries follow a practice, in allocating their quotas among exporting countries, of granting preferential treatment to countries with which their trade balances are

[76] *Commerce Reports,* March 10, 1934, p. 158.
[77] E.g., the revised quotas announced for certain commodities early in 1934 involved substantial reductions in the amounts to be admitted, but it was expected that additional quotas would later be granted to countries offering special facilities to Dutch imports. (*Ibid.,* February 10, 1934, p. 90.)

favorable or with which they have clearing agreements. Some countries, such as Greece, Rumania, and Turkey have tended to build their quota systems around this principle and to carry it out in a relatively systematic fashion. Others, like Hungary, Italy (with respect to most commodities), and (formerly) Poland and Czechoslovakia, have given considerable weight to this factor among others, although the exact basis on which their quotas have been apportioned among exporting countries has not been made known.

The Greek quota system has already been briefly described in connection with private compensation transactions,[78] but it is worth our while, at this stage, to examine it in somewhat greater detail, for it sheds light, not only on the manner in which the principle of "bilateral balancing" may be brought into a quota system, but also on the way in which various types of import restrictions may be utilized side by side. Emphasis on "bilateral balancing" became apparent in the Greek quota regulations at a relatively early stage, especially in provisions subjecting imports of certain types of commodities or imports from certain countries to compulsory compensation. In a series of regulations promulgated during the course of 1935, however, the system was regularized, and all imports were classified into the following categories:

List A. Goods which might be imported without quantitative restriction and irrespective of country of origin (41 items of various types, including certain essential foodstuffs, certain raw materials, and books and newspapers).

List B. Goods which might be imported in full exchange (compulsory compensation) for Greek products, in partial exchange from countries with which Greece had a partial exchange agreement, or freely from countries with which Greece had an active balance of trade. (Items of varied types—predominantly foodstuffs and producers' goods.)

List C. Goods which might be imported from any country and

the import of which was to be subject to quantitative limitation; i.e., global quotas. (Predominantly producers' goods.)

List D. Goods the import of which was to be subject to a special permit. (Various commodities, including numerous types of machines, the import of which is now subject to permit in a number of young industrial countries, in order to facilitate control of the rate of industrial expansion.)

List E. Goods which might be imported from any country and the import of which was to be limited to a certain value in foreign exchange. (Predominantly luxury goods—exchange quotas expressed in Swiss francs.)

List F. Goods falling under the same category as Lists C and E (i.e., goods subject to quantitative limitations or limited to a certain value in foreign exchange), but the import of which was to be allowed only against total or partial exchange of products, or from countries with which Greece had an active balance of trade. (Consumers' goods of luxury or semi-luxury class.)

List G. Goods the import of which was to be subject to quantitative limitation, but which might be imported in excess of quota and without limitation of quantity in exchange for Greek products. (Short list of producers' goods.)

List H. Goods the import of which was to be prohibited. (Goods the sale of which in Greece was subject to government monopoly, goods excluded on sanitary or moral grounds, etc. The monopolized commodities might be imported by permission of the Ministry of Finance.) [79]

In the last few years, Greece has shown a tendency to grant special exceptions in order to facilitate imports from Germany, with which her trade balance has been active, involving the accumulation of large frozen clearing balances in Berlin. These exceptions have taken the form of the granting of permission for extra-quota imports from Germany, a procedure which the Greek regulations have allowed in the case of imports from countries with which Greece has accumulated active clearing

[79] For complete lists of commodities coming under the various categories, see *Board of Trade Journal*, CXXXIV (1935), 226–27, 260–62, and CXXXV (1935), 556–58, 586–87, 616–17, 651–53, 686. Changes made in lists from time to time have also been reported in *ibid., seriatim.*

balances.[80] In fact, it has been reported that imports from Germany have scarcely been subject to quota at all.

Mention has already been made of a group of countries (Hungary, the former Polish and Czechoslovakian governments, and, with respect to most commodities, Italy) which have never revealed the exact basis on which imports subject to licensing systems are apportioned among the various exporting countries. Available evidence seems to indicate that in granting licenses for imports from this or that country, these governments have taken into account a variety of factors, among the more important of which are (1) commitments made in published or secret bilateral commercial agreements, (2) the state of the balance of trade with individual countries, (3) political considerations, (4) the existence or non-existence of a clearing or payments agreement and the nature of the provisions of such agreements, (5) the state of clearing balances, and (6) the provisions of international cartel agreements.

Until we have examined the provisions of recent commercial agreements,[81] however, our picture of the geographical apportionment of quotas will remain relatively incomplete. It is important to take account of the fact that the United States, for example, has insisted on the inclusion in her recent commercial agreements of provisions extending the application of the most-favored-nation clause to quantitative import restrictions and to exchange control. In most cases, she has succeeded, by this means, in securing relatively fair treatment for her exports in accordance with a "base period" formula. A few other countries have secured similar guarantees, at least in some of their agreements. Constant vigilance is required, however, to see that such guarantees are carried out, and protests against violation of treaty provisions are not infrequent. In this connection, it should be noted that the conclusion of

[80] Cf. *Commerce Reports,* November 3, 1934, p. 286.
[81] See Chapters XII–XIII.

secret bilateral commercial agreements or of secret supplements to published agreements has been a rather common practice in Europe in recent years and that many of these arrangements include quota concessions of one kind or another. Such agreements involve perhaps most frequently the countries which in any case allocate their quotas among exporting countries in a rather arbitrary manner. The existence of these secret arrangements greatly complicates the problem faced by countries which are attempting to enforce fair treatment for their exports.

9. *Bilateral Quotas*

The term "bilateral quotas" arose in connection with a system inaugurated by the French government in the latter part of 1931.[82] Restrictions on imports of German industrial products were under consideration, as a means of reducing the growing French deficit in Franco-German trade. Rather than impose unilateral quotas, the French government decided to leave the size of each quota to be determined by negotiation between the French and German dealers or producers most directly concerned. Accordingly, meetings were sponsored between French importers or industrialists, on the one hand, and their German competitors or suppliers, on the other. Once these groups had agreed, in the case of a given German product, on the quantity which would be permitted to enter the French market, the agreement would be submitted to the French and German governments for ratification. If it passed this stage, the restriction would be announced by the French government and given the force of law. A limitation would be placed, not only on imports from Germany, but also on imports from all other sources. Each supplying country would be allotted a proportion of the quota based on its relative posi-

[82] For a more detailed account of bilateral quotas, see Haight, *op. cit.*, pp. 29 ff.; Häfner, "Die Politik der mengenmässigen Einfuhrregulierung," pp. 55 ff.; Heuser, *Control of International Trade*, Ch. IX; and Dietrich, "French Import Quotas," pp. 669 ff.

tion in the French market as compared with that of Germany in a given base period.

Bilateral quotas of this kind were also negotiated with industrial groups or trade organizations in other European countries, especially in cases in which associations capable of carrying on the negotiations were already in existence. Imports of manufactured goods from Great Britain, for example, were usually restricted on the basis of bilateral quotas. It was generally provided that export certificates or licenses would be issued by the foreign government or by a producers' or exporters' association in the foreign country. This relieved the French Government of the responsibility of issuing import licenses and meant that the foreign exporters rather than the French importer, would be obliged to secure a license.

Why did such a system arise? The French Government evidently favored it partly because it meant that some of the troublesome problems involved in fixing quotas and issuing licenses could be avoided. Furthermore, it was felt that these quota agreements might stimulate the formation of international cartels and thereby introduce an element of stability into world markets, a development which the French Government, at that time, was inclined to regard with favor.[83] Exporters' associations in foreign countries were willing to accept this arrangement partly because they feared that unilateral quotas imposed by the French Government might be even more restrictive than quotas determined by negotiation and partly, perhaps, because they recognized that exporters in possession of export licenses would have an excellent chance of acquiring all or part of the "quota-profits" created by the restriction. It is possible, also, that the prospect of securing monopoly-profits, as well as quota-profits, may have been envisioned by some.

The use of this system has not been confined to France, although it has apparently played a relatively minor rôle in other import quota systems. Holland and Belgium employed it

---

[83] Cf. Häfner, "Die Politik der Mengenmässigen Einfuhrregulierung," p. 56.

to some extent, but the Swiss Government has been opposed throughout to the negotiation of bilateral quotas, or industrial *ententes*, as they are sometimes called.[84]

Since bilateral quotas obviously may encourage the formation of international cartels or may provide official sanction for restrictions enforced by cartels already in existence, the attitude taken by European governments toward arrangements of this sort has depended in part on their general attitude toward international cartels. In this connection, it is interesting to note that unilateral import quotas have in a number of instances been set up and administered in such a way as to facilitate the carrying out of international cartel agreements. Thus the former Czechoslovakian government, in allocating individual quotas for nitrate imports by countries of origin, respected the decisions of the International Cartel of Artificial Nitrate Producers and the agreement of this body with the Chilean government. In 1936, the British government introduced an import licensing system for iron and steel, in order to give effect to an agreement between the British Iron and Steel Federation and the Continental Steel Cartel.[85]

Similar to the "bilateral quota" in effect is an arrangement whereby, though the size of the quota is determined unilaterally, the importing country transfers to the exporting country the right to issue licenses. France adopted this method in the administration of some of her agricultural import quotas, for which the "bilateral quota" method was inappropriate in view of the nonexistence of organizations capable of carrying on the negotiations. The exporting countries were generally asked to sign informal agreements containing certain guarantees designed to insure the smooth working of the quota and to prevent the formation of private export monopolies.[86] Nevertheless,

---

[84] Cf. Heuser, *Control of International Trade,* pp. 118–20.

[85] *Commerce Reports,* July 25, 1936, p. 592.

[86] Thus the Dutch authorities undertook to see that (*a*) the quotas were not exceeded, (*b*) shipments were spread evenly over the quota period, and (*c*) normal commercial relations were maintained. The last clause was interpreted

the system evoked widespread protests in France from various
groups who maintained that it made possible the exploitation
of the French consumer by foreigners, while French importers
resented the fact that quota-profits were going, at least in large
part, to foreign exporters. The upshot was the virtual discon-
tinuation of the system at the end of 1933, when it was decided to require import licenses, in most cases, for agricultural
products subject to quota restrictions.[87]

Certain Belgian and French quotas on manufactured products have also been administered in this fashion. The British
worked out a slight variation on this system in connection with
their agricultural import quotas, which have sometimes been
grouped into two classes, compulsory and "voluntary." Under
the former type of arrangement, Britain imposed import license
requirements; under the latter, exporting countries, knowing
that in any event they would have to face eventually a restriction of the British market for the commodity in question,
agreed to impose quantitative limits on their exports to the
United Kingdom.[88] Even in the case of compulsory quotas,
however, certain of the foreign countries affected undertook to
regulate exports of the commodity concerned to the British
market through the issue of export certificates. Thus, when
compulsory quotas were imposed on bacon imports from non-
British sources, it was announced that bacon could be imported
from specified countries (the principal foreign exporting coun-

---

to mean that the Dutch Government would not permit exporters to form
monopolies. Cf. Heuser, *Control of International Trade,* p. 113, and Haight, *op.
cit.,* p. 31.

[87] *Commerce Reports,* December 16, 1933, p. 396.

[88] Cf. Richardson, *British Economic Foreign Policy,* pp. 166–67. At the beginning of 1938, compulsory quotas were in effect for imports from non-
British countries of chilled beef, frozen beef, frozen mutton and lamb, cured
pork, frozen pork, potatoes, and Irish cattle. "Voluntary" quotas had been
applied to imports from non-British countries of canned beef, eggs, condensed
milk, milk powder, and cream and, nominally at least, to imports from the
Empire of fresh, chilled, or frozen beef, veal, and mutton, canned beef, bacon
and hams, processed milk, and Canadian oats. (*Foreign Agriculture,* II [1938],
10.)

tries) only (*a*) under a license issued by the Board of Trade, or (*b*) "under a certificate issued by the Government of a country which has made an arrangement for the purpose with his Majesty's Government in the United Kingdom." [89] According to a later announcement, the former procedure would apply to imports from Argentina and the United States, while imports from all the Continental European countries affected by the restriction would come in under export certificates.[90]

The attitude of exporting countries toward this type of arrangement has varied. Some have preferred not to undertake the responsibility of issuing export certificates, perhaps because of a general aversion to controlling the channels of trade any more than necessary. At the other extreme are certain countries which have not merely responded to the initiative taken by importing countries but have demonstrated a tendency to develop a generalized system of control of exports affected by rigid foreign import restrictions. Their primary object has been to secure, for exporters or producers or the public treasury, some of the benefits of high prices prevailing in restricted import markets. This sort of tendency, which is of considerable significance, will be discussed in a later chapter in connection with export control.[91]

10. *Conclusions*

In the course of our discussion of various instruments of trade control, we have been led to conclude that measures adopted to meet an emergency situation have had such profound repercussions on the internal economic structures and external economic relations of the countries utilizing them

---

[89] *Board of Trade Journal*, CXXXI (1933), 700. "Voluntary" bacon quotas had been introduced in 1932.

[90] *Ibid.*, 795–96.

[91] See pp. 354 ff. below.

that it has become more and more difficult to get rid of them. This conclusion is perhaps justified to an even greater degree in relation to import quotas than to any form of control measure which we have yet considered.

In the first place, once quotas are introduced, there is a tendency to apply them to more and more commodities, for the price-increasing propensities of a restriction on the imports of one foreign commodity tend to lead, in many instances, to the substitution of another foreign commodity, imports of which thereupon become subject to control in their turn. Furthermore, domestic producers, witnessing the benefits conferred by the quota system on producers in other lines, press for a quota on imports of the commodity in which they are interested, while producers whose commodities are affected by import quotas fight to retain their sheltered positions or to secure a reduction of the quota in order to enjoy a still greater degree of protection.

Thus, one is not surprised to find that, while more and more commodities came to be affected by import quotas, especially in the years immediately following 1931, there have been relatively few cases in which quotas, once imposed, have been withdrawn. Up to the beginning of 1934 or thereabouts, moreover, quotas tended to be made progressively more restrictive in their effects. Since that time, a number of conflicting tendencies have been at work. As trade began to recover from the depression, quotas were liberalized to some extent, either autonomously or under the terms of the numerous bilateral commercial agreements which were being negotiated. Many of the intra-European agreements had the effect, however, merely of diverting trade from one country to another rather than of actually enlarging it. After the conclusion of the Tripartite Monetary Agreement, it was expected that removal of quotas would be the next step toward trade liberalization. Actually, the only country which substantially modified its import restrictions following the signing of this agreement was Switzerland.[92] France removed quotas on a relatively small number of products but has made no progress in the direction of relaxation since.[93] The removal of import quotas can be accomplished only through international action; and, since the autumn of 1936, the outlook for effective international action has grown steadily more hopeless.

If we are to weigh the factors which are likely to determine the future of import quotas, we must consider for a moment, from a very general point of view, the purposes which such restrictions were being made to serve at the outbreak of war in 1939. These may be listed, briefly, as follows: (1) the protection of individual industries, (2) the insulation of domestic markets for individual commodities from foreign price developments, in order to permit the carrying through of price or production control schemes, (3) the stimulation of production along particular lines, e.g., agricultural production under self-sufficiency programs, (4) the conserving of supplies of foreign exchange for particular types of foreign purchases, e.g., raw materials for use in armament industries, (5) protection of the currency, in so far as this was not accomplished through exchange restrictions, and (6) commercial bargaining along strictly bilateral lines.

Import quotas, rather than tariffs, were being used to serve these purposes because they permitted the volume of imports to be determined with precision and because they tended to

---

[92] In order to render the system of import restrictions as flexible as possible, the Federal Department of Public Economy issued the following instructions to the proper departmental authorities: Within quota limits, import permits were to be obtained without proof of previous importation; the requirement that local goods be purchased in order to obtain additional quotas was to be restricted or abolished (see Chapter X); importers were to be given greater freedom in the use of their quotas; and, subject to seasonal requirements and the exigencies of commercial policy, exceptions were to be made to the rule of granting quotas quarterly. (*Commerce Reports,* October 10, 1936, p. 819.)

[93] Cf. *ibid.,* pp. 821–22, for modifications of French customs barriers after the 1936 devaluation. Import quotas on approximately 100 products were suspended, effective October 3, 1936.

destroy the price-link between domestic and foreign markets, at least so far as individual commodities were concerned. Countries which have been making wide use of import quotas must be prepared, however, to face certain more or less inevitable consequences of their policies. Their national price levels are likely to become more and more divorced from world price levels. This development is likely to entail (a) a shift away from production for world markets and toward production for internal markets or, in other words, a move in the direction of autarky, and/or (b) rigid internal price control with its corollary of rationing in both consumers' and producers' markets. Another possibility is export subsidization on a wide scale, obviously an expensive process. Extensive use of quotas, as they are administered at the present time, involves, furthermore, the introduction of rigidity into the organization of the import trade. The channels of foreign trade also tend to become rigidified. (This applies to both exports and imports if the country enters into large numbers of commercial agreements involving quota concessions on both sides.) The formation of importers' monopolies and, possibly, producers' monopolies may be encouraged. The monopoly movement may go even farther and involve exporters' monopolies and new international cartels, since the canalization of foreign trade markets will create ideal conditions for such developments.

In short, import quotas are likely to be associated with a continuation of the trends toward organization of economies along nationalistic lines and increased governmental control of economic activity. These two tendencies are, in part, independent of each other, and, in part, closely interrelated. The future of quotas may also depend on whether organized producers in industries catering to the home market will continue to exercise more influence on governmental policy than consumers' groups or representatives of export industries. Obviously, the question is a complicated one, and we shall have more to say about it in the concluding chapter.

CHAPTER X

OTHER FORMS OF IMPORT RESTRICTION

1. *European Control of Agriculture as a Factor Affecting Commercial Policy*

In this chapter we shall be concerned with measures which have been employed mainly in conjunction with European agricultural control schemes. It is hardly necessary to point out that, especially in the years since 1928 or 1929, governments all over the world have attempted one experiment after another in their efforts to mitigate the difficulties under which agricultural producers were suffering. In both agricultural-importing and agricultural-exporting countries, there has, on the whole, been a trend toward enhanced governmental control of the marketing of agricultural commodities, while, in some cases, control has been extended to cover production or consumption, or both. Import restrictions and export subsidies have played an important part in agricultural programs. In fact, in most instances, especially in importing countries, governmental intervention in agriculture initially took the form of measures affecting foreign trade and only later moved into the field of internal control.

It is with the agricultural-importing countries that we shall be primarily concerned in the present chapter, for it is naturally in this group of countries that import restrictions have played an especially important rôle. The policies of agricultural-exporting countries will receive some attention in the following chapter. It is essential, however, to recognize the fact that many European countries are important both as importers and exporters of agricultural products. In fact, such countries as Holland and Denmark might be classified as importing-exporting countries; or, alternatively, they have sometimes been called processing countries, because, as importers of cereals and exporters of animal products, they perform the function of absorbing agricultural raw materials and working them over into a more finished or processed stage for export. In such countries as these, measures to restrict imports and to promote exports have frequently formed inseparable parts of the same program.

Rigid governmental regulation of the trade in cereals, involving price-fixing and, in some instances, complete state monopolies, was a characteristic of the World War period in Europe, when the problem was one of scarcity, not over-production.[1] In fact, the Swiss Government retained its cereal monopoly until 1929 and later adopted a modified form of semi-monopolistic control, while the Norwegian grain monopoly functioned continuously from 1917 on, though its powers were modified from time to time.[2] In most countries, however, freedom of market operations was restored in the early nineteen-twenties. Meanwhile, as we have seen, European tariff rates on agricultural commodities were low or nonexistent in many cases.[3] From 1925 on, and more especially from 1928 on, agricultural imports were subjected to increasingly heavy duties. Sliding-scale tariffs, designed to stabilize the internal price, were adopted in some instances. But, as world prices began to fall very rapidly, protectionists found that, if the home market was to be insulated effectively, duties had to be increased at frequent intervals or made very high once and for all. Where duties were "bound" in commercial treaties, this

[1] Cf. Royal Institute of International Affairs, *World Agriculture: An International Survey* (London, 1932), p. 189.

[2] *Ibid.*, pp. 190–92 and U. S. Congress, Senate, Committee on Agriculture and Forestry, *World Trade Barriers in Relation to American Agriculture*, Sen. Doc. No. 70, 73d Congress, 1st Sess. (Washington, 1933), pp. 451–53, 500–501.

[3] Cf. p. 18, above.

procedure was impossible, and, in any event, very high tariffs on foodstuffs did not find favor with the general consuming public. Seeking alternative means of protecting the domestic agricultural producer, governments began to turn to milling regulations from 1929 on. Through requiring millers, for example, to utilize a definite proportion of home-produced grain in their milling operations, an attempt was made to guarantee the domestic producer a secure position in the home market. This does not mean that tariffs on cereal imports were not raised to very high levels in many instances by the very countries which introduced milling regulations.[4] It means, among other things, that governments were seeing to it that domestic agricultural producers would find a market for their products, *regardless* of subsequent foreign price developments.

But milling regulations, unsupplemented by other measures, proved difficult to enforce. By 1931, moreover, the agricultural crisis, which had at first affected primarily cereals, had spread in acute form to other branches of farm production. It was at this stage that direct quantitative restrictions on imports began to be adopted on an extensive scale. In fact, as we have seen in the preceding chapter,[5] import quota and licensing regulations were, in some European countries, applied first to agricultural products and only later to industrial products. So far as cereals were concerned, import quotas usually did not supplant milling regulations but merely supplemented them. Furthermore, the fact that exchange restrictions had the effect of limiting agricultural imports into exchange-control countries should not be forgotten.

But these attempts to insulate the domestic agricultural producer from the effects of foreign price changes were frequently found to have undesirable results. High prices for staple agricultural commodities injured domestic consumers

---

[4] Cf. p. 23 above, for duty increases during this period. Certain countries, moreover, resorted to sliding-scale duties.

[5] Cf. p. 253, above.

and proved a disadvantage to export industries. The export industries which suffered most directly were those which depended on imported cereals as raw materials, e.g., the animal and animal products industries of Denmark, Holland, and other countries. In some cases, drastic import restrictions were so effective in raising domestic prices and stimulating domestic production that countries which had normally been on an import basis with respect to certain agricultural commodities found themselves developing export surpluses which in turn threatened domestic price-maintenance.[6] These and other factors led to demands for price-stabilization or price-fixing measures. But, because of the close interdependence among markets for various agricultural products, attempts to regulate prices in one market led to a need for price-regulation in other markets. Illegal or "gangster" markets, similar to the "black" bourses associated with exchange control, developed where prices were fixed. It was found that price-fixing or price-stabilizing regulations could be adequately enforced only if combined with production control and/or centralization of buying and selling operations in the hands of a governmental or semigovernmental monopoly. If this monopoly, in addition, took charge of imports, it could not only be made responsible for adjusting the volume of imports to the requirements of the

[6] Various countries which had been obliged to import substantial amounts of wheat during the nineteen-twenties found themselves facing the problem of disposing of wheat export surpluses toward the middle of the nineteen-thirties. On the Czechoslovakian experience, see G. Diller, "Einzelstudien über Marktregulierungen. III. Die Marktregulierungen in der tschechoslowakischen Getreidewirtschaft," *Weltwirtschaftliches Archiv*, XLIV (1936), 561. In the 1934–35 wheat crop year, "France, Sweden, Estonia, and Latvia, hitherto net importers, joined Poland and Lithuania as net exporters with the aid of export bounties or an equivalent." (Stanford University, Food Research Institute, *Wheat Studies*, XII [1935–36], 101.) "France apparently *exported* net almost 10 million bushels of wheat in August–March 1934–35—net exports larger than those of any other European country, even including the Danubian countries and Russia." (*Ibid.*, XI [1934–35], 336.) Actually France *produced* a surplus as early as 1932, but much of this was carried over for future domestic consumption under a government plan for subsidized storage. Cf. *The Economist*, CXVI (1933), 21, and U. S. Department of Agriculture, Bureau of Agricultural Economics, *Foreign Agriculture*, I (1937), 275–89.

internal price-regulating program but could also absorb any abnormally large profits on imports (arising because of the existence of a price-differential between home and foreign markets) for the benefit of domestic consumers or producers.

The extent to which individual control measures have been employed has varied greatly among the different European countries. In some cases, import monopolies were set up relatively early in the depression, while in other cases agricultural imports continued to be regulated by quotas or exchange permits, or even by tariffs. But internal prices and marketing have frequently been subjected to rather rigid control even though no actual monopoly of domestic dealings or of imports has been established. Centralized control of all dealings in agricultural commodities has gone farthest in the Soviet Union, with its collective farms, and in Germany and Italy, where farmers and dealers in agricultural commodities have been organized on a "corporative" basis. In Italy, all agricultural operations have been made subject to the regulation of eight agricultural corporations. Germany has centralized control in the hands of the Reich Food Estate (*Reichsnährstand*), a public corporation or national cartel, organized in 1933 and embracing agriculture, forestry, horticulture, fisheries, and game resources. Within these branches of the national economy, all producers, laborers, processors, importers and wholesale or retail dealers, not excluding agricultural cooperatives, have been required to belong to the cartel. Under the general supervision of the Minister of Agriculture, an attempt has been made to fix prices, and, in many cases, sales quotas, throughout the national cartel from the first producer to the final purchaser.[7]

This brief résumé of agricultural control measures in Europe, especially as they apply to imports, has been included in order to show that the regulations to be discussed in this chapter

---

[7] See *Foreign Agriculture*, I (1937), 233–34; *The Economist*, CXVII (1933), 579; and K. Brandt, *The German Fat Plan and Its Economic Setting* (Stanford University, 1938), pp. 194–96.

should be regarded, not as isolated protectionist devices, but as fitting into a particular setting. Their use has not, however, been confined entirely to European countries or to agricultural commodities, as we shall see.

2. Milling, Linked-Utilization, and Linked-Purchasing Regulations

We shall be concerned in this section with a group of measures which are designed to promote the consumption of a domestic product *at the expense of* a foreign product. *Linked-utilization regulations* render the utilization of a foreign product dependent on the utilization, in some specified proportion, of the same or some other domestic product. Best known and most common of the linked-utilization regulations are the so-called *milling regulations,* which have already been mentioned and which require domestic millers to employ a specified minimum percentage of domestic grain in their milling operations. This minimum percentage is always higher than the proportion of domestic grain that would be employed in the absence of government interference.[8]

Linked utilization of two commodities, one of which is produced abundantly at home, while the other must be imported on a substantial scale, can be required if the commodities are reasonably satisfactory substitutes for each other. Of this nature are the measures, common in petroleum-importing countries, requiring that all gasoline sold on a domestic market must contain a specified percentage of domestic alcohol. This sort of measure performs the dual task of aiding the farmers (especially potato growers) from whose products alcohol is derived and of rendering the country less dependent on imported petroleum.

[8] The term "milling regulations" has been used to cover measures governing various other aspects of the miller's operations, e.g., the extraction ratio. These other measures will not be discussed here, because their effects on international trade, while not negligible, are ordinarily less direct and less important than the effects of the type of milling regulation described in the text.

OTHER IMPORT RESTRICTIONS 291

Linked-utilization regulations may or may not require actual mixing of the domestic and foreign products. Where mixing is required, the term *mixing regulations* has sometimes been employed; but we shall avoid this term, since it is not applicable to all cases in which linked utilization is prescribed. The Swedish milling regulations achieve a compromise on this point. As matters stood in 1938, of the total amount of wheat or rye consumed by any Swedish mill, 90 per cent had to be of domestic origin. Any given quantity of wheat flour, however, might contain a smaller percentage of domestic wheat, but not less than 80 per cent. There was no corresponding minimum percentage for rye.[9]

Let us consider first that class of linked-utilization regulations which applies to units of the same commodity procured from foreign and domestic sources. It is obvious that regulations of this type, like import quotas, tend to provide a relatively secure position on the home market for the domestic producer of the commodity concerned. Yet import quotas, a type of customs barrier, can ordinarily be enforced with considerably greater ease than measures which require supervision of the activities of a large number of domestic traders or processors. In view of this consideration, why should linked-utilization regulations of this class be adopted at all?

The explanation lies partly in the fact that they constitute a method of indirect import restriction which does not formally conflict with commercial treaty obligations.[10] The widespread resort to milling regulations from the middle of 1929 on was certainly not unrelated to the fact that a number of European states had by that time ratified the Convention for the Abolition of Import and Export Prohibitions and Restrictions.[11] By the middle of 1931, on the other hand, it had become clear that

[9] Canada, Ministry of Trade and Commerce, *Commercial Intelligence Journal*, LIX (1938), 384.

[10] In this respect, they may be classed with a number of other more or less indirect import barriers. For a list of such devious protectionist devices, see Haberler, *The Theory of International Trade*, pp. 350–52.

[11] Cf. pp. 14–15 above.

the Convention was destined to be of no practical importance, and the countries which had ratified it began to withdraw in order to adopt direct quantitative restrictions on imports.

Furthermore, the adoption of milling regulations was a rather natural development in view of the fact that control of milling and baking operations in one fashion or another has been an accepted practice on the Continent of Europe, reaching its height during the World War.

It might be argued—though I doubt if this consideration had much practical weight in leading to the adoption of one type of weapon rather than the other—that linked-utilization regulations penalize the domestic consumer less heavily than import quotas, assuming that the same level of domestic production is sought in either case. Let us suppose that milling regulations, as applied to wheat, for example, result in the consumption of a larger quantity of domestic wheat than formerly. Proceeding on the usual assumption that wheat is produced under conditions of increasing cost, the price of domestic wheat will tend to rise.[12] Foreign wheat will still be available at its former price, however, or possibly at a lower price if the reduction in the requirement of the country in question for imported wheat is sufficiently large to affect the world price. The mixing regulations have the effect of limiting the range of substitutability between domestic and foreign wheat, irrespective of whether or not there are significant differences in quality between the

[12] The short-period supply curve will tend, regardless of assumptions concerning the shape of cost curves, to be positively inclined, since the stock of domestic wheat for any one crop year is fixed. In considering the effects of milling regulations, one must take into account the effects of the qualitative differences between the domestic and the imported product. A substantial proportion of the wheat produced in a number of the wheat-importing countries of Continental Europe, being of inferior quality, was used for animal consumption previous to the introduction of milling regulations, which had the effect, of course, of requiring that domestic wheat be used to an increased extent for human consumption. The precise effects of milling regulations on the total consumption of domestic wheat will depend, in part, on the extent to which farmers are forced, because of the rising price of domestic wheat, to shift to other forms of feed, but this would obviously play a similar rôle in the case of quotas.

two products. In other words, an artificial barrier is erected
between the market for domestic wheat and the market for
foreign wheat, creating a price-differential which cannot be
explained by qualitative differences. The price of flour to the
domestic consumer will depend on the price of domestic wheat,
the price of foreign wheat, and the proportion of each type of
wheat employed. Where import quotas are employed, on the
other hand, imported wheat will, as we know, fetch the same
price on the home market as domestic wheat of corresponding
quality.[13]

It must be emphasized in this connection, however, that the
relative effects of quotas and linked-utilization regulations depend largely on their comparative severity. Clearly, milling
regulations which called for the employment of 100 per cent
domestic wheat would tend to raise the domestic price more
than a relatively liberal import quota. Nor does a static
analysis of the effects of trade-control measures of this sort
tell us very much about what is likely to happen in practice,
since both quotas and linked-utilization regulations are subject
to frequent administrative changes. Actually, these changes,
over a period of years, have tended to be in the direction of
greater self-sufficiency, regardless of the type of weapon employed. Over the shorter run, there has been a tendency to
eliminate the effects of crop fluctuations on prices received by
domestic producers. Thus, an exceptionally good domestic
harvest would be likely to result, on the one hand, in a reduction of the import quota, or, on the other, in an increase in the
prescribed proportion of domestic wheat to be employed by
millers.[14]

One must recognize, also, that, as time has gone on, Euro-

[13] Cf. pp. 232 ff. above.

[14] If milling regulations called for the employment of a constant and fixed
proportion of domestic wheat, the price of flour on the domestic market
would remain somewhat more sensitive to world price changes than it would
if imports were subjected to a fixed quota. In practice, this consideration is of
little importance in view of the fact that a change in the world price is very
likely to lead to a change in the milling regulations.

pean countries have in many cases ceased to rely on linked-utilization regulations alone, or on import quotas alone, to control imports of agricultural commodities. Import licensing or quota systems have been employed to supplement and help enforce linked-utilization regulations, while prices of imported agricultural commodities have been subjected to price-fixing regulations on the domestic market. Quota and linked-utilization regulations are administered in such a way as to facilitate the enforcement of the official domestic price. In other cases, an import monopoly regulates the flow of imports in such a way as to facilitate the enforcement of whatever internal regulations have been imposed. Nor should one forget that, in exchange-control countries, the volume of imports of agricultural commodities may be affected by the decisions of the exchange-control authorities.[15]

The spread of milling regulations for wheat was very rapid

[15] The effects of linked-utilization regulations on the qualities of goods sold on the domestic market may under certain conditions be somewhat different from the effects that an ordinary import quota would have. Where the domestic product is inferior to the imported product—linked-utilization regulations frequently apply to cases of this sort—and where actual mixing is required, the result may be the complete exclusion of the better grades of the end-product from the domestic market. Import quotas, by forcing up the prices of these better grades, might simply place them out of reach of the lower-income groups. Here again, however, much depends on the relative severity with which different types of regulations are administered and on the extent to which various restrictions are combined in practice. Furthermore, it is not always easy to determine, on a priori grounds, the nature of the adjustments to which a given form of governmental interference will give rise. Thus, when milling regulations were first applied to wheat, there was some tendency for millers to respond by acquiring a larger proportion of the very hardest foreign wheats than formerly. In this way they succeeded in compensating to some extent for the inferior qualities of the soft domestic wheat which they were now required to use in increased amounts. (Cf. "Economic Nationalism in Europe as Applied to Wheat," Wheat Studies, VIII [1931–32], 261–76.) Later on, regulation of the sources of imports through import licensing or exchange permit requirements, combined with price-fixing on the domestic market and other forms of governmental interference, frequently prevented this sort of adjustment. Meanwhile, however, millers were gradually adopting improved techniques which enabled them to turn out a relatively satisfactory grade of flour even though they were obliged to use a fairly large proportion of soft domestic wheat. (For this last observation, I am indebted to Dr. Joseph S. Davis of the Food Research Institute of Stanford University.)

from the middle of 1929 on, a few countries having adopted them previous to this date.[16] Germany and France resorted to this type of requirement in 1929, while in 1930 Sweden, Czechoslovakia, Latvia, Peru, and Greece, and in 1931 Tunis, Belgium, Luxemburg, Italy, and Holland followed suit.[17] Thus, by the end of 1931, most of the wheat-importing countries of Continental Europe had milling regulations in force. In later years, more countries were added to the list, including, up to August, 1938, the Irish Free State, Mexico, Brazil, and Finland.[18] In most cases, the milling regulations have been retained, even though imports have been taken over by a government monopoly.

In the majority of these countries, the milling regulations called for the utilization of a considerably higher proportion of domestic wheat in the milling industry than had been employed previously. This proportion tended to be increased as time went on, moreover, although the actual required percentages of domestic wheat, which were subject to alteration by administrative bodies, were occasionally reduced for short periods to take account of seasonal variations or harvest fluctuations. In fact, a number of European countries, which had previously been net importers of wheat, rapidly achieved self-sufficiency and even began to produce export surpluses.[19]

[16] Norway inaugurated milling regulations in 1927, while Spain also adopted them prior to 1929, though rendering them virtually inoperative in May, 1930, through a prohibition on further imports of wheat until the domestic price should exceed 53 pesetas per 100 kilos for a month. (*Board of Trade Journal*, CXXIV [1930], 735, and *Wheat Studies*, VIII [1931–32], 173.)

[17] *Ibid.* In Belgium, no governmental regulations were adopted, but an informal agreement, specifying the proportion of domestic wheat to be employed in milling, was reached between the Belgian millers and the Government.

[18] *Foreign Agriculture*, II (1938), 491.

[19] Cf. p. 288 above. In Germany, the proportion of domestic wheat required was increased from 40 per cent in August, 1929, to 97 per cent in August, 1931, and was, in general, maintained close to the latter point in succeeding years. Foreign wheat in excess of 3 per cent could be used, up to a maximum of 30 per cent, if the additional quantities were imported on certificates showing that equal amounts of wheat had been exported. (*Wheat Studies*, VIII [1931–32], 173.) This provision simply represented a con-

The domestic wheat producer would profit little if the milling regulations for wheat simply resulted in increased imports of foreign flour. Hence, the wheat regulations have generally been accompanied either by restrictions on flour imports or by regulations providing that all flour sold in the country or used by bakeries must contain a specified percentage of flour milled from domestic wheat.[20] Countries like France and Italy, which had a flour-exporting business, exempted flour intended for export from the milling regulations or provided that such flour might contain a lower percentage of domestic wheat than flour intended for domestic consumption.[21]

To what extent have linked-utilization regulations been applied to commodities other than wheat? Certain European

---

tinuation of the German government's policy of encouraging exports of soft wheat from East Prussia, even though some hard wheat had to be imported into western Germany.

The proportion of domestic wheat actually employed by Dutch flour mills increased from 3.9 per cent in 1930 to 34.6 per cent in 1934. The Netherlands had produced 17.1 per cent of all wheat consumed in the country on an average in the harvest years 1923/24 to 1929/30, but much of this wheat, which was of inferior quality, had been used for feed. The prescribed milling ratio was gradually increased from 20 per cent in July, 1931, to 35 per cent in February, 1933./ (K. Schiller, "Einzelstudien über Marktregulierung. I. Das niederlandische Marktregulierungssystem für Weizen und Weizenprodukte," *Weltwirtschaftliches Archiv*, XLIV [1936], 353.) Sweden, France, and Italy were by 1933 requiring the employment of close to 100 per cent domestic wheat in milling operations. (*Wheat Studies, seriatim.*) France had required 97 per cent domestic wheat in December, 1929, but this ratio was reduced somewhat in 1930 and the first half of 1931. The increase in the prescribed ratio of domestic wheat in Sweden was spectacular; it rose from 45 per cent in July, 1930, to 95 per cent in January, 1933, although there were some rather marked upward and downward fluctuations in the interim. Later on, it was reduced to 90 per cent.

[20] The Swedish milling regulations adopted in 1930 for wheat and rye specified the proportion of domestic grain *or flour of* domestic grain which had to be respectively present in grain milled or flour sold. (*Commerce Reports,* February 16, 1931, p. 464.)

The percentage applied to flour sold did not always equal that applied to grain milled, since allowance sometimes had to be made for flour imports, owing to the limited capacity of the domestic milling industry.

[21] The Italian regulations, adopted in 1931, called for the employment of 95 per cent domestic wheat in the production of all flour and semolina except that intended for export. (*Commerce Reports,* June 29, 1931, p. 799.)

countries have adopted milling regulations for rye, oats, and other cereals; but these grains have been affected to a less extent than wheat, a natural result of the fact that Continental European countries have tended, on the whole, to be more nearly self-sufficient with respect to these coarser grains than with respect to wheat.[22] The linked utilization of domestic and foreign supplies has been required by Brazil in the case of coal, while Germany has adopted regulations of this type for hops, oil seeds, and wool among other commodities.[23] A number of European countries have employed linked-utilization regulations in order to stimulate the development of domestic cinema industries. In several cases, the regulations date back to the nineteen-twenties but have been made progressively more severe as time has gone on. Thus by a government decree of June 13, 1935, all Italian theaters were required to show one domestic film for every three foreign films. Previously, this requirement had applied only to first- and second-class theaters in the principal cities.[24]

Regulations which call for the linked utilization of two different products are usually employed to achieve one or both of the following objectives: (1) to stimulate the consumption of a commodity of which the country ordinarily produces more than it requires or of which it has a temporary surplus (a result, incidentally, which could not be achieved through import quotas, except perhaps very indirectly), and (2) to promote national self-sufficiency by reducing dependence on imports and at the same time stimulating production of domestic substitutes. The first of these two motives was undoubtedly dominant in influencing several butter-exporting countries, including Holland and Sweden, to require that all margarine sold within their

---

[22] "Europe ex-Russia remains a heavy net importer of wheat, a substantial net importer of corn, and a moderate net importer of barley, while it is largely self-contained as to rye and oats." (*Wheat Studies*, VIII [1931–32], 264.)

[23] *World Trade Barriers in Relation to American Agriculture*, pp. 391–92, and *Commerce Reports, seriatim.*

[24] *Ibid.*, August 10, 1935, p. 105.

respective areas contain a given percentage of butter.[25] Measures requiring that all gasoline sold on the domestic market contain a specified percentage of domestic alcohol frequently seek to achieve both objectives simultaneously, as we have previously noted.[26] Regulations of this sort were adopted by a large number of European countries and several Latin American countries in the years from 1930 to 1937.[27]

Since the coming into power of the Hitler regime, and especially since 1937, Germany has made rather extensive use of measures requiring the linked-utilization or pro-rated consumption of two commodities in her campaign for self-sufficiency. Japan has also employed this type of measure on a considerable scale since the outbreak of the war with China. Regulations put into effect in the latter country in late 1937 and the first half of 1938 provided for the mixing of staple (i.e., an artificial) fibre in cotton and woolen textiles *intended for domestic consumption.* The percentages of staple fibre required were gradually increased, eventually reaching 50 per cent for woolen goods, while the use of raw cotton in the production of goods for the domestic market was banned.[28] In this way, supplies of imported raw cotton and wool could be conserved for use in the

[25] Similarly, a lard-exporting country, Denmark, required the compulsory mixing of lard with domestic margarine and prohibited the importation of margarine, following an increase in the German duty on lard which adversely affected Danish exports. (*Ibid.,* July 8, 1933, p. 27.)

[26] Cf. p. 290 above.

[27] The percentage of alcohol required ranges, for the most part, from 5 per cent to 25 per cent. In Italy, where domestic alcohol production was far from sufficient to permit the addition of alcohol to all imported gasoline at the rate prescribed, the regulations adopted in 1931 included some interesting and unusual features. Sufficient alcohol, 99.6 degrees pure, was to be mixed with gasoline, at the rate of 20 per cent by volume, to consume one-fourth of the annual domestic production of alcohol. Ninety-five per cent of this alcohol was to be reserved for sale to gasoline importers, the remainder for domestic producers of artificial carburants. It was estimated that on this basis domestic alcohol production would yield only enough alcohol to be mixed with 40,000 out of the 500,000 metric tons of gasoline imported annually. (*Commerce Reports,* February 29, 1932, p. 515.)

[28] The regulations applied to cotton yarns, cotton goods, and cotton hosiery and to woolen yarns and cloth. (*Commerce Reports, seriatim.*) By the middle

export industries or for military purposes. In order to enforce
the cotton regulations, however, the Government had to inaugurate rigid control of all domestic dealings in cotton goods
manufactured for export.[29] Indeed, these requirements are now
simply part of an elaborate commodity mobilization scheme,
involving drastic import restrictions, price-fixing, rationing of
domestic consumption, and governmental supervision of production. Raw cotton is not the only material which may not be
used at all for various purposes regarded as unimportant from
a military point of view. Germany has had a similar program
and, moreover, has revived the practice followed during the
World War of requiring that various inferior ingredients be
used, in specified proportions, in the making of flour and
bread.[30]

In some cases, governments do not require actual linked
utilization, but merely linked purchasing of foreign and domestic materials. Linked-purchasing regulations generally take
the form of rendering importation of the foreign product contingent on the purchase of a specified amount of the same or
some other domestic product. Latvia has made considerable
use of this type of measure. Thus, late in 1931, permission to
import foreign sugar was made contingent on the purchase of
ten tons of Latvian-refined sugar from the Government-owned
sugar mill for every ton of foreign sugar to be imported.[31] Imports of wheat and wheat products, rye and rye products, and
certain fats and fatty acids were made subject to similar regu-

---

of 1938 manufacturers of woolen textiles were required to mix staple fibre or
other fibrous material, exclusive of raw cotton, with their wool at the rate
of 50 per cent or more. (*Ibid.*, July 23, 1938, p. 645.)

[29] *Ibid.*, January 15, 1938, p. 52, and July 9, 1938, p. 604.

[30] As matters stood in May, 1938, millers were required to add at least 7
per cent (and might add as much as 10 per cent) corn flour to all wheat flour.
In the case of rye flour, 3 per cent potato starch meal and 3 per cent potato
meal had to be added. Extraction rates were prescribed, and neither wheat nor
rye could be used for feed or for distillation purposes in Germany. (*Wheat
Studies*, XIV [1937–38], 322 n.)

[31] *Commerce Reports*, December 21, 1931, p. 696.

lations.[32] Measures of this sort are simpler and probably, on the whole, easier to enforce than those which call for linked utilization of foreign and domestic products. They have in some cases been employed in place of linked-utilization regulations to encourage domestic cinema industries.[33]

Several governments have been granted a general power to introduce linked-purchasing regulations. The Spanish Government, for instance, was authorized early in 1935 to compel importers of products subject to quotas to purchase similar Spanish merchandise. In the administration of certain of her import quotas, Switzerland has followed a practice of granting additional or "concessional" licenses to importers or to foreign exporters on the basis of their purchases of like Swiss products.[34]

On the whole, outside of Germany and Japan, linked-utilization and linked-purchasing regulations play a relatively minor rôle in comparison with other forms of import restriction, even in the case of agricultural products. In view of the fact that they can be employed to accomplish certain objectives which the more direct import restrictions are incapable of achieving, however, they have gradually received a somewhat wider use as time has gone on, chiefly *in conjunction with* other control measures.

[32] *Ibid., seriatim.*

[33] One can conceive of cases, however, in which linked-purchasing regulations would not be very effective in stimulating the consumption of domestic at the expense of foreign products. Thus, if wheat importers were required to purchase a given amount of domestic wheat for every unit of foreign wheat imported, but no check were made on their subsequent disposal of the domestic wheat, it might be possible for them to satisfy the requirements by purchasing and reselling wheat which would eventually find its way back into the feed market for which it would have been destined in any event.

[34] In 1936, an importer of British cycle saddles, for example, was given, in addition to his basic quota, a concessional quota in proportion to his extra purchases of Swiss saddles. See H. L. Setchell, *Economic Conditions in Switzerland, March, 1936,* p. 22, and *Report on Economic and Commercial Conditions in Switzerland, May, 1938,* pp. 19–20 (Great Britain, Department of Overseas Trade, Reports No. 640 and 706 [London, 1936 and 1938]).

3. *Import Monopolies*

Under an import monopoly, the exclusive right to import a given commodity or group of commodities is granted to the government or to an agency designated by the government. In establishing such a monopoly, a government may be seeking to achieve one or more of a number of objectives:

a. The securing of government revenue. The tobacco and salt monopolies which have functioned for years in various countries both in Europe and outside of Europe, and which apply to domestic sales as well as to importation and/or exportation, have been regarded primarily as revenue-producing agencies. We shall not be concerned with this type of monopoly, for most of those in existence are of long standing.

b. The securing of economies of large-scale buying (especially important in the cases of commodities procured entirely from abroad). Whether a government import monopoly can actually secure substantial economies is a matter which has been much debated. In any event, this consideration seems to have been of little importance in recent years as a factor leading to the establishment of import monopolies, although it was certainly employed as an argument in favor of centralized importing during the World War.

c. Protection of the domestic producer without placing too heavy a burden on the domestic consumer. In order to carry out this objective, a monopoly is usually given control of domestic transactions as well as of imports. In the case of certain European import monopolies for agricultural commodities, a policy of the following sort has been worked out: the monopoly purchases the entire domestic supply of the commodity at a price well above the world price, imports a certain amount at the world price, and sells to the domestic processor at a price somewhere between the two. Over the long run, it hopes to cover its expenses and to show, at the most, moderate profits. Clearly, other things being equal, the burden on the consumer, under such a scheme, will tend to be relatively small where imports are large in relation to domestic production. Any economies of large-scale buying secured by the monopoly are, of course, all to the good.

It was this sort of policy which the Swiss Grain Monopoly followed during the nineteen-twenties, which the Norwegian Grain

Monopoly followed after it was reorganized under a law of 1928, and which has been pursued to some extent by certain of the import monopolies set up since 1930.

   d. Regulation of the volume and sources of imports, with a view to domestic price-stabilization, while avoiding some of the rigidities and other undesirable features of import quota systems. As compared with an import quota or licensing system, a government import monopoly is a flexible instrument for regulating the volume of imports, especially if the flow of imports is to be carefully adjusted in such a way as to permit the maintenance of a fixed price on the domestic market. All the difficult problems connected with distributing import licenses among the various importing firms can be avoided. The government monopoly need not purchase from exporting countries in proportion to the shares contributed by them in some previous period but may purchase strictly on a price and quality basis if it so desires. On the other hand, it will prove a very convenient mechanism for a government which wishes to determine the sources of its imports largely with an eye to commercial bargaining or political considerations. Finally, profits resulting from the restriction of imports (corresponding to the quota-profits which arise under an import quota system) can be prevented from accruing entirely to importers (as they are likely to do under a quota system unless taxed away by a system of license fees). The monopoly can either pass such profits on to consumers in the form of a lower price, as previously indicated, or can retain them, to turn them over eventually to the public treasury or to place them in a special fund for some such purpose as the subsidization of domestic producers of the commodity in question.

   e. Complete integration of control of domestic transactions and of imports. As we have already had occasion to point out, European agricultural control schemes have involved, in a number of instances, granting to the same agency a monopoly control over domestic transactions and imports.

A number of the so-called import monopolies which have been set up in recent years have not actually exercised the sole right to import but merely the sole right to issue licenses to importers. Where this practice is followed, most of the attributes of monopolistic buying are usually absent, and many of the rigidities of an ordinary import licensing system are retained. We shall use the term *import-regulating* monopoly to refer to a control body of this type, with the understanding that monopolistic purchasing is not necessarily implied and that the powers of such bodies vary considerably from country to country. In most cases, these import-regulating monopolies determine from time to time the volume of imports needed in order to carry out an internal price-regulating program and issue licenses to individual importers accordingly.

Outright monopolies or import-regulating monopolies for wheat and flour imports were fairly common on the Continent of Europe by the summer of 1939, while in a number of cases some sort of monopoly control applied to other types of cereals as well. In Norway, as we have seen, the wartime grain monopoly was never altogether given up, though private traders were permitted to import grains from 1927 to 1929, when the import monopoly was re-established.[35] The Swiss Grain Monopoly was abandoned in 1929, to be followed by a compromise between a monopoly and free market system. In 1933, the Swiss Grains and Feedstuffs Coöperative Society was given the exclusive right (1) to issue permits for the import of wheat and rye and (2) to import other cereals.[36] Between the beginning of 1929 and the end of 1936, import monopolies for grain were established by Estonia, Sweden (later abandoned), Latvia, and Czechoslovakia, while Portugal, Italy, and France set up import monopolies for wheat. In Germany and the Netherlands, all agricultural imports of any importance have been controlled through import-regulating monopolies. Sweden, Denmark, and Latvia have rendered the importation of sugar subject to a state monopoly.[37]

[35] Cf. p. 286 above; C. L. Paus, *Economic Conditions in Norway, March, 1932*, Great Britain, Department of Overseas Trade, Report No. 514 (London, 1932), p. 28; and *Board of Trade Journal*, CXXI (1928), 54.

[36] *Commerce Reports*, May 20, 1933, p. 318.

[37] *World Trade Barriers in Relation to American Agriculture*, p. 351, and *Commerce Reports*, March 7, 1932, pp. 578–79. See also "Government Measures for the Relief of Agriculture in Sweden since 1930," Svenska Handelsbanken, *Index*, Supplement, March, 1939, p. 14.

Import monopolies have been established for certain non-agricultural commodities in the years since 1930. Italy rendered the importation of coal, coke, copper, tin, and nickel subject to a state monopoly in 1935 and, toward the end of 1938, adopted the same policy with respect to foreign motion picture films.[38] Several Latin American countries have set up import monopolies for gasoline or for petroleum and petroleum products.[39] In Iceland, the importation of a miscellaneous group of commodities has been monopolized by the government.[40] As in the case of agricultural commodities, these monopolies are usually associated with governmental control of internal prices and marketing.

Switzerland, Estonia, (formerly) Czechoslovakia, and a few other countries have granted the exclusive right to issue licenses for the importation of certain specified commodities to syndicates of importers or of importers and producers. This practice has been followed primarily in connection with imports of foodstuffs and certain highly important minerals or mineral products, such as coal and petroleum. Its purpose in most cases, apparently, has been to facilitate diversion of important foreign purchases to those exporting countries which the government found it desirable to favor in the light of "bilateral balancing" or other commercial bargaining considerations.[41]

On the whole, the proportion of world trade which has actually been carried on by governmental monopolies has been

[38] *Commerce Reports*, August 10, 1935, p. 105, and October 15, 1938, p. 917.

[39] Thus, Chile established a state monopoly for the importation and distribution of petroleum and petroleum products in 1932, while Costa Rica rendered the importation of gasoline subject to governmental monopoly in the same year. (*Ibid.*, May 30, 1932, p. 540, and January 21, 1933, p. 44.)

[40] In 1935, monopolies were set up for imports of matches and cigarette paper, electrical equipment, and seedling shrubs or seeds, while vegetables were added to the list in 1936. (*Ibid.*, February 16, 1935, p. 111; June 8, 1935, p. 384; June 22, 1935, p. 418; and June 27, 1936, p. 508.)

[41] Cf. Heuser, *Control of International Trade*, p. 180. Cf., also, H. C. A. Carpenter, *Economic Conditions in Switzerland* (dated December, 1933), Great Britain, Department of Overseas Trade, Report No. 568 (London, 1934), p. 42, on the Swiss Government's reasons for setting up central purchasing boards for various articles of prime necessity.

relatively insignificant, whether we are referring to imports or to exports. Broadly speaking the conduct of foreign trade in capitalist countries has remained in private hands. Only in Soviet Russia has a relatively complete state monopoly of foreign trade been established, and even here capitalist devices such as tariffs and import licenses have played some part in determining the quantity of imports and in controlling the activities of the firms which have been granted governmental monopolies of the trade in their respective commodities.[42] Iran (Persia) rendered all foreign trade subject to a state monopoly in 1931, but much of the trade has actually been conducted by private firms, subject to the securing, in the case of imports, of permits which have been issued by the Government on a rigid "bilateral balancing" basis.[43] It is worth noting in this connection, however, that German foreign trade has recently been controlled and directed by the state almost as completely as Russian foreign trade, even though no general state monopoly has been proclaimed and the actual conduct of trade has remained largely in private hands.[44] This has been true also of the foreign trade of Japan and, to a somewhat less extent, of that of Italy.

Let us consider, first, the European agricultural import monopolies which have taken over the actual importation of the commodities under their jurisdiction. These monopolies have, I believe without exception, been established in connection with programs of agricultural protectionism. Furthermore, in all instances, a considerable degree of control over

[42] Any detailed discussion of the organization of foreign trade in the Soviet Union must remain outside the scope of this book. A good general survey, together with a bibliography, may be found in K. W. Kapp, *Planwirtschaft und Aussenhandel* (Geneva, 1936). See also J. D. Yanson, *Foreign Trade in the U.S.S.R.* (London, 1934).

[43] Cf. Kapp, *op. cit.*, pp. 133–34. For texts of the Trade Monopoly Law of Feburary 25, 1931, and of the Supplementary Law of March 11, 1931, see *Board of Trade Journal*, CXXVI (1931), 574–76.

[44] Cf. A. Feiler, "International Trade under Totalitarian Governments," *Social Research*, V (1938), 424–41.

internal prices and marketing is exercised. In fact, in the usual case, the monopoly has exclusive control over dealings on the domestic market as well as over imports. Internal prices are fixed, and it is the task of the monopoly to control the flow of imports in such a way as to assist in the enforcement of the official domestic prices.

The monopolies differ considerably, however, in the degree of protection which they are designed to afford the domestic producer, and in the extent to which they permit the domestic consumer to benefit from the fact that world prices are lower than domestic prices. Protection of the foreign exchange position is an important consideration in some countries but not in others. Furthermore, if the country is actively interested in distributing its purchases among exporting countries in accordance with "bilateral balancing" objectives or political aims, the monopoly's purchasing policies are almost certain to be affected.

The degree of self-sufficiency which France has attained with respect to wheat is such that the French National Wheat Office may be expected to import only occasionally or in unusual circumstances. In fact, in normal times, exports (over which it also has control) may be expected to concern it more than imports. The Czechoslovakian Grain Monopoly faced a similar situation during its period of existence. The success which has finally attended Mussolini's "Battle of the Grain" means, presumably, that the Italian wheat monopoly is not likely to import large amounts of wheat in ordinary years. Because of its relatively long history, and because of the fact that it has imported on a significant scale, we shall turn our attention to the Norwegian Grain Monopoly.

The principles under which the Norwegian Grain Monopoly operates (August, 1939) were laid down in a law passed in 1928. The state grain trade was to be managed by a director appointed by the King and a council appointed by Parliament. The latter was to consist of seven members, of which four were to be representatives of co-operative organizations, two of consumers' societies, and two of farmers' societies.[45]

The Monopoly purchases all domestic-grown wheat, rye, barley, and oats offered to it by producers at prices somewhat above world prices for grain of corresponding quality. It has the exclusive right to import (or export) any of these grains or their ground products, and, in exercising this right, it imports at world market prices such quantities of grain or flour as are necessary to meet the requirements of the country. Millers must purchase grain and sell flour at prices fixed by the Monopoly. In fixing the selling price of flour, the Monopoly works on the principle that it shall cover its expenses and earn a moderate profit.[46] The law provides that profits are to be used "to provide for a price-regulating fund, operation fund, or other funds, and for necessary establishments and expansion, or otherwise for the promotion of the activities of the grain monopoly."[47] It would seem that Norwegian consumers, while bearing the burden of the premium (over and above the world price) paid to domestic producers, are nevertheless allowed to benefit to some extent from the fact that foreign wheat is available at lower world prices. Accordingly, they presumably fare better under this system than they would under an import quota system so administered as to yield a corresponding degree of protection to domestic producers.

In purchasing foreign grain and flour, the Monopoly receives offers submitted daily by resident agents of grain exporters and flour millers.[48] It aims, in general, to purchase at the lowest possible price and to take full advantage of market fluctuations.[49] While it was reported in 1936 that the purchasing power of the Grain Monopoly had evidently been utilized to

[45] Royal Institute of International Affairs, *World Agriculture,* p. 192. See also *World Trade Barriers in Relation to American Agriculture,* p. 452.
[46] *Commercial Intelligence Journal,* LIX (1938), 297.
[47] *World Trade Barriers in Relation to American Agriculture,* p. 453.
[48] *Commercial Intelligence Journal,* LIX (1938), 297.
[49] *Ibid.*

some extent in order to secure concessions for Norwegian exports,[50] one gathers that this sort of consideration has been given much less weight by the Norwegian monopoly than by many others.[51]

Turning now to import-regulating monopolies, let us consider first the system in force in the Netherlands, where state monopoly control has been extended to include imports of all agricultural commodities of any importance under the terms of a series of general enabling acts, including the Wheat Act of 1931, the Dairy Crisis Act of 1932, the Hog Crisis Act of 1932, and, finally, the Agricultural Crisis Act of 1933. The internal marketing, as well as the importation and exportation of all important agricultural products, has been rendered subject to centralized control, exercised by agencies or *Centrales,* each of which has been granted monopoly powers with respect to a group of commodities. The actual degree of control employed varies from commodity to commodity. The monopolies are semi-public institutions, administered by representatives of producers' and dealers' associations but subject to strict governmental control and supervision.

In general, the aim of the control schemes has been to bring about the payment of remunerative prices to domestic agricultural producers who, as a result of the drastic decline in world prices during the depression, were suffering severe losses. In the attempt to raise and maintain Dutch prices above world prices, reliance has been placed on a number of regulatory devices, the details of the control scheme varying for the different commodities. Subsidies, mixing regulations, excise and processing taxes, import monopoly fees, official intervention in agricultural markets, outright price-fixing, and, in some cases, production control have all played their parts. The revenue

[50] Cf. C. L. Paus, *Report on Economic and Commercial Conditions in Norway,* June, 1936, Great Britain, Department of Overseas Trade, Report No. 657 (London, 1936), p. 5.

[51] This is the opinion expressed by wheat experts of the Food Research Institute of Stanford University.

derived from the various fees and taxes contributes to a general Agricultural Crisis Fund, from which subsidies are paid and administrative expenses met.[52]

For our purpose, primary interest attaches to the system of "import monopoly fees" which is governed by the terms of the Agricultural Crisis Act of 1933, as subsequently amended. The monopolies or *Centrales* do not, in general, make foreign purchases directly but, rather, exercise the sole right to issue permits for importation. Fees, varying in amount for each commodity, are charged for the issue of licenses. In the case of commodities produced to some extent in the Netherlands, the fee must, in accordance with the terms of the Agricultural Crisis Act, be high enough to remove as far as possible the difference between the world price of the product and the domestic price, in so far as such difference may result from the operation of the various control measures.[53] Fees are also applied to certain commodities not produced in the Netherlands, but regarded as competitive with Dutch products.[54]

In attempting to comply with the terms of the Agricultural Crisis Act, the monopolies have naturally been obliged to alter their permit fees frequently in response to changes in world prices.[55] The fees have also been the subject of negotiation be-

[52] For the terms of the various enabling acts, see the following publications of the International Institute of Agriculture: *Annuaire internationale de legislation agricole*, XXI–XXIII (1931–1933); *The Agricultural Situation in 1932–33*, pp. 245–57; and *The World Agricultural Situation in 1934–35*, pp. 409–19. See also *World Trade Barriers in Relation to American Agriculture*, pp. 437–47; *Foreign Agriculture*, I (1937), 88–97; and the British Department of Overseas Trade Reports on economic conditions in the Netherlands. For an excellent survey of the wheat control scheme, see Schiller, *op. cit.*

[53] International Institute of Agriculture, *Annuaire internationale de legislation agricole*, XXIII (1933), 485–86, and *Commerce Reports*, October 7, 1933, p. 237.

[54] U. S. Tariff Commission, *Concessions Granted by the United States in the Trade Agreement with the Kingdom of the Netherlands* (Washington, 1936), p. XXV.

[55] The alterations, however, have tended to lag behind changes in world prices to some extent. (U. S. Department of Commerce, *The Netherlands: Basic Data on Import Trade and Trade Barriers, Part A, Factors Affecting Imports from the United States* [Washington, 1935], p. 31.)

tween the Dutch and foreign governments. The latter have
tended to regard these fees as analogous to tariffs in their effects
and have secured concessions in the form of fee reductions,
usually for limited quantities of imports, in commercial treaties.[56] In so far as all applications for import permits are satisfied, subject only to the requirement that the fee be paid—and
this is apparently the practice followed at least in some cases—
the fees constitute the active import-restricting agent, operating
somewhat like tariffs. In so far as the monopolies limit the issue
of permits quantitatively, the active import-restricting agent
may be this quantitative limitation; in such a case, everything
depends on the relationship between the height of the fee and
the volume of imports permitted. So far as the effect on the
home market is concerned, this distinction is not particularly
vital. The crucial point is that the Dutch agricultural control
measures envisage the maintenance of a relatively stable, and,
for some commodities, a definitely fixed, price on the home
market. Changes in world market prices are not, in general,
allowed to affect Dutch agricultural prices. Consequently, the
monopoly fees, which are subject to frequent alterations, do
not, like tariffs of the ordinary type, preserve the price-link
between domestic and foreign markets. To the extent that the
fees are "bound" in commercial treaties, the freedom of the
Dutch authorities to pursue a policy of internal price stability
may be somewhat limited, although, where the concessions
apply only to specified quantities of imports, this is not necessarily the case. It should be noted, moreover, that certain
agricultural imports are subject to ordinary quotas or are
affected by mixing regulations. In any event, it would seem that
the Dutch consumer fares much as he would under an import
licensing system, bearing the full burden of the restriction of
imports; while the Government appropriates all "quota-profits"

---

[56] It is the view of Schiller (*op. cit.*, p. 366) that the monopoly fees were
rightly handled as tariffs in the Trade Agreement of December 20, 1935, between the United States and the Netherlands.

secured by importers through what amounts to an import license fee. It is primarily the agricultural producers who, by receiving subsidies from the proceeds of monopoly fees, benefit from the existence of price-differentials between Dutch and world markets for their products.

Although it was reported in 1935, that, as a general rule, reductions of monopoly fees granted in commercial agreements were not applicable to imports from third countries,[57] there have been instances since that time in which such concessions have been extended to countries entitled to most-favored-nation treatment.[58] The Dutch Government has also undertaken, in commercial treaties, to purchase from its treaty partner designated quantities of imports of commodities subject to import monopoly control.[59]

The German import monopolies resemble the corresponding Dutch institutions in some, but not all, respects. In Germany, as in Holland, the primary aim of the control scheme has been support of internal prices, but outright price-fixing has proceeded farther than in Holland and has been made applicable to all agricultural commodities of any importance.[60] Imports

---

[57] U. S. Department of Commerce, *The Netherlands: Basic Data on Import Trade and Trade Barriers, Part A, Factors Affecting Imports from the United States*, p. 44.

[58] Thus, the conventional monopoly fee established on limited quantities of apple and pear imports in the American Agreement was extended to countries entitled to most-favored-nation treatment, applying in each case to the quantity of imports of these commodities from the country in question in 1934, except in the case of Great Britain, for which a total of 1500 metric tons was established. (*Commerce Reports*, April 17, 1937, p. 321.)

[59] In the American Agreement, the Netherlands undertook to purchase annually from the United States a quantity of wheat flour equivalent to not less than 5 per cent of the annual total wheat flour consumption in the Netherlands and a quantity of milling wheat equivalent to not less than 5 per cent of the annual total consumption of foreign milling wheat in the Netherlands. These undertakings were subject to the proviso that the prices of said products delivered in the Netherlands should be competitive with the prices of products of comparable grade and quality from other foreign sources. (*Reciprocal Trade Agreement between the United States of America and the Netherlands*, U. S. Executive Agreement Series, No. 100 [Washington, 1937], p. 50.)

[60] Cf. W. Abel, "Der Preis in der landwirtschaftlichen Marktordnung," *Jahrbücher für Nationalökonomie und Statistik*, CXLV (1937), 22–23.

are centralized in the hands of public bureaus (*Reichsstellen*), established at various dates from 1930, and especially from 1933, on. The control mechanism was developed in connection with the Corn Monopoly, which was set up in 1930 and served as a model for the monopolies inaugurated at later dates. Although this office was granted the exclusive right to introduce corn into internal circulation in Germany, it functioned in practice by requiring importers to offer to it all corn purchased for importation, for which it paid the "monopoly purchase price," i.e., the foreign price (c.i.f. German port, or free on rail, frontier station) plus the duty. This corn was immediately resold to the importer at the "monopoly selling price," which equalled the monopoly purchase price plus a fee or surcharge. Thus the importer in effect paid a tax which was returned to him in the form of a higher price on the internal market, and which varied in accordance with changes in the world market price of corn or in the level at which the Government wished to maintain the internal price.[61] The monopoly was, in general, expected to purchase all corn offered to it, although it was not obliged to do so, and was not permitted to import corn itself except under unusual circumstances.[62]

Under the present arrangement (August, 1939), once the importer of a commodity subject to monopoly control has paid his tax and received a so-called "acceptance certificate" from the appropriate *Reichsstelle,* he must apply for a foreign exchange certificate.[63] From 1933 on, moreover, the *Reichsstellen* took over the actual importation of agricultural commodities to a significant extent.[64] In so far as the importer is still permitted to function, his activities are much more narrowly circum-

[61] The monopoly was set up to get around the terms of a commercial treaty with Yugoslavia which prevented any increase in the corn duty. (*World Trade Barriers in Relation to American Agriculture,* p. 387.)

[62] On all this, cf. *ibid.,* p. 387, and *Board of Trade Journal,* CXXIV (1930), 461–62, and CXXX (1933), 610–11.

[63] Cf. *Commerce Reports,* November 14, 1936, p. 917.

[64] Cf. B. Mehrens, *Die Marktordnung des Reichsnährstandes* (Berlin, 1938), p. 43.

scribed than under the Dutch system. The *Reichsstelle* dictates from whom he is to purchase, to whom he may sell, the price which he may charge, and the profit which he may retain for himself.[65] In other words imports must go through a so-called "sluice" (*Schleuse*) before reaching the domestic market.

With regard to the sources of German imports, the net effect has been that such factors as the available supply of foreign exchange and the state of Germany's trade balance with individual countries have played an important rôle in determining the quantities and geographical sources of Germany's agricultural imports. In addition, Germany has made many commitments in bilateral agreements as to the quotas of specified agricultural commodities which she will purchase from this or that country and the prices which she will pay for them. The centralization of control in the hands of the *Reichsstellen* has, in fact, facilitated the carrying out of the German policy, mentioned in earlier chapters,[66] of paying relatively high prices for agricultural imports from certain countries in order to stimulate the sale of German export products under clearing and compensation arrangements.[67] In view of the fact that German prices for many agricultural commodities have been substantially higher than world prices, the *Reichsstellen* have been in a position to pay more than the world price, for purposes of commercial policy, when exercising their power to import directly. Clearly, a similar path is open to any import monopoly operating in a situation in which the domestic price exceeds the world price by more than transportation costs.

Import monopolies constitute an excellent means of evading the obligations of the most-favored-nation clause, which was never intended to apply to them and cannot, in any satisfactory

---

[65] Cf. *Commercial Intelligence Journal*, LIX (1938), 78.

[66] Cf. p. 161 above.

[67] Cf. Mehrens, *op. cit.*, p. 45. It should be noted that, even before 1933, discrimination was exercised by the Corn Monopoly through a schedule of fees which resulted in preferential treatment for Danubian corn. (*World Trade Barriers in Relation to American Agriculture*, p. 387.)

manner, be made to do so. In the American Reciprocal Trade
Agreements, clauses have been inserted to the effect that monopolies shall, in making their foreign purchases, "accord the
commerce of the other country fair and equitable treatment"
and shall, apart from quantitative limitations permitted in the
Agreements, "be influenced solely by competitive considerations, such as price, quality, marketability, and terms of sale." [68]
Obviously, such clauses are difficult to enforce; but we shall
have more to say about this problem in Chapter XII.

In conclusion, it would seem that the economic meaning of
import monopolies depends largely on how they are set up and
administered. A monopoly which actually exercises its exclusive
right to handle foreign purchases *can* be administered in such
a way as to afford a given degree of protection to the domestic
producer without penalizing the consumer as much as would
an ordinary import quota system administered in such a way
as to yield the same degree of protection to producers. It can,
moreover, distribute its purchases among exporting countries
purely on a price and quality basis, thereby permitting trade to
follow the lines of comparative advantage (in so far as it imports at all) more effectively than would the usual type of
import quota system. On the other hand, differently administered, it could be turned into a very effective instrument for
exploiting the domestic consumer and discriminating among
supplying countries.

Import-regulating monopolies of the Dutch type bear considerable resemblance to an import licensing system under
which quota-profits are taxed away by an appropriate schedule
of license fees. The German system goes considerably farther
in the direction of state control of foreign purchases, leaving
little, if any, initiative to the private importer.

[68] *Reciprocal Trade Agreement between the United States of America and
the Netherlands,* p. 16.

4. *Import Prohibitions*

Before leaving the subject of import restrictions, let us consider briefly the part played by import prohibitions. An outright prohibition of imports is, of course, a more drastic measure than the imposition of a licensing requirement and, accordingly, tends to be employed less frequently. Though common enough during the mercantilist period, import prohibitions were scarcely used during the latter half of the nineteenth century except where protection of the public health or morality was involved. The War and early post-War years were characterized by a vigorous revival of import prohibitions, imposed to defend the currency or purely as protectionist measures, although, as we have seen, the so-called import prohibitions of the War period were not usually outright prohibitions.[69] During the period of currency stability from 1925 on, import prohibitions tended to disappear; the fact that a number of European countries ratified the abortive International Convention for the Abolition of Import and Export Prohibitions and Restrictions, concluded in 1928, acted as a restraining influence for a time, while bilateral commercial treaties embodied, in many cases, undertakings not to impose prohibitions on imports from the other country except where necessary for the protection of the public health, morals, or safety. Since the beginning of 1931, outright import prohibitions have reappeared here and there, although even now there are few countries which make more than an exceptional use of this relatively drastic weapon of restriction.

The growing movement for more thorough protection of consumers has resulted in a host of measures prohibiting the importation of substandard or adulterated commodities of various sorts. One can point to various instances in which import prohibitions intended as protectionist measures have been disguised as sanitary regulations, but this is an old story; and, indeed, such subterfuges have been, to some extent, super-

---

[69] Cf. p. 10 above.

fluous in countries where unwanted imports could be effectively excluded through the operation of the foreign exchange regulations. Moreover, the withdrawal of one country after another from the 1928 Convention removed one of the sanctions against the open employment of import prohibitions.

Customs embargoes on imports of specified luxury goods have not infrequently been adopted as measures of currency defense, usually to supplement or facilitate the enforcement of exchange control regulations.[70] For the rest, import prohibitions have invariably had a protectionist aim of one sort or another. Sometimes, the embargo applies to a commodity which competes with some important domestic product.[71] In at least one instance, the object was to forestall the appearance of technological unemployment, through an embargo on the importation of machines which would displace workers.[72] Temporary import prohibitions have served, in a number of cases, to prevent the rush of imports which ordinarily takes place just previous to the coming into effect of an increased customs duty.[73] One of the more interesting of the embargoes endowed with a protectionist purpose was a measure put into force by the French Government in 1937, whereby imports of a number

[70] Iceland prohibited the importation of a list of articles, mostly of a luxury nature, in October, 1931. (*Commerce Reports,* November 2, 1931, p. 287.) Bolivia has imposed temporary embargoes on various luxury items off and on during recent years, the measures originating during the Gran Chaco War. (*Ibid., seriatim.*) Germany made rather extensive use of import prohibitions on raw materials from March, 1934, to the introduction of the "New Plan" in September of the same year. (*Ibid.*)

[71] Thus Denmark's efforts to stimulate the domestic consumption of lard, already mentioned in a previous connection, involved not only a regulation requiring the mixing of lard in domestic margarine, but also a prohibition on imports of margarine. Cf. p. 298 n. above.

[72] I refer here to a measure introduced by El Salvador in May, 1931, reputedly at the request of a printers' union, prohibiting the importation of linotypes and other similar machines. (*Commerce Reports,* July 20, 1931, p. 18.)

[73] Toward the end of 1933, Sweden prohibited the importation of corn, grain, and other feedstuffs, pending the adoption of taxes on such imports and regulations requiring that they be mixed with domestically produced grains. (*Ibid.,* January 6, 1934, p. 12.)

of products into France *by land* were prohibited, unless they could be proved to have been carried directly from the country of origin. Assistance of French ports was the object, and exceptions could be made only by international agreement.[74]

The effect of import prohibitions, of course, in the case of a commodity produced to some extent or capable of production at home, is to divorce the domestic price completely from the world price, rendering it dependent entirely on domestic supply and demand conditions. Wherever the decisions of a foreign exchange control board result in the effective exclusion of foreign commodities from the domestic market, the same result is secured. "Effective import prohibitions" of this type were common during the period of acute exchange scarcity and have played an important rôle in such countries as Italy, Germany, and Japan in recent years.

[74] *Ibid.*, March 12, 1938, p. 251.

CHAPTER XI

Export Promotion and Control

One way of attempting to "improve" the balance of trade is to restrict imports; another way, obviously, is to stimulate exports. Governments have not hesitated to use both types of approach in recent years. The pressure for governmental aid to individual export industries, moreover, has been almost as insistent as the clamor for protection to industries suffering from the competition of imports from abroad. The degree of interdependence between the two types of developments cannot be over-emphasized. The difficulty of disposing of export surpluses was greatly intensified for all countries by the multiplication of import barriers elsewhere; while, on the other hand, protectionist policies at home tended to have the effect of maintaining or increasing costs of production for the export industries, thereby giving rise to an argument for assistance to exports. As we noted in the preceding chapter, moreover, certain countries which had been on an import basis with respect to wheat or other agricultural commodities found themselves, after several years of highly restrictive import policies, developing export surpluses which could not be sold on world markets except at substantial losses. It need only be added that dumped exports could be very effectively prevented from flowing back to a home market which was protected by a rigid import license system.

Export promotion has assumed a variety of forms, direct and indirect. The various ways in which exchange-control countries manipulated or partially relaxed exchange regulations in order to permit exporters to receive exchange premia in one form or another have been discussed at length in earlier chapters. But other methods of subsidization have been extensively used by both exchange-control and free-exchange countries. The securing of concessions for exports in bilateral agreements, moreover, has assumed great prominence. In addition, the competitive position of export industries has been affected in many cases by the granting of direct and indirect production subsidies of various types. Since any attempt to cover adequately the subject of production subsidies would extend the scope of this book to unmanagable proportions and would take us out of the realm of commercial policy and into the realm of general economic policy, we shall confine ourselves to a consideration of export subsidies.

Of scarcely less importance and certainly not unrelated to the emphasis on export promotion has been the movement toward increased governmental control of exports, which, in at least certain of its aspects, represents merely an extension of a development of considerable importance during the nineteen-twenties. Permit systems have been applied to exports for a variety of purposes, including improvement of standards of quality, the promotion of orderly marketing, and limitation of the outward movement of strategic raw materials. Where one or more countries have been in a position to control a substantial proportion of the world supply of a commodity, export restrictions have been employed to raise the world price. The part played by export permits in exchange control systems has already been described, and the ease with which a control mechanism adopted in connection with exchange control may in time be utilized for purposes not strictly connected with the protection of the value of the currency does not have to be emphasized. As we had occasion to note, moreover, in our survey of clearing agreements, the struggle to balance bilateral trade between individual pairs of countries has involved the subjecting of exports, as well as of imports, to quantitative control. The so-called "bilateral" quotas have been enforced through control exercised in the exporting country. As we shall see in this and the following chapters, this trend toward bilateral trade canalization is closely related, as well, to attempts in certain countries to secure price stability for agricultural exports, and it is impossible to separate completely the subject of export promotion from that of export control.

1. *Direct Export Subsidies and Subsidization of Exports in Connection with Market Control Schemes*

a. The nature of export subsidies. Exports may be said to be officially subsidized when governmental action makes possible the sale of a good abroad at a price that is lower than the price charged for the identical good on the home market at the same time and under the same circumstances, with due allowance for differences in transportation costs.[1] Direct export subsidies have never been as popular as one might suppose, even in the mercantilist period, when governments frequently refrained from adopting them because of the financial drain involved.[2] During the course of the nineteenth century, they tended to disappear, partly as a result of the influence of free trade doctrines and partly because of a growing realization that the effects of subsidies could be offset by parallel action on the part of competing exporting countries.[3] The spread of anti-dumping legislation and its application to governmental export subsidies during the course of the present century have exercised a further restraining influence, though this legislation has

[1] I.e., we apply to governmental action the generally accepted definition of dumping. See, for example, Haberler, *The Theory of International Trade*, p. 296.

[2] Cf. J. Grunzel, *Economic Protectionism* (London and New York, 1916), p. 200.

[3] The meaningless situation created by the widespread competitive granting of export bounties on sugar, counteracted by increased protection in importing countries, led to the conclusion in 1902 of the Brussels Sugar Convention, which remained in effect until the World War. Cf. *ibid.*, pp. 207–12, and Haberler, *The Theory of International Trade*, pp. 317–18, n.

not always been strictly enforced. Clauses precluding the granting of export bounties have sometimes been inserted into commercial treaties.

During the post-War period, direct export subsidies played a relatively minor, though not a negligible rôle.[4] In the years since 1930, however, export subsidies have become a factor of considerable importance in international trade. Certain countries, including a number of agricultural-exporting countries, have utilized them in order to offset an exchange disadvantage. Agricultural exports, moreover, have been subsidized to an increasing extent through the use of sliding-scale bounties designed to assist in the maintenance of a fixed or relatively stable price on the domestic market. These sliding-scale bounties are frequently associated with schemes for centralized marketing of exports. A central marketing board may be permitted to fix a tax on domestic consumption of the commodity in question in order to finance an export bounty. Under another type of scheme, a marketing board or export monopoly fixes the price paid to domestic producers at a point well above export parity, sells to exporters (or directly to foreign importers) at export parity, and reimburses itself for the losses involved in this process by extracting a relatively high price from domestic processors or by drawing on general public funds. In this case, the subsidization is indirect, and in periods of rising world prices the marketing board may be able to minimize its losses on exports through careful timing of purchases and sales, although it is likely to lose heavily during a prolonged period of falling world prices. The payment of subsidies on agricultural exports and, in some cases, domestic price controls as well were abandoned by a number of countries in the 1936–37 season, when world prices rose until they exceeded

[4] For a brief survey of post-War production and export subsidies, see League of Nations, International Economic Conference, Documentation, *1. Direct and Indirect Subsidies; 2. Differential Taxes on Circulation, Consumption, or Handling of Foreign Imported goods; 3. Regulation of Quantities of Imports and Exports Admitted* (Geneva, 1927), pp. 10–13.

the domestic prices these countries were seeking to maintain. The price-decline which ensued during the following year led to the reconstitution of subsidization schemes and to the adoption of export subsidies by certain countries which had up to that point held aloof.

It is clear that export marketing control schemes may be adopted for a variety of purposes. Among the objectives which may conceivably be sought are reduction of marketing costs through the partial or complete elimination of middlemen's profits, spreading the flow of exports evenly over time, or enforcing standards of quality. If a country has a virtual monopoly of the world supply of a particular commodity, it may decide to introduce some sort of control over exports in an attempt to raise the world price. Where no such monopoly exists, a group of countries which together control a substantial proportion of the supply of a commodity may combine in an attempt to regulate the world price. But if no international agreement is concluded and a country must compete with other important suppliers of a given export product, it cannot hope to benefit by attempting to influence the world price upward, even if its position as a supplier is important enough to make such an attempt feasible. If it tries to raise the price on its home market, it must be prepared to lose ground as an exporter of the product or to subsidize exports. It is only with marketing schemes involving subsidization of exports that we shall be concerned in this section, and we shall emphasize the subsidization aspects of such schemes, not because the other aspects are unimportant, but because subsidies have a more serious effect on international commercial relations.

b. Some theoretical considerations. A fixed export bounty tends to raise the price on the domestic market and to depress prices on foreign markets, creating a price-differential between home and foreign markets equal to the bounty rate (after allowing for transportation costs). If the country granting the bounty is a very important world supplier of the commodity in question, the major portion of this adjustment may come about through a fall in the world price, in which case the bounty will be of little benefit to domestic producers of the commodity. Sliding-scale bounties tend to create a variable price-differential, which is likely to have a somewhat disorganizing effect on world markets if the country granting the bounty is an important supplier.

It might be argued that in the particular case in which the domestic price of a commodity is artificially fixed above the world price, an export bounty which merely compensates for this difference will not tend to depress the world price. This is not necessarily true. A great deal depends on the methods by which the internal price is supported, the nature of demand and supply conditions, the relation between the "official" price and marginal production costs at the time the measure is introduced, the importance of the country as a supplier of the world market, and various other factors. This much may be said, however. If the domestic producer is paid a price that is higher than export parity, and no attempt is made to restrict production, the policy will have the effect of encouraging the maintenance of a larger volume of domestic production than is justified in view of the world price and, at the same time, of discouraging domestic consumption. If exporters are now enabled to meet the world price with the help of subsidies, the volume of exports will tend, under most conditions, to exceed that which would take place in the absence of all governmental intervention. If a decline in the world price results, not only will subsidy rates have to be increased, but other countries will be likely to respond with subsidies of their own. We need not elaborate on the additional complications which may ensue— the resistance which domestic producers will tend to display against any attempt to lower the official price, the disadvantages encountered in world markets by domestic manufacturers or processors utilizing the commodity in question as a raw material, the need for tariffs or import restrictions to prevent re-importation of the subsidized exports, and so on. For the most part, the indirect effects will not differ in kind from those which would follow from the imposition of an ordinary subsidy. If restriction of production were involved, as it is in a few cases, it is conceivable that depression of the world price might be avoided, but this would depend in large part on how the scheme was carried out.

What can be said about export subsidies adopted to offset an exchange disadvantage? Clearly, such a policy tends to interfere with the adjustment of domestic prices to world prices; and, unless world prices rise, the country will have to face either indefinite continuation of export subsidies or eventual devaluation. In practice, a number of exchange-control countries have stimulated exports in part through direct export subsidies and in part through partial depreciation of the currency. It is sometimes difficult to ascertain from official information where one form of assistance ends and the other begins. In Germany, as we have seen, straight export subsidies eventually superseded certain of the more indirect forms of assistance. Where depreciated blocked marks of one sort or another were retained, however, as in the trade with Latin America, export subsidies apparently tended to enter into the picture *if* and *when* the discount on these special marks was not sufficient to enable the German exporter to get the business.

A further question of considerable theoretical interest arises in connection with subsidies adopted to offset an exchange disadvantage. Should all exporters be granted uniform compensation, in terms of a specified percentage of the export prices of their commodities, or not? [5]

Country A's currency may be said to be over-valued when, at current exchange rates, its price level is relatively high as

[5] This same problem arises, and can be answered in much the same terms, in connection with exchange premia, of the type utilized in Hungary and Rumania, or in connection with regulations requiring exporters of various commodities to surrender differing proportions of exchange at official rates.

compared with prices in other countries. The extent to which its prices are out of line, however, will tend to vary for different types of goods and services. Those prices which are highly sensitive to international price changes tend to adjust themselves promptly to any change in foreign prices or currency values. Other less sensitive prices tend to respond more slowly, the reaction of any given price depending on a variety of factors, e.g., the rigidity of prices of constituents entering into its cost of production, the nature of competition in the industry, etc. The degree of over-valuation, essentially an average concept, will have to be measured by comparison of some appropriate index of prices in Country A with corresponding prices in other countries;[6] but the extent to which an exporter of any given commodity suffers from an exchange disadvantage will depend on cost and demand factors in his particular industry. Hence, the granting of a uniform bounty or exchange premium does not seem altogether appropriate, especially in the early stages of over-valuation, but it would be almost impossible to find ways of measuring the exact degree of exchange disadvantage suffered by each industry. A policy which seeks to grant to every exporter a bounty or premium precisely equal to the loss he suffers in trying to meet prices charged by his foreign competitors (we have seen in Chapter V that this policy was frequently followed in connection with exchange premia, as in the case of German blocked accounts) is likely to ignore the influence of such factors as technological changes in the industry in question and may result in compensating exporters for disadvantages not connected with the over-valuation of the currency. Furthermore, whatever the theoretical niceties of the case, if the policy adopted involves

---

[6] The question as to what price index is appropriate strikes at the heart of the difficulty and has never been altogether satisfactorily settled. For two recent suggestions, see H. S. Ellis, "The Equilibrium Rate of Exchange," and S. E. Harris, "Measures of Currency Overvaluation and Stabilization," in *Explorations in Economics: Notes and Essays Contributed in Honor of F. W. Taussig* (New York and London, 1936).

the granting of a different premium for each transaction or for each industry, political pressure is likely to play an exceedingly important rôle in determining the degree of assistance received by any given firm or industry. A similar problem arises in connection with any broad subsidy program, whether connected with over-valuation or not.

It is clear that, under any circumstances, unrestrained acceptance of the principle that it is perfectly legitimate to pay a subsidy which will equalize the domestic price with the world price would lead to the *reductio ad absurdum* that any country could export any commodity it liked, subject, of course, to the limitations imposed by its ability to finance the necessary subsidies or by the willingness of domestic consumers to endure the sacrifices involved. The principle of comparative advantage would be thrown completely overboard except as a measure of the magnitude of subsidies needed by the various industries. In a sense, this is the obverse of the theory that tariffs should be imposed to equalize costs of production at home and abroad. It is intriguing to speculate as to what would happen to world trade if both principles were adopted simultaneously everywhere.

a. Export subsidies in Germany. The only industrial country that adopted direct governmental export subsidies on a wide scale during the nineteen-thirties was Germany, although toward the end of 1938 British industries were encouraged by their government to organize in order to meet German competition in foreign markets.[7] Very little official information has been available on the operation of the German scheme. Its legal basis has rested in a law of June 28, 1935, authorizing the Reich Chamber of Economics to issue regulations concerning the imposition and use of levies on groups or associa-

---

[7] Cf. *The New York Times,* December 2, 1938. Of considerable significance, too, were the conversations between British and German industrialists in the early months of 1939, looking toward the formation of agreements for the restriction of competition, but these negotiations broke off after the German invasions of Czechoslovakia in March. See *World Economic Survey, 1938–39,* p. 190.

tions of business men or concerns and concerning the collection of the levies through Chambers of Commerce and other similar bodies.[8] The purpose of the levies was not made public, but it was generally known that the funds collected were to be used for export subsidies. Industrial firms, which have borne the largest share of the burden, have paid a turnover tax of 2 per cent or more on their home sales, the rate apparently varying somewhat among different industries in proportion to net earnings.[9] According to various unofficial reports, the total levy on German banking, industrial, and commercial firms has amounted to approximately one billion marks *per annum,* or not quite 25 per cent of the total value of German exports in 1935 and rather less than this in later years.[10] Such an overall average conceals a wide variation in the proportionate amount of assistance granted on individual export transactions, for the rate of benefit has apparently varied not only from commodity to commodity but from country to country.[11] In general, an exporter has evidently received the amount required to enable him to meet foreign competition, but he has tended to receive more than this in cases in which the Government has happened to be sponsoring a campaign to increase particular branches of German trade or drive out foreign competitors in a given area. It should be remembered that, under the exchange control regime, exports have been subject to permit, and considerable government supervision has been exercised over prices quoted.[12]

[8] See *Commerce Reports,* August 3, 1935, p. 84, and *The Economist,* CXXI (1935), 13. Actually, this act merely regularized a procedure which had apparently been followed for some time previously.

[9] Cf. *ibid.,* and H. B. Killough, *International Trade* (New York and London, 1938), p. 485.

[10] The contribution of industrial firms has amounted to 700 to 800 million marks a year. (*Ibid.,* p. 486; *The Economist,* CXXXIII [1938], 694; and *The Statist,* CXXVIII [1936], 376.)

[11] Cf. Rawlins, *Economic Conditions in Germany to March, 1936,* p. 158. In the case of a patented article obtainable only in Germany or a product in which Germany has a virtual international monopoly, no subsidy whatever has been granted.

[12] Cf. p. 265 above.

The secrecy surrounding the original adoption of export subsidies was intended to forestall the application of anti-dumping duties.[13] No secret, however, was made of the fact that the 1939–40 budget contained a specific appropriation of 1,500 million marks "for the promotion of German foreign trade."[14] This was apparently to be used, at least in part, for direct subsidies, supplementing the fund raised through "voluntary" contributions from German business firms.[15]

d. Agricultural export subsidies. For the most part, export subsidies outside of Germany have applied to agriculture commodities, the producers of which are not ordinarily in a position to organize for the purpose of controlling prices or meeting foreign competition without government support or coercion. Some of the most extensive subsidization schemes have been adopted by certain of the British Dominions, where they have been associated with price-fixing and market-control programs.

[13] Cf. P. B. Taylor, "Problems of German-American Relations," *Foreign Policy Reports,* XIV (1938), 103. Business firms have not been permitted to enter contributions to the export fund as separate items in their financial statements nor to publish or transmit to foreign customers any information about subsidies received by them. (Rawlins, *op. cit.,* p. 157, and *The Statist,* CXXVIII [1936], 376.)

Germany was forced to take measures to stop the payment of public and private bounties or subsidies and the use of various types of indirect subsidization in connection with exports to the United States, in order to bring about the removal of certain countervailing duties imposed by the United States Treasury in June, 1936. (U. S. Treasury Department, Treasury Decisions, LXX [1936], 201–202 [T.D. 48479].) Later, a carefully defined compensation procedure was approved by the Treasury. (Cf. p. 182 n., above.) It was on the ground of the alleged misuse of this procedure that the Treasury justified the much wider application of countervailing duties to all dutiable imports from Germany, announced in March, 1939. The German Government, it was charged, had, in connection with compensation transactions, been causing goods imported from the United States to be sold at a premium in Germany and using the proceeds to subsidize exports to the United States. There was no implication in the Treasury announcement that German exports to the United States had been assisted under the direct subsidy program. See *The New York Times,* March 19, 1939, and *Opinions of the Attorney General of the United States,* March 18, 1939 (39 Op. 65) for the opinion rendered to the Treasury by Attorney General Murphy on the nature of German subsidies.

[14] *The New York Times,* April 4, 1939.

[15] Evidently the 1938–39 budget contained an item of 100 million marks earmarked for foreign trade promotion. (*Ibid.*)

Governmental control of the marketing of agricultural commodities was introduced in these countries during the War, or even earlier, was revived or continued on a minor scale during the nineteen-twenties, and has been greatly extended in scope since 1930. The feasibility of the inclusion of export subsidies as an integral part of certain of these control schemes has depended in part on the fact that Empire products have not been subject to anti-dumping laws in the important British market.[16]

One of the first countries to introduce direct export subsidies on a wide scale during the depression was South Africa. Adopted late in 1931, the Export Subsidies Act was intended to "assist the primary producers in the extremely difficult position brought about by a continued decline in the price level and accentuated by Great Britain's departure from the gold standard." [17] Subsidies were granted on a wide variety of primary products, including processed farm products, but excluding gold, diamonds, and sugar. It was originally intended that the measure should be purely temporary and that subsidies in general should equal 10 per cent of the f.o.b. value; but actually the measure was renewed year after year until 1937, while shortly after the adoption of the act, amendments were put through to permit subsidies up to 25 per cent, or 35 per cent in the case of beef and mutton.[18] Certain modifications were made following South Africa's departure from the gold standard at the end of 1932, and from May, 1934, on the rates were reduced at intervals until the scheme was finally abandoned in 1937. Meanwhile, however, more and more of South Africa's agricultural export commodities became subject to market-control schemes involving the payment of bounties on exports. A few of these schemes dated back to the nineteen-

[16] Cf. p. 217 n., above, on the British anti-dumping legislation.
[17] Quotation from Hansard, XVIII, 39, as cited in *Official Year Book of the Union of South Africa*, 1931–32, p. 1058.
[18] *Ibid.*, 1938, p. 786; *Commercial Intelligence Journal*, XLV (1931), 952–53; and *Board of Trade Journal*, CXXVII (1931), 583.

twenties, but most of them were adopted after the outbreak of the depression. They have been administered by control boards which have exercised varying degrees of power over the marketing of the commodities under their jurisdiction. In most cases, internal production, processing, or transactions taxes have been levied on the commodity in question and the proceeds used, at least in part, for export bounties. In some cases, internal prices have been fixed; in others, compulsory export quotas, designed to bring about the export of a larger proportion of domestic production than would be exported under the normal operation of market forces, have been established.[19] Whatever the methods used, the effect has been to maintain the domestic price above export parity, so that in most cases subsidies have had to be paid if exports were to continue. As might be expected, duties have had to be levied on imports of the commodities concerned to prevent the reimport of subsidized exports. Under the Marketing Act of 1937, a broad enabling measure, provision was made whereby new control boards might be set up without special legislation.[20]

In New Zealand, the primary aims of market control schemes for export products have been elimination or limitation of competition among individual exporters, regulation of the flow of exports, and improvement of the quality of New Zealand products.[21] Although some degree of price-regulation has been attempted, price-discrimination between home and foreign markets has not, on the whole, been a characteristic of the New Zealand system of control, at least until recently. Passage of the Primary Products Marketing Act by the Labor Government in 1936, however, marked the beginning of a new approach to New Zealand's export problem. Up to the outbreak

---

[19] Cf. *Foreign Agriculture,* I (1937), pp. 72 ff.

[20] South Africa, Department of Agriculture and Forestry, *The Marketing Act, 1937, in Summary* (Pretoria, mimeo., 1937).

[21] Cf. R. G. Hampton, "Export Control Boards in New Zealand," in W. L. Holland, ed., *Commodity Control in the Pacific Area* (Stanford University, 1935), especially pp. 333–34.

of war in 1939, the provisions of the Act had been applied only to the dairy industry, but a broader application was contemplated. Under the new scheme, exports of butter and cheese were made a government monopoly, to be handled by the Primary Products Marketing Department. The Government paid dairy farmers fixed prices for butter and cheese intended for export—but sold the products abroad at world prices.[22] Any deficit incurred when the official price was above export parity became an overdraft on the Dairy Industry Account at the Reserve Bank of New Zealand, but it was hoped that profits realized in periods of high world prices would offset losses encountered when world prices were low.[23] Obviously, for true export subsidization to be involved at any time, prices of dairy products sold on the home market would have to be held above prices realized on exports. The Act provided the power to fix prices in the home market, and this power was utilized with respect to butter prices toward the end of 1937. It was apparently the intention of the Government to keep local prices in line with the official prices paid for units destined to be exported.[24]

Certain other British countries have employed export subsidies to a significant extent. Australia has a long tradition of government control over the marketing of primary products, dating back, for some commodities, to pre-War years. Many of

[22] Farmers were paid through their creameries or factories on the basis of f.o.b. prices paid by the Government at ports of exportation. (*Foreign Agriculture*, I [1937], 198, and H. Belshaw, "Guaranteed Prices for New Zealand Exports," *The Economic Record*, XIII [1937], 171.)

[23] The achievement of such a result would obviously depend on the successful gauging of future world price movements; but the act provides that in the fixing of official prices, account is to be taken of such factors as "costs involved in the efficient production of dairy produce" and the "general standard of living of persons engaged in the dairy industry in comparison with the general standard of living throughout New Zealand" in order that an "efficient producer" shall under "normal circumstances" be assured of a "sufficient net return from his business to enable him to maintain himself and his family in a reasonable state of comfort." (*Foreign Agriculture*, I [1937], 198-99.)

[24] Cf. Belshaw, *op. cit.*, pp. 173-74.

her recent subsidization schemes have resembled those of South
Africa, but enforcement of a uniform domestic price by the
Australian Federal Government was held unconstitutional in
1936. This interfered seriously with the operation of some of
the marketing schemes, which have, however, attempted to
carry on with the help of voluntary control exercised by producers' organizations.[25] Under a new wheat control scheme,
adopted at the end of 1938 and involving export subsidization
when the export price fell below a certain point, the Federal
Government agreed to raise the necessary funds through the
imposition of an excise tax on flour sold for domestic consumption, while the state governments enacted the legislation required for maintaining a fixed domestic price.[26]

Subsidization of agricultural exports played a rather important rôle in the Irish Free State from 1932 on, but a number
of these subsidies were abolished in 1938 after the conclusion
of the Anglo-Irish agreement which settled the long-standing
trade dispute between the two countries.[27] Canada has not, on
the whole, followed the example of other British countries in
subsidizing agricultural exports. Her well known wheat marketing scheme, adopted in 1935, has involved the subsidization of
production but not of exports.[28] It is interesting to note that

[25] For further details, see D. B. Copland and C. V. Janes, *Australian
Marketing Problems: A Book of Documents, 1932–1937* (Sydney, 1938);
W. M. Smith, *The Marketing of Australian and New Zealand Primary Products* (London, 1936), especially Chapter III; J. B. Brigden, "Control in the
Australian Sugar Industry" and G. L. Wood, "Control of Primary Commodities in Australia," in Holland, *op. cit.;* and *World Trade Barriers in Relation
to American Agriculture,* pp. 300–306. See also *Foreign Agriculture,* III (1939),
65–66.

[26] This fixed domestic price was to be maintained even if it was at times
exceeded by the export price. In fact, the scheme was based on the theory that
in periods of low world wheat prices flour consumers would subsidize wheat
growers, while in periods of high world prices wheat growers would subsidize
flour consumers. For further details, see *Foreign Agriculture,* III (1939),
509–24.

[27] Many of the subsidies had, in fact, been intended primarily to offset
British import duties on Irish products.

[28] The Canadian Grain Board has purchased wheat from farmers at prices
which have at times been above export parity prices, but the wheat has been

in August, 1939, Canada was the only major wheat-exporting country in which prices for wheat sold for domestic use were no higher than those for export wheat.[29]

Direct export subsidization has not been an important feature of the recent commercial policy of Latin American countries which, as we have seen in Chapter V, have learned to utilize differentiation of exchange rates as a means of export promotion. A few countries, including Venezuela and Chile, have subsidized agricultural exports to some extent,[30] however, while the subsidization of grain exports by Argentina has been of considerable importance for world trade. Mention has already been made of the Argentine Grain Regulating Board, which functioned from November, 1933, to January, 1937, and was reconstituted in November, 1938.[31] To carry out a government policy aimed at permitting producers to cover their production costs, the Board has purchased wheat, corn, and flaxseed whenever market prices fell below certain guaranteed minima established by the Government. Any losses entailed in selling to exporters at international prices have been met from the Government's profits on foreign exchange operations. Actually, the Board's losses on exports were very small from 1933 to 1936, owing to the worldwide rise in grain prices.[32]

---

sold by the Board at market prices, for *either* export or domestic consumption, through the regular grain-exchange channels. See *Foreign Agriculture*, II (1938), 62 and III (1939), 68.

[29] Cf. *ibid.*

[30] The Chilean Agricultural Export Board, set up in 1930, was given power to fix minimum prices and to subsidize agricultural exports through the granting of (1) bounties, (2) variable bounties designed to cover the difference between the domestic market price and international quotations in the case of commodities affected by the Board's price-fixing regulations, and (3) special bounties for the purpose of developing new foreign markets. (*World Trade Barriers in Relation to American Agriculture*, pp. 335–36.) These powers have been utilized from time to time in connection with exports of wheat, oats, beans, and other products.

Since 1935, Venezuela has been utilizing profits derived from foreign exchange operations to subsidize exports of coffee, cacao, and certain other agricultural products. (*Commerce Reports*, May 22, 1937, p. 420.)

[31] See p. 106 n. above.

[32] Cf. p. 108 above.

The subsidization of agricultural exports by the United States
Government, regarded by many as antithetical to the spirit
of the Reciprocal Trade Agreements Program, has been the
subject of considerable controversy within the country. Up
to August, 1939, only wheat and cotton had been affected, but
other agricultural producers were pressing for assistance on
their products. The administration seems to have been motivated, at least in part, by the hope of convincing other nations of the necessity of concluding international wheat and
cotton agreements.[33]

Although exports of wheat and flour from the Pacific Northwest benefited from subsidies to some extent from 1933 on,[34]
it was not until 1938 that a general subsidy policy was announced for wheat and flour exports. Under this program,
exporters purchased at the domestic price, sold at the lower
export parity price, and were compensated for the difference
by the Federal Government.[35]

The cotton program, announced on July 22, 1939, and ef-

[33] Cf. the statement of Acting Secretary of Agriculture Wilson in announcing
the wheat subsidy program. (U. S. Department of Agriculture, Agricultural
Adjustment Administration, *Information for the Press*, August 29, 1938.) An
international cotton conference met in Washington in September, 1939, but
rejected the American proposal for a price-control scheme on the ground that
such a course was impracticable in view of the existing international situation.
See *The New York Times*, September 10, 1939.

[34] See J. S. Davis, "Pacific Northwest Wheat Problems and the Export Subsidy," *Wheat Studies*, X (1933–34), 353–426, and *On Agricultural Policy* (Stanford University, 1939), pp. 265–66 and 364.

[35] The procedure was slightly modified at the time the 1939–40 program was
announced. (*The New York Times*, August 21, 1939, and August 22, 1939.)
The wheat control program as a whole, of course, with its crop loans, export
subsidies, and other features, operates to hold the domestic price above export
parity.

The 1938–39 program was designed to bring about the export of 100 million
bushels of wheat, including that exported in the form of flour. This, it was
calculated, would amount to about 18 per cent of the estimated world trade
in wheat for the crop year, as compared with a U. S. share of 20 per cent for
1937–38 and of 25 per cent on an average for the years 1920–29. Actually, something over 100 million bushels were exported, of which 94 million received
subsidies totalling $27,000,000 (i.e., averaging 28.7¢ a bushel). (*Ibid.*, August
22, 1939.)

fective for one year, was to involve the payment of an export subsidy of 1.5 cents a pound net weight on lint cotton. In addition, exports of cotton goods were to receive an equivalent subsidy, in order to eliminate any competitive disadvantage which might result from the raw cotton subsidy.[36] This rate, intended to offset price disparities between domestic and foreign markets, was to be subject to alteration, but the Department of Agriculture announced that, as a matter of policy, no changes would be made unless they were essential to the success of the program.[37]

Agricultural export subsidies in Europe, as elsewhere, have been closely associated with attempts to stabilize or maintain domestic prices of farm products. Because of the importance of import quotas in European commercial bargaining, however, European agricultural-exporting countries find that the amounts and destinations of their chief exports are to a large extent determined well in advance. As such countries have gradually learned to control the flow of exports to specified markets, they have found that the need for export subsidies has, at least in some cases, disappeared. What has been happening, roughly, is that agricultural-exporting countries have gradually found ways of taking advantage, at least partially, of the high prices prevailing in the restricted markets of agricultural-importing countries. Through controlling the flow of exports and through preferential agreements, they have been enabled to acquire a share of the "quota-profits" arising from the restrictions imposed in importing countries. We shall have more to say about this tendency in a later section of this chapter.

Most of the agricultural-processing countries of northern Europe have been subsidizing their exports of animal and dairy products on an appreciable scale in recent years. In

[36] *Ibid.*, July 23, 1939. Subsidies were not to apply to specified neighboring countries, pending the possible setting up of barriers to cotton imports.

[37] Representatives of the cotton trade had expressed opposition to a variable rate, on the ground that it would seriously interfere with the operation of cotton markets in this country. (*Ibid.*, July 14, 1939.)

nearly all cases, the subsidies have been associated with domestic price-stabilization schemes.[38] Regulation of prices of agricultural commodities in the Netherlands has been mentioned in the previous chapter. The *Centrales* have been given monopoly control over certain exports, and export subsidies have been granted where necessary to offset the effects of internal price control; but every effort has been made to take advantage of possibilities of obtaining remunerative prices in markets affected by import quota restrictions, and restriction of production has been practiced in some cases.[39]

In Southeastern Europe, exchange premia in one form or another have been utilized far more extensively than direct subsidies to stimulate exports, but the latter have played some part, especially in connection with schemes to raise the domestic price above export parity. To the extent that Germany, Italy, and certain other countries have entered into agreements to purchase specific quantities of Danubian and Balkan products at prices above world prices, however, the need for export

[38] In Sweden, domestic prices of butter, bacon, and eggs have been stabilized, while exporters have been paid the difference between the "controlled" domestic prices and the prices at which their products have been exported. Though exports of live hogs and cattle have been subsidized under the livestock control scheme, the amounts required for this purpose have declined in the last few years, owing to an increase in prices obtained in Germany, which has been purchasing these products from Sweden on a contract basis for periods of as much as a year in advance.

Finland commenced to subsidize animal and dairy exports in 1932 and 1933, while Norway has been subsidizing egg exports in the last few years. Government or government-regulated monopolies have been handling exports of livestock from Estonia, Lithuania, and Latvia. Export subsidization has been involved in some cases.

[39] Certain exports have benefited from the payment of equalization fees, intended to compensate for import or internal taxes affecting the commodity concerned or some material entering into its production. (*Commerce Reports, seriatim.*) Refunds of this type are commonly granted in various countries, although there is a danger that concealed export subsidization may result if the rate of refund exceeds the tax rate. Cf. Grunzel, *op. cit.*, p. 202. It is to be noted, further, that the country's position as an exporter of the commodity in question may not be unaffected by the combination of tax and refund even though the two are precisely equal. It is conceivable that, under certain demand and supply conditions, the volume of exports might be larger than it would be in the absence of any governmental intervention.

subsidies to help enforce domestic price-maintenance schemes in Southeastern Europe has become less urgent.[40] In some cases, the payment of high prices by clearing countries has facilitated the subsidizing of exports to free-exchange countries, while the countries in this region have controlled exports in order to take advantage of high prices in restricted export markets.

The conclusion of the Rome Agreements of 1934, with their clauses committing Austria and Italy to purchase specified quantities of Hungarian wheat at prices far above the world price, enabled Hungary to abolish her "grain ticket" system for subsidizing wheat exports and to adopt a domestic price-stabilization scheme.[41] At about the same time, an Agricultural Relief Fund, derived mainly from taxes on flour and certain other products, and amounting recently to about 50 million pengös *per annum,* was inaugurated for the subsidization of agricultural exports in general.[42] Exports of a number of important commodities have been handled by export syndicates which have been set up with the active coöperation of the Government and have exercised a considerable degree of control over prices in the domestic market.

Yugoslavian exports to clearing countries have been carefully

[40] Preferential tariff agreements with western European countries have performed the same function.

[41] On the "grain ticket" or *Boletta* system, see *World Trade Barriers in Relation to American Agriculture,* pp. 401–403, and *Foreign Agriculture,* II (1938), 102 ff. Under the Rome Agreements, Hungary obtained an outlet for over 15 million bushels of wheat (including wheat flour), at a price of 16 pengös per quintal for Austria and 17 pengös per quintal for Italy. (These prices were later raised somewhat.) The Hungarian Government thereupon concluded contracts with *Futura* (the central marketing body of the Union of Hungarian Cooperatives), the Hungarian Cereal Exporters' Association, and the Grain Trade Company, whereby these organizations agreed to carry through open-market purchases of wheat at fixed minimum prices whenever weakness threatened to develop in the market. This guaranteed price system was given up, and the agreements with Italy and Austria were modified somewhat, in 1936–37 when world prices rose above Hungarian minimum prices. (*Ibid.*) For a fuller discussion of Hungarian export policies, see Ellis, "Exchange Control in Austria and Hungary," Ch. III.

[42] *Foreign Agriculture,* II (1938), 108, and Royal Institute of International Affairs, *South-Eastern Europe* (London, 1939), p. 118.

controlled and it has been possible to utilize part of the profits from exports sold at high prices to subsidize exports fetching low prices. Rumania has granted direct subsidies on the export of wheat and a few other commodities to free-exchange countries.[43] Bulgarian wheat exports have been handled by the Government Grain Monopoly, which has bought wheat from domestic producers at prices well above world market prices and sold to domestic millers at still higher prices, utilizing the profits derived in this way to cover its losses on sales to exporters at prices enabling them to compete in world markets. In general, wheat exports have been permitted only to free-exchange countries.[44]

Although European agricultural-exporting countries have sometimes succeeded, through introducing export controls, in taking advantage of high prices prevailing in countries enforcing import restrictions, one should not conclude that the spread of import controls necessarily tends to render the employment of export subsidies superfluous. The control of exports will benefit the exporting country only in cases in which it has been guaranteed a definite position in the market of the importing country. As we have seen in Chapter IX, however, it is by no means true that the geographical sources of imports are predetermined with absolute rigidity in all countries with quota

[43] *Ibid.*, p. 132.

[44] See League of Nations, *Trentième Rapport du Commissaire de la Société des Nations en Bulgarie* (Geneva, 1934), pp. 14–15, and *Foreign Agriculture*, I (1937), 632.

Among European countries which have not been mentioned, France has paid premiums to exporters of hogs and certain hog products and has in some years subsidized wheat and butter exports, while Switzerland recently began to subsidize livestock exports. (*Commerce Reports* and *Government Measures Affecting Agricultural Prices, seriatim.*) Italy has utilized direct subsidies to some extent, apparently in a rather flexible manner, but apart from the bounties on exports of rice and raw silk, little official information has been available on Italian subsidies. The rice bounties have been paid in conjunction with a domestic price-fixing scheme and have varied according to the destination of exports. (*World Trade Barriers in Relation to American Agriculture*, pp. 417–20.) The United States Government imposed countervailing duties on imports of certain silk products from Italy in July, 1939. (*The New York Times*, July 6, 1939.)

or permit systems. Secondly, even when exporting country B is entitled to a specific share of importing country A's quota for a given commodity, importers in country A cannot be forced to make unprofitable purchases in country B. Hence, if an exporting country wishes to maintain the price of a given commodity above export parity through price-control measures, it may under certain conditions be forced to subsidize exports to maintain its markets *even* in countries with rigid import quota systems.[45] Thirdly, export subsidies may be a very effective way of expanding exports of a given commodity to a country in which imports of that commodity are handled exclusively by a government monopoly; for it will be to the monopoly's advantage, in general, to purchase as cheaply as possible and yet the fact that the goods it purchases have been subsidized at the source will not interfere, except perhaps very indirectly, with its ability to enforce its official price on the domestic market. This is a consideration of some practical importance, especially with respect to such a commodity as wheat, exports of which have recently been subsidized by almost every important exporting country and imports of which have in many cases been handled by government monopolies.

2. *Other Forms of Export Promotion*

Probably no method of indirect export stimulation has been as important since 1931 as exchange rate manipulation. In fact, so far as exchange-control countries were concerned, the utilization of this device to some extent removed, at least for a time, the need for other indirect means of subsidizing exports. But governments have provided indirect assistance to exporters in a great variety of ways, some of which may be classified as involving indirect subsidization. Special attention has been

[45] A country employing import quotas will not be likely, moreover, to penalize exports which have been subsidized at the source by imposing penalty duties or tighter import restrictions, since the price on its domestic market will not be affected, except perhaps very indirectly, by the fact of such subsidization.

given to improving export credit facilities. This movement has manifested itself particularly in the spread of export credit guarantee systems, which may under certain conditions involve indirect export subsidization.

Governmental export credit guarantee systems came into being in the years immediately following the World War, when economic and currency conditions in many European countries were so unstable that exporters could not themselves assume the risks involved in selling to such countries nor could they pay the premiums asked for credit insurance by private companies. Led by the United Kingdom, which began to guarantee export credits on a relatively small scale in 1919, twelve European countries adopted export credit insurance schemes previous to 1930. After the beginning of the depression, the system spread to Japan, Latvia, Poland, Sweden, and Switzerland, while the Export-Import Bank which was established by the United States Government in 1934 performs certain of the functions elsewhere assigned to export credit guarantee authorities.[46] In addition, the highly unstable trade conditions which characterized the depression and which, in certain respects, still prevail, have led to considerable extension of the scope of these export credit insurance systems. Particularly ticklish has been the problem of transfer risks, arising in connection with exchange restrictions, but the handling of this problem has been facilitated by the spread of clearing and payments agreements, which, as we have seen, earmark the proceeds of Country A's exports to Country B for repayment of Country A's trade debts to Country B, the major risk for Country B's exporters being the risk of delay in repayment.

We shall not attempt to describe in any detail the provisions of the different schemes, which vary considerably with respect to such matters as the duration of credits covered, the types and percentages of risks underwritten by the government, and

[46] For a list of countries having export credit guarantee systems, see Dietrich, *World Trade*, p. 178.

the total resources available. There is one general issue, however, which should be considered. The object of governmental export credit guarantee schemes, in general, is to assist exporters through supplementing the facilities offered by private insurance companies. But the most difficult question which a government seeking to guarantee export credits must settle concerns the extent to which it will depart, in fixing premium rates and accepting various types of risks, from the principles which would be followed by a conservative private insurance company.[47] In so far as a government accepts abnormal risks which would not be accepted by a private company and in so far as its premiums are lower than those which would be charged by a private company, it encourages exports which could not otherwise take place. The more liberal its policy, the greater will be the probability that the scheme will operate at a loss, in which case indirect export subsidization will be involved. But the mere fact that the government's rates are lower than those which would be charged by a private company, or that its policy in general is more liberal, does not necessarily mean that the government runs the danger of suffering a loss. In abnormally unstable periods, market risk premiums may exaggerate the degree of actual risk involved. In addition, the danger of loss tends to be smaller for the government in many cases than it would be for a private company, since a government may have access to more reliable sources of information with respect to credit conditions abroad and may be in a better position to press its claims in case of nonpayment of debts. This latter advantage is of special importance in connection with the class of risks which the government is best equipped to handle, the so-called political risks. An export credit risk may be said to be political in nature when the decision of a foreign government may play an important part in determining the outcome, as in the case of transfer and

[47] For an interesting discussion of this problem, see E. M. Shenkman, *Insurance against Credit Risks in International Trade* (London, 1935), pp. 162 ff.

conversion risks, arising in connection with exchange restrictions and transfer moratoria, or in cases where the debtor is a foreign government.[48] It is easy to see, therefore, that while a government insurance department may be able to pursue a considerably more liberal policy than a private company without operating at a loss, it is quite possible for a government to turn an export credit guarantee scheme into an instrument for aggressive export promotion if it so desires.

The British scheme, which has formed a model for many of the other schemes, transacted a very small volume of business during the nineteen-twenties and accordingly played an almost negligible rôle in the promotion of British exports. During the present decade the Government has extended the maximum limit placed on the total liabilities of the Board of Trade in connection with export credit insurance and, in addition, has permitted the guaranteeing of types of risks which were formerly not acceptable. The result has been a huge increase in the amount of credits guaranteed. A small part of this increase occurred between 1931 and 1934 and was largely attributable to the liberal manner in which Russian contracts, included since 1929, were guaranteed.[49] The major portion of the increase, however, has taken place since 1934, when the British Government decided upon a radical departure from the policy which it had been pursuing for a number of years and began to assume transfer and conversion risks on a limited basis.[50] This step was taken, be it noted, only after the passage of the Debts Clearing Act and the conclusion of the Anglo-German Pay-

[48] That government export credit schemes are especially well adapted to deal with risks of a political nature is perhaps best illustrated by the fact that a number of schemes originated in order to promote trade with the Soviet Union and that a substantial proportion of the business of certain of the schemes consists in guaranteeing export credits to the Soviet Union. Cf. S. K. Margold, *Export Credit Insurance in Europe Today, 1934,* U. S. Sen. Doc. No. 225, 73d Cong., 2d sess., p. 48 (insert).

[49] Cf. Shenkman, *op. cit.,* p. 238.

[50] The annual value of British exports effected under governmental credit guarantees increased from about $38,500,000 in 1933–34 to roughly $250,000,000 in 1938–39. (*The New York Times,* July 24, 1939.)

ments *Agreement* in 1934. An important extension of the
scheme occurred early in 1939, at a time when the British
Government was concerned over the political and economic implications of German foreign trade promotion, especially in
Southeastern Europe. It was decided to increase the aggregate
liability which the Board of Trade might incur from £50 million
to £75 million for credits guaranteed after consultation with the
Export Credits Guarantee Department's Advisory Council of
business men.[51] In addition, the 1939 Act set up a new category of export credit insurance, in connection with which
consultation with the Advisory Council was not required.
Total liabilities under this new heading were not to exceed
£10 million. It was generally expected that this sum would be
used to guarantee credits which would not be regarded by
the Advisory Council as altogether sound commercially and
financially but which, in the phrase of government spokesmen,
might "on the long-term view be expedient in the national interest." [52]

Export credit guarantee schemes which are of the pure insurance type may be distinguished from those which are not.[53]
Under the former type of system, an exporter applies for government credit insurance and, having received it, can approach
his bank for credit accommodation with considerable confidence
that his request will be granted. In some countries, however,
the export credit guarantee department performs the functions
of a bank by furnishing the actual credit. An important function of many of the schemes is the provision or guaranteeing
of medium-term credits, a type of accommodation which has
come to be increasingly in demand in connection with exports of
certain types of capital goods but which the financial institu-

[51] 2 and 3 Geo. 6, 1–5, Ch. 5 (*The Law Journal Reports*, CVIII [August, 1939], 17 ff.).

[52] See *The New York Times*, December 9, 1938. This special fund was raised to £60 million after the German invasion of Czechoslovakia. Cf. Tasca, *World Trading Systems*, p. 134.

[53] Cf. Dietrich, *World Trade*, p. 181.

tions in most countries are not yet fully equipped to handle.

The American scheme, administered by the Export-Import Bank of Washington, which was set up by the Government in 1934, is not primarily an insurance scheme but is intended rather to furnish, in connection with both import and export transactions, types of credit which cannot be secured through the regular banking channels. The Bank will, however, undertake to underwrite some proportion of the risk in connection with transactions involving "terms beyond those usually experienced in export and import business." [54] Short-term credits are considered only when commercial banks, "because of unusual circumstances, are unable or unwilling to provide such accommodations." [55] In connection with intermediate credits (180 days to 12 months) which are granted for either consumers'-goods or capital-goods transactions, the Bank endeavors to supplement existing facilities. Long-term credits, ordinarily confined to capital-goods transactions, may be extended for periods of one to five years and "under special conditions for such longer periods as may be warranted." [56] So far as possible, existing financial institutions are given an opportunity to participate in commitments undertaken or to coöperate with the Bank in various ways. [57]

Export credits, especially of the medium-term variety, have, in the last few years, partially fulfilled the functions formerly performed by long-term foreign issues. [58] Creditor countries regard them as having the advantage of insuring, in a way that is not always possible in connection with publicly issued foreign loans, that the funds made available to the borrowing country will be utilized for purchases in the lending country. The necessary adjustments in the balances of payments of both

[54] *General Policy Statement of Export-Import Bank of Washington,* June 15, 1938.

[55] *Ibid.*

[56] *Ibid.*

[57] *Ibid.*

[58] Cf. E. Staley, *World Economy in Transition* (New York, 1939), p. 276.

lending and borrowing countries thus tend to take place more smoothly.

In this connection, mention should be made of a practice which seems to be increasing in importance, that of extending governmental or semi-governmental export credits under the terms of bilateral intergovernmental agreements, whereby the borrowing country, in return for the credit, grants certain concessions to the lending country. Some of these credits have been granted or guaranteed by export credit insurance departments. Whether such arrangements involve indirect subsidization of the creditor country's exports depends largely on the terms of the agreement, which might conceivably, for example, force the borrowing country to purchase from the lending country goods which could be more economically purchased elsewhere.

Of special interest are the credit agreements concluded in the last few years by Germany, the United Kingdom, and the United States with certain exchange-control countries. The rôle played by political motives in leading to the conclusion of these agreements is immeasurable but highly important. Germany's credits have formed part of her campaign to increase her economic and political influence in certain areas, while England and the United States have quite obviously been seeking to combat the spread of German influence. Mention has already been made of Germany's 1938 credits to Turkey and Poland, which were to be repaid in the form of goods, and of the British credit of May, 1938, to Turkey.[59] The well known German-Rumanian Economic Agreement of March, 1939, provided for German financial assistance of a more positive sort, designed to develop Rumanian industries capable of supplying Germany with needed primary products as well as to provide outlets for German exports of machinery and other goods.[60] The United Kingdom promptly responded by con-

[59] Cf. p. 188 above.
[60] Cf. pp. 425–26 below.

cluding an agreement with Rumania, under which the Export Credits Guarantee Department was to underwrite Rumanian Government sterling notes to the value of £5,000,000, issued to finance Rumanian Government expenditures in the United Kingdom. The maturities of these notes were to be so arranged as to insure the repayment of the entire sum over a period of twenty years, while the nature of the expenditures to be made by Rumania was to be settled by agreement between the British Export Credits Guarantee Department and the Rumanian Legation in London.[61] Provision was likewise made for government coöperation directed toward the establishment in Rumania and Britain of trading companies for the promotion of trade between the two countries.[62]

The financial soundness of these credits, from the point of view of the creditor countries, depended in part on the fact that both Britain and Germany conducted their trade with the countries mentioned under the terms of clearing agreements which made specific provision for debt repayments out of the proceeds of the borrowing country's exports to the lending country.[63] This element has been lacking in connection with the American credits, which have been extended to certain Latin American countries. The United States Government's policy has been to use its credits as a lever to bring about the relaxation of foreign exchange restrictions in the borrowing countries. The first agreement of this type was concluded with

[61] *Board of Trade Journal*, CXLII (1939), 740.

[62] *Ibid.*, p. 738. It is scarcely necessary to draw attention, also, to the German-Russian Trade Agreement of August 19, 1939, whereby Germany granted to Russia a credit of 200 million marks, to be repaid over the course of seven years and to be utilized for Russian purchases of German goods over the course of two years. The credit was sufficiently large to bring about a substantial increase in Russian purchases, as compared with 1937 or 1938, but not as compared with 1935 or earlier years. (*The New York Times*, August 21, 1939, and August 22, 1939.)

[63] It should also be noted that the borrowing country under such agreements may be forced to advance funds to its exporters, since the fact that its importers purchase on a credit basis may mean that clearing funds will not suffice to pay exporters. (Cf. pp. 162–63 above.)

Brazil in March, 1939. Brazil agreed to free her foreign exchange market for commercial transactions and, under a separate arrangement with Foreign Bondholders' Protective Council of New York, to resume service on a temporary basis on her dollar bond indebtedness.[64] The freeing of the commercial exchange market was to be facilitated by an undertaking on the part of the Export-Import Bank to establish, in coöperation with commercial banks, acceptance credits in favor of the Bank of Brazil to the amount of $19,200,000, such credits to be gradually repaid over a period of two years. This financial assistance would make possible the transfer of frozen commercial debts; but, in addition, the Export-Import Bank agreed to assist in the improvement of Brazil's transportation facilities and in the development of her other domestic undertakings by granting further credits, to the extent that its funds might be available for such purposes, to American manufacturers or exporters engaged in supplying Brazil's requirements.[65] The "domestic undertakings" to be assisted were those designed to increase Brazil's "productive capacity" and her "trade with the United States." It was evidently understood that particular attention would be paid to the development of the Brazilian rubber industry, with a view to rendering the United States less dependent on other areas for its supplies and to mitigating the price shifts which had proved so upsetting to American rubber-consuming industries.[66] The American Government also undertook to coöperate in the establishment of a Brazilian Central Reserve Bank by asking Congress for authority to place at the disposal of the Brazilian Government gold up to the amount of $50 million, repayment to be made from Brazil's future gold production.

[64] Cf. pp. 76–77 above. It was the expectation of the Brazilian Government that a permanent settlement with respect to its dollar bond indebtedness might be effected at the end of two years. (See text of the notes exchanged between Brazilian and American officials, *The New York Times*, March 10, 1939.)

[65] *Ibid.*

[66] *Ibid.*

Among methods of indirect or concealed export subsidization which have received considerable attention from students of commercial policy in the past, some have recently been utilized on an extended scale while at least one, the "import certificate" system, has recently faded into insignificance.[67] The practice of fixing preferential freight rates for export shipments, which has long been utilized to some extent by countries which operate their own railway systems, has been fairly common.[68] Concern over the position of the balance of payments has led, in some cases, to the adoption of an analogous practice designed to stimulate "invisible" exports, the fixing of preferential passenger rates for foreign tourists. Here again, however, the sale of blocked currencies at a discount has probably been a more important means of attracting business, on the whole, than the fixing of preferential railway rates. Tourists have been permitted to use their depreciated travel marks or lira to purchase all sorts of services incidental to their journeys.[69]

During the early nineteen-thirties the "import certificate" system was of some importance as a means of indirectly subsidizing grain exports from Central and Eastern Europe, but this practice has almost disappeared since 1934 or 1935, partly as a result of the spread of more direct methods of subsidization and partly because of the growing emphasis on self-sufficiency in certain countries. Under this system exporters were issued so-called "import certificates" which could be tendered in payment of import duties on the same commodity or on other

[67] For a discussion of direct and indirect export bounties, see Grunzel, *op. cit.*, Part II, Chapter III.

[68] On bilateral agreements containing concealed import preferences in the form of permission granted by one country to the other to fix preferential freight rates on its export shipments to the first country, see p. 452 below.

[69] Another form of "invisible" export promotion which has received considerable attention since the beginning of the depression but which, however, has been motivated as much by political as by economic considerations is the practice of granting shipping subsidies.

designated commodities. These certificates could be sold to importers or cashed in at customs offices.[70]

Before concluding this section, we should at least mention the fact that governments everywhere are steadily improving and extending the general services offered to exporters and that this sort of development received great impetus during the depression. Some countries do not attempt much more than the provision of adequate information about foreign markets and credit conditions, but in other cases governments participate in foreign advertising campaigns designed to enhance the general reputation of the nation's products or appropriate sums of money to assist in the investigation and opening up of new markets.

3. *Export Duties*

The levying of export duties constitutes an important means of raising revenue in non-industrialized countries and colonial areas.[71] Such countries do not have at their disposal all the varied sources of income which are available to a modern industrial state and, in addition, occasionally find themselves strategically placed to derive considerable revenue from an export duty on some primary product without causing material harm to domestic producers of the commodity. A situation of this sort may arise when a country has a virtual monopoly in the production of a given commodity, especially one for which the foreign demand is relatively inelastic. In the most favorable cases, the burden of the price adjustment necessitated by the imposition of the duty may be borne almost entirely by the foreigner; but it is obvious that if an exporting country goes too far in exploiting its advantageous position, foreigners may be stimulated to search for natural or synthetic substitutes

---

[70] For a more extended discussion, see *World Trade Barriers in Relation to American Agriculture*, pp. 81–82.

[71] Cf. E. Staley, *Raw Materials in Peace and War* (New York, 1937), pp. 67–71, and League of Nations, International Economic Conference, Documentation, *Export Duties* (Geneva, 1927), pp. 3–11.

for the commodity in question.[72] In practice, export duties in most of the countries employing them for revenue purposes cover a fairly wide range of primary products and are moderate in amount (usually not exceeding 10 per cent ad valorem and often much less than this), but there have been examples of high duties in cases in which the tax-levying country exercised, at least for a time, a substantial degree of monopoly power, e.g., Chilean nitrates.

Clearly, except in extremely favorable circumstances, export duties are something of a disadvantage to the export industries concerned. Consequently, as more and more countries become industrialized and develop varied sources of revenue, taxes of this sort tend to be looked upon with increasing disfavor. There have been a number of cases, moreover, in which the power of a country to exploit its monopolistic position with respect to some commodity has been materially weakened by the development of substitutes or of new sources of supply abroad. To these long-run tendencies toward removal of export duties were added, in the early nineteen-thirties, the effects of the depression; for the drastic decline in the prices of agricultural products and raw materials meant a sharp increase in the burden imposed on producers by export taxes on their products, especially where specific rather than ad valorem duties were imposed or where competition with other exporting countries was intense. Consequently, during these years the cases in which export duties were reduced or removed tended, in spite of budgetary difficulties in the countries levying them, to exceed in number and importance those in which duties were increased.[73]

[72] It is clear that, following the imposition of an export tax, the price of the commodity in world markets will tend to exceed the price in the duty-levying country by the amount of the duty (with due allowance for transportation costs). The adjustment is likely to come about partly through a fall in the price on the exporting country's market and partly through a rise in prices on world markets, but the exact nature of the adjustment will depend on various demand and supply factors.

[73] E.g., Brazil lowered her export duties in her 1931 budget; Panama, as an

Export duties are occasionally levied for purposes other than the raising of revenue. Raw material exports are sometimes taxed in order to benefit domestic processing or fabricating industries.[74] Colonial export tax schedules may grant preferential status to exports of materials to the mother country, in order to assist the latter's industries. Export duties may be designed to limit the outflow of materials of strategic wartime importance or to discourage the export of substandard products. They have played an important part in certain commodity restriction schemes. All these objectives, however, may be accomplished, sometimes more effectively, through export license systems or even, in some cases, through outright embargoes on exports. Quantitative control of exports, moreover, may be employed for other purposes for which export duties would prove a cumbersome weapon. While the conditions which have prevailed since 1931 have tended to encourage an increased resort to export restrictions, they have also favored the employment of quantitative or absolute methods of restriction rather than export duties. We shall proceed, therefore, to a discussion of this sort of weapon.

4. *Export Quotas and Embargoes*

The imposition of any sort of restriction on the export of a commodity clearly tends to create a price-differential between domestic and foreign markets for the commodity, with prices quoted abroad exceeding those on the home market

---

aid to exporters in view of low world prices, suspended indefinitely the export duties on cacao, balata, and sarsaparilla; in March, 1931, Mexico materially reduced her export duties on many products; in April, 1931, the Rumanian Government abolished export duties on salted hides and skins, in line with its policy of reducing gradually and finally removing all export duties; while Bulgaria abolished nearly all its export duties and taxes in 1934. (*Commerce Reports, seriatim.*)

[74] Cf. Staley, *Raw Materials in Peace and War*, p. 67, for a list of purposes for which export duties are levied.

(after allowing for transportation costs). Whether the price-adjustment will come about primarily through a fall in the home price or through a rise in the foreign price will depend on demand and supply factors both at home and abroad. These factors will also determine the amount of the price-differential in the case of a quantitative or absolute export restriction, whereas an export duty will tend to create a price-differential of its own magnitude. The differences between export duties and quantitative export restrictions are analogous in other respects to the differences between tariffs and quotas on imports. Export quotas, so long as they remain effective in restricting exports, tend to sever the price-link between domestic and foreign markets for the commodity concerned. Like import quotas, moreover, they give rise to difficult problems concerning the distribution of exports among exporting firms and among countries of destination.

We may distinguish at the outset between two broad classes of export restrictions: those designed primarily to control the value of exports to a particular area and those designed primarily to control the volume of exports of individual commodities. Regulations of the former type have occasionally been introduced to prevent the accumulation (1) of foreign credits blocked by exchange restrictions, or (2) of an inconveniently large credit balance under the terms of a clearing agreement. They are usually enforced through existing or newly-adopted export permit requirements, but they are ordinarily intended, at least in theory, to affect all exports alike. We have had occasion to discuss regulations of this sort in earlier chapters and will not be particularly concerned with them here,[75] except in the case of Japan, whose situation has been somewhat unusual.

Control over the flow of exports of individual commodities has been introduced for a number of reasons in the years since 1931. The practice of enforcing inspection regulations to pre-

[75] Cf. pp. 358–61 above.

vent the outflow of substandard products which might injure the reputation of a whole national industry seems to be growing, especially in connection with exports of fresh fruits and vegetables. Restrictions have occasionally been placed on exports of staple foodstuffs during bad crop years in order to conserve supplies for the domestic population and mitigate price increases. But regulations of this sort do not tend to entail fundamental changes in the conditions under which international trade is carried on. Of far greater significance are the export restrictions which have been imposed (1) to limit the outflow of materials of wartime importance, (2) to regulate the flow of exports which are affected by import quotas in the country of destination, and (3) to help give effect to market control or commodity restriction schemes.

In view of the widespread restrictions placed on exports of strategic materials during the World War,[76] one should not be surprised to find that the threat of war has, since 1933 or 1934, led to the re-introduction of many measures of this sort. Some degree of control over exports of arms and munitions has been retained by a number of countries ever since the War, but new or more stringent regulations have been widely adopted in the last five or six years. Countries in all parts of the world, moreover, have prohibited, or placed under license, exports of scrap iron, and in many cases the restrictions have been extended to cover scrap metals of all kinds. Other strategic raw materials widely affected by export restrictions, especially in Europe, are crude and refined metals of various kinds and textile raw materials. Italy and Germany, with their thoroughgoing self-sufficiency programs, have gradually extended restrictions of this type until they cover a wide range of commodities. Japan, too, has naturally made extensive use of this type of measure since 1937. But even such countries as France, former Austria, and former Czechoslovakia extended control over numerous commodities of possible wartime importance

[76] See Chapter I.

from 1934 or 1935 on.[77] The Italian sanctions episode and the various controversies over embargoes on the export of war materials to Spain are too familiar to require mention.[78] The Dutch, Swiss, and French Governments temporarily prohibited exports of long lists of commodities during the Munich Crisis. Export restrictions of this sort are intended to serve the dual purpose of assisting domestic military preparations or operations and hampering corresponding activities abroad. As might be expected, the formation of alliances and alignments or the outbreak of actual war invariably gives rise to discrimination in the application of these measures to the various countries of destination.

More interesting, from a purely economic point of view, is a tendency mentioned earlier for governments to exercise control over exports which have been subjected to quantitative restrictions in import markets. To some extent, such control has been adopted merely in response to initiative taken by importing countries that wished to transfer the responsibility of issuing licenses to exporting countries. Certain governments, however, have demonstrated an unmistakable tendency toward the adoption of a generalized policy of regulating exports which are affected by import quotas in foreign markets. Through

[77] In 1935, France, for example, prohibited exports, re-exports and transshipments of cotton, wool, rubber, certain woods, rifle stocks, and other products; rendered the exportation of munitions subject to license; undertook to control the importation and exportation of electric current; and prohibited the importation or exportation of carrier pigeons. Additional measures followed in succeeding years, including a prohibition on exports of war materials to Spain. Although absolute export prohibitions imposed during the Munich Crisis were later removed, export license requirements remained in effect for many of the commodities concerned. Germany's export permit requirements, applied previously to various individual commodities, were extended in 1935 to cover a wide range of foodstuffs and raw materials, including edible fats, potatoes, textile materials, metals, rubber, hides, skins, and oils. Later, such commodities as bauxite, certain types of waste leather, phenol, cresol, and copper sulphate were added to the list. (*Commerce Reports, seriatim.*)

[78] On the sanctions question, see E. Atwater, *Administration of Export and Import Embargoes, 1935–36,* Geneva Research Centre, Geneva Studies, IX, No. 6 (December, 1938), and Royal Institute of International Affairs, *International Sanctions* (London and New York, 1938).

a system of export permits, the quantities of such exports have been made to conform to the amounts permitted under the quota regulations of the various importing countries. Considerable emphasis has been placed, also, on spreading the flow of exports evenly over the quota period, while, in some cases, export prices have been regulated. A policy of this kind, as we have seen, has little point except in cases in which the exporting country is definitely allocated, either through autonomous action on the part of the importing country or through the terms of a bilateral agreement with that country, a specific share of the import quota or a pre-determined absolute quantity of imports. This accounts for the apparently piece-meal fashion in which control of this sort has been applied. Where the exporting country *is* entitled to a definite quota, an export permit system has certain clear advantages. Exporters are placed in a position to acquire at least a substantial proportion of the quota-profits created by the import quota.[79] These profits may, indeed, be taxed away *in toto* by the exporting country through an appropriate system of export license fees. Where prices of agricultural export products are held above export parity, the exporting country may, in same cases, as we have noted above, partially or wholly avoid the burden of granting export subsidies by regulating the flow of exports affected by foreign import quotas. In fact, export control may facilitate domestic price control in the case of a commodity which is exported largely to markets in which the amounts and sources of imports are determined in advance. These advantages all hold for the case in which the exporting country has received from the importing country a concession in the form of a preferential duty on a limited quantity of imports. Export regulation in certain Danubian and Balkan countries has applied to some cases of this sort.

One of the first countries to set up machinery for control

[79] It is obvious, of course, that the price-differential in a case of this sort is attributable entirely to the import quota and not to the export permit system.

of exports affected by foreign import quotas was the Netherlands. In accordance with a law of December 24, 1931, as amended by legislation enacted early in 1932, the Dutch Government was given the power to institute license requirements for exports affected either by foreign import quotas or by any foreign regulation tending to disturb the regular flow of imports.[80] Permits were distributed among exporters in accordance with the volume of exports (of the designated commodity to the country in question) handled by them in some previous period. Permit fees of not more than 5 per cent might be levied to meet administration costs. In accordance with later regulations, if exporters holding permits received excess profits as a result of the existence of a price-differential between the Dutch market and foreign market in question (over and above transport costs), the Government was to impose export license fees which, together with the fees levied to cover administration costs, would amount to not less than 70 per cent and not more than 100 per cent of the price-differential.[81] Proceeds, apart from those allocated for administration costs, were to be employed for the assistance of producers of the commodities concerned. In other words, a primary function of the Dutch scheme was to see that the ultimate benefits arising from the existence of a price-differential should go largely to Dutch producers, rather than to Dutch exporters or foreign importers. At first the regulations were applied only to exports of various agricultural products to France and Belgium-Luxemburg. Later, control was extended to cover a considerable range of exports, including some industrial products, to Germany and Netherlands India. There have been scattered instances of regulation of exports to other markets.

Other countries of Northern Europe have also employed this type of export control to some extent. The Finnish Government was authorized, in 1934, to regulate the exportation

[80] *Deutsches Handels-Archiv*, LXXXVI (1932), 1090.
[81] *Ibid.*, 1264–65 and 1438–39.

of any commodity to countries subjecting importation of that commodity to quotas or other restrictions. Sweden and Denmark have regulated certain exports affected by foreign quota restrictions, especially those of Britain and Germany. Particularly interesting is the Danish hog control scheme, which represents one of the few attempts to integrate export regulation of this type and production restriction.[82] The scheme was adopted in 1932, when the market for Danish bacon was drastically restricted by the introduction of British import quotas. It has involved the purchase from producers, at prices determined on the basis of British bacon prices, of a sufficient number of hogs to fill the British and German quotas for Danish bacon and to satisfy the home market.[83] Production over and above these requirements has been discouraged by paying producers a substantially lower price for surplus hogs, the products of which have been sold on other foreign markets, at a loss if necessary.[84] The overwhelming importance of the British market as an outlet for Danish bacon has been at once a source of strength and weakness for the working of this scheme. So long as the British quota has remained relatively stable, the Danes have had a reasonably simple planning problem on their hands, but sudden, unpredictable changes in the British quota have on occasion thrown the whole scheme out of gear.[85]

Danubian and Balkan countries, as indicated earlier in this chapter, have also tended to extend control over exports affected by rigid import restrictions. In this region, govern-

[82] The Netherlands hog control scheme has somewhat similar aims but is not as closely integrated with quota restrictions in foreign markets as is the Danish.

[83] Each producer has periodically been allotted cards entitling him to sell a certain number of hogs at this price. (*Foreign Agriculture,* III [1939], 69–70.)

[84] Underselling on the home market has been prevented by forcing bacon factories and slaughterers to pay into the control agency's fund the difference between the prices of hogs sold with cards and those without cards. (*Ibid.*)

[85] Thus, the very effectiveness of the Danish scheme of production restriction proved a drawback in 1937, when the Danes were unable to take advantage of a sudden increase in the British bacon quota. (*Ibid.*)

ment intervention has in several cases taken the form of encouraging or requiring the formation of export syndicates which have regulated the flow of exports of individual commodities, under governmental supervision. Thus, an Austrian government decree of May 12, 1933, provided for the setting up of government-regulated export organizations for certain commodities, "in order to take full advantage of export possibilities for Austrian goods which may result from international agreements." [86] It was reported that the activities of these organizations, which might be limited to exports to individual countries, were to be aimed at preventing Austrian exporters from dissipating, by competition among themselves, the benefits which might accrue to them through preferential agreements. Resolutions were to be binding among members but might be vetoed by the Government when contrary to the public interest. The Hungarian export syndicates have been mentioned earlier in this chapter.[87]

Yugoslavia has controlled exports to clearing countries with a view to deriving the maximum benefit from concessions granted by these countries. The majority of agricultural exports have been regulated through the issue of licenses by the Institute for Promoting Foreign Trade, which has attempted to discourage competition among exporters. Wheat exports to countries with which Yugoslavia has preferential agreements have been legally monopolized by *Prizad* (Privileged Corporation for the Export of Yugoslavian Agricultural Products), which has fixed prices at which it would buy wheat largely on the basis of what Germany paid.[88]

One of the most interesting and thoroughgoing systems of export regulation is to be found in Japan, whose export problems, at least from 1932 to the outbreak of the war with China,

[86] *Commerce Reports,* July 8, 1933, p. 26.
[87] P. 337 above.
[88] *Prizad* has also handled plum exports. On its activities and history, see V. Pertot, "Einzelstudien über Marktregulierungen: V. Die Weizenregulierungen in Jugoslavien," *Weltwirtschaftliches Archiv,* XLV (1937), 628–59.

were somewhat unusual. As in some of the countries of South-eastern Europe, control has been exercised by private exporters' organizations subject to governmental supervision.[89] The scheme is based on the Export Association Law of 1925 and subsequent amendments. Organizations may be formed by exporters of a staple article of commerce or by those who export to a given foreign area. During the late nineteen-twenties, emphasis was placed on export promotion, and the only regulatory activity undertaken by the associations to any important extent involved the enforcement of standards of quality. From the end of 1931 on, however, there came a change in the problems confronting Japanese exporters. A conjunction of favorable factors permitted Japanese goods to be sold abroad at extremely low prices, with the result that Japan's exports underwent a marked expansion at a time when export industries in other countries were still suffering severely from the depression. The rapidity of Japan's export advance soon began to be threatened by a tendency on the part of foreign countries to apply tariff and quota restrictions with special severity to Japanese goods. Supported by the Government, which effected certain changes in the Export Association Law, Japanese export organizations responded with a more positive type of export control, the primary aims of which were to forestall the tightening of import barriers against Japanese goods and to regulate the flow of exports in conformity with restrictions already in existence. The number of export organizations increased rapidly, especially from 1933 on.

Chief emphasis came to be placed on control of the quantity of exports, but other important functions of the associations have included the setting of minimum prices and regulation of

[89] See, in particular, S. Ogata, "Probleme der Exportkontrolle in Japan," *Weltwirtschaftliches Archiv*, XLIII (1936), 472–507; Mitsubishi Economic Research Bureau, *Japanese Trade and Industry: Present and Future* (London, 1936), pp. 46, 117–18, 125–26, 618; and Z. Takidani, "The Development of the Japanese Commercial Policy," *Journal of the Kobe University of Commerce,* I (May, 1938), 21–23.

the conditions of sale (to prevent concealed price-cutting). The execution of these restrictions has frequently been simplified by the existence of production controls instituted by manufacturers' associations, though the functions of manufacturers' associations and export associations sometimes overlap one another in a confusing fashion.

The extent to which the different types of export control have been employed has varied among individual export organizations. Even associations composed of exporters of a particular commodity have confined their activities, in certain cases, to goods destined for a single market or group of markets.[90] Varying conditions in sheltered import markets have led to the setting of different minimum prices for exports to different countries. The Japanese Government has on a number of occasions succeeded in forestalling or mitigating the tightening of import barriers in foreign countries by undertaking, in a formal or informal ("gentlemen's") agreement, to impose quantitative limits on the exportation of a given commodity or commodities to the country in question. To the export associations has fallen the chief responsibility for carrying out the terms of these agreements; while voluntary export restrictions have sometimes been undertaken by the associations themselves under the terms of agreements concluded with private interests abroad.[91]

An important function of some of the export associations composed of those who export to a given country or region has been to keep an eye on Japan's balance of trade with any coun-

---

[90] For a list of export organizations and the types of control exercised by each, as of May 3, 1935, see Ogata, *op. cit.,* pp. 478–80.

[91] Among the more important agreements of this nature was that concluded in January, 1937, between representatives of Japanese and American textile interests, providing for a definite two-year quota on exports of cotton piece goods to the United States. (*The New York Times,* January 23, 1937.) For an illuminating discussion of Japanese trade negotiations with foreign countries, see T. Uyeda, *The Recent Development of Japanese Foreign Trade,* Prepared for the Sixth Conference of the Institute of Pacific Relations, Yosemite, California, Aug. 15 to 29, 1936, Japanese Council Papers, No. 3 (Tokyo, 1936), Ch. II.

try whose commercial policies emphasize the desirability of "bilateral balancing." Attempts have been made to control the total value of exports to such markets, and certain of the associations have accumulated reserve funds to assist in promoting Japanese imports from such countries.[92] This sort of activity has been especially important in the trade with Latin America.

We come finally to a consideration of export quotas introduced in connection with market control or commodity restriction schemes. There have been cases in which market control schemes have involved a special type of export quota imposed in order to bring about a larger quantity of exports than would result from the free operation of market forces. Of this nature are the compulsory export quotas which have been enforced by certain South African and Australian export control boards.[93] Far more common have been export quotas designed to reduce the quantity of exports in order to raise the world price. This sort of action can be advantageously undertaken by one country acting alone only under certain rather unusual conditions —the country must have a virtual monopoly in the production of the commodity, the foreign demand must be relatively inelastic, and so on.[94] Cases of this sort exist, but they are relatively rare and tend, indeed, to become more rare as new sources of supply or satisfactory substitutes are found for commodities formerly subject to successful monopolistic exploitation by a single country. Export quotas are being used on an increasing scale in conjunction with attempts to raise or control world prices of primary products, but the important developments in this field since the outbreak of the depression have depended on joint action by a number of supplying countries. We shall therefore consider them in Chapter XIV, which will be concerned with multilateral negotiations and agreements.

[92] Cf. Ogata, p. 483.
[93] Cf. pp. 330–32 above.
[94] Cf. p. 322 above.

The depression, and the rigid import restrictions to which it gave rise, created difficult problems for export industries all over the world. Governments have responded by providing exporters with various forms of state assistance and by subjecting exports to a considerably enhanced degree of official guidance and control. So far as the technique of trade control is concerned, certain developments stand out as being particularly significant. These are (1) the various attempts to protect export industries from the effects of world price changes, even though this may involve export subsidies, and (2) the tendency to encourage exporters to sell at different prices in different markets. If carried very far, these policies would radically change the nature of international competition.

In our survey of the methods of import control which have become so popular since 1931, we emphasized the fact that these devices tend to divorce domestic price movements from world price movements. The attempts to insulate export industries from the effects of international price movements constitute a further move in the same direction and, to a very considerable degree, have grown out of the situation created by the import controls. They have applied primarily to agricultural commodities, but it should be remembered that the prices of many manufactured goods tend to be relatively rigid without government intervention, owing to the nature of competition among large scale industrialists and the prevalence of combinations or cartels. Just as industrialists have found, however, that international agreements or cartels must be formed if prices of internationally traded commodities are to be effectively controlled, so governments find it exceedingly difficult to control prices of agricultural commodities or other primary products in the absence of international agreements. For commodities on an import basis, the difficulties may not be insuperable if the government is willing to extend its control over economic life to a sufficient degree. Where export products are involved, the difficulties are considerably greater. In periods of falling world prices, subsidies must be increased, a process which is not only expensive but may prove futile if the country is an important supplier or if several countries pursue a simultaneous policy of subsidization. In periods of rising world prices, on the other hand, producers press for removal of the price controls, thereby rendering it difficult for the government to accumulate the reserves needed to combat the next price-decline.

But, in the absence of multilateral agreements, nations have found that the division of markets along bilateral lines sometimes makes it easier for them to control the prices of their export products. If Country A's exports are guaranteed a fixed position in the markets of important importing countries, Country A can, by controlling the flow of exports, secure the advantages of high prices ruling in these markets. Abnormal profits acquired in this fashion can be used to subsidize exports to other markets. It is just here that the second important development noted above enters the picture, the tendency to encourage exporters to sell at different prices in different markets. It is only the existence of quantitative import restrictions (whether enforced through exchange permits or import control systems) that makes this sort of export policy possible. We shall have a clearer picture of the nature and extent of bilateral trade canalization after we have examined bilateral agreements in the next chapter. For the present, it is worth emphasizing the fact that arrangements of this sort certainly do not provide complete protection against the impact of economic fluctuations especially when the fluctuations are of a substantial order of magnitude.

PART IV

INTERNATIONAL COMMERCIAL BARGAINING

1

CHAPTER XII

Bilateral Agreements

1. *Recent Trends in Bilateral Bargaining*

The progress of commercial bargaining during the nineteen-twenties has been sketched in an earlier chapter.[1] We saw how the most-favored-nation clause eventually reasserted itself as the basis of commercial treaties after the rather chaotic conditions of the early post-War years. On the whole, however, tariff changes were predominantly upward throughout the post-War period, and this movement was greatly intensified from 1929 on. As the depression deepened, a primary purpose of bilateral negotiations was to restore freedom to raise duties, through deconsolidating tariff rates that had been "bound" in earlier treaties. Tariff reductions were regarded as practically out of the question. An important concern in many countries was to "improve" the balance of trade by restricting imports, whether through tariffs or more drastic devices. It was not until trade began slowly to recover from the depression that much thought was given to the possibility of seeking expansion of exports by negotiating for the lowering of foreign trade barriers. That these negotiations should proceed along bilateral lines appeared inevitable after the failure of the World Economic Conference of 1933.[2] There followed, from the autumn of 1933 to the late summer of 1939, a period of unprecedented activity in bilateral commercial bargaining. The

[1] See pp. 24–26 above.
[2] Cf. pp. 428–30 below.

367

intensity of the activity, however, was largely to be explained by the fact that, partly because of the prevalence of nontariff trade barriers and partly because of the political and economic instability of the period, agreements were of short duration and had to be frequently renewed and revised.

So far as the lowering of trade barriers was concerned, the results of all this bargaining were somewhat disappointing. Though some progress was made, many of the agreements, especially between pairs of countries in Central and Eastern Europe, were trade-diverting rather than trade-enlarging in their net effects. Concessions were frequently of a preferential or exclusive nature, especially where nontariff trade barriers were concerned. The period was characterized by an unwonted degree of emphasis on the balancing of bilateral trade between individual pairs of trading nations. Substantial injury to, and often outright discrimination against, the trade of third countries generally resulted from agreements of this character.

There have been a number of elements in the international situation since 1931 which have encouraged the employment of discriminatory methods in commercial bargaining. The tariff history of the late nineteen-twenties gave rise to considerable disillusionment over the efficacy of the most-favored-nation clause as an instrument for encouraging the reduction of tariff levels. Part of this disillusionment was directly attributable to the commercial policy pursued by the United States after the World War. As a great creditor nation, the United States should have been ready to undertake a reduction in her relatively high tariff level. Actually, revisions of the American tariff were in an upward direction; and, although the United States demanded unconditional most-favored-nation treatment from foreign countries, she refused to enter into bilateral negotiations for the reduction of tariff rates on the ground that her single-column tariff schedule was autonomous and not subject to alteration by negotiation. This attitude was completely contrary to the Continental European conception of commercial bargaining.[3] With the passage of the Hawley-Smoot Tariff Act in 1930, European disillusionment was intensified.[4] It was at about this time that the campaign for intra-European tariff preferences got under way and that one began to note the appearance of "buy from those who buy from you" attitudes. As early as 1930, Italian importers and industrialists were apparently subjected to private pressure by their Government to boycott the United States and to buy from countries which were willing to purchase Italian products, although outwardly Italy remained at this time one of the most loyal supporters of the most-favored-nation clause.[5]

The complete failure of multilateral action to reduce tariffs in the early nineteen-thirties (see Chapters I and XIV) also had much to do with the growth of a strong movement, at first for regional tariff preferences, and later on for agreements of an exclusively bilateral nature.

The influence of political developments on the growth of discriminatory practices in international commercial relations was of the utmost importance, especially from 1933 on. As numerous writers have pointed out, the commercial policy of a country that is preparing for war must of necessity be very different from that of a country which anticipates peacetime conditions for an indefinite future and is interested primarily in increasing economic welfare measured in terms of goods and services. In this connection, it does not greatly matter whether a country is deliberately pursuing an aggressive foreign policy or merely expects to be *drawn* into war to defend its interests.[6] In either case, it is likely to seek political alliances or friend-

---

[3] In Anglo-Saxon countries there has been a tendency to regard most-favored-nation treatment as a right to which a state is entitled by natural law; whereas, on the Continent, especially in France and Germany, the exchange of most-favored-nation guaranties has been regarded as the final step in tariff bargaining. Cf. Haberler, *Liberale und Planwirtschaftliche Handelspolitik,* p. 20.

[4] Cf. pp. 31–32 above.

[5] Cf. Jones, *Tariff Retaliation: Repercussions of the Hawley-Smoot Bill,* pp. 87–103.

[6] Cf. Staley, *World Economy in Transition,* pp. 206–12.

ships with other powers and may find it desirable to purchase or cement these friendships with trade concessions of a preferential or exclusive nature. The cheapest market may become, from a long-run point of view, a less advantageous place in which to buy than one which can be relied on for supplies in time of war. Impressive arguments may be put forward for commercial policies directed specifically toward expansion of trade with markets of the latter type, even though these policies may involve discrimination. A clear case in point, of course, is the German attempt to expand trade with the countries of Southeastern Europe and to build up these countries as sources of supply for certain raw materials and foodstuffs needed by Germany.

The widespread adoption of nontariff trade barriers [7] provided a convenient means of evading the most-favored-nation clause, a possibility which was in some cases recognized at the time these measures were introduced but which was not, in general, fully exploited until somewhat later. The employment of such methods also had much to do with the trend toward "bilateral balancing," with which we shall deal specifically in a later section.

2. *The Position of the Most-Favored-Nation Clause since 1931*

It is not our intention to enter into the controversy over the advantages and disadvantages of the most-favored-nation clause. There is a voluminous literature on the subject.[8] Evaluation of recent trends in bilateral commercial bargaining, how-

[7] The term *nontariff trade barriers,* as used in the present chapter, refers to those types of trade restriction which do not take the form of tariffs, taxes, fees, etc., levied by the customs authorities. It embraces primarily exchange restrictions, import and export quota and license systems, import and export monopolies, and import and export prohibitions.

[8] Cf., e.g., G. Haberler, *The Theory of International Trade,* pp. 377–93; J. Viner, "The Most-favoured-nation Clause," Svenska Handelsbanken, *Index,* VI (1931), 2–17; S. H. Bailey, "Reciprocity and the Most-Favoured-Nation Clause," *Economica,* XIII (1933), 428–56; and L. Sommer, *Neugestaltung der Handelspolitik: Wege zu einem intereuropäischen Präferenzsystem* (Berlin, 1935).

ever, entails a careful consideration of the extent to which recent developments have changed the position of the clause.

There is little question that the most-favored-nation clause played a less important rôle in international commercial relations at the end of the nineteen-thirties than at the close of the preceding decade. This did not come about, however, as a result of a wholesale abandonment of the clause. One can point to few countries which openly departed from the clause as an instrument of policy. The United States Tariff Commission reported as late as the end of 1936 that most-favored-nation agreements existed between nearly one-half of the "possible bilateral country combinations" and were applicable to "much more than half" of the world's trade.[9] The movement away from the clause may be said to have taken *chiefly* the following forms: (1) adoption of new or additional exceptions to the clause; (2) employment of nontariff trade barriers, which cannot be rendered consistent with the clause in a very satisfactory manner and which, in any case, are frequently held by the governments administering them to be outside the scope of the clause; (3) conclusion of "secret" agreements or "secret" supplements to published agreements. It is sometimes maintained that the clause has been weakened through refinement of tariff classifications undertaken for the purpose of creating artificial distinctions between the products of different countries, but whether this sort of activity has really made possible extensive discrimination is a debatable point.

[9] U. S. Tariff Commission, *Extent of Equal Tariff Treatment in Foreign Countries*, p. 10. The great majority of these agreements were unconditional rather than conditional in form. In so far as nontariff trade barriers have rendered tariffs more or less inoperative in the trade between countries having most-favored-nation agreements, however, and in so far as the most-favored-nation clause is ignored in the administration of such barriers, the proportion of world trade governed by the clause is correspondingly reduced. The compilation of adequate statistics on this point would be a difficult task, since account would have to be taken of the fact that, even where quotas or other nontariff trade barriers exist, they do not affect the entire trade of the country concerned nor is the most-favored-nation clause always ignored in their administration.

Against these factors tending to limit the applicability of the clause should be placed at least one development which has tended to strengthen the clause. This was the entry of the United States in 1934 into the field of active tariff bargaining on the basis of a broad interpretation of the unconditional most-favored-nation clause. It is true that the United States adopted the unconditional form of the clause in 1923, but it was not until the inauguration of the Reciprocal Trade Agreements Program in 1934 that this country was willing to agree to conventional reductions in its single-column tariff schedule. Through its championship of the clause and through its insistence that most-favored-nation treatment be extended, as far as possible, to include the administration of quotas and other nontariff trade barriers, the United States has attempted to forestall the spread of discriminatory methods in commercial policy.

Let us now consider, one by one, the developments which have tended to limit the scope of the clause.

a. The adoption of new or additional exceptions to the clause. It has long been customary to recognize certain so-called *regional exceptions* to the most-favored-nation clause, where such exceptions are expressly stated in commercial agreements embodying the clause.[10] One (or both) of the contracting countries renounces its right to claim the benefit of any concession granted by the other country to certain designated states bound to it by geographical, ethnic, or historical ties. Thus the Scandinavian countries, Norway, Sweden, and Denmark, in their agreements with third countries, exclude from the operation of the most-favored-nation clause any preferences which they may grant to each other. Similar reservations have been made by the Baltic states, the Central American countries, and other groups.[11]

[10] Two exceptions which are generally recognized and need not be expressly stated are those relating to "border traffic" and to the formation of "customs unions." As we shall see in Chapter XIV, there has been at least one unsuccessful attempt to take initial steps toward a customs union since 1931.

[11] For a list of such groups, see R. Riedl, *Exceptions to the Most-Favoured-*

As we have noted in Chapter I, the practice of restricting the scope of the most-favored-nation clause in this manner showed a tendency to increase in the years following the World War.[12] The extent to which countries included in groups of this sort actually grant preferential treatment to one another, however, has been, and still is, very limited.[13] We shall deal with the recent developments in this field in the following chapter. It is sufficient to note here that, in spite of much talk of the need for regional economic *blocs,* especially in Europe, there are still relatively few cases of tariff preferences on a regional basis, and most of those which have been granted have taken the form of preferential tariff quotas.

Another closely related and generally recognized exception to the most-favored-nation clause concerns preferential tariff arrangements between the different parts of an empire. This question, too, will be treated in the next chapter, but it should be noted here that this exception to the most-favored-nation clause, unlike the one just discussed, is of considerable importance and has tended to become more important in recent years. The Ottawa Agreements are well known, but the fact that preferential arrangements between mother countries and colonies have been on the increase since the end of the nineteen-twenties is perhaps less well known. Many of these new preferential arrangements, however, have appeared in conjunction with the adoption of nontariff trade barriers.

Next we come to the question of commodity exceptions to the most-favored-nation clause. The practice of restricting the applicability of the clause to (*a*) a list of specified commodities, or (*b*) to all commodities except those appearing on a list of exceptions was adopted by several countries during the depression. Where this type of exception is introduced, the *limited*

Nation Treatment, Report presented to the International Chamber of Commerce (London, 1931), pp. 12–18.

[12] Cf. p. 25 above.

[13] Cf. U. S. Tariff Commission, *Extent of Equal Tariff Treatment in Foreign Countries,* p. 14.

form of the clause is said to be employed.[14] Adoption of the limited most-favored-nation clause might conceivably, if many commodities were excepted in each agreement, lead to a situation in which all concessions were absolutely exclusive, i.e., in which the principle of pure reciprocity was applied. In practice, nothing of the sort has tended to happen. Commodity exceptions are usually few and tend to consist of items which are of little or no importance in the trade between the two countries concluding the agreement. This result is likely to ensue because nations refuse to permit commodities which are of any importance in their export trade to be excluded from most-favored-nation treatment on entry into foreign markets. Unless a country's bargaining power is very weak, it can usually enforce its demand for most-favored-nation treatment with respect to its leading exports. Even so, the limited most-favored-nation clause seems to find favor with a few countries as a means of retaining greater freedom in bargaining.

French commercial treaties concluded during the early nineteen-twenties generally contained a grant merely of limited most-favored-nation treatment on France's part, but in a number of agreements the commodity exceptions were of negligible importance in the other country's exports.[15] France has adhered to the limited form of the clause in the years since 1931, but again in many instances she has been obliged to grant most-favored-nation treatment on all products actually exported by the other country or at least on all products of any interest to the other country.[16] By a decree of December 23, 1931, the Spanish Government also reverted to a limited most-favored-

[14] Obviously, there are other ways of limiting the applicability of the clause, but for the sake of convenience we shall use the term *limited most-favored-nation clause* in its narrower sense, confining it to those cases in which commodity exceptions are prescribed.

[15] Cf. Viner, "The Most-favoured-nation Clause," p. 4.

[16] Cf. U. S. Tariff Commission, *Extent of Equal Tariff Treatment in Foreign Countries,* p. 90.

nation policy, to which it had adhered for a time during the nineteen-twenties.[17] A few other countries have limited their grants of most-favored-nation treatment in certain instances, especially in dealing with countries which consistently do so. On the whole, this method of restricting the applicability of the clause in tariff matters has not achieved any widespread popularity; but, as we shall see, a limited form of most-favored-nation treatment is frequently granted in connection with quantitative import restrictions.[18]

b. The most-favored-nation clause and nontariff trade barriers. As we have already had occasion to note, tariffs constituted practically the sole barrier to international trade during the greater part of the nineteenth century.[19] The most-favored-nation clause was intended to apply primarily to customs questions, and the question of its applicability to nontariff trade barriers did not arise.[20] In response to the employment of import and export prohibitions and restrictions during the first World War and the early post-War period, a number of the treaties concluded during the nineteen-twenties contained clauses specifically extending the most-favored-nation

---

[17] *Ibid.*

[18] The applicability of the clause has been restricted in certain other ways in recent years. On the right of nations to claim, through the clause, the benefits of multilateral conventions which they have not signed, see pp. 432–33 below. The practice of inserting provisions into commercial agreements specifically exempting anti-dumping duties from the operation of the clause has been growing, as has that of including a reservation designed to permit arrangements to eliminate double-taxation.

[19] Cf. pp. 7–8 above.

[20] "According to the general practice in commercial treaties, the term 'Customs questions' includes the scales of Customs duties and the method of levying them — i.e., import and export duties, supercharge coefficients, where they exist, and subsidiary charges of every sort levied on imports and exports. The term also covers all the rules, formalities and charges inseparable from Customs operations of every description (including, for instance, the regulations for the treatment of passengers' luggage or commercial travellers' samples; the procedure and time limits for appeals to administrative, judicial or arbitral authorities against Customs decisions relating to the application of tariffs)." (League of Nations, *Recommendations of the Economic Committee Relating to Tariff Policy and the Most-favoured-nation Clause* [Geneva, 1933], p. 8.)

obligation to trade barriers of this sort.[21] By no means all treaties in force in 1931, however, included clauses of this nature, and, in any event, the interpretation of such clauses in relation to import quota or license systems was difficult and controversial, since the treaties did not include any specific formula to serve as a guide in this matter. Furthermore, as we have seen in an earlier chapter, no completely satisfactory formula for this purpose exists. The "base period" formula (under which exporting countries are allotted shares of the quota corresponding to their relative contributions to imports of the commodity into the country imposing the quota in a given

[21] Typical of such clauses was that appearing in a commercial treaty of May 28, 1930, between the Netherlands and Yugoslavia:

Article 5.

1. "The High Contracting Parties undertake not to hamper their reciprocal commercial relations by any import or export prohibitions or restrictions.

2. Exceptions to this rule, which must in any case apply to all countries or to the countries in which identical conditions prevail, may be made in the following cases only:

(*a*) For reasons of public security or the safety of the State;

(*b*) On moral or humanitarian grounds;

(*c*) In regard to traffic in arms, ammunition and implements of war or, in exceptional circumstances, all other military supplies;

(*d*) In regard to sanitary police measures and for the protection of animals and useful plants from extinction or degeneration and against disease and noxious insects or parasites, in accordance with the international principles adopted with regard to such matters;

(*e*) For the protection of national treasures of artistic, historic, or archaeological value;

(*f*) For the purpose of preventing or restricting the import or export of gold, silver, coins, currency notes, banknotes or securities;

(*g*) For products which are subject to State monopolies and for the application to foreign goods of prohibitions and restrictions which are or may hereafter be imposed on the production, sale, or consumption within the country of the same native goods.

3. Nothing in the present Article shall affect the right of the High Contracting Parties to adopt measures prohibiting or restricting importation or exportation for the purpose of protecting, in extraordinary and abnormal circumstances, the vital interests of the country. Nevertheless, the High Contracting Parties mutually guarantee each other most-favored-nation treatment in the above matters and undertake reciprocally not to impose prohibitions or restrictions on importation, exportation or transit, which are not applicable to all other countries without distinction." (League of Nations, *Treaty Series,* CXXIX [1932] 77.)

base period) has been most frequently employed, but, in addition to its rigidity, it has the disadvantage of leading to disputes over the choice of appropriate base periods.[22]

A similar problem arose in connection with exchange restrictions which were also not usually covered by the most-favored-nation clause and which could easily be held to be outside its scope, since customs barriers were not necessarily involved. Yet exchange regulations, as we have seen, could be administered in such a way as to render most-favored-nation guaranties completely meaningless. Discrimination was often involved in decisions affecting the allocation of exchange or the particular exchange rate to be applied to purchases from different countries. Exchange regulations lent themselves to administrative secrecy which in turn made possible favoritism and arbitrary preferences; but whether the basis of allocation was made public or not, "bilateral balancing" considerations usually came to be given great emphasis.

Exchange-control countries, moreover, became involved in a network of clearing and payments agreements, under which the proceeds of sales to a given country were earmarked for remittances to that country. In so far as such arrangements limited the funds available for remittances to third countries, they tended to discriminate against the exports of such countries. The sources of imports ceased to be determined by competitive factors alone. It is for this reason that clearing and payments agreements can be said to violate the spirit of the most-favored-nation clause. Some of these agreements, of course, provide not merely for the earmarking of funds but also for preferential exchange rates or exchange premia.

In view of the general uncertainty regarding the scope of the most-favored-nation clause and in view of the danger of retaliation, a number of countries attempted in 1931 and 1932 to adhere to the principle of equality of treatment, in one form or another, in the administration of quotas or exchange

[22] Cf. p. 271 above.

restrictions. As time went on, however, more and more countries turned to discriminatory methods, defending their policies on the ground that nontariff trade barriers were not covered by the clause. This tendency has been opposed, not always with complete consistency, by a number of countries which have refrained from employing nontariff trade barriers on any extensive scale. These countries have succeeded in securing guaranties of equality of treatment, at least for their chief exports, in many instances. But even countries which have employed quotas or exchange restrictions in a discriminatory fashion on their own part have sometimes secured guaranties of equality of treatment from other countries, where it seemed in their interest to do so.

On the whole, however, especially on the Continent of Europe, when two countries, both employing extensive quota or exchange restrictions, proceed to bargain over these restrictions, the most-favored-nation clause is ignored. Any attempt to observe it would doubtless lead merely to prolonged higgling over the choice of base periods. These countries seek to protect their export markets, not so much from discrimination as from drastic curtailment, by totally different methods. Among the more important of such methods are the following:

(1) Insisting on the inclusion in commercial agreements (or clearing agreements) of some sort of compensation clause, whereby each country is assured that its purchases in the other country will lead to sales to that country;

(2) Getting other countries to agree to make advance commitments with respect to their total purchases in Country A.

(3) Insisting on provisions for the reopening of negotiations in the case of any complaints or of material changes in import regulations.

(4) Setting up mixed or joint commissions to supervise the working of bilateral agreements.

In so far as countries *have* secured pledges that their exports shall receive fair treatment under the exchange regulations, import licensing systems, or monopoly regimes of other countries, these guaranties have assumed a variety of forms. In some cases specific formulas of fair treatment, such as the "base period" formula in connection with quotas, have been written into agreements. In other cases, the pledge has taken the form of a grant of most-favored-nation treatment, without any definite provision as to how this most-favored-nation guaranty is to be interpreted.[23] In still other cases, all that has been granted has been a vague pledge of equitable treatment. More often than not, these guaranties, especially in relation to import quotas, have applied only to specified commodities. In some cases, the list of commodities covered is quite short. The net result of all this has been a highly confused situation in which discrimination is widely practiced, *except* where it is precluded either by safeguards written into bilateral agreements or by tactical considerations.

The most consistent and thoroughgoing campaign against the employment of discriminatory methods in connection with nontariff trade barriers has been waged by the United States under its Reciprocal Trade Agreements Program. This country has worked out definite formulas of fair treatment with respect to the administration of exchange restrictions, import quota and license systems, and import monopolies. In each agreement, it seeks to secure pledges of fair treatment for its exports in accordance with these formulas. Among other countries which have frequently secured guaranties of fair treatment for their exports under foreign import or exchange regulations are the United Kingdom, the Netherlands, Soviet Russia, Norway, Sweden, and Brazil. Many of these countries, however, have on occasion, in somewhat inconsistent fashion, granted or received special favors in the form of preferentially large quotas or entered into clearing and pay-

---

[23] In some cases, as, e.g., when it is merely a matter of what exchange rate is to be employed, no such definite provisions are necessary.

ments agreements which endowed their exports with what amounted to a preferential status.[24]

c. Secret agreements and protocols. The number of secret commercial agreements concluded on the Continent of Europe, and particularly in Central Europe, has apparently been by no means insignificant in recent years. In some cases, the contents of these agreements have become more or less generally known, although they have never been officially published. In other cases, such information as is available is based largely on newspaper speculation. In addition, there may be some unpublished agreements whose very existence has been successfully kept secret. There is little question, however, that an important purpose of most secret agreements has been to make possible concessions of a discriminatory nature, which the countries involved preferred not to make public for fear of subjecting their exports to retaliatory action. Some of these concessions were clearly motivated by political considerations.

One country, or rather ex-country, which is known to have concluded a large number of secret agreements during the nineteen-thirties is Czechoslovakia. According to a report of the United States Tariff Commission, quotas granted to certain countries by Czechoslovakia in unpublished special agreements were so large as to "involve an abnormal curtailment of imports from other countries." [25] Another country which went in extensively for secret agreements from about 1934 on was Germany.[26]

d. Weakening of the clause through the narrowing of tariff classifications. It has long been charged that the most-favored-nation clause can be rendered virtually meaningless through the artificial narrowing of tariff classifications in such a way

[24] The United States has also received special favors in a few instances. Cf. p. 403 below.

[25] U. S. Tariff Commission, *Extent of Equal Tariff Treatment in Foreign Countries,* p. 74.

[26] These secret agreements often took the form of unpublished supplements to published agreements.

as to permit the application of different tariff rates to essentially the same goods coming from different countries. Commercial treaties have been known to include tariff concessions on items so narrowly defined that third countries could not possibly benefit from the concessions. Probably the extent to which this procedure has been deliberately employed in order to make possible discrimination among different countries has been greatly exaggerated.[27] With the progress of industrialization and the development of more and more highly specialized products, tariff schedules have naturally become increasingly complicated. Furthermore, the possibility of retaliation tends to discourage the deliberate elaboration of tariff schedules for the purpose of discrimination.[28] In some cases, clauses have been inserted into commercial treaties to prevent this type of procedure.[29]

It should be recognized, moreover, that tariff bargaining on the basis of the unconditional most-favored-nation clause presents certain inherent difficulties which can sometimes be partially overcome through the narrowing of tariff classifications. A country may find that it is not worth its while to enter into commercial agreements involving "sacrifices" on its part if its exports are, through the operation of the clause, benefiting extensively from concessions embodied in agreements to which it is not a party. Hence, governments which are anxious to secure concessions from many countries frequently limit the concessions which they will offer in any particular agreement to those commodities which are supplied chiefly by the other party to the agreement. If this policy is carefully followed, there will usually remain important items on which tariff reductions can be offered to countries with which negotiations are

[27] Cf. Viner, "The Most-favoured-nation Clause," p. 10.

[28] Cf. H. J. Tasca, *The Reciprocal Trade Policy of the United States: A Study in Trade Philosophy* (Philadelphia, 1938), p. 142.

[29] Thus the Dutch-Yugoslav treaty of May 28, 1930, extended the most-favored-nation guaranty to "the classification and interpretation of tariffs." (League of Nations, *Treaty Series,* CXXIX [1932], 77.)

to be conducted at a later stage. The narrowing of tariff classifications sometimes facilitates the carrying out of such a procedure. As we shall see, these tactics have been employed in the carrying out of the United States Reciprocal Trade Agreements Program, and American tariff classifications have been narrowed in many instances.[30] Clearly, the net effects of such a policy will depend in large part on the spirit in which it is carried out.

On the whole, there is little question that the weakening of the most-favored-nation clause during the nineteen-thirties came about *chiefly* through the employment of nontariff trade barriers. The use of such weapons, in turn, had a profound influence on the adoption of "bilateral balancing" policies, which we shall now consider.

3. *Bilateral Balancing Policies*

A "bilateral balancing" policy may be defined broadly as a policy based on the theory that *bilateral payments* between any given pair of trading nations should *approach a balance*. Actually, the extent to which invisible items in the balance of payments are taken into account is somewhat limited. Policies do not tend to be very consistent in this respect; and, in general, it may be said that the country which has an "unfavorable" balance of commodity trade *vis à vis* the other country has the upper hand in the bargaining, *regardless* of the status

[30] Cf. p. 397 below. For illustrations of reclassifications of American tariffs, see Tasca, *Reciprocal Trade Policy,* p. 315. Frequently a tariff reduction will apply to all items of a given class which are above or below a certain value or size. In many such cases, the effect of the reclassification is to benefit primarily the products of the other country concerned in the agreement.

It is interesting to note, in this connection, that, in the Anglo-Swedish agreement of May 15, 1933, Sweden reduced the duty on passenger automobiles "with engines having a cylinder capacity of less than 1600 cm^3." (League of Nations, *Treaty Series,* CXL [1933–34], 355.) The intention, apparently, was to favor the characteristically small British car over, e.g., American cars which characteristically have a total cylinder capacity much greater than 1600 cubic centimeters.

of invisible items in the bilateral balance of payments. Hence, in practice, bilateral balancing policies often seem to aim at the equalization of bilateral trade, rather than of bilateral payments.

That the trend toward bilateral balancing should have been an outstanding development of the past decade must be attributed in considerable part to the spread of exchange control (or, ultimately, to the factors which gave rise to exchange control). We have seen how regulation of the foreign exchanges led to the introduction of clearing agreements, which in turn could not be made to work unless accompanied by compensation clauses or other provisions designed to secure the achievement of a fixed trade ratio. These provisions were often included in commercial agreements associated with the clearing agreements. Payments agreements, which eventually replaced clearing agreements in some instances, were sometimes less rigid than clearing agreements but were definitely based on a bilateral balancing principle.

It should be recognized, as we have taken pains to point out in an earlier connection, that countries which sought to remain aloof from bilateral payments arrangements nevertheless found their trade becoming more rigidly bilateral in nature as a result of the existence of these arrangements in other parts of the world.[31] Furthermore, even countries which refused to adopt a "bilateral balancing" policy in any form, inevitably found their commercial negotiations tending, to some extent, in that direction. For, unless they were prepared to grant to countries with which they had "favorable" trade balances, concessions which were not fully compensated by corresponding counter-concessions, they ran the risk, in some cases, of seeing their exports to such countries drastically curtailed. In view of these considerations, it is easy to see how the spread of bilateral balancing policies may become a cumulative process.

Unlike exchange restrictions, import quotas and monopolies

[31] Cf. pp. 200–201 above.

cannot be said to have led directly to bilateral balancing, but they certainly lend themselves to the carrying out of such policies; and, on the whole, it would appear that bargaining on the basis of extensive quota or monopoly systems can most easily be conducted on bilateral balancing principles. In any event, the detailed governmental control over the quantities of goods moving in international trade which the employment of quotas and monopolies implies is likely to be accompanied by increased attention to the state of the trade balance with individual countries.[32]

It is important to emphasize the fact that bilateral balancing policies have here been defined as being based on the theory that bilateral payments should *approach* a balance. They do not invariably call for the establishment of a rigid trade or payments ratio in each and every agreement. In fact, they range all the way from very flexible policies to those which are carried out with the utmost rigidity. One might draw up a list of the various forms which bilateral balancing policies may take, with the understanding that in practice the policy pursued by any given country may combine elements of several types. Such a list would have to include at least the following types of policies:

(*a*) *Conduct of treaty negotiations on the theory that the country which has a "favorable" balance of trade or payments in its economic relations with the other country should make all or most of the sacrifices.* This theory lies behind all bargaining on a bilateral balancing basis, but we refer here to the cases in which no other mechanism, such as a rigid compensation clause, is employed to cause bilateral trade or payments to approach a balance. The disproportionate "sacrifices" of one of the two countries are alone relied on to achieve this end.

[32] A spectacularly "unfavorable" development in the trade balance with particular countries may give rise to "buy from those who buy from you" sentiments. Thus, the marked increase in the passive trade balances of Latin American countries with Japan, which accompanied the rapid expansion of Japanese exports to this area from 1932 on, had something to do with the adoption of bilateral balancing tariff systems by certain of these countries. Cf. p. 222 n. above and p. 385 below.

This is the type of policy which the United Kingdom has shown some tendency to follow since 1931. Britain has a large passive balance in her trade with many countries and has taken advantage of this situation to extract disproportionately large concessions from other countries, meanwhile imposing unilateral restrictions on imports from these countries. This policy has been combined with a fairly strict adherence to the unconditional most-favored-nation clause in the administration of British tariffs and quotas.[33] In fact, there is nothing about a bargaining policy of this type which is *necessarily* inconsistent with the clause, so long as concessions are generalized to countries entitled to most-favored-nation treatment. It is in the character of the bargaining conducted on the basis of the clause that a departure from traditional methods of commercial policy is taken; for, in the past, negotiations have usually been conducted on the theory that *reciprocal concessions,* rather than bilateral trade or payments, should be balanced.[34]

(*b*) *Administration of tariffs, exchange regulations, import quota and licensing systems or import monopolies on a bilateral balancing basis, combined with the sort of bargaining policy described under (a).* In this category must be grouped the multiple-column tariff systems recently adopted by certain Latin American countries, which subject imports of the same items from different countries to higher or lower tariff rates in accordance with the state of the balance of trade with those countries.[35] Here, also, must be grouped all exchange control systems which tend to favor, in the allocation of exchange or in the determination of the exchange rate or premium to be paid, imports from countries with which the trade balance is active. Here, too, belong most import quota and permit systems, and many governmental import monopolies, since we have found that under the majority of these control schemes, "buy from those who buy from you" policies are followed.

All the policies in this group are inconsistent with the spirit of the most-favored-nation clause, although outright violations of the letter of the clause are not usually involved. In the case of

[33] As we shall see, Britain has permitted her exports to receive preferential treatment under the quantitative and exchange restrictions of other countries in certain instances. Preferences to the Empire are, of course, regarded as outside the scope of the most-favored-nation clause.

[34] Large countries, however, have generally had some superiority in bargaining power.

[35] Cf. pp. 222–23 above.

the Latin American countries which have adopted multiple-column tariff schedules based on a bilateral balancing principle, the benefits of the minimum tariff are generally extended to the few (in some cases, *very few*) countries which are entitled by treaty to most-favored-nation treatment, irrespective of the state of the trade balance with those countries. (Significantly enough, Cuba denounced her most-favored-nation agreements with Japan, Portugal, and Italy just previous to embarking on her bilateral balancing tariff policy.[36]) The countries which administer exchange control or quantitative import restrictions on a bilateral balancing basis usually maintain that the most-favored-nation clause applies only to tariffs, although they are occasionally forced to broaden the application of the clause in their relations with certain countries.

The policies in this group may but do not necessarily lead to equalization of bilateral trade or payments. Clearly, it is easier to achieve such equalization through quantitative or exchange restrictions than through tariffs.

(*c*) *Conclusion of clearing or payments agreements.* The nature of such arrangements and the way in which they violate the most-favored-nation clause have already been discussed.

(*d*) *Inclusion of compensation clauses in bilateral agreements, whether in connection with clearing or payments agreements or not.* Compensation clauses may: (*a*) call for a fixed trade ratio, (*b*) provide that bilateral trade must be conducted wholly or partly on a compensation basis, or (*c*) fix the total value or detailed composition of trade on each side in such a way as to achieve a fixed trade ratio. It is where agreements include compensation clauses that bilateral balancing is most rigidly carried out. Even in such cases the actual trade ratio may deviate from the prescribed ratio, unless trade movements are subjected to rigid and detailed control in order to prevent such an occurrence. Compensation clauses sometimes apply only to a portion of the trade between the two countries.

The extent to which bilateral balancing policies have gained acceptance may perhaps best be indicated by mentioning the countries which have avoided them. Almost the only country of any importance which has sought to remain aloof from bilateral balancing in all its manifestations is the United States,

---

[36] U. S. Tariff Commission, *Extent of Equal Tariff Treatment in Foreign Countries,* p. 115.

although this country deviated from its accepted policy to some slight extent in 1939 when it concluded a compensation (barter) agreement with the United Kingdom. Among countries which have, for the most part, paid tribute to bilateral balancing theories only to the extent of entering into a very small number of clearing or payments agreements are Norway, Sweden, and some of the British Dominions. Brazil has taken various steps away from bilateral balancing in the last few years, steps which culminated in the undertaking, embodied in the United States-Brazilian Credit Agreement of 1939, to free her foreign exchange market for commercial transactions.[37] With these exceptions, most countries of any importance in world trade have been involved, at least to an appreciable extent, in bilateral balancing programs of one sort or another. The strongholds of bilateral balancing are Central and Eastern Europe and, in less rigid fashion, Latin America.

Despite the widespread acceptance of bilateral balancing theories, agreements which called for a rigid bilateral trade ratio were in the minority at the outbreak of World War II. Even the countries which were most definitely committed to bilateral balancing policies, moreover, sometimes found it to their advantage to permit trade to deviate somewhat from rigid bilateral channels, for a number of reasons. In the first place, the disadvantages of a policy which forces trade into rigid bilateral channels become painfully obvious when, as a result, exorbitant prices have to be paid for imported goods. Even a totalitarian state will, on occasion, compromise with its bilateral balancing principles in order to secure goods at favorable prices. Secondly, one of the chief obstacles confronting industrial countries, like Germany, which have sought to expand trade on a strictly bilateral basis, has been the relative lack of purchasing power in agricultural and raw material-producing countries. Such countries, though they form the chief sources of supply for the staple imports of industrial states, do

[37] Cf. pp. 346–47 above.

not always constitute the best markets for industrial goods. A third major obstacle to attempts to force trade into rigid bilateral channels—and one which has been mentioned at earlier stages in our study—is the tendency for trade currents to shift, both in the long and in the short run. Clearly, none of these obstacles is insuperable, but all three tend to give rise to a need for rigid and detailed control of trade, if equalization on a bilateral basis is to be secured.

4. *Specific Quota Provisions of Bilateral Agreements*

With the spread of import quota systems, it was natural that quotas should become a subject for bilateral bargaining. In this section we shall be concerned, not with the general guaranties which countries have given each other with respect to the operation of their quota systems, but with specific concessions relating to the quotas for individual commodities. The extent to which such concessions have appeared in the various agreements has naturally depended to a very large degree on the extent to which import quotas have been employed by the countries concerned. Agreements between countries with comprehensive quota systems have tended to relate very largely to the quantities of goods which each country would admit from the other. On the whole, as we have seen, there has been a tendency for such agreements to be based on a bilateral balancing principle, but this is not necessarily the case.

Individual quota concessions have usually taken one of the following forms:

- (*a*) an undertaking to permit imports of a specified quantity of a given commodity from the other country;
- (*b*) allocation to the other country of a definite share of the quota for a given commodity;
- (*c*) an undertaking to permit imports of a given commodity amounting to a specified total value (in terms of currency units) from the other country, i.e., allocation of a value quota.

Of these, commitments of the third type have not been very common except in conjunction with exchange control systems, in which they have taken the form of an undertaking to issue exchange permits amounting to a given value for importation of a specified commodity from the country in question.[38]

Quota concessions may or may not be exclusive or preferential in nature, as we have seen. Furthermore, they may or may not signify an increase in imports from the other country. In some cases, quota concessions merely give to the exporting country: (1) a fixed share of a quota that is in process of being reduced, or (2) an assurance that its quota will not be reduced below a certain minimum. This sort of concession, of course, is more likely to appear in periods of trade depression than in periods of trade expansion.

It is by no means an infrequent occurrence that actual imports of a specified commodity from a given country during a certain period turn out to be greater or smaller than the amount designated in the agreement with that country. If they are less than the agreed amount, the exporting country *may* have cause for complaint. Let us assume that Country A has agreed to admit a definite *quantity* of imports from Country B, but actual imports prove to be less than the amount specified in the agreement. Country B's grounds for protest will not be very strong if Country A's imports of the commodity in question have declined all round, owing, say, to a shift in demand conditions within Country A. Country B may have cause for complaint, however, if it can show that the authorities in Country A have prevented full utilization of Country B's quota by, (1) issuing permits on an unwontedly generous scale for imports from Countries C or D, (2) levying an import license fee or other tax so high as to prevent full utilization of Country B's quota, or (3) exerting secret pressure on importers not to apply for

[38] The Netherlands, however, has made considerable use of value quotas, and her concessions in commercial treaties have sometimes involved this type of quota.

permits to import the commodity in question from Country B.[39]

Where Country A has allocated to Country B a specified *share* of the quota for a given commodity, Country B will have cause for complaint if it fails to receive its due share, *regardless* of the size of total imports of the commodity into Country A.

A further complication may arise in connection with quota commitments. Country B may have been promised a specified quota by Country A but may fail to supply the prescribed amounts at competitive prices, owing perhaps (1) to some unforeseen development such as a strike or harvest failure, or (2) to a combination of Country B's exporters deliberately formed for the purpose of extracting a monopolistic price from Country A. Because of this possibility, governments often insist, before undertaking to allocate definite quotas in their commercial agreements, on the inclusion of protective clauses relating to the prices at which goods are to be supplied.[40] We shall have occasion to examine some clauses of this type in the following chapter.

Finally, something needs to be said about the part played by tariff quotas in recent commercial agreements. The fact is that tariff quotas have originated much more frequently in commercial agreements than they have in autonomous import regulations. They are occasionally employed by countries which make little use of other types of quotas, usually for the purpose of permitting a tariff reduction in an agreement with another country while definitely limiting the increase of imports which will result from the reduction. In this way, tariff

[39] Illustrations of all these types of occurrence can be found in practice. The influence of France's license fee on the utilization of the American quota for apples and pears has been mentioned in Chapter IX. The existence of a tariff on the commodity in question may also affect the outcome and complicate the negotiations.

Germany and Italy seem to have been the most frequent offenders in failing to live up to their quota obligations. In these two countries, the control of the state over importation is so direct that failure to carry out a quota commitment can usually be attributed to governmental action.

[40] Cf. p. 311 n. above, on the Dutch undertaking to procure a specified proportion of its wheat and flour requirements in the United States.

concessions are sometimes made more acceptable to vested interests in the importing country while at the same time opening up the possibility of a sufficient increase in imports to make the concession of real value to the exporting country.[41]

Tariff quotas have also been employed in commercial agreements for a variety of other purposes, among which the following may be mentioned:

(1) To grant preferential treatment, on a limited basis, to another country. Most preferential tariff quotas have applied to imports into Western European countries of the agricultural products of Eastern Europe. (See pp. 447–51 below.)

(2) To permit a country to participate, on a limited basis, in privileges enjoyed by certain other countries. Thus, as we shall see, France granted Soviet Russia the benefits of her minimum tariff for limited quantities of certain commodities.

In the administration of tariff quotas, the most-favored-nation clause has sometimes been ignored, generally by countries which have failed to observe it in conjunction with ordinary quotas. Tariff quotas have played a rôle, also, in secret agreements.

[41] See pp. 397–98 below, on tariff quotas in American agreements.

CHAPTER XIII

BILATERAL BARGAINING POLICIES OF FOUR LEADING COUNTRIES

This chapter will be devoted to a discussion of the bilateral bargaining policies of the United States, Britain, France, and Germany. The commercial policies of these four countries have always exerted an important influence on policies followed elsewhere. Most of the attitudes and techniques which have characterized bilateral bargaining in recent years, moreover, may be illustrated by reference to these four countries. It would be desirable, if space permitted, to examine in detail the policies of other countries, but to a very large extent the nature of these policies has been indicated in discussions of exchange control, clearing agreements, tariff policies, import quotas, and other instruments of trade control.

1. *The United States*

The Reciprocal Trade Agreements Program represents, as we have already indicated, a highly significant departure in American commercial policy. The program was inaugurated with the passage in June, 1934, of "An Act to amend the Tariff Act of 1930." [1] This act gave the President power (1) to "enter into foreign trade agreements with foreign governments or instrumentalities thereof" and (2) to "proclaim such modifica-

---

[1] Public No. 316, 73d Congress (H.R. 8687). The act was to remain in force for three years, but it was extended, in January, 1937, for a further period of three years, or until June, 1940, and has recently been renewed for an additional three-year period.

tions of existing duties and other import restrictions, or such additional import restrictions, or such continuance, and for such minimum periods, of existing customs or excise treatment of any article covered by foreign trade agreements, as are required or appropriate to carry out any foreign trade agreement that the President has entered into hereunder." [2] Existing rates of duty could not, however, be raised or lowered by more than 50 per cent, nor could any article be transferred between the dutiable and free lists.[3] The "proclaimed duties and other import restrictions" were to apply to the products of all countries; or, in other words, generalization of concessions was prescribed. It was provided, nevertheless, that the President might suspend their "application to articles the growth, produce, or manufacture of any country because of its discriminatory treatment of American commerce or because of other acts or policies which in his opinion" tended "to defeat the purposes" of the act.[4] Continuation of preferential tariff arrangements with Cuba was authorized; in other words, we would continue to regard our tariff relations with Cuba as constituting a "regional exception" to the most-favored-nation clause.

Agreements concluded under the act were to be subject to termination, upon due notice, at the end of three years, but if not then terminated, were to be subject to termination upon not more than six months' notice. Under a further provision of the act, "reasonable public notice of the intention to negotiate an agreement" had to be given in order that interested persons might have an opportunity to present their views to the President or an agency designated by him. Finally, and of the utmost importance, was the absence of any provision requiring Senate ratification of agreements concluded under the act. In the light of the history of previous American attempts to conclude reciprocal trade treaties, it is doubtful if any progress

[2] *Statutes of the United States of America,* Session Laws, 73d Congress, 2d Sess., 1934 (Washington, 1934), p. 943.
[3] *Ibid.,* pp. 943–44.
[4] *Ibid.,* p. 944.

could have been made under a reciprocal trade program which called for Senate ratification of agreements.[5]

By November, 1939, Reciprocal Trade Agreements were in force with twenty foreign countries, with which, in all, close to 60 per cent of the foreign trade of the United States was conducted.[6] The names of these countries and the dates on which agreements were concluded are given in Table X, together with the names of countries with which intention to negotiate agreements had been announced. Of the agreements in force, eleven were with Latin American countries, six with Continental European countries, and the remaining three were with the United Kingdom, Canada, and Turkey. In addition, Newfoundland, the British Colonies, and most of the French and Dutch Colonial Empires were covered by the agreements. Of the countries not included in this list, many had most-favored-nation agreements with the United States. We shall have something to say about the countries with which the American Government has been having trade difficulties at a later stage.

In attempting to summarize the contents of these agreements, let us consider first the concessions granted by the United States, bearing in mind the fact that this country entered into the Trade Agreements Program with an exceedingly high tariff level. Apart from the broad guaranties of most-favored-nation treatment which have been given in each agreement, in return for corresponding guaranties from the other country concerned, the concessions of the United States have related almost exclusively to individual tariff rates, since this country employs nontariff trade barriers only to a very minor extent. These concessions have resulted in an appreciable modification of the American tariff level. According to a compilation prepared by the United States Tariff Commission following the conclusion of the agreements of November 17,

---

[5] Cf. Tasca, *Reciprocal Trade Policy*, pp. 43–44.
[6] Cf. *Commerce Reports*, February 18, 1939, p. 151.

TABLE X

AGREEMENTS CONCLUDED UNDER U. S. RECIPROCAL TRADE AGREEMENTS PROGRAM,
NOVEMBER, 1939 [a]

COUNTRY	DATE SIGNED	DATE EFFECTIVE
Cuba	August 24, 1934	September 3, 1934
Belgium	February 27, 1935	May 1, 1935
Haiti	March 28, 1935	June 3, 1935
Sweden	May 25, 1935	August 5, 1935
Brazil	February 2, 1935	January 1, 1936
Canada (see revised agreement below)	November 15, 1935	January 1, 1936
Kingdom of the Netherlands (Netherlands in Europe, Netherlands India, Surinam, and Curacao)	December 20, 1935	February 1, 1936
Switzerland	January 9, 1936	February 15, 1936
Honduras	December 18, 1935	March 2, 1936
Colombia	September 13, 1935	May 20, 1936
Guatemala	April 24, 1936	June 15, 1936
France and its colonies, dependencies, and protectorates other than Morocco	May 6, 1936	June 15, 1936
Nicaragua [b]	March 11, 1936	October 1, 1936
Finland	May 18, 1936	November 2, 1936
El Salvador	February 19, 1937	May 31, 1937
Costa Rica	November 28, 1936	August 2, 1937
Czechoslovakia [c]	March 7, 1938	April 16, 1938
Ecuador	August 6, 1938	October 23, 1938
United Kingdom, including Newfoundland and the British Colonial Empire	November 17, 1938	January 1, 1939
Canada (revision of agreement of 1936)	November 17, 1938	January 1, 1939
Turkey	April 1, 1939	May 5, 1939
Venezuela	November 6, 1939	December 16, 1939

COUNTRIES WITH WHICH INTENTION TO NEGOTIATE HAD BEEN ANNOUNCED,
NOVEMBER, 1939 [d]

COUNTRY	DATE OF ISSUANCE OF NOTICE
Cuba (supplemental agreement)	November 30, 1938
Belgium [e]	August 16, 1939
Argentina [f]	August 23, 1939
Chile	October 2, 1939
Uruguay [f]	October 20, 1939

[a] Adapted from *Commerce Reports*, November 18, 1939, p. 1072.
[b] Certain provisions of the trade agreement ceased to be in force as of March 10, 1938.
[c] The operation of this agreement was suspended as of April 22, 1939.
[d] Negotiations previously announced with Italy and Spain were inactive.
[e] A new trade agreement to supersede the agreement signed February 27, 1935, was to be negotiated.
[f] Negotiations with Argentina and Uruguay were later terminated.

1938, with Britain and Canada, the trade agreements had by that time resulted in the reduction of 1,077 out of 3,200 odd rates in the American tariff schedule.[7] Nearly half of these reductions had amounted to 40–50 per cent of the previous rates, and nearly nine-tenths of them to at least 20 per cent.[8] In addition, eighty-two rates had been consolidated at existing levels and numerous commodities had been "bound" on the duty-free list. American tariffs remained quite high in many instances, but the post-War trend toward the building of a higher and higher tariff wall around this country had been definitely reversed.

The duty reductions undertaken by the United States have been based on an exhaustive study of the nature of our imports. Considerable emphasis has been placed on the desirability of lowering rates on import items which do not compete with American products to any appreciable extent.[9] Reductions on competitive items have generally been rather moderate in amount.[10] The administration has followed the policy, moreover, of confining concessions to commodities of which the other country concerned is the "chief supplier."[11] This procedure has been designed to facilitate the process of tariff bargaining, as we have seen.[12] It has also been intended to answer the objections of those who maintain that generalization of concessions on the basis of the unconditional most-favored-

[7] *The New York Times,* December 10, 1938.

[8] Cf. *ibid.,* for the table from which these statistics have been calculated. Cf., also, Dietrich, *World Trade,* p. 444.

[9] A study undertaken by the United States Tariff Commission in 1933 indicated that many items of import were of a more or less non-competitive nature. See U. S. Tariff Commission, *Economic Analysis of Foreign Trade of the United States in Relation to the Tariff,* Sen. Doc. No. 180, 72d Congress, 2d Sess. (Washington, 1933).

[10] For a complete list of changes in rates, covering all agreements concluded up to the end of 1938, see United States Tariff Commission, *Changes in Import Duties since the Passage of the Tariff Act of 1930,* Miscellaneous Series (Washington, 1939).

[11] According to State Department officials, this practice has been adhered to with a considerable degree of consistency, though not with absolute rigidity.

[12] Cf. p. 381 above.

nation clause permits third countries "to get something for nothing," since they share in the benefits of tariff reductions contained in agreements to which they are not parties.[13] As a result of the application of the "chief supplier" formula, third countries rarely derive the major benefit from an American concession, though the benefits are seldom confined exclusively to the country which has "received" the concession.[14] Furthermore, many of the agreements contain an "escape clause," which permits either country to withdraw a concession from which a third country is deriving the major benefit.[15]

In the process of lowering the American tariff level by negotiation, tariff classifications have been narrowed in numerous instances.[16] Here, again, we are dealing with a device which is designed to facilitate the process of tariff bargaining. There is little question, also, that it has sometimes been utilized to protect the American producer at his more vulnerable points. Another practice which has been followed in a few instances, in order to permit reductions in the American tariff level without subjecting the domestic producer to what he might regard as an undue amount of foreign competition, has been that of limiting the duty reduction on a particular item to a specified quantity of imports, i.e., that of setting up tariff quotas. A number of tariff quotas on agricultural imports were set up in the first

[13] Actually, the United States generalizes concessions to all countries (except those on the "black list"), irrespective of whether or not they are entitled to most-favored-nation treatment. Cf. p. 398 below.

[14] See U. S. Senate, *Extending Reciprocal Trade Agreements Act,* Hearings before the Committee on Finance, 75th Congress, 1st Sess. (Washington, 1937), pp. 53–54.

[15] Before the concession is withdrawn, written notice must be given to the other government. If, after consultation, the two governments can reach no agreement on the matter, provision is made whereby the entire agreement can be terminated on thirty days' written notice. See, for example, U. S. Department of State, *Reciprocal Trade Agreement between the United States and Sweden,* May 25, 1935, Article XIV. (Hereafter, in referring to a provision of a particular American trade agreement, we shall simply cite the name of the foreign country concerned and the number of the article in which the provision is contained, e.g., Sweden, XIV.)

[16] The first fifteen agreements involved 173 new tariff classifications. (Tasca, *Reciprocal Trade Policy,* p. 182.)

trade agreement with Canada.[17] Some of these tariff quotas were liberalized or removed, while additional tariff quotas were set up, in the second agreement with Canada.[18] Another important example of a tariff quota was a provision of the Agreement of November 6, 1939, with Venezuela, whereby the American excise tax on imports of crude petroleum and fuel oils was reduced from ½ cent to ¼ cent a gallon on an annual amount of imports "not in excess of 5 per cent of the total quantity of crude petroleum processed in refineries in continental United States during the preceding calendar year." [19] Until recently, tariff quotas set up in the American trade agreements have been administered on a *global* basis, or, in other words, have not been allocated by countries. They have applied, however, to commodities imported very largely from the country to which the concession has been granted. Early in 1939, the tariff quota on heavy cattle was allocated among countries in accordance with the "base period" formula, in response to the request of Canada, a request which Canada was entitled to make under a provision of the agreement of November 17, 1938.[20] The tariff quota on petroleum (Venezuelan agreement) has also been allocated by countries.

The benefits of concessions granted by the United States in its trade agreements (with the exception of that with Cuba) are extended to all countries except those placed on the "black list" because of their "discriminatory treatment of American commerce" or because of "other acts or policies" tending "to defeat the purpose" of the Trade Agreements Program.[21] At the outbreak of war in 1939, the only country on the "black

[17] They applied to cattle weighing over 700 pounds, cattle weighing under 175 pounds, cream, certain types of lumber, and certified seed potatoes. (Canada, Agreement of November 15, 1935, Schedule II.)

[18] Canada, Agreement of November 17, 1938, Schedule II.

[19] U. S. Department of State, *Bulletin,* I (1939), 534. For information on excise taxes on imports, see U. S. Tariff Commission, *Changes in Import Duties since the passage of the Tariff Act of 1930,* pp. 167–70.

[20] U. S. Department of State, *Press Releases,* XX (1939), 163.

[21] Cf. p. 393 above.

list" was Greater Germany.[22] The chief cause of complaint against Germany has been that country's failure to allocate for imports from the United States an amount of foreign exchange proportionate to the amount employed for this purpose in a previous "representative period." [23] In fact, under Germany's bilateral clearing and other payments arrangements, proceeds of German exports are largely earmarked for imports from the countries concerned. It should be recalled, in this connection, that imports into the United States from Germany have, since early in 1939, been subject, not merely to the "general" rates of the American tariff schedule, but also to penalty duties levied to counteract concealed subsidization of German exports.[24]

Turning to the concessions which the United States has

[22] Australia was also on the "black list" from August 1, 1936, to February 1, 1938. Under an import licensing system introduced on May 22, 1936, the importation of a substantial number of commodities from non-British countries was made subject to license. The declared object of the new policy was to divert Australia's purchasers to the countries which were "good customers" for Australian exports. In practice, the system was employed to discriminate against American and Japanese products, but on December 7, 1937, the Australian Government announced its intention of removing the license requirements. Cf. N. F. Hall, "Trade Diversion—An Australian Interlude," *Economica,* V (New Series) (1938), 1–11, and U. S. Department of State, *Press Releases,* XVIII (1938), 144.

Australia and Germany are by no means the only countries which have discriminated against American exports since the inauguration of the Reciprocal Trade Agreements Program. But it has been necessary to employ the "black-listing weapon" with considerable discretion because of the danger of retaliation. If a country is found to be discriminating against American trade, the first step taken is to enter a protest with the foreign government concerned, and an attempt is made to settle the matter by negotiation. (Cf. U. S. Senate, *Extending Reciprocal Trade Agreements Act,* Hearings before the Committee on Finance, p. 83.)

The fact is that constant vigilance is required to prevent discrimination against American trade under the quota or exchange control systems of some foreign countries, even in cases in which satisfactory agreements have been concluded with these countries. Protests against this or that act of open or concealed discrimination are constantly being made.

[23] For a history of the trade controversy with Germany, see P. B. Taylor, "Problems of German-American Relations," *Foreign Policy Reports,* XIV (1938), 103–105, and Tasca, *World Trading Systems,* Ch. V.

[24] Cf. p. 328 n. above.

received from foreign countries, the first thing to note is that this country has sought to secure in each case a broad guaranty of unconditional most-favored-nation treatment, covering non-tariff trade barriers as well as customs matters. She has not in all cases secured all that was desired in connection with the various types of quantitative and exchange restrictions, but by and large the trade agreements have effected a substantial improvement in the treatment accorded American exports in foreign markets.

Considering first the question of tariffs, it should be noted that the mere procuring of most-favored-nation treatment in tariff matters represented a distinct gain in some cases. This was conspicuously true of the French agreement, for previously many American products had been subject to the intermediate or maximum rates of the French tariff, paying duties which amounted in some cases to several times the minimum rate.[25] The United States has also received numerous valuable tariff concessions. But, in many of the agreements concluded with countries employing exchange control or import quota systems, by far the most important concessions received by this country have concerned the operation of those systems. In addition to general guaranties of fair treatment in the allocation of exchange or import permits, the United States has secured important specific concessions on individual commodities, such as (1) enlargement of quotas or exchange quotas allocated to this country, (2) removal of restrictions, or (3) safeguards or guaranties against the introduction of new restrictions.

Let us examine the handling of quotas in the American

---

[25] See U. S. Department of State, *Trade Agreement between the United States and France,* May 5, 1936, Analysis of the General Provisions and Reciprocal Concessions, pp. 1–2, and U. S. House of Representatives, *Extending Reciprocal Foreign Trade Agreement Act,* Hearings before the Committee on Ways and Means, 75th Congress, 1st Sess. (Washington, 1937), p. 121.

Actually, the French Government, in accordance with its usual practice, granted the United States only limited most-favored-nation treatment in the agreement of May, 1936, but the commodity exceptions listed were unimportant to American trade. (France, I, and Schedule I—Section A.)

trade agreements. The United States has sought to secure certain general guaranties with respect to quantitative import restrictions both from countries employing quotas on an extensive scale and from those which have made little use of this weapon of trade control. Corresponding guaranties have been given by this country. In the first place, a standard provision prevents the imposition by either country of any prohibition or quantitative restriction on the importation of any article on which the duty has been consolidated in the agreement, except as specified or "in conjunction with governmental measures operating to regulate or control the production, market supply, or prices of like domestic articles, or tending to increase the labor costs of such articles." [26] Obviously, if no such safeguard were included, a country could destroy the value of a duty concession by imposing a quantitative restriction on imports of the article concerned. This, it will be recalled, was just what France and certain other European countries did in 1931 and later years when they applied import quotas to commodities on which duties had been "bound" in commercial agreements.[27]

Secondly, the American agreements provide that neither country shall subject imports from the other to any prohibition or restriction "which is not applied to the importation of any like article originating in any third country." [28] Furthermore, if either country does maintain or establish quantitative import restrictions, the other country shall be allocated a share equiva-

[26] Cf., e.g., Switzerland, VI. It was provided, however, that the Government imposing quantitative restrictions in conjunction with such measures had to give sympathetic consideration to any representations made by the other country with respect thereto, and that the latter might terminate the entire agreement after a specified time period if the negotiations were unsuccessful. Clearly, the consistent inclusion of this exception relating to market control measures in the earlier American agreements was designed, on the part of the United States, to permit the American Government to employ quantitative import restrictions in conjunction with the A.A.A. or N.R.A., if this seemed necessary.

[27] Cf. pp. 245 ff. above.

[28] E.g., Sweden, II.

lent to the proportion of the trade which it enjoyed in a "previous representative period." [29] This provision applies also to tariff quotas in most of the agreements.[30] Clearly, as we have noted in earlier connections, a country must be prepared, in order to protect its interests under such a clause, to enter into a considerable amount of bargaining over the selection of base periods. Even then, it may be obliged to compromise frequently, for no base period will be satisfactory to all exporting countries interested in a given product. Furthermore, as we have seen, application of the base period formula tends to rigidify the channels of trade and to render them, in many instances, more and more remote from existing competitive conditions as time goes on. In this connection it is interesting to note that, in the Provisional Commercial Agreement of November 15, 1938, between the United States and Greece, the previous representative period formula was discarded in favor of a more flexible arrangement whereby import quota allocations were to be based on the share of imports (of a given commodity) supplied by the other country "during past years, account being taken in so far as practicable in appropriate

[29] The precise wording of this clause varies. In many agreements, including most of those with countries having extensive quota systems, it applies only to import restrictions imposed by either country on products *of interest* to the other. Thus, a quota country may retain considerable bargaining freedom with respect to products of no interest to the United States. Some of the agreements (e.g., France, VI; Netherlands, VI) call specifically for the selection of a base period prior to the imposition of any quantitative restriction on the product concerned.

In any event, a "representative period" has been officially defined as "a series of years during which trade in the particular article under consideration was free from restrictive measures of a discriminatory character and was not affected by unusual circumstances such as, for example, a crop failure in the case of an agricultural product." (U. S. Department of State, *Press Releases,* XII (1935), 213.) Cf., also, Tasca, *Reciprocal Trade Policy,* p. 130.

[30] In the French agreement, however, it does not apply to tariff quotas employed by France. (France, VI.) Cf. p. 418 below, on the use of tariff quotas by France. The United States, moreover, agrees not to invoke the most-favored-nation clause in relation to preferences granted by France subject to the recommendations of the Stresa Conference but reserves its right to reopen negotiations if such preferences impair materially the benefits obtained in the French agreement. (France, XV.)

cases of any special factors which may have affected or may be affecting the trade in that article." [31]

Significant, likewise, is the fact that in the Greek agreement, allocation of quotas into national contingents was left optional with the country imposing the quota.[32] Thus the Greek Government, which in any case enforced licensing requirements, was to be permitted to employ the global or unallocated quota combined with a licensing system, i.e., the type of quota which we characterized in Chapter IX as that best calculated to conform with the most-favored-nation clause.[33] The agreement contained, however, certain additional clauses designed to prevent concealed evasion of the principle of equality of treatment through the exertion of secret governmental pressure on importers.[34]

Other agreements with quota countries likewise contain safeguards against the issue of import licenses or permits on a discriminatory or secretive basis and, in some cases, include additional clauses designed to prevent specific abuses likely to be associated with the quota systems of individual countries.[35] In addition, the agreements regularly extend the application of the most-favored-nation clause to all rules, formalities, and charges imposed in connection with quantitative restrictions.

Supplementing these general provisions, the United States has received from quota countries important specific concessions enlarging individual quotas or consolidating them at existing levels. It is interesting to note that under the French agreement, the United States obtained a number of "supplementary"

---

[31] U. S. Department of State, *Provisional Agreement between the United States of America and Greece*, Executive Agreement Series, No. 137, p. 2. For a discussion of the implications of this change in wording, see Tasca, *World Trading Systems*, p. 12.

[32] Cf. *ibid.*, p. 10 and p. 268 n. above.

[33] Cf. p. 268 above.

[34] Cf. Tasca, *World Trading Systems*, p. 14.

[35] E.g., the Netherlands agreement provides that each country will take appropriate steps to "facilitate as much as possible the exhaustion" (i.e., complete utilization) of quotas. (Netherlands, VI.)

quotas, in addition to a general assurance of a fair share of all quotas on products in which it had an interest in accordance with the representative period formula.[36] Thus, the champion of fair and equitable treatment was granted in this instance, in somewhat inconsistent fashion, what amounted to preferential treatment.[37]

Coming to the question of exchange control, most of the agreements specifically extend the application of the most-favored-nation clause to exchange regulations. Some agreements go farther and provide that, with respect to exchange made available for commercial transactions, each country shall allot to the other a share of the "total available exchange" which shall not be less "than the share employed in a previous representative period prior to the establishment of any exchange-control for the settlement of commercial obligations to the nationals of such other country." [38] Certain of the more recent agreements with exchange-control countries, however, adopt a rather different approach to the problem of equality of treatment under foreign exchange regulations. Each country is precluded from imposing any "prohibition, restriction, or delay, on the transfer of payment" for imports of the other country's products or "of payments necessary for and incidental to the importation of such articles." [39] In addition, in connection with payments for imports, unconditional most-favored-nation treatment is specifically extended to cover rates of exchange, taxes, surcharges, and all rules and formalities applicable to such

[36] These supplementary quotas were to be subject to revision by the French Government every year. (France, VI, and Schedule III.) Certain other countries have also been granted "supplementary quotas" by the French Government. Cf. p. 418 below.

[37] It is argued by the American authorities, however, that, since such supplementary quotas are stated in terms of absolute quantities rather than in terms of percentages of total imports, the American Government does not, in fact, receive an exclusive concession which cannot be extended to other countries. Cf. Tasca, *World Trading Systems*, pp. 15–16.

[38] Sweden, IX.

[39] Ecuador, X, and Czechoslovakia, X. Similar provisions appear in the provisional commercial agreements with Italy and Greece.

transactions. It had been found that, under the "representative period" formula, not only was it difficult to work out a satisfactory method of calculating the total amount of exchange which should be allotted to the other country, but further questions arose in connection with the problem of distributing this exchange for individual transactions from day to day. Nor did the "representative period" formula offer adequate protection against delays or blockages of transfer or against discrimination through the employment of differential exchange rates or premia.[40] Under the new arrangement, if an exchange-control country wishes to restrict purchases in the United States, it must do so not through direct limitation of exchange purchases, but through quantitative restriction of imports, in which case American exports are protected under the quota provisions of the agreement.[41] Thus, the American Government would seem, rather inconsistently, to be sanctioning the spread of the quota system in exchange-control countries, but it has been led to adopt this attitude by the apparent impossibility of obtaining, through any other means, satisfactory treatment for its exports under the exchange regulations of foreign countries. In the view of the American authorities, apparently, definite quantitative limitations on American exports are preferable to the unexpected blockages and concealed forms of discrimination which may, sometimes inevitably, occur under exchange control systems. It remains to be seen whether this newer approach to the exchange problem will prove reasonably satisfactory in operation or acceptable to large numbers of exchange-control countries.[42]

Finally, with respect to the foreign purchases of govern-

---

[40] For a full discussion of the implications of the new type of exchange provision, see Tasca, *World Trading Systems,* Chapter IV.

[41] An exchange-control country may enforce exchange permit requirements but it must issue permits freely for all imports other than those excluded under quota regulations.

[42] It proved impossible to apply this approach in the case of the Turkish agreement. Cf. *ibid.,* p. 31.

mental monopolies, the agreements provide that each country shall accord the commerce of the other country "fair and equitable treatment."[43] Furthermore, in making their foreign purchases, such monopolies shall be influenced solely by "competitive considerations, such as price, quality, marketability, and terms of sale."[44] Such a formula is, of course, difficult to enforce, as we have previously noted.[45]

The American Government has received from individual countries certain valuable concessions designed to improve the treatment accorded American exports under specific laws or administrative regulations of those countries. An important concession of this sort was the undertaking on the part of Canada to accord American exports better treatment under its "arbitrary valuation" system.[46] The agreements make definite provision for consultation in connection with disputes over sanitary regulations.[47]

In addition to the formal trade agreements, the United States has concluded a number of less formal executive agreements designed to improve its trade relations with certain countries, with some of which, it was expected, formal trade agreements would later be concluded. Among these were the Temporary Commercial Arrangement of December 17, 1937, with Italy and the Provisional Commercial Agreement of November 15, 1938, with Greece, both of which dealt with most-favored-nation treatment, incorporating the broad and precisely defined most-favored-nation provisions of the Reciprocal Trade Agreements (including those relating to nontariff trade barriers) but pro-

[43] Switzerland, VIII.
[44] *Ibid.*
[45] Cf. p. 314 above.
[46] Cf. pp. 226–27 above.
[47] The longstanding dispute between Argentina and the United States over the administration of American sanitary regulations affecting the importation of Argentine meat has been an obstacle to the conclusion of a trade agreement between the two countries. (Cf. p. 416 below). The United States has complained, furthermore, against Argentina's application of the principle of "bilateral balancing" in connection with her exchange regulations, a practice which has operated to the disadvantage of this country. (Cf. pp. 105–10 above.)

viding for no specific trade concessions.[48] Also of interest are
the series of agreements concluded with Soviet Russia. The
first of these was signed in July, 1935, and provided that Russia
would purchase American goods to the value of at least 30 million dollars in the following year while the United States on its
part would accord to the commerce of the Soviet Union unconditional most-favored-nation treatment.[49] Under an arrangement of August 6, 1937, which has been renewed in succeeding
years, Russia agreed to increase her purchases to 40 million
dollars for the following year.[50] The United States, like other
countries, has apparently taken the attitude that, in dealing
with a country whose foreign trade is subject to a state monopoly, the securing of a most-favored-nation guaranty is of
little value and the best way to assure adequate sales to such a
country is to procure a definite purchase commitment in advance.

Although the Reciprocal Trade Agreements Program has
been remarkably successful, it has had to face, from the beginning, two serious obstacles. The first of these has been the
strength of the forces, both economic and political, working
toward bilateral balancing. In particular, the refusal of Germany to modify her strongly bilateral program has proved a

[48] An interesting feature of the Italian agreement was the following provision:
"The total amount of any permitted import, of which a share is to be
assigned by either country to the other, shall include all imports of the regulated article, including such imports as may be made through public or private
clearing, compensation, or payment arrangements." (U. S. Department of State,
Temporary Commercial Arrangement between the United States and Italy,
December 17, 1937.) It was expected that the provisions of this Temporary
Arrangement would later be incorporated in a comprehensive trade agreement,
but negotiations for such an agreement were afterwards abandoned. There
is some evidence that Italy, in carrying out her "bilateral balancing" policies,
has not lived up to the terms of the temporary agreement with the United
States.
[49] Actually, the precise value of goods which Russia would purchase was
stated in a separate communication accompanying the exchange of notes between
the two governments.
[50] U. S. Department of State, *Bulletin,* I (1939), 96. Actually Russian purchases have exceeded the specified amounts.

major stumbling block. As a matter of fact, this resistance on
the part of Germany, and to some extent on the part of Italy
and certain other countries, has proved more serious from a
political than from an economic point of view. The Trade
Agreements Program, often defended as an instrument for
world peace, has perhaps helped to draw the democracies closer
together but it has certainly done little to iron out the differences between the democracies and the totalitarian states.[51]

The other major obstacle which the Program has had to face
has been the opposition of protectionists within the United
States. Because of the strength of this opposition, the administration has had to proceed with great caution in lowering the
American tariff level through negotiation with foreign governments. Nevertheless, the cry has frequently been raised that
this or that American industry has been injured through the
Trade Agreements Program. The attacks of these opposition
groups tend to be intensified when the Trade Agreements Act
comes up for renewal, as was well illustrated in the early months
of 1940.

2. *The United Kingdom*

As a low tariff or virtually free trade country, Britain never
had any difficulty in securing most-favored-nation treatment
for her exports in foreign markets during the latter half of the
nineteenth and the early part of the present century. The British frequently complained, on the other hand, that without tariffs of their own to use as bargaining weapons they had no way
of resisting the upward movement of tariffs abroad. True,

[51] There is considerable evidence that the American Government has recently
been veering toward a policy of employing tariff weapons to exert economic
pressure on countries with aggressive foreign policies. It is significant that
countervailing duties were applied to German products and to certain Italian
products in 1939, while in the same year notice was served on Japan that the
1911 commercial treaty would be terminated. On the other hand, considerable
restraint has been shown in employing penalty duties or the "black list"
weapon against democratic nations.

through the operation of the most-favored-nation clause, they received the benefits of tariff reductions embodied in commercial agreements in which they were not concerned, but these reductions often applied to commodities which were not of much importance in the British export trade.

British disillusionment with this state of affairs was intensified during the early years of the depression, as each new effort to halt the world-wide increase in tariff barriers failed. It was partly to provide herself with a bargaining weapon that Britain went over to tariffs in 1931 and 1932. Under the tariff policy which she has followed since that time, primary consideration has been given to the provision of adequate protection to domestic producers, while Empire products have been guaranteed a margin of preference over foreign (non-British) products. The tariff system has been supplemented by the enforcement of quantitative restrictions on agricultural imports, which likewise have been administered in such a way as to guarantee the home producer first place, and the Empire producer second place, in the British market. Foreign countries have accordingly been obliged to accept a diminished share in a restricted British market. Furthermore, although the British Government has continued to uphold the unconditional most-favored-nation clause as the basis of its commercial relations with other states, it indicated, in 1933, that most-favored-nation treatment would not be extended indefinitely to countries which refused to grant concessions to British exports in a spirit of reciprocity.[52]

[52] The altered attitude of the Government toward the clause was made clear by Mr. Runciman in the course of a debate on commercial policy in the House of Commons on March 15, 1933, in which he maintained that a country with "such world-wide interests" as Great Britain could not easily drop the most-favored-nation clause but went on to point out that in any negotiations to be undertaken, concessions must be made by both sides. Further, he said: "I want to make it clear that if any nation sits back in the hope that we will enter into successful negotiations with another Power and that they will be able to achieve most-favored-nation treatment without consideration coming from them, they will come to a deadlock. If they gain any advantage from us, they must be reciprocal in their action. They must be ready to make concessions similar to

Britain has concluded a long series of trade agreements with foreign countries since 1933, in an attempt to use her newly acquired bargaining weapons to secure enlarged outlets for her exports. She has, as we have seen, shown considerable tendency to take advantage of her "unfavorable" balance of trade with many of these countries in order to secure substantial concessions for British exports in return for disproportionately small concessions on her own part.[53] In fact, British concessions have consisted in large part of guaranties not to worsen the treatment accorded to her treaty partners.[54] Where the other country was a large net debtor to the United Kingdom, as in the case of Argentina or Germany, it was the bilateral balance of payments which was apparently kept in view.

Thus Britain has demonstrated some inclination toward a flexible form of bilateral balancing but at the same time has formally adhered to the unconditional most-favored-nation clause. Apart from her preferential treatment of Empire products, she has treated the products of all countries alike in the administration of her import tariffs and quotas.[55] Her import quotas on agricultural products have, in general, been administered in accordance with the "base period" formula. In so far as individual foreign countries have been granted specific minimum quotas in commercial agreements, the size of these quotas has been determined, on the whole, in accordance with the share of the given country in British imports of the com-

---

ours and to those of other countries. Unless they do that, we cannot agree to most-favored-nation treatment being retained as a permanent element in the conditions which control their traffic and ours." (Great Britain, *Parliamentary Debates, Commons*, CCLXXV [1932–33], 2020, 2024.) Cf. also Richardson, *British Economic Foreign Policy*, pp. 118–19, and Jones, *op. cit.*, pp. 240–44.

[53] Cf. pp. 384–85 above and Richardson, *op. cit.*, pp. 101–14.

[54] Cf. P. W. Bidwell, *Our Trade with Britain: Bases for a Reciprocal Trade Agreement* (New York, 1938), p. 85.

[55] Products of foreign countries have been subjected temporarily to penalty duties in a few instances. Cf. p. 220 above. In the Anglo-French agreement of June 27, 1934, France was granted *limited* most-favored-nation treatment, but the commodity exceptions were unimportant, and it was apparent that in limiting the application of the clause, the British Government was merely following the lead of the French Government.

modity from all *foreign* countries in the base period. Where a country has failed to receive specific quotas on products in which it is interested, it has usually received a grant of equitable treatment on the "base period" principle. These guaranties have sometimes applied only to specified commodities, usually those of most interest to the other country. Thus, Britain has retained some bargaining freedom in connection with her quotas, without indulging in any serious discriminations.

When we come to examine the concessions which Britain has *received* from foreign countries, we find a somewhat different situation. By entering into a limited number of clearing and payments agreements, Britain has become a partner to arrangements whereby foreign countries earmark most of the proceeds of their sales to the United Kingdom for remittances to that area. So far as these agreements are concerned, Britain has gone in for a rather rigid type of "bilateral balancing" and has permitted her interests to be safeguarded at the expense of third countries, in violation of the spirit of the most-favored-nation clause. In addition, under the quota provisions of certain of Britain's bilateral agreements, foreign countries have been obligated to shift some of their purchases to the United Kingdom. Thus, the Scandinavian countries were obliged to secure an increased proportion of their coal supplies from the United Kingdom under the terms of a series of trade agreements concluded in 1933 and 1934. A protocol to the Anglo-Danish agreement of April 24, 1933, contained the following provision:

> "The Government of the United Kingdom shall have the right to terminate the Agreement upon three months' notice, if in any one year the amount of coal of United Kingdom origin imported into Denmark is less than 80 per cent of the total imports of coal into Denmark in that year, as shown by the official statistics issued by the Danish Government." [56]

[56] Great Britain, *Treaty Series*, No. 34 (1933), Cmd. 4424, p. 14. The Danish Government, however, was to be given an opportunity to discuss the matter and a period of grace during which the deficiency might be made good.

412   INTERNATIONAL COMMERCIAL BARGAINING

Denmark had secured 58 per cent of her total coal imports from Britain in 1932, the year preceding the conclusion of the agreement.[57] The other Scandinavian countries likewise agreed to increase their coal purchases from the United Kingdom in similar fashion.[58] These arrangements worked to the immediate disadvantage of Germany and Poland, which had been supplying large amounts of coal to these countries.[59] On the other hand, they had the effect of restoring British coal exports to the position they had occupied in these markets of Northern Europe previous to the British coal stoppage of 1926.[60] Thus, by choosing a sufficiently remote base as a reference point, one can argue that the United Kingdom did *not* receive preferential treatment under these agreements.

A further issue of considerable interest arises in connection with these coal quotas. As we have seen, when a country pledges itself to import a specific quota or to satisfy a designated proportion of its import requirements for a given commodity from a particular country, it opens itself to the danger of being supplied inferior goods or of being charged exorbitant prices, or both. Hence, it usually seeks to protect itself by insisting that some sort of safeguarding clause relating to the prices and qualities of the goods to be supplied be inserted in the agreement. Clauses of this nature sometimes, but not always, require that prices be strictly competitive. Evidently the Scandinavian countries, in return for the concessions which

[57] *The Economist,* CXVI (1933), 901.

[58] Norway, having procured 43 per cent of her coal imports from Britain in 1932, pledged herself to acquire 70 per cent of her imports from that source in an agreement concluded May 15, 1933; for Sweden, the corresponding percentages were 30 per cent in 1932 and 47 per cent under the agreement concluded on the same date as that with Norway. (*The Economist,* CXVI [1933], 1061, and Great Britain, *Treaty Series,* No. 32 [1933], Cmd. 4421, p. 10, and *ibid.,* No. 4 [1934], Cmd. 4500, p. 26.)

[59] Apparently, however, the British gain in the Scandinavian and Baltic markets was to some extent offset by enhanced Polish and German competition in certain other markets. Cf. P E P (Political and Economic Planning), *Report on International Trade* (London, 1937), pp. 280–81.

[60] *Ibid.*

they received from the United Kingdom, expected to pay something more than the competitive price for British coal imported under the quota commitments of 1933.[61] Nevertheless, care was taken to safeguard their importers from excessively unfavorable price developments. The Anglo-Danish Agreement of April 24, 1933, contained the following clause:

> "The Contracting Governments take note of a letter to the Danish Consul-General in London dated this day and signed on behalf of the United Kingdom coal industry by the Chairman of the Central Council of Colliery Owners and the Chairman of the British Coal Exporters' Federation, wherein they have expressed their desire and firm intention to fulfill the requirements of Danish buyers and users of coal by every means within their power; and for this purpose have given to Danish buyers and users the assurances contained in that letter with regard to prices, qualities, availability of supplies, and other matters. The right of the Government of the United Kingdom, as stipulated above, to terminate the Agreement upon 3 months' notice in the circumstances set out is conditional upon those assurances being implemented." [62]

Similar clauses were contained in the other Scandinavian and Baltic agreements.[63]

Quite apart from the clearing and payment agreements, which had, of course, definite bilateral balancing implications, some of the British agreements have included clauses specifically giving expression to bilateral balancing objectives. In

[61] Cf. *The Economist*, CXXXIII (1938), 694.

[62] Great Britain, *Treaty Series*, No. 34 (1933), p. 14. For additional safeguarding clauses, cf. *ibid.*, p. 16.

[63] The Norwegian Government, as is indicated clearly in an exchange of notes appended to its agreement, sought to secure the inclusion, in the Protocol containing the coal arrangements, of a clause providing against an increase in the price of United Kingdom coal by 30 per cent or more. It was found impossible "to adopt such a course," but His Majesty's Government did agree to enter into consultation with the Norwegian Government in the event of "the minimum free on board prices in sterling of United Kingdom coal exported to Norway having risen for a calendar month above the minimum free on board prices for such coal ruling during the calendar month immediately prior to the date of signature of the agreement, to an extent which exceeds any increase in the general level of prices by 30 per cent or more." (Great Britain, *Treaty Series*, No. 4 [1934], p. 35.)

the Anglo-Danish Agreement of 1933, the two Governments merely agreed that, in administering the provisions of the Agreement, they would "keep in view the balance of trade between the two countries." [64] The Anglo-Russian Agreement of February 16, 1934, representing the opposite extreme, contained a rigid compensation clause. It was provided that bilateral payments (as defined in the agreement) were gradually to be balanced in accordance with a definite formula, whereby Russian payments to the United Kingdom should bear to proceeds accruing to the Soviet Government in the United Kingdom the following proportions:

> "In the year ending December 31, 1934 .... 1:1.7
> In the year ending December 31, 1935 .... 1:1.5
> In the year ending December 31, 1936 .... 1:1.4
> In the year ending December 31, 1937 .... 1:1.2
> Thereafter an approximate balance of payments measured by the ratio 1:1.1 shall be maintained." [65]

But the British Government's leanings toward the principle of bilateral balancing left no mark on the Anglo-American Agreement of November, 1938, in which reciprocal concessions were approximately balanced despite Britain's markedly "unfavorable" trade balance with the United States.[66] The Agree-

[64] Great Britain, *Treaty Series,* No. 34 (1933), p. 12. At the same time, they took note (1) of conversations which had taken place in regard to steps for increasing the sales in Denmark of United Kingdom iron and steel, and (2) of certain private agreements between organizations in Britain and Denmark whereby the Danish organizations undertook to employ exclusively certain British supplies in the production of specified products destined for the British market; e.g., wrappers "made exclusively of jute cloth woven in the United Kingdom" were to be used for bacon and hams exported to the United Kingdom. (*Ibid.*)

[65] Great Britain, *Treaty Series,* No. 11 (1934), Cmd. 4567, p. 9.

[66] Britain reduced tariffs on American imports amounting in 1936 to 50 million dollars, while the United States reduced duties on British imports amounting to 59.9 million dollars in 1937. If we take into account commodities on which tariffs or duty-free status were bound, we find that British concessions exceeded American in value. This was offset, however, by the fact that American concessions (consisting mostly of bindings of duty-free status) affecting British colonial products exceeded concessions received for American goods in

ment was notable, also, for the removal or reduction of certain preferences formerly extended to Empire products, a procedure which was in large part made possible by the coöperation of Canada, which concluded at the same time an agreement with the United States removing certain preferences formerly extended to British products.

On the whole, the British have shown no great consistency in their recent commercial bargaining efforts but have demonstrated, rather, a tendency to seek the utmost advantage from each individual agreement.[67] Thus, while the Government has struggled to secure equitable treatment for British exports under foreign exchange or quota regulations in cases in which discrimination has been exercised, it has not hesitated to accept what has amounted to preferential treatment where the balance of bilateral trade or payments has warranted it. Other examples of similar inconsistencies could be cited. At the outbreak of war in 1939, it was not easy to see in what direction British commercial policy was heading.

3. *France*

France, as already indicated, has adhered to the limited form of the most-favored-nation clause since 1931, although frequently the commodities excepted from most-favored-nation treatment in her commercial agreements are few and unimportant to the other country concerned. In addition, many of the agreements concluded by France during the worst years of the depression restored to her the freedom to raise tariff rates which had been consolidated during the latter part of the nineteen-twenties. France has been willing to consolidate her tariffs to a limited extent during the nineteen-thirties, but on a somewhat provisional basis. The *modus vivendi* concluded

---

British colonies. (U. S. Department of State, *Press Releases,* XIX [1938], Supplement A, *The Trade Agreement with the United Kingdom,* pp. 2–4; and *The Economist,* CXXXIII [1938], 357–58.)

[67] For a similar view, see Tasca, *World Trading Systems,* pp. 145–46.

with Italy on March 4, 1932, indicated the turn which French policy was to take in this regard.[68] Each country granted the other most-favored-nation treatment on an extensive list of commodities. In addition, each country specified with respect to a second substantial list of commodities the rates which were to be applicable to goods coming from the other country. It was provided, however, that if either country increased the duty on any of the products in this second category, so as to destroy the "tariff equilibrium" to the disadvantage of the other, the injured party might request the immediate opening of negotiations in order to restore that equilibrium. If no agreement was reached within ten days, the injured party might thereupon increase its duties on any products in its corresponding list to an equivalent extent.[69]

If the French Government has attempted to restrict the applicability of the most-favored-nation clause in tariff matters, it has taken the attitude, at least since the latter part of 1933, that the clause is not applicable at all in the case of quotas. As we have seen in an earlier chapter, under the new policy which went into effect at the beginning of 1934, 25 per cent of each quota was to be apportioned among the various exporting countries in accordance with the "base period" formula, but the remaining 75 per cent was to be distributed in accordance with corresponding advantages offered to French exports by other nations.[70] In other words, France intended to employ her quotas as bargaining weapons on a principle of reciprocity. For a number of reasons, however, it was found impossible to adhere rigidly to this policy. Certain countries were in a position to secure guaranties of their full share of all French

---

[68] Cf. Haight, *French Import Quotas,* p. 96.

[69] For the text of the agreement, see *Journal Officiel de la République française,* LXVI (1934), 281–91. See also *Commerce Reports,* May 9, 1932, p. 357.

[70] Cf. Haight, *op. cit.,* pp. 104–105, and A. Marvaux, "La politique commerciale de la France," *Revue Économique internationale,* XXVI (1934), 255–56.

quotas, on the "base period" principle, in return for relatively small concessions or no concessions at all to French exports.[71] These were countries whose markets were of vital importance to the French export trade or whose imports were not, in general, subject to quantitative restrictions. In some cases, their demands for fair treatment were backed up by retaliation or threats of retaliation against French products. Furthermore, France found it difficult to apply the new policy rigorously in the case of commodities supplied exclusively by a few countries; nor could she expect to exact "equivalent concessions" from countries which furnished essential raw materials but lacked sufficient purchasing power to import French goods on a large scale.[72]

Thus, in certain of the agreements which she has concluded since 1933, notably those with the United States and the United Kingdom, France's most important concession has consisted of a guaranty to allocate to the other country its full share of all quotas on the "base period" principle.[73] In other cases, as in the commercial treaty of December 21, 1935, with Spain, France has committed herself to no general guaranty with

---

[71] Cf. *ibid.*, p. 259.

[72] Cf. *ibid.*, p. 257.

[73] Anglo-French commercial relations were settled, after considerable controversy in an agreement concluded June 27, 1934, in which France guaranteed to the United Kingdom the "full share of all quotas . . . which is mathematically attributable to the United Kingdom in accordance with the proportion of the total foreign importation into France of the goods in question in the basic period which was represented by United Kingdom goods."

In the Reciprocal Trade Agreement with the United States, concluded May 13, 1936, France's undertaking applied simply to products of commercial interest to the United States and guaranteed to that country "a share of the total quantity or value of any such product permitted to be imported or sold during a specified period equivalent to the proportion of the total importation of such product from foreign countries which the United States of America supplied in a basic period *prior* to the imposition of any quantitative restriction on such product." (U. S. Department of State, *Reciprocal Trade Agreement between the United States and France,* May 13, 1936, Article VI.) Actually, the United States had received most-favored-nation treatment under the French quota system since 1932, through the terms of a note sent to Ambassador Edge by the French Government in that year.

respect to quota allotments but has allocated to the other country specified percentages of a limited number of quotas.[74] In addition, a number of countries, both in the first and second categories, have been granted supplementary quotas on products of special interest to them.

France has made some use of tariff quotas in her commercial agreements. In line with the recommendations of the Stresa Conference of 1932, which will be discussed in the next chapter, she has granted to certain of the Danubian countries exclusive preferences in the form of reduced duties on limited quantities of what in each case was a leading agricultural export of the country in question.[75] Another purpose for which she has used tariff quotas has been to permit a country to share to a limited extent in privileges enjoyed by third countries. Thus, Soviet Russia, most of whose products had formerly been subject to the French maximum tariff, obtained, in the agreement signed January 11, 1934, the privilege of the French minimum rates on lists of specified products, in some cases within *fixed quota limits*.[76]

An interesting feature of a number of recent French agreements is the emphasis on "tariff equilibrium" or "trade equilibrium." We have already mentioned the provisions for the maintenance of a tariff equilibrium, at least with respect to the commodities on which tariff rates were provisionally consolidated, in the Franco-Italian Agreement of March 4, 1932.[77] This same agreement contained the following clause:

> "In case one of the two countries should subject to quantitative restriction one or more products of interest to the export trade of the other country, the latter may, if it considers the equilibrium of reciprocal exchanges to be disturbed to its disadvantage, either adopt analogous measures of quantitative restriction or raise the

---

[74] League of Nations, *Treaty Series*, CLXVII (1935), 41–47.

[75] Actually, the duty has not usually been reduced, but a tariff rebate has been granted.

[76] Cf. *Commerce Reports*, March 3, 1934, p. 142.

[77] Cf. p. 416 above.

tariff rates indicated respectively in lists C and D—annexed to the present agreement—for one or more products included in the same lists, in such a way, however, as to employ only measures which will have equivalent repercussions on the exchanges. . . ." [78]

Similarly, an agreement concluded with Norway in February, 1936, provided that the contracting parties, in case either of them imposed higher duties or import restrictions which threatened to disturb to any considerable extent the trade equilibrium aimed at by the agreement, might demand the reopening of negotiations with a view to reëstablishing the equilibrium by corresponding compensations. [79] Clearly, these provisions aimed at the maintenance of a relatively stable ratio in the bilateral trade between the two countries concerned. The French payments agreements which have been concluded in recent years, as we have seen, go farther than this and call for the maintenance of a fixed trade ratio.

On the whole, the predominant tendency in recent French commercial bargaining policy has been an emphasis on reciprocity. The French Government has been inclined toward the attitude that concessions are to be granted to other countries only in return for equivalent concessions to French exports, while any restrictions imposed on French trade, of such a nature as to cause the bilateral trade balance to move against France, are to be answered in kind. To be sure, France has found that, for the protection of her exports, she must adhere by and large to the most-favored-nation clause in tariff matters; but she has sought, though not always successfully, to retain as much bargaining freedom as possible by limiting the application of the clause to selected commodities. Finally, it is quite evident that most of the agreements which France has recently negotiated with other countries have been designed to achieve and

---

[78] *Journal Officiel,* LXVI (1934), 291. (My own translation of the French text.) Both this clause and the clause relating to the raising of the provisionally bound duties appear in the *Protocole de Signature.* Lists C and D covered the commodities on which duties were bound.

[79] *Commerce Reports,* April 11, 1936, p. 293.

maintain a relatively stable trade ratio. That this is likely to be an inevitable development in bargaining between quota countries has already been indicated.

4. *Germany*

Until the accession to power of the Nazis early in 1933, Germany adhered, on the whole, to the most-favored-nation clause. When objections were raised, by countries entitled to most-favored-nation treatment from Germany, to the tariff preferences granted in 1931 to certain Danubian countries, these preferences were not put into effect.[80] In the administration of her exchange regulations, Germany sought to maintain a policy of fair treatment by enforcing, until 1934, a scheme whereby exchange was allocated to importers on the basis of their 1931 imports and no attempt was made to apportion these allotments by countries.[81] Considerable difficulty arose, however, over the tariff quotas on certain agricultural imports employed by Germany from 1930 on. At the time, there were few precedents to indicate just how the most-favored-nation guaranty was to be interpreted in connection with quantitative import restrictions. The policy pursued by Germany for a time, of apportioning her tariff quotas among the principle exporting countries on an "equal share" basis, may have represented a sincere attempt to adhere to a system of fair treatment, but its actual effect was to discriminate against the countries which had constituted the chief suppliers of the commodities in question in previous years.[82]

Although the Nazi policies have led to the severing of certain of Germany's most-favored-nation agreements, many of the commercial treaties to which Germany was a party in the summer of 1939 still contained the most-favored-nation clause. The sources of German imports, however, have been largely

[80] Cf. p. 449 n. below.
[81] Cf. pp. 81–82 above.
[82] Cf. p. 270 n. above.

determined, since the adoption of the New Plan in September, 1934, by the all-embrasive "exchange permit" system, to which the most-favored-nation clause is held not to apply. Exchange permits have been issued on a relatively rigid "bilateral balancing" basis, under the terms of the numerous clearing and payments agreements which Germany has concluded. In fact, it is these clearing and payments agreements, rather than the many basic commercial treaties inherited from former periods, which provide the chief clue to the commercial bargaining policy pursued by the German Government from 1934 on.

Although Germany's early clearing agreements were apparently forced on her by creditor countries, the Nazis gradually turned to a system of rigid bilateral balancing in a deliberate attempt to achieve certain important objectives, among which were:

(1) Economizing reserves of free foreign exchange for purposes essential to the success of the autarky program;

(2) Encouraging expansion of trade with certain countries (Japan, Italy, and countries of Southeastern Europe and Latin America) for political reasons;

(3) Promotion of economic stability through linking of exports and imports by countries, in order, it was argued, that a decline in exports to a given market would be accompanied automatically by a restriction of imports from that country.[83]

Germany's clearing and payments agreements, together with the commercial agreements which have sometimes accompanied them, have usually determined not merely the amount of exchange which the German Government would apply to purchases from the other country, but the manner in which this exchange would be allocated among different categories of imports or types of payments. In a number of cases, a rigid compensation clause was included, as in the Czech-German

[83] Cf. F. Huhle, "Die Meistbegünstigung in der Aussenhandelspolitik der deutschen Nationalwirtschaft," *Jahrbücher für Nationalökonomie und Statistik,* CXLVIII (1938), 209.

quota, tourist, and transfer agreement of November 10, 1937, under which each country agreed to import goods from the other to the value of about 145 million RM.[84]

In addition to her commitments to allocate foreign exchange in specified ways, Germany has undertaken, in some of the agreements concluded since 1934, to import specified quantities of given commodities from the other country or to accord the other country a reduced tariff rate on specified quotas of goods. Certain of these ordinary quotas and tariff quotas have been embodied in unpublished agreements, apparently in an attempt to avoid any difficulties which might arise in connection with most-favored-nation guaranties.[85] In certain other cases, the concessions have applied to commodities exported more or less exclusively by the other country, e.g., Chilean natural nitrates.

As we have already noted, when a country definitely commits itself to import a specified *quantity* of a particular commodity from a second country, it often seeks to secure guaranties with respect to the prices and qualities of goods to be supplied. One gets the impression, from newspaper accounts and other unofficial sources, that in the last few years Germany has sought to exert a considerable degree of control over the prices and qualities of goods supplied her under quota arrangements, particularly with the countries of Southeastern Europe. Provisions of this nature, however, rarely appear in the published portions of her agreements. In Germany's case, the motive has

---

[84] Cf. *Commerce Reports*, December 25, 1937, p. 1030. Germany was to allocate 15.3 million RM for the import of coal, 44 million for agricultural products, 72.7 million for manufactured products, 10 million for "general compensation," and 5.7 million for the reduction of the Czech clearing balance. In return, Czechoslovakia agreed to allocate a sum equivalent to 15.3 million RM for coal imports from Germany, a further sum of 15 million for "general compensation," and the remainder for all other imports, to be divided between manufactured and semi-manufactured goods and raw materials. We have discussed in Chapter VII the terms of the German-Canadian payments agreement of October 22, 1936, under which Germany undertook to apply, out of the total sum allocated for imports from Canada, fixed percentages for imports of specified commodities. (Cf. pp. 197–98 above.)

[85] Cf. p. 380 above.

not always been protection, but rather a desire to promote trade through increasing the clearing balances held by other countries in Berlin.[86] She has apparently undertaken to purchase specified quantities of agricultural products from various Danubian and Balkan countries at fixed prices, paying, in the typical case, considerably more than the world market price.[87] It should be noted in this connection, however, that Germany has not always lived up to the terms of her quota commitments.

An elaborate program for the control of prices of goods supplied to Germany on a quota basis has been developed under the terms of a series of agreements between Germany and Denmark. An agreement concluded early in 1934 was reported to contain an unpublished portion allocating to Denmark specified shares of the German butter, cheese, and egg import trade, corresponding in general to the Danish shares in earlier years.[88] The two countries signed an agreement early the following year, prolonging the previous arrangement and providing for the establishment of a "Joint Commission to consider the supplying of the German market with unsmoked bacon, slaughtered poultry, lard, butter, cheese and hens' eggs, together

---

[86] Cf. p. 161 above.

[87] Germany was reported to have agreed to take practically all of Rumania's agricultural surpluses at fixed prices under the terms of the agreement concluded in March, 1939 (*Foreign Agriculture*, III [1939], 155). No such arrangement, however, appears in the published portion of the agreement, which is discussed below. (Pp. 425–26.) It has also been reported that Germany undertook, in this same agreement, to purchase a specified quantity of Rumanian cattle at a fixed price which was appreciably higher than that originally asked by the Rumanians. (Royal Institute of International Affairs, *South-Eastern Europe*, p. 136.) Germany has apparently been prepared, in general, to purchase as much as Bulgaria wanted to sell, even in excess of agreed import quotas, at prices fixed from time to time by the appropriate *Überwachungsstelle*. (Cf. *ibid.*, p. 175.) In some cases, evidently, prices have been fixed under the terms of agreements between private or semi-official interests in the two countries concerned. It is important to recall, in this connection, the rôle played by semi-official export syndicates and monopolies in the Danubian and Balkan countries. (Cf. pp. 336–38 above.)

[88] *Commerce Reports*, April 21, 1934, p. 253. The conclusion of this agreement, and of similar agreements with Finland and Estonia, followed the extension of the German import monopoly control system to apply to butter, cheese, and eggs. (Cf. pp. 311–13 above.)

with the fixing of prices and other matters pertaining to the marketing of the said goods." [89] This Commission was to consist of experts appointed by both Governments and was empowered to set up Sub-Commissions for particular commodities or groups of commodities.[90] It was to be the duty of the Joint Commissions "to fix, from time to time, maximum and minimum prices for the sale of unsmoked bacon, butter, and hens' eggs to German buyers . . ." [91]

These Joint Commissions, set up to handle a particular problem, are not to be confused with the more general Government Commissions which were frequently set up, from about 1934 on, under the terms of agreements between countries employing quantitative methods of trade control. In fact, Germany and Denmark had each undertaken, in their agreement of March 1, 1934, to set up a Government Commission. These Commissions were to keep "in direct touch with each other in order to deal with questions connected with the application of the Agreement . . ." [92] We have mentioned in Chapter VI the similar commissions which were often set up under terms of clearing agreements. In some cases, as in the Franco-German Agreements of July 10, 1937, two sets of commissions were established, one under a clearing or payments agreement and the other under a commercial agreement which accompanied it.[93] Each set of commissions was expected to take up questions arising in connection with the carrying out of the agreement under which it was established. It is obvious that a need for some such arrangement as this is likely to appear wherever bilateral commercial agreements call for detailed official control of the movements of trade between two countries. This is one

[89] League of Nations, *Treaty Series*, CLX (1935), 163.

[90] These Sub-Commissions were to be set up with the approval of the General Government Commissions to be mentioned below.

[91] *Ibid*. They were likewise empowered to take similar steps "in respect of hard cheese, not in separate packets, of 2½ kilogrammes gross weight or less."

[92] *Ibid.*, CL (1934), 41.

[93] See *Journal Officiel*, LXIX (1937), 8165–232.

way in which governments seek to render rigid bilateral balancing policies workable.

But Germany has proceeded much farther than this, and indeed farther than any other country, in her attempts to render her bilateral balancing policy workable. I have in mind here, in particular, her campaign to develop the countries of Southeastern Europe as sources of supply for the commodities Germany needs and as markets for German industrial goods. In this way, Germany has sought to become less dependent on commerce of a world-wide character and to procure needed materials on a bilateral clearing basis from countries which could continue to supply her in time of war. The origins of such a policy may be found in a German-Hungarian agreement of February 21, 1934, which provided, among other things, for a partial shift in Hungarian agricultural production from wheat to oil seeds, the entire crop of oil seeds to be purchased by German firms.[94] Similar provisions were included in later agreements with most of the other countries of Southeastern Europe, but the policy found its fullest expression in the well-known five-year Treaty for the Promotion of Economic Relations between Germany and Rumania, concluded on March 23, 1939, in the midst of an atmosphere of extreme international tension. This treaty called for the drawing up of a long-range plan for the development and adjustment of the mutual economic relations of the two countries.[95] Account was to be taken on the one hand of Germany's import needs, while, on the other hand, attention was to be paid to the possibilities for developing Rumanian production, to Rumanian internal needs, and to the exigencies of Rumania's economic relations with other countries. The plan was to make particular provision, among other things, for the following:

[94] Cf. R. P. F. Edwards, *Economic Conditions in Hungary, 1933–35,* Great Britain, Department of Overseas Trade, Report No. 629 (London, 1936), p. 21, and *Commerce Reports,* April 21, 1934, p. 254.
[95] *Reichsgesetzblatt,* Teil II, Nr. 22 (May 26, 1939), 780.

(1) The expansion and direction of Rumanian agricultural production, special attention being paid to the production of feedstuffs, oil seeds, and fiber plants;

(2) The development of existing, and the organization of new, agricultural industries and processing establishments;

(3) The development of Rumanian forestry and lumber industries;

(4) The supplying of machinery and equipment for mining firms in Rumania;

(5) The establishment of mixed German-Rumanian companies for the exploitation of particular mineral resources in specified regions of Rumania and the formation of an additional mixed company for the investigation and exploitation of Rumanian mineral oil resources;

(6) Industrial and banking coöperation;

(7) The supplying of armaments and other equipment for the Rumanian army, navy, air force, and armament industry;

(8) The development of Rumanian facilities for transportation and communication.

The responsibility for carrying out the terms of the agreement was given over to the Government Commissions set up under the German-Rumanian commercial treaty of March 23, 1935.[96] Payments were to take place under the terms of existing bilateral payments arrangements between the two countries. It was further provided that the Government Commissions might agree to permit certain payments—presumably from Germany to Rumania—to take place in the form of capital goods.

Clearly, then, some of Germany's agreements, particularly those with the countries of Southeastern Europe, represent an important departure in the sphere of bilateral commercial bargaining, in the direction of positive, long-range planning of bilateral economic relations. This planning takes place within a framework of rigid bilateral canalization of trade, involving strict control of prices and quantities of goods exchanged and offsetting of payments.

[96] *Ibid.*, pp. 780–81.

CHAPTER XIV

Regional and Multilateral Negotiations

1. *Multilateral Negotiations*

During the course of our discussion in earlier chapters, we have had occasion to observe, at several points, that multilateral attempts to lower trade barriers in recent years have been virtually a complete failure. The precedents which had been established during the nineteen-twenties were by no means encouraging. The World Economic Conference of 1927 had succeeded in agreeing on recommendations looking toward the liberalization of international trade barriers, but the concrete results of these recommendations had, as we noted in Chapter II, been meagre indeed. The Convention for the Abolition of Import and Export Prohibitions and Restrictions, concluded in 1927, never obtained the requisite number of ratifications, while the attempt to secure a multilateral tariff truce in 1930 and 1931 failed altogether. Only in such matters as the unification of customs formalities was the League able to secure some degree of multilateral economic coöperation.

The severe financial crisis of 1931 shocked the world into realization of the need for some sort of joint effort. Though trade barriers were erected on an unprecedented scale from the middle of 1931 on, the standstill agreements did provide some relief for Germany in the financial sphere, while, in June, 1932, the Lausanne Agreements affected a belated, provisional settlement of the reparations question.[1]

---

[1] See Great Britain, Parliamentary Papers, *The Final Act of the Lausanne Conference,* Cmd. 4126 (London, 1932) and *Further Documents Relating to*

Meanwhile, plans were being made for a world economic con-ference to be held in London under the auspices of the League of Nations, and the Lausanne Conference passed a resolution listing the main questions to be taken up by such a conference. Arrangements were made for the appointment of a Preparatory Commission of Experts which would undertake a preliminary study of these issues. In a somewhat indecisive Draft An-notated Agenda for the conference, submitted to the League in January, 1933, the experts emphasized the need for (a) res-toration of an effective gold standard, (b) readjustment of prices and costs of production, (c) abolition of exchange re-strictions, and (d) relaxation of the barriers to international trade.[2] All these problems, they maintained, were closely inter-related and had to be attacked simultaneously.[3] Furthermore, many of the essential adjustments depended on the taking of appropriate action by individual governments.

The World Monetary and Economic Conference finally met in London in June, 1933. At the suggestion of the United States Government, eight countries had, on May 12, 1933, signed a "tariff truce," in which they agreed not to adopt, prior to the conclusion of the Conference, any new measures which might enhance the difficulties adversely affecting inter-national trade.[4] Virtually all the governments represented at

---

the Settlement Reached at the Lausanne Conference, Cmd. 4129 (London, 1932). A separate "Gentlemen's Agreement," which was not published until some days after the publication of the official agreement, made ratification by the signatory creditor countries (Belgium, Great Britain, France, and Italy) contingent on the reaching of a satisfactory settlement between those countries and their own creditors (chiefly the United States). Pending such an agreement, the tempo-rary arrangements suspending all payments would remain in force. It is hardly necessary to add that, up to the outbreak of war in 1939, no agreement with the United States over the War Debts question was ever reached.

[2] League of Nations, Monetary and Economic Conference, Draft Annotated Agenda: Submitted by the Preparatory Commission of Experts (Geneva, 1933), pp. 8–9.

[3] Ibid., p. 7.

[4] See Royal Institute of International Affairs, Survey of International Affairs, 1933 (London, 1934), pp. 43–44, and M. S. Stewart, "Problems before the World Economic Conference," Foreign Policy Reports, IX (1933), 77 n. Cf.,

the Conference later adhered to the truce. Yet the United States must be assigned a considerable share of responsibility for the fact that the Conference adjourned without having accomplished any of its major purposes. In a message submitted to the Conference on July 3, the President characterized the immediate achievement of exchange stability as an objective of relatively minor importance. The United States, he maintained, in an oft-quoted sentence, was seeking "the kind of dollar which a generation hence" would "have the same purchasing and debt paying power as the dollar value we hope to attain in the near future." [5] This view of the situation was utterly unacceptable to the gold *bloc* delegations, whose currencies were being threatened by the uncertainty regarding the future of the dollar and who contended that the securing of some agreement looking toward the achievement of exchange stability in the near future was a necessary prerequisite to the relaxation of trade barriers.

Following the disclosure of this serious rift, the Conference attempted to carry on, but the discussions were half-hearted and adjournment took place on July 27. Perhaps the disagreement over the question of exchange stabilization might not have been so serious had the delegates been in substantial agreement over other fundamental objectives of the Conference; but the discussions revealed marked divergences of opinion, especially as to methods of achieving a relaxation of trade barriers.[6] Some countries inclined toward multilateral action to lower tariffs; others held out for bilateral agreements. The old difficulty which had long stood in the way of multilateral tariff reductions again cropped up, some delegations favoring gradual reductions by uniform annual percentages, others maintaining that nations with relatively high tariffs

---

also, p. 210 above. Some of the states which adhered to the tariff truce did so with various reservations.

[5] U. S. Department of State, *Press Releases*, July 8, 1933, p. 16.

[6] See League of Nations, *Journal of the Monetary and Economic Conference* (London, 1933), *passim*.

should make the more substantial reductions.[7] Finally, all countries favored removal of nontariff trade barriers, but few seemed ready to take immediate steps toward this end.

Did the Conference accomplish anything of a concrete nature? Significantly enough, the field in which the greatest degree of progress was made was that of coördinating production and marketing by international agreement.[8] In other words, the Conference seemed better able to agree on measures designed to effect a more comprehensive regulation of movements of commodities across international boundaries than on proposals aimed at the liberalization of international trade barriers. A number of special sub-committees were set up to deal with commodities which seemed to lend themselves to international control. The one concrete agreement which was concluded during the course of the Conference was an international silver agreement; and not long after the adjournment of the Conference, on August 25, 1933, a wheat agreement was signed by twenty leading wheat importing and exporting countries. These measures will be discussed in the following section, but it is appropriate to note at this stage that international commodity control schemes have constituted practically the only significant multilateral economic agreements concluded in recent years.

The adjournment of the World Economic Conference was followed by a period of unprecedented activity in bilateral commercial bargaining. Some of the agreements negotiated, as we saw in the preceding chapter, were primarily trade-liberalizing in their net effects; many others were trade-diverting in nature.

With the devaluation of the chief gold *bloc* currencies and the conclusion of the Tripartite Monetary Agreement in 1936, the problem of currency adjustment was tentatively settled and the stage seemed set for a further determined effort to relax

---

[7] See League of Nations, Monetary and Economic Conference, *Reports Approved by the Conference on July 27th, 1933, and Resolutions Adopted by the Bureau and Executive Committee* (London, 1933), p. 23.

[8] Cf. M. S. Stewart, "The Work of the London Economic Conference," *Foreign Policy Reports*, IX (1933), 205.

trade barriers on a multilateral scale. In fact, the statements issued to the press by the British, French, and American Governments at the time of the signing of this agreement emphasized the importance of "action being taken without delay to relax progressively the present system of quotas and exchange controls with a view to their abolition." [9] The matter received further attention at the meeting of the League of Nations Assembly in October, but in terms of concrete accomplishment, the results of these discussions were disappointing.[10]

In April, 1937, it was announced that M. van Zeeland, the then Belgian Premier, had accepted a joint invitation from the British and French Governments to undertake "an enquiry into the possibility of obtaining a general reduction of quotas and of other obstacles to international trade." [11] Van Zeeland proceeded to interview government officials in all the leading countries in an endeavor to work out a set of recommendations which would have some chance of general acceptance. His report was not presented until January, 1938. In the meantime, a trade recession had set in, and international political tension had increased. While all the governments consulted by van Zeeland had appeared to recognize the desirability of a restoration of international trade, "the attitude, almost everywhere, became qualified by a very marked reserve" as soon as concrete suggestions or practical proposals were requested.[12] Nevertheless, the report recommended the conclusion of a "pact of economic collaboration" which would embrace "the largest possible number of states," and would "in any case" be "open to all." [13] Signatories of this general pact would then

[9] Bank for International Settlements, *Seventh Annual Report* (Basle, 1937), Annex VII.

[10] Cf. p. 213 above.

[11] Great Britain, Parliamentary Papers, *Report Presented by Monsieur van Zeeland to the Governments of the United Kingdom and France on the Possibility of Obtaining a General Reduction of the Obstacles to International Trade, January 26, 1938,* Misc. No. 1 (1938), Cmd. 5648 (London, 1938), p. 27.

[12] *Ibid.,* pp. 30–31.

[13] *Ibid.,* p. 48.

proceed to work out more detailed arrangements for the purpose of carrying out the report's further proposals, which included: (a) gradual reduction of exceptionally high tariffs, (b) removal of arbitrary and abusive measures of indirect protectionism, (c) gradual abolition of import quotas, with certain possible exceptions, (d) revision and extension of the Tripartite Monetary Agreement, and (e) suppression of exchange control.[14] It is small wonder, in view of the unfavorable atmosphere in which the report was published, that no action was taken on its recommendations and that the years 1938 and 1939 were characterized by intensification rather than relaxation of trade barriers.

Although multilateral attempts to lower trade barriers in the nineteen-thirties were a failure, steps were taken to remove one of the obstacles to the conclusion of multilateral economic pacts. This was the possibility that states which refused to participate in multilateral conventions to relax trade barriers might claim for their exports the benefits of any advantages mutually conceded in such conventions, on the basis of their right to receive most-favored-nation treatment from states participating in the convention in question. Clearly, if the benefits of multilateral agreements were to be shared by all states having most-favored-nation agreements with the participants, countries which were reluctant to lower their trade barriers would find it to their advantage to remain aloof from multilateral negotiations involving "sacrifices" on their part, knowing that they could eventually participate in the benefits without any sacrifices. This was a difficulty that the World Economic Conference of 1927 had not foreseen when it ad-

---

[14] *Ibid.*, pp. 32–42. It might be necessary, the report maintained, to retain the following types of quotas: (a) those set up to resist "dumping" methods, (b) those designed as protection against the competition of countries with abnormally low standards of living, and (c) certain types of agricultural quotas. The suppression of exchange control could probably best be accomplished if steps were taken to adjust debts and if banks of issue were to set up credits in favor of each other at the Bank for International Settlements.

vocated the conclusion of both multilateral pacts and bilateral agreements based on the most-favored-nation clause.

The Economic Committee of the League considered this question and concluded, in a report issued in 1929, that bilateral agreements based on the most-favored-nation clause might legitimately contain a reservation to the effect that the clause could not be invoked by one of the contracting parties to claim the benefits of concessions or privileges granted by the other party under the terms of multilateral conventions in which the first country did not participate. Such reservations, however, should be applicable only in the case of multilateral conventions of "a general character and aiming at the improvement of economic relations between peoples." [15] In line with this proposal, many of the most-favored-nation agreements concluded since 1929 have contained a reservation to this effect.

In addition, as a result of a resolution of the 1933 Conference of American States at Montevideo, the Pan American Union has on file for signature a multilateral treaty under which the signatory parties undertake to refrain from invoking, in their relations with one another, the obligations of the most-favored-nation clause in order to obtain the benefits of multilateral economic conventions of general applicability.[16] Significantly enough, by November, 1938, only six American states (the United States, Cuba, Panama, Nicaragua, Guatemala, and Colombia) and two European nations had signed the treaty.[17]

There is little doubt that the failure of the Monetary and Economic Conference of 1933 gave rise to widespread disillusionment over the possibility of securing multilateral economic agreements and that, since that time, proposals for multilateral action in the economic sphere have been half-hearted and

[15] League of Nations, *Recommendations of the Economic Committee Relating to Commercial Policy* (Geneva, 1929), p. 13.

[16] *Commerce Reports,* October 20, 1934, p. 252.

[17] The United States and Cuba were the only countries which had ratified the treaty. (*Bulletin of the Pan American Union,* LXXII [1938], 717.)

timid. Only with respect to regulation of the production and marketing of individual commodities, as we shall see in the following section, have nations succeeded in reaching agreement on a multilateral basis.

2. *International Raw Commodity Control Schemes*

Our survey of recent commercial policy would hardly be complete without some reference to international commodity restriction schemes, but this subject has been so extensively covered by other writers that we shall attempt no more than a brief summary of the leading developments here.

The violent fluctuations in raw material prices which have characterized the years since 1914 have given rise to numerous attempts to control the world prices of these commodities. A few international restriction schemes had been adopted before the World War, but the movement really got under way during the nineteen-twenties and proceeded at an accelerated pace during the "great" depression. Many of the schemes adopted during the post-War decade broke down after a few years' trial, only to be renewed, usually in modified form, in the early 'thirties. According to J. W. F. Rowe, who has studied this problem extensively, the following commodities were subjected to an appreciable degree of artificial control at one time or another during the decade from 1925 on:

(*a*) 1925–29—wheat, sugar, copper, rubber, petroleum (partial), coffee, zinc (Europe), lead (partial), iron and steel (partial), potash, aluminum (Europe).

(*b*) Since 1929—cotton, wheat, sugar, copper, rubber, petroleum, coffee, zinc, tin, lead, iron and steel (very slight), nitrate, potash, wood pulp (partial), sawn wood goods (partial), aluminum, tea.[18]

[18] "Artificial Control Schemes and the World's Staples," Svenska Handelsbanken, *Index*, X (1935), 76–77. In addition some degree of control was exercised in the case of certain other, less important commodities.

The second group, it should be noted, comprises all the commodities appearing in the first and a number of additional ones. Between 1935 and the summer of 1939, a few of these schemes broke down, while others were made more effective. The outbreak of war in September, 1939, meant, of course, that at least those agreements participated in by Germany and one or more of the Allies ceased to function.

The fact that international restriction schemes first began to be adopted on a significant scale in the nineteen-twenties is not difficult to explain. Under the stimulus of a spectacular rise in prices, raw material production and productive capacity outside of areas of conflict had undergone, in many cases, a marked expansion during the War years. With the gradual return to normal peacetime conditions, a number of these industries began to suffer from over-capacity. The fact that technical improvements were simultaneously taking place on a wide scale simply intensified the tendency for prices to decline. Under these conditions, it is not surprising that producers sought a solution in artificial restriction of supply. Nor is it altogether surprising that when raw material prices collapsed in the early years of the depression, the adoption of international restriction schemes seemed to offer a way out, despite the failure of earlier arrangements.

It may be argued that producers should have relied on the price mechanism to bring about an eventual adjustment between supply and demand. In their defense, it should be pointed out that the price mechanism is not at all times and under all circumstances capable of accomplishing the adjustments expected of it under ideal conditions. Producers of raw materials, in particular, frequently suffer from a tendency for supply and/or demand for their products to respond in a sluggish or perverse fashion to changes in price. Recurring cycles of prosperity and depression tend to obscure the influence of long-run factors and to cause periodic over-expansion and over-contraction. The disturbances which have characterized the years since 1914 have imposed an especially severe strain on the price mechanism.[19] In addition, producers of many of the more important raw materials entering into international trade find themselves operating under oligopolistic conditions and turn naturally to monopolistic combination as the way out of an uncertain price situation.[20]

In a few exceptional instances, production of a raw commodity is concentrated very largely in one country, and restriction of supply on a national scale suffices, at least for a time, to control the movements of the world price.[21] In the typical case, however, an agreement among producers in widely separated national areas is necessary if the world price is to be controlled. When the producers in each country are relatively few in number and are well organized, they may be in a position to enter into a private international agreement or cartel. If the number of producers in each national area is large, however, governmental intervention or support is usually necessary before price control on either a national or international scale can be sought or enforced. In such cases international restriction agreements are likely to be intergovernmental in form and to be enforced by governmental action. Even private international cartels frequently find it impossible to enforce their agreements without governmental coöperation or support.

Control by a single government, or government-supported combination of producers, has been attempted, for varying periods of time, in the case of coffee (Brazil), natural nitrates

---

[19] For a fuller discussion along these lines, see Staley, *Raw Materials in Peace and War,* pp. 89–100.

[20] For further discussion of this point, see Ellsworth, *International Economics,* pp. 424–45, as well as the standard works on imperfect competition. Oligopolistic competition in the strict sense prevails when a staple commodity, incapable of any appreciable degree of product-differentiation, is marketed by few sellers. While this condition does not prevail for all raw commodities, some, like wheat and cotton, which are produced and sold within national boundaries by many small producers, have been subjected to governmental control along national lines. In such cases, competition in the international sphere takes on the attributes of oligopoly, and intergovernmental agreements are likely to be sought.

[21] Cf. p. 322 above.

(Chile), cotton (United States), cinchona bark (Netherlands East Indies), and other commodities. Aluminum, copper, mercury, diamonds, and nickel are examples of commodities which have been brought under private international control through the formation of producers' cartels or through virtually complete domination of available supplies by a unified concern.[22] The international tea restriction scheme has depended on governmental support for its enforcement.[23] Rubber and tin, however, have been controlled under the terms of intergovernmental agreements. Finally, the abortive International Wheat Agreement of 1933, the International Silver Agreement, and the International Sugar Agreement of 1937 were intergovernmental agreements concluded under the auspices of the League of Nations and growing out of the discussions initiated at the London Monetary and Economic Conference of 1933.[24]

Price control, usually the central aim of international restriction schemes, is generally sought, as already indicated, through limitation of supply. This most frequently takes the form of a restriction of exports from each national area, supplemented in certain cases by some degree of control of production within such areas. Private international cartels sometimes employ more elaborate devices such as division of markets and fixing of prices.[25] It should be noted, in this connection, that private international cartels have been formed in a number of industries producing fabricated articles as well as in raw material industries. Such arrangements, though very important, lie outside the scope of this study, which is concerned with those aspects of international trade control in which governments have been directly involved.

[22] In some of these cases, American producers coöperate with European cartels through "gentlemen's agreements."
[23] Cf. Dietrich, *World Trade*, pp. 351–53.
[24] Cf. p. 430 above.
[25] Cf. U. S. Temporary National Economic Committee, *Transcript of Testimony of Dr. Theodore J. Kreps on Cartels*, January 15, 1940 (Washington, 1940), p. 6.

International restriction schemes are, it has been maintained, most clearly justified if their aim is merely to tide an industry over a severe depression or to meet a temporary decline in demand.[26] Producers may thereby avert unnecessarily painful readjustments and maintain their purchasing power without, in the final accounting, inflicting injury on consumers. Actually, raw material producers, once united in a control scheme, have rarely been content with such limited objectives but have attempted to maintain the price well above its natural equilibrium point for long periods. This tendency does not always reflect merely a desire of producers as a group for monopoly profits. It often is attributable, to an important degree, to pressure exerted by high-cost producers who must secure a relatively high price in order to maintain their position in the industry. One of the outstanding weaknesses of restriction schemes, indeed, is the fact that they tend to prevent low-cost, efficient producers from expanding operations at the expense of their high-cost rivals.

But prolonged attempts to enforce an artificially high price have frequently ended in disaster. In order to maintain a monopoly price successfully, certain conditions are essential.[27] The control scheme should take in all (or nearly all) actual or potential sources of supply of the commodity in question. Otherwise, the maintenance of an artificially high price tends to encourage the expansion of production in uncontrolled, "outside" areas.[28] The more elastic the conditions of supply in these outside areas, the greater the danger. In addition, an attempt

[26] Cf. J. W. F. Rowe, *Markets and Men: A Study of Artificial Control Schemes in Some Primary Industries* (New York, 1936), pp. 216–18.

[27] Cf. Staley's discussion of monopoly power, *Raw Materials in Peace and War*, Appendix B.

[28] The increase of production in "outside" areas has proved a source of serious difficulty in numerous instances, e.g., coffee (Brazil), natural nitrates (Chile), sugar (Cuban restriction scheme and Chadbourne Plan), and rubber (Stevenson scheme). In the majority of these cases, the "outside" areas eventually were brought into a more comprehensive scheme. The Chilean nitrate industry, which suffered from the development of the artificial nitrate industry, has recently operated under an agreement with the European Nitrate Cartel.

to raise the price above the equilibrium point may not prove very profitable unless the demand for the product is relatively inelastic.[29]

It is altogether conceivable that control schemes which, analyzed from the point of view of the particular industries concerned, appear profitable might be regarded as ultimately unprofitable if producers could take full account of their broader repercussions on the economy as a whole. Many economists have argued that the existence of rigid "controlled" prices in an economy which is subject to violent "ups and downs" tends to interfere with a smooth adjustment of the price system and to prolong periods of depression. This problem, obviously, cannot be settled here. It has been mentioned primarily for the purpose of indicating the complicated questions which must be considered before one can reach a final judgment on the merits of international restriction schemes.

The gradual accumulation of experience in the organizing and administering of control schemes has resulted in various adaptations designed to prevent some of the mistakes which were made in the nineteen-twenties. Among these changes, the following are especially important:

(a) Production and export quotas have tended to be altered in accordance with variations in the size of stocks rather than with movements in the market price. Thus an attempt has been made to avoid the maintenance of an unduly high price in the face of rapid accumulations of stocks.[30]

(b) Vigorous efforts have been made to bring into the control schemes all producing areas of any importance, even if special inducements had to be given to reluctant countries.

(c) There has apparently been a greater realization of the need for restraint in enforcing monopolistic prices, although this has not as yet been clearly demonstrated in the administration

[29] The relative elasticity of the demand for raw silk (for which rayon, of course, has formed an increasingly important cheaper substitute) has limited the power of the Japanese Government to support the price of this commodity.

[30] Cf. League of Nations, *Report of the Committee for the Study of the Problem of Raw Materials* (Geneva, 1937), p. 18.

of controls. Some schemes have begun to provide for the maintenance of buffer stocks, which may be thrown on the market at times when prices threaten to rise too rapidly and replenished when prices are low.

(d) In a few cases, consumers have been represented, though merely in an advisory capacity, on regulatory bodies set up to administer the control schemes.

(e) Some attention has been given to the need for maintaining or expanding demand as well as for limiting supply. To this end, importing as well as exporting countries have been brought into some of the recent agreements (wheat and sugar) as active participants, in order to prevent the erection of further barriers to importation or even to bring about some relaxation of import restrictions. In addition, attempts have been made to stimulate consumption through advertising or educational campaigns.

Some of these tendencies are well illustrated in the history of international sugar restriction, which originated as a result of maladjustments growing out of the World War. Beet sugar production in Europe fell off drastically during the War, partly because many of the best fields lay within the actual areas of conflict and partly, of course, because of scarcity of labor in the fields.[31] Cuba responded by rapidly expanding her output, only to find herself faced with an acute overproduction problem once the European beet sugar industry, with the aid of high protection, began to get back on its feet. In the latter half of the nineteen-twenties, therefore, we find Cuba attempting a unilateral restriction scheme, which completely failed to raise the price or to prevent it from falling. Not only did Cuba's competitors in the export field gain ground at her expense, but sugar-importing countries continued to grant increased aid to producers through higher tariffs and bounties. This, it will be recalled, was a period of growing agricultural protectionism, and beet sugar had long been a favorite subject of protection, especially in Europe.[32]

[31] Cf. Rowe, *Markets and Men*, p. 78.
[32] Cf. pp. 18–19 above. The cultivation of beet sugar has been encouraged

By 1931, the price of sugar had fallen to disastrous levels, and the other leading sugar-exporting countries were ready to join with Cuba in a restriction scheme. An international agreement, known as the Chadbourne Plan, was signed in May of that year by the producers' associations of Cuba, Java, Germany, Czechoslovakia, Poland, Hungary, Belgium, and Peru (the leading exporting countries). Yugoslavia joined later. Production in each of the participating countries was to be limited to current requirements for internal consumption plus an agreed export quota.[33] This scheme, too, failed to prevent a further fall in the world price, although it did bring about some reduction in stocks, which had totalled 7½ million tons, or about one-quarter of annual consumption, in 1931. Again the chief cause of failure was a marked increase in production in areas outside the agreement, i.e., primarily in countries which did not export to the world market. While the Chadbourne countries reduced their production by nearly 7 million tons per annum, output in the rest of the world increased by 4½ million tons, largely as a result of the influence of intensified measures of protection on production in the British Empire and in the United States and its territorial possessions.[34] The 1931 agreement was not renewed when its expiration date arrived on September 1, 1935.

Meanwhile, however, the countries participating in the Chadbourne scheme had sought to secure, at the Monetary and Economic Conference of 1933, the conclusion of a more comprehensive agreement which would bring in importing as well as exporting countries. Only in this way, it was recognized, could the progressive narrowing of the world market for sugar

---

partly as a measure of economic preparedness for war and partly as a social measure (it requires large amounts of labor and hence helps to keep the agricultural population on the land).

[33] For details and text of agreement, see V. Gutierrez, *The World Sugar Problem, 1926–1935* (London, 1935), Ch. VII and Appendix I.

[34] Cf. Rowe, *Markets and Men*, pp. 83–85.

be forestalled. Although no agreement was reached at the Conference, negotiations were continued from time to time, and the International Sugar Agreement which was concluded in May, 1937, under the auspices of the League of Nations, was a direct outgrowth of the 1933 discussions.[35]

The 1937 agreement was signed by twenty-one governments, representing nearly all the importing and exporting countries of any importance. Its *declared* objective was to "assure consumers of an adequate supply of sugar on the world market at a reasonable price not to exceed the cost of production, including a reasonable profit, of efficient producers." [36] In order to understand its provisions, one needs to take account of the fact that markets of certain of the leading importing countries (especially the United States and the United Kingdom) were in considerable part reserved for importations from colonies, Dominions, and territorial possessions through quota and preferential tariff systems.[37] In other words, through these preferential arrangements, the scope of which had been broadened during the nineteen-thirties, the free world market for sugar had been greatly restricted. In order to put a stop to this trend, the 1937 agreement embodied a series of guarantees, given by importing countries and countries exporting only to preferential markets, designed to stop further contraction of the free world market and perhaps even to enlarge it. The United States, for example, agreed to maintain that part of its imports derived from foreign countries (not enjoying a preferred status in its market) at the level fixed under the Sugar Quota Regulations of December, 1936, while the Philippines undertook not to export to countries other than the United States and its territorial possessions, so long as the Islands were entitled to a specified minimum quota in the American

---

[35] Cf. League of Nations, *International Sugar Conference: I. Text of the Agreement, II. Proceedings and Documents of the Conference* (Geneva, 1937), p. 5.

[36] *Ibid.*, p. 8.

[37] In addition, Cuba is given a preferential status in the American market.

market.[38] All the contracting governments, moreover, were to give favorable consideration to proposals having for their object the stimulation of an increase in the consumption of sugar.

Exports to the free world market were to be regulated through basic export quotas, totalling 3,622,500 metric tons, which were apportioned among the countries regularly exporting to this market in previous years.[39] These quotas might be increased by a uniform percentage when, in the judgment of the regulatory body set up under the agreement, market conditions seemed to call for such action. They might also be reduced by not more than 5 per cent during the first two years of regulation and thereafter without limit provided the consent of the countries concerned was secured. Unutilized quotas could not, as under some schemes, be carried over to the following year. In fact, each country which did not expect to use its full quota was to notify the regulatory body as early as possible, in order that the unused portion might be allocated among the remaining exporting countries. Except under special circumstances, stocks were not to exceed 25 per cent nor to fall below 10 per cent of annual production in each country entitled to a basic export quota. This result was to be secured through the imposition of appropriate production controls by the various exporting countries.

The agreement was to be administered by a General Council composed of delegates of all the contracting governments and by an Executive Committee of nine members. The exporting countries were given a majority (55 per cent) of the votes in the General Council, while on the Executive Committee importing countries, cane-sugar producing countries, and beet-sugar producing countries were to have three representatives each.

Of all the international restriction schemes which have thus

[38] The Philippines were, however, to be granted a quota for exportation to the free market if the basic quotas of the countries regularly exporting to that market were enlarged. (*Ibid.*, pp. 9–10.)

[39] A small reserve quota was also set up for countries which occasionally exported to the free market.

far been adopted, the International Sugar Agreement is one of the most comprehensive. On the supply side, it provides for control of exports, production, and stocks, while on the demand side it seeks to prevent any further narrowing of the world sugar market. It does not, like some agreements, place any restrictions on new planting as such, nor does it provide for representation of consumers, even in an advisory capacity. The fact that the agreement is inter-governmental in nature does not necessarily guarantee representation of consumer interests, for producers, even in the importing countries, are generally in a position to exert more influence on governmental policies than are consumers.

Raw material producers evidently learned many valuable lessons about regulatory schemes from the experience of the nineteen-twenties. Whether they as yet fully appreciate the dangers of seeking to maintain an excessively high price is questionable. Prices of many "controlled" commodities rose abruptly in late 1936 and early 1937, and while export quotas were in many cases raised, increased supplies were apparently not thrown on the market quickly enough. Certainly, the relatively new practice of maintaining buffer stocks needs to be rendered more effective and more widely applicable.[40]

International restriction schemes are probably in a relatively early stage of their development. If current tendencies continue, they are likely to become more prevalent in the future than they have been in the past. It is almost certain, moreover, that governments will undertake more active supervision of such schemes, in order to see that they are administered in the interests of the national economy as a whole.

3. *Regional Groups*

In the terminology of commercial policy, a "region" is a group of two or more states which are bound to each other

[40] Cf. League of Nations, *Report of the Committee for the Study of the Problem of Raw Materials*, pp. 56–62.

by ethnic, geographic, or historical ties. States belonging to such a region may seek an increased degree of economic integration or coöperation in a variety of ways, through the formation of a customs union, the granting of tariff preferences or preferential quota arrangements, the adoption of coördinated export policies, and so on.

Regional tariff preferences are recognized as legitimate exceptions to the most-favored-nation clause if the commercial agreements between the countries concerned and outside states contain specific reservations to that effect.[41] Among the regional exceptions which have been generally recognized for some time are those relating to the Scandinavian states and the Central American countries.[42] In the years following the World War, the number of such recognized "regional" groups tended to increase, but the extent to which the countries involved actually exercised their right to extend tariff preferences to each other's products was relatively limited.

During the early years of the depression, the failure of successive attempts to secure a multilateral agreement which would halt the upward movement of trade barriers naturally led nations to consider the alternative possibility of combatting rampant economic nationalism through the conclusion of regional economic pacts. Such pacts would aim at the liberalization of trade barriers between the states concerned, thereby permitting the region to enjoy the fruits of a more widespread division of labor. Thus, world trade as a whole would, it was argued, indirectly benefit. As time went on, political developments tended to encourage the formation of regional *blocs,* which would coöperate economically *and* politically. It is doubtful, in fact, if regional economic coöperation could ever be achieved in the absence of fairly strong political friendship between the states involved.

It is not our purpose here to analyze in detail the effects of

[41] Cf. p. 372 above.
[42] Cf., also, the discussion on p. 372 above.

preferential tariff arrangements. This task has been admirably performed by other writers.[43] Suffice it to say that regional economic pacts cannot be expected to lead to an expansion of world trade if the countries concerned grant each other preferential treatment by erecting higher trade barriers against the rest of the world while leaving the barriers affecting their mutual trade virtually unchanged. In fact, the effects of such an agreement on world trade are likely to be harmful. Even if trade barriers *within* the region are liberalized, this may not benefit world trade if the relaxation of restrictions takes a form which involves no increase in *total* imports into the countries concerned.[44] In a period when trade restrictions are being intensified all round, regional agreements are not likely to be trade-liberalizing in nature, at least to any marked degree. Even so, they may in some instances perform important functions in helping to revive business confidence and in reversing the trend toward economic nationalism.

One must draw a sharp distinction, moreover, between regional agreements of an exclusive nature and those which are open to all nations willing to undertake the same obligations as the original signatories. Agreements of the latter type are potentially multilateral and might conceivably constitute an effective approach to multilateral action in a world in which nationalistic tendencies dominate the economic scene.

The remainder of this section will be devoted to a discussion

[43] Cf., in particular, Haberler, *Theory of International Trade,* pp. 383–90; A. C. Pigou, *Protective and Preferential Import Duties* (London, 1906), pp. 85 ff.; and F. W. Taussig, *Free Trade, the Tariff, and Reciprocity* (New York, 1920), pp. 120 ff.

[44] Thus, many recent preferential arrangements have involved lowering the tariff rate on a limited quantity of imports of a given commodity from the country to be favored. Such a preferential tariff quota does not have the effect of increasing the *total* quantity of imports of the commodity concerned into the country granting the preference, unless the quota exceeds the amount which would normally be admitted from *all* sources. If it has the effect merely of increasing imports from the country receiving the preference, it simply diverts trade from third countries. Even tariff preferences which are not quantitatively limited may not involve any increase in total imports of the commodity.

of some of the more important attempts in the direction of regional economic *rapprochement* during the nineteen-thirties.[45]

a. *The Danubian countries*. From 1930 on, the plight of the agricultural countries of Eastern and Southeastern Europe attracted considerable attention, and many of the schemes put forward to meet the economic problems of this area revolved around some form of regional economic coöperation. The more important of these schemes were designed to assist the agricultural countries of the Danubian basin—Hungary, Rumania, Yugoslavia, and Bulgaria. Austria and Czechoslovakia were likewise included in some of the proposals for Danubian collaboration.

It was natural that plans for economic rehabilitation of this area should have emphasized the need for some sort of regional pact, for it had long been recognized that the breaking up of the old Austro-Hungarian Empire into a number of separate agricultural and industrial states, each with its independent tariff system, had played havoc with the economic structure of the region. In fact, the peace treaties had contained provisions permitting the setting up of preferential commercial relations between Czechoslovakia, Austria, and Hungary, and these countries had taken advantage of the privilege to some slight extent during the nineteen-twenties.[46]

In 1930, as we have seen in Chapter III, a series of agrarian conferences was held in Eastern Europe.[47] Out of these conferences came two main proposals: (*a*) for centralized control of exports from the four Danubian countries and Poland, and (*b*) for agreements between European industrial and agricultural countries providing for preferential tariff treatment by the former of the leading agricultural products of the latter. No

---

[45] In order to confine the discussion to manageable proportions, it will be necessary to omit certain regional groups, such as the Little Entente, which had barely initiated serious efforts toward economic coöperation when it began to collapse politically.

[46] Cf. U. S. Tariff Commission, *Extent of Equal Tariff Treatment in Foreign Countries*, p. 75.

[47] Cf. p. 34 above.

definite action was taken, a number of countries opposing the second proposal on the ground of its incompatibility with the most-favored-nation clauses of existing trade agreements. During the course of 1931, however, Rumania, Yugoslavia, Hungary, and Bulgaria negotiated individually with Western European countries for tariff preferences on grain. Their efforts were attended with some degree of success.[48]

In the spring of 1932, the four leading European powers—Britain, France, Germany, and Italy—held a conference in London to discuss the economic problems of the Danubian area. Considerable divergence of opinion came to light at this meeting. The Tardieu (French) Plan, which contemplated the establishment of reciprocal tariff preferences by the five Danubian states—Austria, Czechoslovakia, Hungary, Rumania, and Yugoslavia—encountered much opposition.[49] Germany maintained that, because of the importance of her trade with the Danubian area, she should be permitted to participate in any scheme for regional preferences. Italy, disliking some of the political implications of the plan, held out for bilateral agreements between Danubian and non-Danubian states.[50] Great Britain was reluctant to waive her rights under the most-favored-nation clause, except possibly in favor of Austria.

An important meeting was held at Stresa in September, 1932, attended by the members of a committee appointed at the Lausanne Conference to submit to the Committee of Enquiry for European Union proposals for the relief of the countries of Central and Eastern Europe. The chief recommendation of this conference took the form of a draft multilateral convention, to be participated in by all European states. The

---

[48] Cf. p. 449 below.

[49] Royal Institute of International Affairs, *Survey of International Affairs, 1932* (London, 1933), pp. 22–23. The plan also provided that certain other countries, including Germany and Italy, should grant the Danubian countries preferential tariffs on agricultural products and that an international loan of $50 million should be raised for the protection of the budgets and foreign exchanges of the Danubian countries.

[50] Cf. Royal Institute of International Affairs, *South-Eastern Europe*, p. 24.

convention called for the raising of a fund for the support of prices of cereals produced in Central and Eastern Europe, the contribution of each state to the fund to be reduced in proportion to preferences on cereal importations from the grain-producing countries granted by it under the terms of bilateral agreements.[51] Like most matters considered by the Commission of Enquiry for European Union, these proposals came to nothing.

Out of this series of rather fruitless discussions, however, a few concrete results did emerge. The four agricultural countries of the Danubian area succeeded in obtaining tariff preferences for their chief products in a number of individually negotiated bilateral agreements with European industrial states.[52] As time went on, however, the question of preferential tariff arrangements to benefit the Danubian area became, to a

[51] League of Nations, Commission of Enquiry for European Union, *Report by the Stresa Conference for the Economic Restoration of Central and Eastern Europe* (Geneva, 1932), pp. 23–24. Preferences should in no case affect the most-favored-nation rights of third states and should apply to quotas based on average exports of the cereals concerned during the years 1929, 1930, and 1931. They were to be granted on wheat, barley for fodder, maize, rye, barley for brewing, and oats. Germany would acquit herself of any contribution to the fund through the conclusion of appropriate bilateral agreements.

[52] Under the terms of agreements concluded late in 1931 and early in 1932, France accorded to Hungary, Rumania, and Yugoslavia preferential tariff quotas on wheat. In return, these countries reduced their duties on various industrial products of interest to French exporters. Later, preferences were granted to the same three countries on feed corn, in the cases of Hungary and Yugoslavia at a time when a large French wheat crop rendered the wheat preferences valueless. (*Commerce Reports, seriatim,* and L. Sommer, *Neugestaltung der Handelspolitik,* p. 214.) Austria was also granted a preferential tariff quota on lumber.

Germany negotiated a number of bilateral agreements providing for preferential tariff treatment of Danubian agricultural products from 1931 on. The preferences were not always confined to specified quotas of imports, as were those conceded by France. Some of these preferences were not put into effect, at least ostensibly, owing to the opposition of countries having most-favored-nation agreements with Germany. Cf. Jones, *Tariff Retaliation,* p. 298, and *Commerce Reports,* April 1, 1933, p. 203.

Austria and Czechoslovakia also extended certain tariff preferences to Danubian agricultural countries, some of which were in time made effective. Meanwhile, France, Germany, Austria, and Czechoslovakia began to seek insertion in their new commercial agreements of provisions exempting from the opera-

very large extent, a dead issue. More and more, foreign trade within this region and with such outside countries as Germany and France came to be governed by exchange regulations, clearing agreements, or import quotas. Under these arrangements, as we have seen, the most-favored-nation clause was largely ignored and the movement of commodities across national boundaries was regulated on "bilateral balancing" principles.

The 1930 proposal for centralized control of exports from the four Danubian states and Poland was never adopted,[53] but a few limited steps in this direction were later taken. The Bulgarian central grain-marketing organization entered into an agreement with the corresponding organizations in Rumania and Yugoslavia to inform each other daily as to their sales prices.[54] A number of years later, in 1937, exporters of cattle from Hungary, Yugoslavia, and Rumania agreed to set up a central organization to coördinate their selling activities.[55]

From the beginning, and to an increasing extent as time went on, attempts to work out a rational solution of the Danubian problem were impeded by political conflicts. The interests of France, Germany, and Italy, all seeking to maintain or acquire political influence in this region, were frequently at variance. For a time, the Danubian countries which had benefited from the Versailles Treaty tended to align them-

---

tion of the most-favored-nation clause all preferences granted to certain states of Central and Eastern Europe.

Italy, as we shall see in the following section, entered into preferential arrangements with Austria and Hungary.

[53] Cf. p. 447 above.

[54] U. S. Tariff Commission, *World Trade Barriers in Relation to American Agriculture*, p. 327.

[55] H. Hantos, "Le Regionalisme économique en Europe," *Revue économique internationale*, XXXI (1939), 72. The German-Polish rye agreement of 1931, which was later extended to cover wheat and participated in by the Soviet Union, represented another interesting instance, though one not directly traceable to the Danubian conferences, of an attempt to restrain competition in the export of cereals. See K. Colegrove, "The German-Polish Rye Agreement," *Journal of Political Economy*, XXXIX (1931), 213–228, and *Commerce Reports*, December 29, 1934, p. 413.

selves with France, while Austria and Hungary had more in common with Germany and Italy. Later on, French influence waned throughout the region, as Germany recovered her military might and developed her policy of stimulating purchases from the countries to the southeast. Meanwhile, the increasing self-sufficiency of certain European industrial countries, with respect particularly to wheat, nullified some of the advantages granted to the Danubian countries under earlier preferential arrangements and forced them to readjust their agricultural production.

b. The Rome Agreements. At the various conferences held in 1930 and 1931 to consider the Danubian problem, Italy had been inclined to favor the conclusion of bilateral preferential agreements between Danubian and non-Danubian countries. She proceeded, at a relatively early date, to put a modified version of this policy into practice in her economic relations with Austria and Hungary, two neighboring countries with which Italy had close political ties.

The first manifestation of this policy was the conclusion of the so-called Brocchi Agreements. Though bilateral in form, these agreements embodied similar principles and were apparently worked out, at least partially, in triangular negotiations.[56] They are notable chiefly for their application of a novel type of concealed tariff preference, designed to avoid formal violation of the most-favored-nation clause. Each of the agreements contained a clause whereby the countries concerned reciprocally recognized their mutual right to subsidize certain exports to each other. The subsidies were to take the form of preferentially low export credits. Austrian exporters, for example, were enabled to secure credits on sales of specified goods

---

[56] Cf. Jones, *op. cit.*, p. 296. The Austro-Hungarian treaty was concluded in June, 1931, while those between Italy on the one hand and Austria and Hungary on the other were not signed until February, 1932. For the text of the Austro-Hungarian treaty, see League of Nations, *Treaty Series*, CXXII (1931–1932), 123–319; for the Austro-Italian, *Gazzetta ufficiale del Regno d'Italia*, LXXIII (1932), 2000–2003; and for the Italo-Hungarian, *ibid.*, 3410–12.

to Hungary at rates sufficiently low to enable them to undersell competitors from third countries in the Hungarian market.[57] The agreements also called for preferential freight rates.

The Rome Agreements of March and May, 1934, went considerably farther in bringing these three countries into a regional economic pact. They comprised, in the first place, two triangular agreements concluded March 17, the one calling for consultation in political matters of mutual interest to the three countries, the other providing the basis for the more detailed bilateral economic agreements which were later to be concluded.[58] In these later detailed agreements, signed May 14, preferential tariffs were openly introduced on a limited scale.[59] In addition, the system of reciprocal export credit privileges set up in the earlier agreements was continued, although again the lists of goods affected were not published. Austria benefited chiefly from the preferences extended by Italy to her industrial products. Hungary expected to gain primarily from the provisions whereby Austria and Italy undertook to purchase specified amounts of Hungarian wheat at prices well above the world price.[60] Italy, in turn, was to derive her main advantage from increased utilization of her Adriatic shipping ports by Austria and Hungary, a development which these two countries were to encourage through the extension of credit favors.

For a number of reasons, the effects of the Rome Agreements, particularly for Hungary and Italy, were not as favorable as had been anticipated. Owing to a rise in the world price

[57] In some cases, the export credit applied to a commodity which entered the importing country duty-free. In such a case, the effect was not that of a preferential tariff, but rather of an export premium applicable to a single country. (Cf. Haberler, *The Theory of International Trade*, p. 387 n.) The Austro-Hungarian Agreement of 1931 was replaced by a revised arrangement in 1932, but the system of reciprocal export privileges was continued.

[58] See League of Nations, *Treaty Series*, CLIV (1934–1935), 281–95. In addition, Austria and Italy on the same day signed a protocol calling for the extension of preferential treatment to Austrian products exported to Italy.

[59] The preferences, some of which were on a tariff quota basis, were later extended somewhat.

[60] Cf. p. 337 n., above, for further details concerning this arrangement.

of wheat, the wheat provisions of the agreements eventually proved disadvantageous to Hungary and were substantially modified in 1936–37.[61] By the middle of 1937, scarcity of foreign exchange reserves had become such an acute problem for Italy that she was forced to denounce the provisions for export credit and freight rate preferences in her agreements with Austria and Hungary.[62] But the final breakdown of the Rome Agreements followed the absorption of Austria by Germany in March, 1938. Of the economic portions of the agreements, all that remained after this event was an undertaking on the part of Italy to absorb a portion of Hungary's grain surplus at a reasonable price.[63]

   c. The Balkan states. The six Balkan states—Yugoslavia, Rumania, Albania, Bulgaria, Greece, and Turkey—do not carry on an extensive foreign trade with each other, for their exports are largely competitive, consisting primarily of cereals and tobacco. Long separated by political differences, they first began to seek coöperation in 1930, when all were suffering from the severe agricultural crisis. A series of Balkan Conferences was held in 1930, 1931, 1932, and 1933.[64] In the economic sphere, the most important accomplishment of these conferences was the conclusion, at Salonika in 1933, of "The Draft of a Regional Economic Understanding," which aimed at an expansion of intra-Balkan trade and at coöperation for the protection of Balkan foreign markets. The contracting parties agreed:

   (*a*) to base their mutual trade relations on the most-favored-nation clause;
   (*b*) to grant each other preferential tariff quotas, inserting a "Balkan clause" in their most-favored-nation agreements with extra-Balkan states;

[61] Cf. p. 337 n., above.
[62] Cf. Hantos, *op. cit.*, p. 86.
[63] *Ibid.*, p. 84.
[64] See R. J. Kerner and H. N. Howard, *The Balkan Conferences and the Balkan Entente, 1930–1935* (Berkeley, 1936).

- (*c*) to reach an understanding concerning trade in products handled by state monopolies;
- (*d*) to take steps toward the unification of customs nomenclature and formalities;
- (*e*) to adopt a common commercial policy toward extra-Balkan states, with a view to protecting the markets for Balkan exports;
- (*f*) to create a Chamber of Compensations which would facilitate the regulation of payments and transfers on a basis of intra-Balkan preferential treatment and would permit the exchange of merchandise on a bilateral, trilateral, or multilateral basis;
- (*g*) to set up a Permanent Balkan Commission for International Commerce which would serve in an advisory capacity.[65]

Following the formation of the Balkan Entente in 1934, an Economic Advisory Council was set up by the participating states (Greece, Rumania, Turkey, and Yugoslavia).[66]

The concrete results of all the steps that were taken in the direction of Balkan economic coöperation were actually rather modest.[67] While the governors of the Balkan central banks adopted a practice of meeting periodically to discuss mutual problems, it was only to a very limited extent that the provisions of "The Draft for a Regional Economic Understanding" were put into effect. From 1934 on, the Balkan states were to a large extent preoccupied with the problem of adjusting their economies to the marked expansion of German imports from this region.[68]

d. The Oslo Group. The countries of Northern Europe—Denmark, Norway, Sweden, Finland, the Netherlands, Belgium, and Luxemburg—have been drawn together in part by geographical proximity and common traditions, in part by similar economic interests, and in part by their time-honored attitude of neutrality in European conflicts. Before the depression,

[65] *Ibid.*, pp. 217–21.

[66] Cf. Dietrich, *World Trade*, p. 246. Bulgaria remained aloof from the Balkan Entente because of her political differences with the four countries concerned, while Albania had long been under the political domination of Italy.

[67] Cf. Hantos, *op. cit.*, p. 82.

[68] Cf. pp. 159–65 above.

moreover, these countries maintained relatively moderate tariffs; and, although they have all utilized nontariff trade barriers to a greater or less degree since the outbreak of the depression, their tariffs remained, on the whole, relatively low at the end of the nineteen-thirties.

The original Oslo Convention, concluded December 22, 1930, represented an attempt to put into effect on a regional scale an agreement much like the abortive multilateral economic convention which was drawn up under League auspices in 1930.[69] It was open to outside states, subject to approval of the original signatories. Finland, not a party to the original convention, was the only country later to take advantage of this clause.

In June, 1932, Holland, Belgium, and Luxemburg went a step farther by concluding at Ouchy an International Convention for the Lowering of Economic Barriers. Although essentially a regional preferential agreement, the Convention was potentially multilateral in that it was open to outside states.[70] The signatory states undertook, moreover, not only to refrain from increasing customs duties in their reciprocal relations, but also to impose no new or higher duties against the products of third states with which they had commercial conventions unless injured by the raising of trade barriers in such states. They also agreed:

(a) to lower their customs duties on each other's products by 10 per cent annually for five successive years, provided the duties on semi-manufactures were not reduced below 10 per cent ad valorem and those on finished manufactures below 8 per cent ad valorem;

(b) to apply no new trade restrictions in their reciprocal relations and to eliminate as soon as possible all existing restrictions, with certain exceptions.

[69] Cf. pp. 32–33 above. The contracting states were to notify each other of projected tariff changes.

[70] For text, see U. S. Department of State, *Treaty Information Bulletin*, No. 37 (October, 1932), pp. 16–23.

This agreement clearly did not provide for the formation of a complete customs union, although its provisions tended in that direction. Despite its potentially multilateral character, it encountered opposition from the United Kingdom—engaged at the time in negotiating the Ottawa Agreements—on the ground that it conflicted with existing most-favored-nation obligations.[71] Apparently for this reason, the agreement was never ratified.

Five years later, when both the Belgian and Dutch currencies had been devalued and international trade was staging a rapid recovery, the Oslo powers decided to take a decisive step toward the reduction of their mutual trade barriers. A Convention signed at The Hague, May 28, 1937, contained the following provisions:

(a) Belgium, Luxemburg, and the Netherlands (the only members of the Oslo Group with extensive quota systems) undertook to waive import restrictions on extensive lists of products originating in and coming from the signatory states.[72] Furthermore, no new or increased customs duties or charges were to be made applicable to the products listed.

(b) Denmark, Finland, Norway, the Netherlands (for the Netherlands Indies), and Sweden undertook not to impose new or increased customs duties or charges or new quantitative restrictions on specified goods originating in and coming from the signatory states.

(c) All agreed to take further steps toward removing trade barriers by negotiating bilateral agreements with each other.

(d) They further agreed to notify each other of proposed restrictions or special charges on the importation of commodities not previously affected by such measures.

(e) Finally, they agreed to examine jointly any measure likely to terminate "abnormal" competitive practices in foreign trade and to make a joint enquiry into conditions governing the award of governmental contracts or orders with a view

[71] Cf. Royal Institute of International Affairs, *Survey of International Affairs, 1932*, p. 40.

[72] In some cases, import permit requirements might be continued, but permits would be granted freely for goods originating in the Oslo region.

to determining to what extent preferences were given to domestic production.[73]

The agreement was to be open to all states and was to be operative for one year from July 1, 1937, subject to the provision that any country might give notice of withdrawal in case of changes in economic conditions which made such a course necessary.

Unlike the Ouchy Convention, this agreement contained no clauses which involved formal violation of the most-favored-nation clause. Removal of import quotas by Holland and Belgium-Luxemburg in favor of the Oslo countries only could hardly be regarded as conflicting with the clause, since restrictions of this character were generally held to be outside the scope of the clause. In fact, Belgium extended her quota concessions gratuitously to the United Kingdom, France, Germany and the United States, while Holland extended hers to the United Kingdom and Germany.[74]

The agreement remained in force for only one year. On May 11, 1938, the participating states signed a declaration in which they recognized that the "state of world conditions" prevented them for the time being from renewing the 1937 Convention but declared themselves ready as soon as economic conditions permitted to resume their efforts toward the reduction of trade barriers.[75] Probably the failure to renew the agreement must be attributed primarily to three factors: (a) the trade recession which commenced in the autumn of 1937, (b) increasing international tension in the political sphere, and (c) the fact that the movement in the direction of

[73] League of Nations, *Treaty Series*, CLXXX (1937–1938), 5–31.

[74] Cf. Royal Institute of International Affairs, *Survey of International Affairs, 1937* (London, 1938), I, 99, and League of Nations, *World Economic Survey, 1936–37*, p. 198.

[75] League of Nations, *Treaty Series*, CLXXXIX (1938), 239. They agreed to notify each other, not only of impending increases in tariff duties, as stipulated in the 1930 Convention, but also of any projected import quotas, exchange restrictions, or special import charges on goods not previously affected by such measures.

lower trade barriers for which the Oslo states had hoped to provide a stimulus had not "caught on"—in fact, the reverse had happened.

e. *The Ottawa Agreements.* The world-wide tariff increases of the late nineteen-twenties and the growing trade barriers of the early 'thirties, rendering ever more precarious Britain's dependence on multilateral trade, tended to add force to the arguments of those groups within the United Kingdom which had long favored Imperial preference. The leading colonies (later Dominions) had established preferences for British products in the years from 1897 to 1907.[76] Britain herself had shown some tendency, since the World War, to set up moderate preferences for Empire products.[77]

Britain was not, however, in a position to extend substantial preferences to the Empire without taking the unpopular step of taxing importations of foreign foodstuffs.[78] It was largely this consideration which had defeated the Empire Free Trade movement in the early years of the century.[79] The Dominions, moreover, could not absorb greatly increased quantities of British goods unless they were willing to abandon the idea of fostering rapid industrialization with the aid of high tariffs. The probabilities of any such shift in Dominion sentiment appeared increasingly slight as Dominion tariffs moved upward during the post-War period. But if Imperial preference could be achieved only through the erection of higher tariff barriers against the rest of the world, it was doubtful if the gains of the Empire, and particularly of the United Kingdom with her world-wide trading interests, would equal the losses.

In spite of these apparent obstacles, it was decided to take

[76] Cf. Richardson, *British Economic Foreign Policy*, p. 131.

[77] Cf. p. 217 above.

[78] Cf. W. H. Beveridge and J. R. Hicks, "The Possibilities of Imperial Preference" in W. H. Beveridge and others, *Tariffs: The Case Examined*, p. 138.

[79] Cf. p. 216 above. Nor would the levying of taxes on foreign imports help the Empire producer (or necessarily injure the British consumer) in the case of such commodities as wheat and wool, of which the Empire as whole produced a surplus. Cf. Beveridge and Hicks, *op. cit.*, pp. 138–41, 143–44.

up the question of Empire preferences at the Imperial Economic Conference at Ottawa in the summer of 1932. Britain had meanwhile armed herself with an extensive tariff system and was contemplating a program of agricultural protectionism based largely on import restrictions rather than on out and out taxation of foreign food imports.[80] Relative stability of currencies within the sterling area also helped to provide a favorable atmosphere for trade negotiations. In his opening speech at the Conference, Mr. Baldwin, the leader of the British delegation, emphasized the need for lowering trade barriers within the Empire instead of "raising them against others." [81] But the eleven bilateral agreements which were signed at Ottawa showed little evidence that this warning had been heeded.

Let us examine, first, the provisions of the agreements between Britain on the one hand and Australia, Canada, New Zealand, South Africa, India, Newfoundland, and Southern Rhodesia on the other. Britain's concessions consisted primarily of the following:

(a) Continued exemption of Empire products from the duties imposed under the provisions of the Import Duties Act of 1932, except for eggs, poultry, and dairy products on which Britain reserved the right to impose a preferential duty or quantitative import restrictions after three years.

(b) Imposition of new or increased duties on a number of commodities imported from foreign countries (chiefly foodstuffs), including wheat, eggs, butter, and copper.

(c) Maintenance, except with the consent of the Dominion governments concerned, of the 10 per cent general ad valorem duty imposed by the Import Duties Act of 1932 on imports from foreign countries of a number of commodities of interest to the Dominions (chiefly foodstuffs and raw materials).

[80] Cf. p. 246 above, on the popular misconception that import restrictions do not raise prices as much as tariffs.

[81] Great Britain, Parliamentary Papers, *Imperial Economic Conference at Ottawa, 1932: Appendices to the Summaries of Proceedings,* Cmd. 4175 (London, 1932), p. 75.

(*d*) Quantitative regulation of certain meat imports—imports from the Dominions to be maintained without restriction at least until June, 1934, and imports from foreign countries to be substantially reduced.[82]

(*e*) Certain additional specific concessions.[83]

The concessions granted to the United Kingdom by the Dominions varied considerably but may be summarized as follows:

(*a*) Maintenance of existing margins of preference on a wide range of commodities imported from the United Kingdom and concession of increased margins of preference on specified items.[84]

(*b*) Removal of certain crisis surcharges and restrictions applicable to United Kingdom goods (in some cases, as soon as conditions permitted).

(*c*) Adoption (by Australia, Canada, and New Zealand) of the principle that tariff protection against United Kingdom products should be given only to industries reasonably assured of sound opportunities of success. Duties on United Kingdom

---

[82] Australia and New Zealand, however, were to impose certain voluntary regulations on the export side.

[83] *The Economist, Ottawa Supplement,* October 22, 1932, pp. 3–7. The British Government reserved the right to remove the new duties on wheat and copper if at any time Empire producers failed to furnish adequate supplies at world prices. The same proviso applied to Britain's undertaking to maintain the existing 10 per cent duty on foreign zinc and lead.

[84] Australia adopted a formula whereby margins of preference for United Kingdom products were to equal specified proportions of the ad valorem duty on such products. The application of the formula resulted, in nearly all instances, in raising the general duty on foreign goods. Canadian margins of preference were raised in one hundred and thirty-two cases by lowering the rates on United Kingdom goods and in eighty-three cases by raising the rates on foreign goods. The Indian Government granted the United Kingdom a 7½ per cent preference on motor cars and a 10 per cent preference on a long list of manufactured goods, to be secured either by lowering the duty on United Kingdom products, raising the duty on foreign products, or by a combination of both. The other agreements provided for increasing the margin of preference on relatively short lists of goods, to be achieved in some cases by raising the rate on foreign goods, in other cases by lowering the rate of United Kingdom goods.

For the sake of simplicity, we use the term Dominions to refer to all the governments, other than that of the United Kingdom, participating in the Ottawa Agreements. Actually, some of them had not acquired Dominion status, though they enjoyed a substantial degree of self-government.

products, furthermore, were to be fixed at a level which would give British producers an opportunity for reasonable competition on the basis of "relative costs of economical and efficient production," except for "infant" industries. Existing duties would be revised by recommendation of the Tariff Board in each country, and no duties in excess of those recommended by the Board would be imposed. United Kingdom producers would be granted an audience before the Tariff Board with respect to proposed changes.[85]

In addition to the agreements in which the United Kingdom was involved, certain inter-Dominion agreements, providing for increased margins of preference on products of interest to the participating countries, were concluded. The non-self-governing colonies were also affected by the terms of the Ottawa Agreements, but of this we shall have more to say in the following section.

To summarize, then, the Ottawa Agreements involved no reduction in the tariff level of the United Kingdom and, in fact, increased it in important instances. Furthermore, by agreeing to impose certain new or increased duties and to maintain the existing 10 per cent rate on a number of products, Britain limited for a period of five years her power to bargain with foreign countries. The Dominions agreed to lower certain duties on British goods, but there were many cases in which their duties on foreign products were to be raised.

Of considerable *potential* significance was the undertaking by certain of the Dominions to confine protection to those industries which had a reasonable chance of success and, in general, to base their tariffs on British goods on the principle of "relative costs." Clearly, the value of this feature of the Agreements would depend on the spirit in which it was carried out. Rigid application of the principle of "relative costs of production" as a basis for fixing tariffs would, of course, remove the *raison d'être* of international trade. Furthermore, as American

[85] *Ibid.*, pp. 7–15. On Australian tariff changes, see *Commerce Reports,* October 29, 1932, p. 74.

experience with this so-called "scientific principle" of tariff-making has demonstrated, it is almost impossible to ascertain relative costs of production in two countries with any degree of precision. It is not surprising, therefore, that the Canadian Tariff Board failed to recommend many substantial reductions in the British preferential tariff, partly because of its inability to make accurate comparisons of production costs.[86] In Australia and New Zealand, however, where the Tariff Boards did not attempt to measure relative costs with a fine degree of precision, some progress was made in lowering duties on British goods.[87] Canada later abandoned the relative costs principle and granted the United Kingdom numerous important tariff reductions outright under the terms of the revised Anglo-Canadian Agreement of 1937.[88]

The preferences set up under the Ottawa Agreements were not to be extended to foreign countries.[89] Nevertheless, there was general agreement among the governments represented at Ottawa "that foreign countries which had existing treaty obligations to grant most-favored-nation treatment to the products of particular parts of the Commonwealth could not be allowed to override such obligations by regional agreements of the [exclusive] character in question."[90] This attitude, of course, was altogether consistent with that displayed by the United Kingdom toward proposals for a Danubian regional agreement and even toward the Ouchy Convention which had not been of an exclusive character.

[86] Cf. *The Economist*, CXXVII (1937), 263.

[87] *Ibid.* Cf., also, Richardson, *op. cit.*, pp. 148–51.

[88] Cf. p. 463 below.

[89] This was made clear in a resolution of the Conference which took note of the fact that the representatives of the various governments "stated that it was their policy that no treaty obligations into which they might enter in the future should be allowed to interfere with any mutual preferences which Governments of the Commonwealth might decide to accord to each other. . . ." (Great Britain, Parliamentary Papers, *Imperial Economic Conference at Ottawa, 1932: Summary of Proceedings and Copies of Trade Agreements*, Cmd. 4174 [London, 1932], pp. 10–11.)

[90] *Ibid.*, p. 11. (Matter in brackets mine.)

In spite of the fact that inter-Imperial trade tended to expand in relation to world trade after the conclusion of the Ottawa Agreements (a development which must be attributed in part to relative currency stability within the sterling area), some of the drawbacks of preferential arrangements of this character became increasingly apparent to the participants in the course of time. Britain, committed to a policy of agricultural protectionism from 1933 on, found that free entry of Dominion farm products tended to interfere with attempts to raise British agricultural prices. Empire products had a way of replacing foreign products which were excluded by import restrictions, and the Dominions resisted, not always with complete success, British proposals involving restrictions on agricultural imports from the Empire. For both Britain and the Dominions, the principle of maintaining minimum margins of preference for Empire goods proved a handicap in bargaining with foreign countries. Canada partially abandoned this principle, in the revised agreement which she concluded with the United Kingdom in 1937, by transferring a large number of items from the list of those on which a minimum margin of British preference was guaranteed to a list on which merely a maximum rate of preferential duty was conceded.[91] In the following year, she helped to bring about the conclusion of the Anglo-American Agreement by agreeing to renounce certain preferences formerly enjoyed in the British market.[92]

With the imposition of wartime trade controls in the British Empire in 1939, imports into British countries came to be governed to a large extent by exchange and import restrictions rather than by tariffs. Though inter-Imperial preference had necessarily to assume a somewhat different form, it appeared likely to take on increased significance, owing in part to the need felt by all British countries for conserving foreign exchange reserves by directing purchases to the sterling area.

[91] *The Economist*, CXXVI (1937), 514.
[92] Cf. p. 415 above.

f. The Pan American Conferences. The American states have been drawn together by a common interest in the welfare of the western hemisphere, but regional economic coöperation has been impeded somewhat by the fact that the economies of the countries of the American continents are to a considerable degree competitive rather than complementary. Trade with European nations is in many cases considerably more important than trade with other American countries.

The International Conferences of American States date back to 1889.[93] They are held with more or less regularity every five years, while in the intervals there have been a number of conferences of business men and experts to consider commercial, financial, and other special problems. Each of the twenty-one American Republics (this does not include the Dominion of Canada, of course) belongs to the Pan American Union, which performs the functions of a permanent secretariat for the Conferences of American States.

Following an abortive attempt by the first conference to stimulate the negotiation of bilateral reciprocal trade agreements between American countries, the problem of trade barriers received very little attention until 1933, when the Seventh International Conference met at Montevideo.[94] By this time, the Roosevelt administration had made clear its intention of lowering tariffs, and the Conference proceeded to adopt a number of resolutions based on proposals of the United States delegation and aimed at modification of the barriers to international trade. They may be summarized as follows:

(*a*) The governments undertake to reduce high trade barriers through the negotiation of bilateral reciprocity treaties based upon mutual concessions.

(*b*) They subscribe to the policy of gradually reducing tariffs and other trade barriers, through the simultaneous initiation of

[93] Earlier conferences had been held by some of the Latin American states.
[94] The failure of the American Senate to ratify various reciprocal trade agreements negotiated by the United States in the eighteen-nineties served to intensify Latin American distrust of American tariff policy. Cf. p. 393 above.

negotiations for bilateral and multilateral agreements to remove prohibitions and restrictions and to reduce tariff rates to
a moderate level.

(c) As part of the preceding undertaking, they will revive and
revise the convention of 1927, or agree upon a new convention,
for the abolition of import and export prohibitions and restrictions.

(d) They declare that the principle of equality of treatment
"stands and must continue to stand as the basis of all acceptable commercial policy" and accordingly undertake that whatever agreements they enter into shall be based on the
most-favored-nation clause in its unconditional and unrestricted form, to be applied to all types of international trade
control.[95]

The Conference further declared itself in favor of special
commercial advantages between neighboring American states as
an exception to the most-favored-nation clause.[96] As we have
seen, moreover, it was in response to a resolution of the
Montevideo Conference that the Pan American Union placed
on file a multilateral convention binding the signatory states
not to invoke the most-favored-nation clause in order to obtain
the advantages of multilateral agreements in which they did
not participate.[97]

Later Pan American Conferences have reaffirmed the principles enunciated at the Montevideo Conference and have emphasized the need for modification of trade barriers.[98] At the
Lima Conference of 1938, it was recommended that the Amer-

[95] U. S. Department of State, *Report of the Delegates of the United States
of America to the Seventh International Conference of American States,* Conference Series, No. 19 (Washington, 1934), pp. 56 and 196–98.

[96] *Ibid.,* pp. 57 and 275.

[97] Cf. p. 433 above.

[98] See U. S. Department of State, *Report of the Delegation of the United
States of America to the Inter-American Conference for the Maintenance of
Peace,* Conference Series, No. 33 (Washington, 1937), pp. 29–30, and "Eighth
International Conference of American States: Explanatory Introduction by
George A. Finch and Texts of Declarations, Resolutions, and Recommendations
Adopted by the Conference," *International Conciliation,* No. 349 (April, 1939),
pp. 163–64.

ican states substitute reasonable tariffs for other types of trade restrictions as rapidly as possible.[99]

To what extent have these various resolutions been carried out? During the years from 1933 on, trade barriers of the American nations were lowered to a significant extent under the terms of bilateral agreements, but it is difficult to determine the extent to which this movement was attributable to the stand taken at the Montevideo Conference.

Of the twenty reciprocal trade agreements concluded by the United States previous to November, 1939, eleven were with Latin American countries.[100] Argentina and Chile, however, were conspicuous absentees from the list, as were some of the other more important countries of South America.[101] In most of these cases, there have been two leading difficulties. American industrial and agricultural interests have vigorously opposed tariff reductions on items competing with American products; yet the leading exports of these countries, i.e., the items on which reductions would have to be conceded if a significant agreement were to be secured, have been commodities extensively produced in the United States (e.g., Argentine livestock products or Chilean copper). Secondly, these countries have been pursuing "bilateral balancing" policies, either through their exchange regulations or through their tariffs; and, since the trade balance of the United States with most of them has been distinctly "favorable," they have been willing to concede equal treatment for American goods only in return for very substantial American tariff concessions. As we have seen, however, the United States recently succeeded in inducing several Latin American countries to relax their exchange restrictions in return for sizable credits.[102]

A number of trade-liberalizing agreements have been con-

---

[99] *Ibid.*, p. 163.

[100] Cf. p. 394 above.

[101] Negotiations with Argentina have since broken down, while negotiations with Chile have given rise to vociferous opposition on the part of American copper interests.

[102] Cf. pp. 346–47 above.

cluded between pairs of Latin American countries. Far more numerous, however, have been the bilateral agreements concluded between Latin American and European countries, a fact which is not surprising in view of the relative importance of European countries in Latin American trade. In this latter group of agreements, as we know, are many which are based on "bilateral balancing" principles.[103] The agreements with Germany and Italy, in particular, have aimed at rigid bilateral canalization of trade. In fact, it is quite apparent that the recent commercial policies of a substantial number of Latin American countries, both in their autonomous and contractual aspects, have violated the principles enunciated at the Montevideo Conference. Of especial significance has been the failure to apply the most-favored-nation clause to "all types of international trade control." [104]

Clearly, the resolutions of the recent Pan American Conferences have been aimed at the expansion of trade on a worldwide basis and have not contemplated the formation of a regional economic *bloc* comprising all the American states. Special commercial advantages between neighboring states are, however, admissible. In so far as such arrangements exist, they tend to be limited in scope and, in most cases, antedate the Montevideo Conference. Under the authority of the "Central American clause," which has long been included in their commercial treaties, a number of the Central American Republics extend preferential treatment on an autonomous basis to the products of other Central American states. The significance of this practice has increased in recent years, for under the new "bilateral balancing" tariffs which have been adopted by several of these countries, products of Central American states are entitled to the minimum tariff rate, irrespective of the state of the bilateral trade balance.[105] In a few cases, preferential agree-

---

[103] Cf. p. 387 above.
[104] Cf. p. 465 above.
[105] See U. S. Tariff Commission, *Extent of Equal Tariff Treatment in Foreign Countries*, pp. 119, 121. The Guatemalan regulations provide that the minimum

ments have been concluded between pairs of Central American Republics. The United States has maintained preferential tariff relations with Cuba since 1902. Tariff preferences between neighboring South American states have not been very common, although a few have been established since 1931.[106] There has been a growing tendency for most-favored-nation agreements between South American nations and countries elsewhere to include clauses permitting such preferences. It should be noted in this connection, however, that some of the South American countries, e.g., Peru, have concluded very few most-favored-nation agreements and hence are not obliged to generalize tariff concessions very widely.

Apart from the broader issues of commercial policy, Pan American economic coöperation has yielded significant results in such important matters as (a) provision for the settlement of commercial disputes by arbitration and (b) standardization of commercial legislation.[107]

The "Good Neighbor" policy of the Roosevelt Administration has done much to remove Latin American distrust of the ambitions and motives of the United States in the political sphere. But the fact that, on the whole, Latin American countries have stronger economic and cultural ties with Europe than with the United States has proved an obstacle to Pan American economic coöperation. Nothing is so likely to draw the states of the Western Hemisphere together as recurrent interruption of or interference with these ties brought on by

rate shall apply to products of Central American countries which have established or may establish preferential rates for Guatemalan products.

[106] As a result of resolutions adopted at a tripartite economic conference at Montevideo in the winter of 1931–32, Brazil, Argentina, and Uruguay concluded a group of bilateral agreements in which they agreed to grant each other free entry or preferential rates for a few products. (*Commerce Reports*, January 18, 1932, p. 138, and December 30, 1933, p. 428; U. S. Tariff Commission, *Extent of Equal Tariff Treatment in Foreign Countries*, pp. 33–34, 60–61, and 108–109.) In agreements concluded in 1932 and 1934, Peru granted Chile substantial tariff concessions which were not generalized. (*Ibid.*, pp. 76–77.)

[107] For a fuller discussion of these and other problems, see Dietrich, *World Trade*, pp. 286–98.

European wars. In this connection, it is interesting to note that one of the resolutions adopted at the Consultative Meeting of Foreign Ministers of American Republics at Panama in September, 1939, provided for the immediate establishment of an Inter-American Financial and Economic Advisory Committee.[108] This step had been repeatedly discussed at earlier conferences, but now there was recognition of an urgent need for an organization which would take up the special economic problems created by the war as well as the more permanent questions of economic relations.

4. Colonial Policy

The recent demands of the "have-not" powers for a redistribution of colonial territories have focused attention on the colonial policies pursued by the "have" powers. If the latter nations have been treating their colonial possessions as more or less exclusive economic preserves, to be administered first and foremost for the benefit of the mother country, then the "have-not" powers have some ground for complaint. For, broadly speaking, the lack of colonial possessions represents a distinct economic disadvantage to a country only if its nationals are barred from trading or investing in colonial areas on equal terms with the nationals of other powers (including the suzerain of the area in question).[109]

---

[108] For information on the functions of this body, see *International Conciliation*, No. 356 (January, 1940), pp. 14–17.

[109] The "have-not" powers have recently made much of the argument that the possession of colonies permits a country to economize on foreign exchange reserves, since raw materials can be purchased in colonial areas whose currency systems are unified or integrated with that of the mother country. This argument raises some complicated problems, but, in general, it is pertinent only for countries which have adopted exchange control as a permanent basis of currency regulation, since other currency systems are based on the theory that in the long run natural equilibrating forces must be primarily relied on to correct an "unfavorable" balance of payments. Whether the acquisition of colonies would actually relieve the pressure on the currency of an exchange-control country would depend on a number of factors, including: (*a*) the extent to

An open-door colonial policy is one which permits of no discrimination in favor of the mother country or against any other country in the regulation of the economic affairs of the colony. Nationals of all other countries alike may buy and sell goods, develop resources, or establish industries in the colony on equal terms with nationals of the mother country.

Under the influence of the prevailing laissez-faire economic philosophy, Great Britain led the way toward the establishment of an open-door colonial policy in the latter half of the nineteenth century. Holland, Germany, and Belgium followed Britain's lead in the last two decades of the century, but the other colonial powers were never won over to a policy of equality of treatment except in so far as they participated in international treaties stipulating an open-door policy in certain African areas.[110] Since the World War, and especially since the beginning of the "great" depression, the open-door policy has gradually been abandoned except in mandated territories and in a few areas in which it is still required by international treaty.[111] This tendency must be attributed in part to post-War

---

which the colonies could supply raw materials needed by such a country, (*b*) the nature of the balances of payments of the colonies, and (*c*) the currency policy pursued by the mother country both before and after the acquisition of new territory. For further discussion of these problems, see League of Nations, *Report of the Committee for the Study of the Problem of Raw Materials*, and M. A. Heilperin, *The Monetary Aspect of the Raw Materials Problem and the Revival of International Trade* (Paris, 1938).

It is interesting to note that Japan's attempt to bring Manchukuo and North China within her currency system has not, thus far, relieved the pressure on the yen—in fact, quite the contrary. Cf. M. Farley, "Impact of War on Japan's Foreign Trade," and "Japan between Two Wars," *Far Eastern Survey*, VIII (1939), 126–27 and 245–46.

[110] See B. Gerig, *The Open Door and the Mandates System: A Study of Economic Equality before and since the Establishment of the Mandates System* (London, 1930), Chs. I–III, and U. S. Tariff Commission, *Colonial Tariff Policies* (Washington, 1922), *passim*.

[111] It had been violated in certain British non-self-governing colonies before the War, while, as we have seen, the Dominions began to grant preferences to British goods at the end of the nineteenth century. (Cf. p. 458 above.) The open door is stipulated under the terms of Class A and Class B Mandates. (Cf. Gerig, *op. cit.*, pp. 109–12.)

forces making for increased protectionism and in part to a growing emphasis on the value of Imperial economic integration in a warlike world. The movement away from the open door may also be regarded as one aspect of the trend toward regionalism. A special factor which played an important rôle from 1931 on, moreover, was the impact of Japanese competition in colonial areas in the Far East and elsewhere.

Alternatives to an open-door policy in tariff matters are complete tariff assimilation between the mother country and its colonies or a regime of tariff preferences. The former policy is pursued by France, the United States, and Japan in relation to certain of their colonies, while tariff preferences are extensively employed within the British, French (non-assimilated colonies), Portuguese, Spanish, and Italian Empires. Import quotas and foreign exchange regulations provide convenient openings for discrimination in favor of intra-imperial trade, as do the various forms of indirect protectionism. Regulations designed to favor the shipping industry of the mother country are frequently enforced, while foreigners often suffer a disadvantage under laws governing the ownership of land or the exploitation of resources in the colonies. In the following survey of developments since 1931, we shall confine our discussion to matters directly bearing on the control of imports and exports.

Nowhere has the recent movement away from the open door been more marked or more far-reaching in its implications than in the British Empire. Prior to the World War, Britain granted no preferences to Empire products; and although certain of the self-governing colonies (later Dominions) began to extend tariff preferences to British goods after 1897, the open-door policy was retained in the British dependent Empire, with minor exceptions, until 1914.[112] After the War, not only did Britain, as we have seen, establish certain preferences for

<hr>

[112] Cf. Richardson, *op. cit.*, p. 135, and A. Zimmern, "The Open Door and Reciprocity: As Illustrated by Developments within the British Colonial Empire," Svenska Handelsbanken, *Index*, VIII (1933), 126.

Empire products, but through her Colonial Office she was able to secure preferences for British goods in many of the non-self-governing colonies. By 1922, twenty-six out of the fifty-five British Crown colonies had extended tariff preferences to the mother country.[113] In fact, the open door in tariff matters was violated throughout the Empire except in the mandated territories and in those areas where it was maintained because of treaty obligations.

Prior to the conclusion of the Ottawa Agreements, however, tariff preferences in the British colonies were not very broad in scope. The Ottawa Conference resulted in a substantial extension of colonial preferences for British and Dominion goods, while colonial products were granted important preferences by both Britain and the Dominions. The colonies, though not represented at the Conference, were affected by the terms of the agreements concluded between Britain, on the one hand, and the self-governing portions of her Empire, on the other. The Conference marked, apparently, a definitive break with the open-door policy, except where treaty obligations or the terms of Mandates stood in the way. At the same time, somewhat more extensive application was given to the most-favored-nation principle as the basis of commercial relations *within* the British Empire. Colonial products receive the same preferences as Dominion products on entry into the United Kingdom. Under the Ottawa Agreements, moreover, each of the Dominions undertook to extend to the non-self-governing colonies, protectorates, and mandated territories any preferences accorded to the United Kingdom, if the latter so requested.[114] In return, the United Kingdom undertook to "invite" the non-self-governing colonies and protectorates to extend to each of the

---

[113] Cf. *ibid.*, p. 129.

[114] The Dominions did not, however, bind themselves to extend preferences to colonies which did not grant preferential treatment to their products or which refused to extend to their products all preferences granted (with certain exceptions) to other parts of the Empire. Cf. U. S. Tariff Commission, *Extent of Equal Tariff Treatment in Foreign Countries*, p. 60.

Dominions any tariff preferences granted to any other part of the Empire. (The colonies have varying degrees of autonomy in fiscal matters but generally comply with the wishes of the Colonial Office.)

In 1934, Britain took a further decisive step away from the open door by imposing quantitative restrictions on imports of cotton and rayon textiles into the British colonies. From 1932 on, exports of cheap Japanese textiles to the British colonial possessions in Africa and the Far East had been undergoing a marked expansion. Japan could sell her goods at prices which were within reach of the poor native populations in these areas, much to the consternation of the Lancashire cotton industry. To put a stop to this Japanese expansion and to restore the Lancashire industry to the preëminent position it had occupied in the British colonies before 1932, the British Government brought about the introduction, throughout the Colonial Empire (except for the mandated territories and treaty areas) of import quota restrictions on foreign cotton and artificial silk goods. The quotas were to be allocated among foreign countries on the basis of average imports in the years 1927–31, the period preceding Japan's spectacular advance.[115]

The Dutch Empire, too, has moved away from the open-door policy since 1931, not through tariff alterations but largely through the introduction of import quotas in the Netherlands East Indies. Under the Crisis Import Ordinance of 1933 and later enactments, the Dutch East Indies Government has subjected a number of leading imports to quantitative restriction. Imports of inexpensive Japanese goods had proved a threat, not only to the market for goods from the mother country, but also to certain colonial industries. Accordingly, the restrictions cover a fairly wide range of products.[116] The quotas have been allocated by countries, a generous share going to the mother

[115] Cf. p. 271 n. above.
[116] Cf. *Commerce Reports, seriatim,* and Royal Institute of International Affairs, *The Colonial Problem* (New York and London, 1937), p. 304.

country in most cases but no specific shares being accorded to Japan, whose goods have had to come in under the unallocated portion of the quota.[117] In some cases, foreign countries have succeeded in increasing their shares of the quotas under the terms of commercial agreements concluded with the Netherlands, which has been actively bargaining for concessions for East Indian exports.

In the French Colonial Empire, the open door has been observed only in those areas in which it has been required by treaty or under the terms of Mandates. In accordance with a law of April 13, 1928, which consolidated a number of previous regulations, the French colonies are divided into two groups, assimilated and non-assimilated. Trade between the mother country and colonies belonging to the former group (French Indo-China, Madagascar, Reunion, French Guiana, and certain islands in the Atlantic) has not been obstructed by tariffs, while the rates of the French customs tariff have applied in general to imports into these assimilated colonies from foreign countries.[118] Algeria, in a class by itself, has been regarded as part of the French customs territory. Between the non-assimilated colonies and France, a preferential tariff regime has prevailed except in so far as the open door has had to be observed in a few colonies and in the mandated territories.

Since 1928, the need for Imperial economic integration has been increasingly emphasized in France, and changes in the intra-Imperial tariff structure have been largely directed toward removing or lowering tariff barriers between France and the non-assimilated colonies (tariffs against the outside world, having been raised). After denouncing the Anglo-French Con-

---

[117] Cf. *ibid.*, and A. Barber, "Six Years of Economic Planning in Netherlands India," *Far Eastern Survey*, VIII (1939), 199.

[118] Cf. B. Ischboldin, "Die neue Aussenhandelspolitik des französischen Imperiums," *Weltwirtschaftliches Archiv*, XLI (1935), 179. The assimilated colonies have been permitted, subject to the approval of the French Government, to modify for their own purposes the rates laid down in the French tariff schedule if they have not seemed adapted to local conditions. This privilege has been little used, however. Cf. *ibid.*, p. 181.

vention of 1898 which provided for equality of opportunity in certain West African areas, the French Government proceeded, in 1938, to authorize the Minister of Colonies to establish local customs rates in French West Africa, a non-assimilated colony which had previously fixed its own rates subject to approval of the mother country.[119] Thus a step was taken away from the open door and in the direction of assimilation of a formerly non-assimilated colony. At the same time, the power to establish colonial export duties, previously lodged with the colonial governments subject to approval of the French Government, was transferred to the French Minister of Colonies, avowedly with the purpose of guiding "certain commercial currents from the colonies in the direction of France" and giving the mother country authority to establish "export duties of a preferential character in the French colonies." [120]

But perhaps the most important single element making for increased economic integration in the French Empire since 1931 has been the fact that imports from the colonies have been generally exempt from French quota restrictions. Some of the French colonies, moreover, have been permitted to place quantitative restrictions on imports of various articles from foreign countries.[121]

In common with certain other colonial powers, France has recently turned her attention to the need for encouraging production in the colonies of agricultural commodities needed by the mother country. This type of problem received particular attention at the *Conference de la France Métropolitaine et de la France d'Outremer* of 1934–35.[122] The movement represents the French corollary to Germany's attempts to develop an economic hinterland in Southeastern Europe and to similar tendencies in other parts of the world.

[119] Cf. Royal Institute of International Affairs, *The Colonial Problem,* p. 51, and *Commerce Reports,* July 9, 1938, p. 613.

[120] *Ibid.*

[121] Cf. Haight, *French Import Quotas,* pp. 63 ff.

[122] Cf. Royal Institute of International Affairs, *The Colonial Problem,* pp. 302–303.

Interest in the open-door issue in very recent years has been stimulated chiefly by Japanese policy in China. Japan, handicapped by a relative scarcity of raw material resources within her own boundaries, has had to depend on an expansion of her export industries in order to procure the raw materials needed for her industrial development. Wherever Japanese fabricated exports made marked inroads in foreign markets, however, import barriers were erected to protect domestic producers from the menacing competition of the products of "sweated Oriental labor." Japan's reply has been to seek political domination in Manchuria, North China, and perhaps other portions of China, in order to bring these areas within a Japanese economic *bloc* or *Grossraumwirtschaft*.[128] Her violations of the open door in Manchukuo and North China have not taken the form of discriminatory tariff rates erected against foreign products. Rather has she adopted the policy of seeking to exclude foreigners from economic activity in these areas by setting up government or government-supported monopolies in various industries. Likewise, she has attempted, not altogether successfully, to displace the former currencies in these areas by a currency unit (the yuan) which is maintained at parity with the yen. Since 1937 Manchukuo and various portions of China have been brought within a rigid exchange control regime which is to a considerable degree integrated with that of Japan and under which purchases are directed to other portions of the yen *bloc* rather than to outside areas in so far as possible. Import permit systems are also administered to the same end. Export embargo or license systems direct the flow of certain of China's raw products to Japan. Trade between North China

---

[128] The problem is, of course, actually not as simple as this brief statement of the Japanese position would suggest. It is virtually impossible to evaluate the relative importance of political and economic factors as motivating forces behind the Japanese campaigns in Asia. As we have seen, moreover, Japan has attempted to resist the erection of further foreign import barriers against her exports by developing an elaborate system of export control and by entering into agreements which involve voluntary restriction of her exports to foreign countries. Cf. pp. 358–61 above.

and Japan has been further encouraged by the lowering of import duties on commodities of particular importance in that trade.[124] All these measures must be interpreted, however, as giving little more than an indication of the nature of Japan's aims in China. The sort of regime which will eventually be set up in the economic sphere will clearly depend in part on the terms of Japan's settlement with China and in part on the success of western powers in preventing a complete closing of the "open door."

Colonial products do not often compete with those of the mother country, but in the cases in which they do, producers within the mother country demand protection from colonial competition. On occasion, this sort of situation presents a formidable obstacle to assimilation of the colony within the tariff system of the mother country. In fact, demands of American producers for protection from Philippine competition were primarily responsible for the passage of the Tydings-McDuffie Act of 1934, which provided the basis for eventual Philippine independence from the United States.

As multilateral efforts to lower trade barriers have broken down, interest in the formation of regional economic *blocs* has grown apace. It is easier for a great imperial power, however, to strengthen the economic ties with its colonies or with those areas over which it has some degree of political authority than it is for a group of independent political entities to achieve economic *rapprochement* in any considerable degree. Thus far, regional economic agreements involving groups of independent national states have been quite limited in scope and in a number of conspicuous instances have broken down altogether.

Nevertheless, it is quite possible that regionalism in the years to come may become increasingly important as a force capable

[124] On all this, see E. A. Ch.-Walden, "Sino-Japanese War and the Open Door," *International Affairs*, XVII (1938), 629–54; N. Hanwell, "Economic Disruption in Occupied China," *Far Eastern Survey*, VIII (1939), 61–66; and other articles in the *Far Eastern Survey*.

of modifying the more extreme forms of economic nationalism. The net economic effects of such a movement would depend in large part on the height and nature of the trade barriers erected between the various regions. Regionalism is undoubtedly preferable to the more pronounced manifestations of economic nationalism, but it would to a very considerable extent cut across the lines of maximum comparative advantage in international trade. Perhaps more important is the danger that inter-regional political rivalry might prove to be even more intense than is international rivalry today. Each region would doubtless strive to expand territorially in order to acquire control of as many natural resources as possible. Whatever happens in this broader field, the struggle over colonies is not likely to cease as long as colonial areas are administered by individual national states for their own economic advantage.

CHAPTER XV

CONCLUSIONS

The network of restrictions which threatened to obliterate international trade in the years from 1931 on appeared at first to be a depression phenomenon. Clearly these measures had been adopted largely in response to falling world prices and currency stringency. The passing of the crisis, however, did not lead to the removal of the new weapons of control. Exchange restrictions were somewhat relaxed, and as trade began slowly to recover from the depression, some of the import barriers were gradually lowered under the terms of bilateral commercial agreements. Governments were loath to relinquish their newly acquired powers, however, and there were very few instances in which nontariff trade barriers, once adopted, were actually removed. Meantime, the technique of control was refined and elaborated, and increasing emphasis was placed on employing quantitative import restrictions as bargaining weapons. The sharp recession in trade which got under way toward the end of 1937 led to a tightening of controls, a process which tended to continue during 1938 and 1939 as the threat of war became more and more serious.

Looking back over the history of commercial policy during the present century, one becomes impressed with the fact that, ever since the World War and to some extent even before, there has been a growing tendency for governments to exert more direct control over the movements of commodities in international trade as part of their normal, peacetime activity. To a very large extent the actual instruments of control have been adopted in the midst of war or depression, but restrictions, once adopted, are difficult to remove and tend to weave themselves into the fabric of ordinary governmental activity.

Summarizing the situation at the beginning of September, 1939, elaborate and rigid systems of trade control were being enforced in a number of important nations. Easily the most complete and well-established regime of state control was to be found in Soviet Russia, but Germany, Italy, Japan, and Spain had proceeded far in the direction of centralized direction of all foreign trade. Elsewhere the proponents of trade liberalization were waging a struggle against potent forces making for increased governmental regulation. Many of the democracies made considerable use of quantitative trade restrictions, and no country of any importance was altogether free of them. Even the United States, which was leading the campaign against the employment of arbitrary and discriminatory restrictions, found it necessary, among other things, to make some of her tariff reductions applicable to merely a limited quantity of imports and to subsidize two of her leading agricultural exports in order to help support the domestic price.

Viewing world trade as a whole, governmental regulation had apparently proceeded farthest in the case of agricultural commodities. Throughout Europe, the great agricultural-importing area, quotas, monopolies, and other import-regulating devices dominated the scene.[1] Agricultural-exporting countries all over the world were experimenting with export-marketing schemes, involving in many cases price control and subsidization of exports. It was estimated in 1938 that, leaving tariffs out of account, 55 per cent of world trade in agricultural commodities was directly or indirectly affected by governmental measures of "control or guidance."[2]

Turning to nonagricultural raw materials, we find those of

---

[1] To refer to Europe as an agricultural-importing area does not mean, of course, that all European countries are net importers of agricultural products.

[2] Cf. discussion by G. Mackenroth, *Proceedings of the Fifth International Conference of Agricultural Economists,* Macdonald College, Canada, August 21 to 28, 1938 (London, 1939), p. 289.

wartime value affected by export restrictions, especially in Europe. In addition, a number of raw materials, including some agricultural commodities, were exported under the terms of international restriction schemes, in most of which governments participated more or less actively. Imports of raw materials, however, were not ordinarily subject to severe restrictions, except in countries suffering from acute exchange scarcity and operating under self-sufficiency programs.

World trade in manufactured articles was regulated chiefly by high tariffs or by import quotas. In some cases, exports of finished goods were restricted under bilateral quota arrangements, while nongovernmental cartels regulated the trade in many manufactured products, especially in Europe. One important country, Germany, was subsidizing exports of manufactured articles on a generous scale.

Nor should one forget that commodity movements of all types were subject to exchange restrictions, which were generally less severe than during the worst years of the depression but were still an important force to be reckoned with in Central and Eastern Europe, Latin America, and parts of the Far East.

The employment of nontariff trade barriers, together with other factors, had tended to encourage a bilateral canalization of world trade. The spread of exchange control had led to the conclusion of clearing and payments agreements which, at the beginning of 1939, played a very important rôle in the trade of certain countries though they affected only a relatively minor portion of world trade as a whole. Commercial agreements, too, had been subjected to the influence of bilateral balancing principles in varying degrees. The net result had been a significant decline in the relative importance of triangular or multiangular trade.[3] The movements of individual commodities through

[3] Although it is impossible to arrive at accurate statistics of triangular trade, figures published by the League of Nations showed that that portion of triangular trade which represented offsetting active and passive trade balances of individual countries declined from 18.4 per cent of world trade in 1929 to 13.8 per cent in 1935. (*Review of World Trade, 1935* [Geneva, 1936], p. 65.)

these bilateral trade channels, moreover, had been rigidified by the enforcement of restrictions on both the import and the export side. Multilateral negotiations had failed completely to stop this trend, while the widespread interest in regionalism had resulted in the actual liberalization of trade barriers on a regional basis only in the case of a few agreements which, for the most part, had eventually broken down. Within the world's great empires, economic integration between the mother country and its colonies or dominions was being increasingly emphasized, but in many cases this was being accomplished through the erection of higher and more rigid trade barriers against the rest of the world. On the whole, the most important force working against the bilateralization and rigidification of world trade was the insistence of certain countries, notably the United States, on the negotiation of bilateral commercial agreements based on a broad application of the most-favored-nation clause and having as their object the lowering of trade barriers on a multilateral basis.

However we evaluate the significance of the various forces at work in the field of commercial policy in the summer of 1939, we must not fail to emphasize the fact that probably not far from half of all world trade was still subject to no restriction other than tariffs. The outbreak of hostilities in September meant the spread of rigid trade regulations to areas formerly relatively free of such measures. To what extent these restrictions would be retained after the war was, of course, anyone's guess, but for the time being the sphere of nontariff trade barriers had greatly widened.

Viewing the period since 1914 as a whole, one discerns two broad sets of forces, to some extent related, to some extent not, which seem to have been chiefly responsible for the extension of governmental control over international trade. First, there are those forces making for increasing governmental control of all aspects of economic life. Second, and possibly even more important, are the forces tending toward economic nationalism.

Governmental control of the economic system has in recent years frequently taken a form which is incompatible with the maintenance of a laissez-faire attitude toward international trade. Regulation of prices, wages, working conditions, rents, and other elements in the domestic economic structure tends to interfere with the competitive position of a nation's industries in international trade and to lead to a demand for protection or subsidization from producers who find their competitive power weakened. The trend toward regulation, moreover, by introducing rigidities into the price structure, renders it more difficult for a nation to adhere to an international monetary system. The greater the emphasis on internal price stability, whether for individual industries or for the nation as a whole, the greater the likelihood that governmental intervention in international trade will take the form of quantitative restrictions rather than tariffs. But the introduction of quantitative trade restrictions is likely to lead, as we have seen, to internal price-fixing and rationing which, in turn, give rise to other controls.

There is every indication that the trend toward governmental control may continue until integrated planning of the entire economic system is achieved. Is it inevitable that such planning, assuming that it continues to take place along predominantly national lines, must be associated with, and in part ushered in by, an attitude of narrow restrictionism toward international trade? The answer would seem to be in the affirmative, unless socialists and economic planners give more attention to the international aspects of their problem than many of them as yet seem inclined to do. In the interests of maximizing the national income, careful consideration must be given to the possibilities of benefiting from the international division of labor. It is highly probable that protectionism may here and there seem desirable for the sake of greater security or of maintaining certain branches of economic activity regarded as particularly advantageous from a social point of view. In such cases, difficult value judgments will be necessary.

A second set of problems concerns the technique of administration of foreign trade. From many points of view, governmental monopolies constitute more flexible instruments of foreign trade regulation than quota and licensing systems but they represent a relatively advanced stage of control since their establishment means the elimination of private importers and exporters. Whatever instruments of regulation are chosen, the economic advantages of adhering to the principle of equality of treatment in trade with other states would seem to be as important for a planned economy as for a laissez-faire economy.[4] But the technical difficulties involved in rendering nontariff trade barriers compatible with equality of treatment are great, as we have had frequent occasion to observe in the course of our study. There seems to be a strong tendency for governmental control or operation of foreign trade to lead to bilateral balancing. Nowhere is this tendency more apparent than in the foreign trade of Soviet Russia. Yet, in the writer's opinion, there is no reason why state trading bodies could not seek out opportunities for triangular or even multiangular trade provided some mechanism for clearing foreign balances along other than strictly bilateral lines were available to them.

This brings us to consideration of the second set of forces which have tended to lead to increasing governmental regulation of international trade—the forces making for economic nationalism. To a very considerable degree, as we have already indicated, these forces are inseparable from the forces making for increased state control of economic life. In part they are purely economic, but to a very important degree they are political and social in nature. The economist regards many of the economic arguments for protection as fallacious, but when he is confronted with the contention that political and social considerations outweigh those of a strictly economic nature, he is powerless to reply.

[4] Decisions on this matter, however, would probably depend on the nature of the plan's objectives.

Whether the cessation of the present conflict will be accompanied by an intensification of economic nationalism or a movement in the opposite direction depends on many factors which cannot be properly weighed at the present time. There are certain elements in the situation which seem to indicate that if international economic integration is sought at all, it will be sought along imperialist, and perhaps regional, lines.

As a number of recent writers have pointed out, the progress of technology has greatly increased the potential advantages to be derived from world economic integration.[5] International trade has shown remarkable vitality in spite of the rigid restrictions placed upon it. But a continuation of the present trend toward economic nationalism is likely not merely to result in a progressive contraction in the volume of trade but also to stifle economic development. For the more rigid types of trade restrictions, as we have seen, tend to discourage the development of new low-cost areas of production for commodities entering into world trade.

One may, at this stage, properly raise the question as to whether the high degree of coördination and integration required for the most effective functioning of the world economic system can ever be achieved if the pertinent decisions continue to be made exclusively by national governments. Is world economic integration conceivable in the absence of an effective international political organization?[6] Under the aegis of such an organization, economic planning along international lines might gradually develop. Thus the apparent dilemma between national planning and the maintenance of a world economic order might be solved. Even the conflict between the pro-

---

[5] Cf., for example, Staley, *World Economy in Transition*, Part I, and E. Boehler, "Memorandum on the Technical Long Term Factors in the Reduction of the Volume of Overseas Trade" in Joint Committee of the Carnegie Endowment and the International Chamber of Commerce, *The Improvement of Commercial Relations between Nations* and *The Problem of Monetary Stabilization*, pp. 14–26.

[6] This question has been raised by W. Röpke in *International Economic Disintegration* (London, 1940).

ponents of internal and external economic stability might cease if the problem of stabilization could be attacked along international lines.

In the autumn of 1940, such a world seems very remote. Perhaps the only hopeful element in the situation is the growing realization on the part of many people that failure to achieve some degree of political coöperation among nations is likely to mean economic chaos and the periodic recurrence of ever-more-serious military struggles.

SELECTED BIBLIOGRAPHY

I. Books and Pamphlets

Allix, Edgard. *Les droits de douane: traité théorique et pratique de législation douanière* (Paris: Rousseau, 1932). 2 vols.

Amini, Ali. *L'institution du monopole du commerce extérieur en Perse* (Paris: Rousseau, 1932).

Angell, James W. *Financial Foreign Policy of the United States* (New York: Council on Foreign Relations, 1933).

—— *The Recovery of Germany* (rev. ed.; New Haven: Yale University Press, 1932).

Ashley, Percy W. L. *Modern Tariff History: Germany–U. S.–France* (3d ed.; New York: E. P. Dutton, 1926).

Atwater, Elton. *Administration of Export and Import Embargoes, 1935–36*, Geneva Research Centre, Geneva Studies, Vol. IX, No. 6 (December, 1938).

The Australian Tariff: An Economic Enquiry, Report of an informal committee set up by the Prime Minister of Australia (Melbourne: Melbourne University Press, 1929).

Barczewski, Max. *Kompensationsgeschäfte im Rahmen der Kontingentierungspolitik* (Berlin: Junker u. Dünnhaupt, 1936).

Bataille, J. *Les Offices de Compensation et leur rôle dans la restauration du commerce extérieur* (Paris: Lib. du Recueil Sirey, 1934).

Baudin, Louis. *Free Trade and Peace* (Paris: International Institute of Intellectual Coöperation, 1939).

Beckerath, Herbert von, and Kern, Fritz. *Autarkie oder internationale Zusammenarbeit?* (Berlin: S. Fischer, 1932).

Beveridge, Sir William H., and others. *Tariffs: The Case Examined* (New York and London: Longmans, Green, 1931).

Bidwell, Percy W. *The Invisible Tariff: A Study of the Control of Imports into the United States* (New York: Council on Foreign Relations, 1939).

—— *Our Trade with Britain: Bases for a Reciprocal Trade Agreement* (New York: Council on Foreign Relations, 1938).

—— *Tariff Policy of the United States*, Report to the 2d International Studies Conference (New York: Council on Foreign Relations, 1933).

Bonn, Moritz J. *The Crumbling of Empire: The Disintegration of World Economy* (London: Allen & Unwin, 1938).

488   SELECTED BIBLIOGRAPHY

Brandt, Helmut. *Die Durchbrechung der Meistbegünstigung* (Berlin: C. Heymann, 1933).

Brandt, Karl. *The German Fat Plan and Its Economic Setting* (Stanford University, Food Research Institute, 1938).

Brandt, Karl, and others. *Autarkie?* (Berlin: C. Peterson, 1932).

de Cock Buning, Emilie. *Die Aussenhandelspolitik der Niederlande seit dem Weltkriege* (Bern: Paul Haupt, 1936).

Cordier, A. W. *European Union and the League of Nations,* Geneva Research Centre, Geneva Special Studies, Vol. II, No. 6 (June, 1931).

Condliffe, J. B. *Markets and the Problem of Peaceful Change* (Paris: International Institute of Intellectual Coöperation, 1938).

Copland, Douglas B., and Janes, C. V. *Australian Marketing Problems: A Book of Documents, 1932–1937* (Sydney: Angus & Robertson, 1938).

—— *Australian Trade Policy: A Book of Documents, 1932–1937* (London: Angus & Robertson, 1939).

Culbertson, William S. *Commercial Policies in Wartime and After: A Study of the Application of Democratic Ideas to International Commercial Relations* (New York: Appleton, 1919).

—— *International Economic Policies: A Survey of the Economics of Diplomacy* (New York and London: Appleton, 1925).

—— *Reciprocity: A National Policy for Foreign Trade* (New York: McGraw–Hill, 1937).

Dalton, John E. *Sugar: A Case Study in Government Control* (New York: Macmillan, 1937).

Davis, Joseph S. *The Farm Export Debenture Plan* (Stanford University, Food Research Institute, 1929).

—— *On Agricultural Policy, 1926–1938* (Stanford University, Food Research Institute, 1939).

Delle Donne, Ottavio. *European Tariff Policies since the World War* (New York: Adelphi, 1928).

Deutsche Agrarpolitik im Rahmen der inneren und äusseren Wirtschaftspolitik, Veröffentlichungen der Friedrich List–Gesellschaft, e. V., Band V–VII (Berlin: Hobbing, 1932).

Devisenbewirtschaftung in Ungarn (8th ed.; Budapest: Verlagsabteilung der Sparkassen und Banken, April 20, 1937).

Dietrich, Ethel B. *World Trade* (New York: H. Holt, 1939).

Donaldson, John. *International Economic Relations: A Treatise on World Economy and World Politics* (New York and London: Longmans, Green, 1930).

Einzig, Paul. *Bloodless Invasion: German Economic Penetration into the Danubian States and the Balkans* (London: Duckworth, 1938).

—— *The Exchange Clearing System* (London: Macmillan, 1935).

—— *Exchange Control* (London: Macmillan, 1934).

—— *Foreign Balances* (London: Macmillan, 1938).

—— *The World Economic Crisis, 1929–1931* (London: Macmillan, 1931).

—— *World Finance, 1914–1935* (New York: Macmillan, 1935).
—— *World Finance, 1935–1937* (New York: Macmillan, 1937).
—— [Also later volumes in same series.]
Elliott, William Y., and others. *International Control of the Non-Ferrous Metals* (New York: Macmillan, 1937).
Ellsworth, P. T. *International Economics* (New York: Macmillan, 1938).
Eulenburg, Franz. *Aussenhandel und Aussenhandelspolitik (die internationalen Wirtschaftsbeziehungen)* (Tübingen: Mohr, 1929).
—— *Grossraumwirtschaft und Autarkie* (Jena: G. Fischer, 1932).
Feis, Herbert. *Europe: The World's Banker, 1870–1914* (New Haven: Yale University Press, and London: H. Milford, Oxford University Press, 1930).
Findlay, R. M. *Britain under Protection* (London: Allen & Unwin, 1934).
Fischer, Werner A. *Devisenclearing: Die Entwicklung der Zahlungs- und Verrechnungsabkommen in Deutschland*, Schriftenreihe zum "Devisenarchiv," Heft V (Berlin: Joachim Berger Verlag, 1937).
Fisk, George M., and Peirce, P. S. *International Commercial Policies, with Special Reference to the United States* (New York: Macmillan, 1930).
Forstmann, Albrecht. *Der Kampf um den internationalen Handel* (Berlin: Haude u. Spenersche buchhandlung M. Paschke, 1935).
Fouchet, Paul. *Les accords de clearing: leurs origines, leurs repercussions* (Paris: Pedone, 1936).
Gantenbein, J. W. *Financial Questions in United States Foreign Policy* (New York: Columbia University Press, 1939).
Geiser, A. *Die Compensation als Mittel der Aussenhandelspolitik unter besonderer Berücksichtigung der Schweiz* (Zürich: Schulthess, 1939).
van Gelderen, J. *The Recent Development of Economic Foreign Policy in the Netherlands East Indies* (London: Longmans, Green, 1939).
Gerig, Benjamin. *The Open Door and the Mandates System: A Study of Economic Equality before and since the Establishment of the Mandates System* (London: Allen & Unwin, 1930).
Gøtrik, H. P. *Danish Economic Policy, 1931–1938: The Repercussions of Modern Commercial Policies on Economic Conditions in Denmark*, Report submitted to the International Studies Conference, 12th sess., Bergen, Norway, 1939 (Copenhagen: Institute of Economics and History.)
Graham, Frank D. *Protective Tariffs* (New York and London: Harper, 1934).
Gregory, T. E. G. *Tariffs: A Study in Method* (London: C. Griffin, 1921).
Greiff, Walter. *Der Methodenwandel der europäischen Handelspolitik während des Krisenjahres 1931* (Berlin: Junker u. Dünnhaupt, 1932).
—— *Die neuen Methoden der Handelspolitik* (Berlin: Junker u. Dünnhaupt, 1934).
Grünfeld, Ernst. *Die deutsche Aussenhandelskontrolle (die Politik der*

Sperren) *vom Kriegsausbruch bis zum Inkrafttreten des Friedenvertrages* (Bonn: Schroeder, 1922).

Grunzel, Josef. *Economic Protectionism,* ed. by Eugen von Philippovich (Oxford: Clarendon Press, and New York and London: H. Milford, 1916).

Guillebaud, C. W. *The Economic Recovery of Germany from 1933 to March, 1938* (London: Macmillan, 1939).

Gutierrez, Viriato. *The World Sugar Problem, 1926–1935* (London: Norman Rodger, 1935).

Haberler, Gottfried. *Liberale und planwirtschaftliche Handelspolitik* (Berlin: Junker u. Dünnhaupt, 1934).

—— *The Theory of International Trade: With Its Application to Commercial Policy* (London: W. Hodge, 1936).

Haight, F. A. *French Import Quotas: A New Instrument of Commercial Policy* (London: P. S. King, 1935).

Hantos, Elemér. *Die Handelspolitik in Mitteleuropa* (Jena: G. Fischer, 1925).

Harris, Charles R. S. *Germany's Foreign Indebtedness,* with the assistance of the Information Department of the Royal Institute of International Affairs (London: Oxford University Press, 1935).

Harris, Seymour E. *Exchange Depreciation: Its Theory and Its History, 1931–35, with Some Consideration of Related Domestic Policies,* Harvard Economic Studies, No. 53 (Cambridge, Mass.: Harvard University Press, 1936).

Heilperin, Michael A. *International Monetary Economics* (London: Longmans, Green, 1939).

—— *The Monetary Aspect of the Raw Materials Problem and the Revival of International Trade* (Paris: International Institute of Intellectual Coöperation, 1938).

Heuser, Heinrich. *Control of International Trade* (London: Routledge, 1939).

Hoffherr, René. *La politique commerciale de la France* (Paris: Centre d'études de politique étrangère, 1939).

Holland, W. L., ed. *Commodity Control in the Pacific Area: A Symposium on Recent Experience* (Stanford University: Stanford University Press, 1935).

International Chamber of Commerce. *Accords de Compensation* (Paris: International Chamber, 1936).

—— Joint Committee of the Carnegie Endowment for International Peace and the International Chamber of Commerce. *International Economic Reconstruction: An Economists' and Businessmen's Survey of the Main Problems of Today* (Paris: International Chamber, 1936).

—— Joint Committee of the Carnegie Endowment for International Peace and the International Chamber of Commerce. *The Improvement of Commercial Relations between Nations* and *The Problem of Monetary Stabilization: Separate Memoranda from the Economists Con-*

sulted by the Joint Committee and Practical Conclusions of the Expert Committee Appointed by the Joint Committee (Paris: International Chamber, 1936).

—— World Business Information Centre. *Clearing and Payments Agreements* (Stuttgart: J. Hess, and Basel: Verlag für Recht und Gesellschaft, A. G., 1938) [Supplements issued from time to time.].

—— [See also other publications of this body.]

International Economic Relations, Report of the Commission of Inquiry into National Policy in International Economic Relations (Minneapolis: University of Minnesota Press, 1934).

International Institute of Agriculture. *The World Agricultural Situation in 1931–32* (Rome: The Institute, 1933). [Similar volumes for later years—title varies somewhat.]

International Institute of Intellectual Coöperation. Danubian Group of Economic Experts. *Danubian Studies I. Chronology of Political and Economic Events in the Danube Basin, 1918–1936. Bulgaria* (Paris: International Institute of Intellectual Coöperation, 1938). [See also separate volume with similar title for Hungary.]

—— *Études danubiennes I. Chronique des événements politiques et économiques dans le bassin danubien, 1918–1936. Autriche* (Paris: International Institute of Intellectual Coöperation, 1938). [See also separate volumes with similar titles for *Roumanie, Tchécoslovakie,* and *Yougoslavie.*]

—— International Studies Conference. 5th, Milan, 1932. *A Record of a First International Study Conference on the State and Economic Life,* Milan, May 23–27, 1932 (Paris: International Institute of Intellectual Coöperation, 1932). [See also records of later conferences.].

Jolly, Pierre. *L'Office franco-allemand de Paiements commerciaux et le commerce franco-allemand* (Paris: Lib. générale de droit et de jurisprudence, 1936).

—— *Traité des opérations de compensation: Les clearings commerciaux* (Paris: Lib. Hachette, 1935).

Jones, Joseph M., Jr. *Tariff Retaliation: Repercussions of the Hawley-Smoot Bill* (Philadelphia: University of Pennsylvania Press, 1934).

Kapp, Karl W. *Planwirtschaft und Aussenhandel* (Geneva: George et cie., 1936).

Kerner, Robert J., and Howard, Harry N. *The Balkan Conference and the Balkan Entente* (Berkeley, Calif.: University of California Press, 1936).

Killough, Hugh B. *International Trade* (New York and London: McGraw-Hill, 1938).

Korek, V., and Stark, J. *Mitteleuropa-Bibliographie: Eine Übersicht des Schrifttums der Jahre 1919 bis 1934, Teil 1: Agrarfrage, Handelspolitik und Zusammenschlussbestrebungen in Mitteleuropa,* Mitteleuropäische Wirtschaftsfragen, Neue Folge, Band II (Berlin: C. Heymann, and Vienna: Oesterreichischer Wirtschaftsverlag, 1935).

Lachaze, Jean. *L'office français de compensation et les reglements internationaux, avec textes des accords* (Paris: Lib. du Recueil Sirey, 1934).

Landry, Adolphe. *La politique commerciale de la France* (Paris: Lib. du Recueil Sirey, 1934).

Larkin, J. D. *The President's Control of the Tariff* (Cambridge, Mass.: Harvard University Press, 1936).

Lawrence, O. L., and Palmer, G. H. *The Economic Consequences of Otatawa in the Pacific Dominions,* prepared for the 5th International Conference of the Institute of Pacific Relations (London: Royal Institute of International Affairs, 1933).

de Leener, Georges. *La politique commerciale de la Belgique* (Paris: Lib. du Recueil Sirey, 1934).

——— *Théorie et politique du commerce international* (Brussels: M. Samertin, 1933).

Liepmann, H. *Tariff Levels and the Economic Unity of Europe: An Examination of Tariff Policy, Export Movements and the Economic Integration of Europe, 1913–1931* (London: Allen & Unwin, 1938).

Lockwood, William W., Jr. *The Foreign Trade Policy of the United States,* prepared for the 6th International Conference of the Institute of Pacific Relations (New York: American Council, Institute of Pacific Relations, 1936).

Loveday, Alexander. *Britain and World Trade, Quo Vadimus and Other Economic Essays* (New York and London: Longmans, Green, 1931).

McGuire, E. B. *The British Tariff System* (London: Methuen, 1939).

Machlup, Fritz. *Führer durch die Krisenpolitik* (Vienna: J. Springer, 1934).

Mackenroth, G., and Krebs, F. *Die Wirtschaftsverflechtung des Britischen Weltreiches* (Berlin: Junker u. Dünnhaupt, 1935).

Madgearu, Virgil N. *Mémoire sur le contrôle des changes en Roumanie,* étude collective par un comité d'experts, Report submitted to the 12th International Studies Conference, Bergen, Norway, 1939 (Paris: International Institute of Intellectual Coöperation, 1939).

——— *La politique économique extérieure de la Roumanie (1927–1938),* Reported submitted to the 12th International Studies Conference, Bergen, Norway, 1939 (Paris: International Institute of Intellectual Coöperation, 1939).

Mayer, J., Horna, M., and Sourek, A. *Neue Wege der Handelspolitik: Wirtschaftlicher Nationalismus, Clearing-Kompensationen* (Prague: Orbis-Verlaga, 1936).

Mehrens, Bernhard. *Die Marktordnung des Reichsnährstandes* (Berlin: Verlag Franz Vahlen, 1938).

Meisner, Andreas. *Einführung in die Zoll- und Handelspolitik: Mit besonderer Berücksichtigung der Tschechoslowakei* (Prague: Deutsche agrarische Druckerei, 1932).

Milhaud, Edgard. *Le chèque-compensation international devant l'opinion* (Paris: Lib. du Recueil Sirey, 1936).

SELECTED BIBLIOGRAPHY   493

—— *Une idée en marche—La compensation organisée* (Paris: Lib. du Recueil Sirey, 1935).

Mitsubishi Economic Research Bureau. *Japanese Trade and Industry: Present and Future* (London: Macmillan, 1936).

Moye, Marcel, and Nogaro, Bertrand. *Le régime douanier de la France: Politique douanière, législation douanière et traités de commerce: Administration et réglementation* (Paris: Lib. du Recueil Sirey, 1931).

Murray, K. A. H., and Cohen, Ruth L. *The Planning of Britain's Food Imports* (Oxford, Agricultural Economics Research Institute, 1934).

Naldoni, Nardo. *La politica economico-coloniale d'Europa nell' epoca moderna* (Rome: A. Signorelli, 1930).

Oualid, William. *International Raw Materials Cartels: Causes, Effects, Regulation* (Paris: International Institute of Intellectual Coöperation, 1938).

Oulès, Firmin. *Le méchanisme des échanges internationaux et la politique commerciale en temps de crise* (Paris: Lib. du Recueil Sirey, 1936).

Panaïtesco, P. N. *Les contingentements dans les relations commerciales avec les pays agricoles* (Paris: Lib. du Recueil Sirey, 1935).

Paranagua, O. *Tariff Policy* (London: H. Milford, Oxford University Press, 1935).

Pasvolsky, Leo. *Economic Nationalism of the Danubian States* (New York: Macmillan, 1928).

Patterson, Ernest M. *The Economic Basis of Peace* (New York and London: McGraw-Hill, 1939).

—— *The World's Economic Dilemma* (New York and London: McGraw-Hill, 1930).

Peek, G. N., and Crowther, S. *Why Quit Our Own?* (New York: Van Nostrand, 1936).

PEP (Political and Economic Planning). *Report on International Trade: A Survey of Problems Affecting the Expansion of International Trade with Proposals for the Development of British Commercial Policy and Export Mechanism, May, 1937* (London: PEP, 1937).

Phelps, Vernon L. *The International Economic Position of Argentina* (Philadelphia: University of Pennsylvania Press, 1938).

Piatier, André. *Le contrôle des devises dans l'économie du III° Reich*, Centre d'études de politique étrangère, Section d'information, Publication No. 9 (Paris: P. Hartmann, 1937).

—— *L'économie de guerre* (Paris: Lib. générale de droit et de jurisprudence, 1939).

Pigou, A. C. *Protective and Preferential Import Duties* (New York and London: Macmillan, 1906).

Plaut, Theodor. *Deutsche Handelspolitik* (2d ed.; Leipzig and Berlin, B. G. Teubner, 1929).

Poole, Kenyon E. *German Financial Policies, 1932–1939*, Harvard Economic Studies, No. 66 (Cambridge, Mass.: Harvard University Press, 1939).

Porri, Vincent. *La politique commerciale de l'Italie* (Paris: Lib. du Recueil Sirey, 1934).

Proceedings of the Fifth International Conference of Agricultural Economists, Macdonald College, Canada, August 21 to 28, 1938 (London: H. Milford, 1939).

Rappard, William E. *Post-War Efforts for Free Trade*, Geneva Research Centre, Geneva Studies, Vol. IX, No. 2 (March, 1938).

Report of the Committee Appointed on the Recommendation of the London Conference (also known as the First Basle Report or Wiggin Report), August 18, 1931.

Report of the Foreign Creditors' Standstill Committee, January 23, 1932.

Report of the Special Advisory Committee (also known as the Second Basle Report), December 23, 1931.

Respondek, Erwin. *Grundzüge europäischer Handelspolitik zwischen den beiden Weltwirtschaftskonferenzen* (Berlin: C. Heymann, 1933).

Richardson, John H. *British Economic Foreign Policy* (London: Allen & Unwin, 1936).

—— *Economic Disarmament: A Study on International Co-operation* (London: Allen & Unwin, 1931).

Riedl, Richard. *Aussenhandel und Währungsschutz* (Vienna: Oesterreichischer Wirtschaftsverlag, 1936).

—— *Exceptions to the Most-Favoured-Nation Treatment*, Report presented to the International Chamber of Commerce (London: P. S. King, 1931).

Robbins, Lionel. *Economic Planning and International Order* (London: Macmillan, 1937).

—— *The Great Depression* (New York: Macmillan, 1934).

Röpke, Wilhelm. *German Commercial Policy* (New York, London, and Toronto: Longmans, Green, 1934).

—— *Die internationale Handelspolitik nach dem Kriege* (Jena: G. Fischer, 1923).

—— *International Economic Disintegration* (London, 1940).

Rowe, J. W. F. *Markets and Men: A Study of Artificial Control Schemes in Some Primary Industries* (New York: Macmillan, 1936).

Royal Institute of International Affairs. *British Commonwealth Relations: Proceedings of the First Unofficial Conference at Toronto, 11–21 September, 1933*, ed. by Arnold J. Toynbee (London: Oxford University Press, H. Milford, 1934).

—— *The British Empire: A Report on Its Structure and Problems* (2d ed.; New York and London: Oxford University Press, 1938).

—— *The Colonial Problem* (New York and London: Oxford University Press, 1937).

—— *International Sanctions* (New York and London: Oxford University Press, 1938).

—— *The Problem of International Investment* (New York and London: Oxford University Press, 1937).

—— *The Republics of South America* (New York and London: Oxford University Press, 1937).

—— *Survey of International Affairs*, annual.

—— *World Agriculture: An International Survey* (London: Oxford University Press, H. Milford, 1932).

—— Information Department. *Anglo-American Trade Relations* (London: The Royal Institute, 1938).

—— —— *Memorandum on the Most-favored-nation Clause as an Instrument of International Policy* (London: The Royal Institute, 1933).

—— —— *Raw Materials and Colonies* (London: The Royal Institute, 1936).

—— —— *South-Eastern Europe: A Political and Economic Survey* (London: The Royal Institute, and New York: Oxford University Press, 1939).

Salter, Sir Arthur. *Recovery: The Second Effort* (New York: Century, 1932).

—— *The United States of Europe and Other Papers*, ed. with notes by W. Arnold Foster (London: Allen & Unwin, 1933).

—— *World Trade and Its Future* (Philadelphia: University of Pennsylvania Press, 1936).

Sarkar, Benoy K. *Imperial Preference vis-à-vis World Economy in Relation to the International Trade and National Economy of India* (Calcutta: N. M. Ray-Chowdbury, 1934).

Sayre, Francis B. *The Protection of American Export Trade* (Chicago: University of Chicago Press, 1940).

—— *The Way Forward: The American Trade Agreements Program* (New York: Macmillan, 1939).

Schacht, Hjalmar. *The End of Reparations*, trans. by Lewis Gannett (New York: Jonathan Cape and Harrison Smith, 1931).

Schlie, Hans. *Die britische Handelspolitik seit Ottawa und ihre weltwirtschaftlichen Auswirkungen*, Probleme der Weltwirtschaft, Schriften des Instituts für Weltwirtschaft an der Universität Kiel, No. 59 (Jena: G. Fischer, 1937).

Shann, Edward O. G. *Quotas or Stable Money? Three Essays on the Ottawa and London Conferences, 1932–33* (Sydney: Angus & Robertson, 1933).

Shenkman, Elia M. *Insurance against Credit Risks in International Trade: Principles and Organization of State and Private Insurance against Credit Risks* (London: P. S. King, 1935).

Smith, James G. *Economic Planning and the Tariff: An Essay on Social Philosophy* (Princeton: Princeton University Press, 1934).

Smith, W. Millar. *The Marketing of Australian and New Zealand Primary Products* (London: Pitman, 1936).

Sommer, Louise. *Neugestaltung der Handelspolitik: Wege zu einem inter-*

europäischen Präferenzsystem (Berlin: C. Heymann, and Vienna: Oesterreichischer Wirtschaftsverlag, 1935).

Staley, Eugene A. *Raw Materials in Peace and War* (New York: Council on Foreign Relations, 1937).

—— *World Economy in Transition: Technology vs. Politics, Laissez Faire vs. Planning, Power vs. Welfare* (New York: Council on Foreign Relations, 1939).

Tasca, Henry J. *The Reciprocal Trade Policy of the United States: A Study in Trade Philosophy* (Philadelphia: University of Pennsylvania Press, 1938).

—— *World Trading Systems* (Paris: International Institute of Intellectual Coöperation, 1939).

Taussig, Frank W. *Free Trade, the Tariff, and Reciprocity* (New York: Macmillan, 1924).

—— *The Tariff History of the United States* (7th ed.; New York and London: Putnam's, 1923).

Taylor, Alonzo E. *The New Deal and Foreign Trade* (New York: Macmillan, 1935).

Upgren, A. R. *Reciprocal Trade Agreements* (Minneapolis: University of Minnesota Press, 1937).

Urba, J. *Das Getreidemonopol in der landwirtschaftlichen Praxis* (Prague: K. Ludvík, 1935).

Uyeda, Teijiro. *The Recent Development of Japanese Foreign Trade: With Special Reference to Restrictive Policies of Other Countries and Attempts at Trade Agreements,* Prepared for the Sixth Conference of the Institute of Pacific Relations (Tokyo: Japanese Council, Institute of Pacific Relations, 1936).

Vakil, C. N., and Maluste, D. N. *Commercial Relations between India and Japan* (London: Longmans, Green, 1938).

Van Woerden, F. A. *La Société des Nations et le rapprochement économique international* (The Hague: M. Nijhoff, 1932).

van Zeeland, Paul. *Economics or Politics?* (Cambridge, England: Cambridge University Press, 1939).

Viner, Jacob. *Dumping: A Problem of International Trade* (Chicago: University of Chicago Press, 1923).

—— *Studies in the Theory of International Trade* (New York and London: Harper, 1937).

Wallace, Henry A. *America Must Choose: The Advantages and Disadvantages of Nationalism, of World Trade, and of a Planned Middle Course,* World Affairs Pamphlets, No. 3 (New York: Foreign Policy Association, 1934).

Wang, Yuan Chao. *German Exchange Control, 1931–36: A Study of Its Origin, Development, Technique and Economic Effects* (unpublished Ph.D. thesis, Harvard University, 1937).

Welk, William G. *Fascist Economic Policy: An Analysis of Italy's Eco-*

nomic Experiment, Harvard Economic Studies, No. 62 (Cambridge, Mass.: Harvard University Press, 1938).

Whittlesey, Charles R. *Government Control of Crude Rubber: The Stevenson Plan* (Princeton: Princeton University Press, 1931).

—— *International Monetary Issues* (New York: McGraw-Hill, 1937).

Williams, Benjamin J. *Economic Foreign Policy of the United States* (New York: McGraw-Hill, 1929).

Winslow, E. M. *The League and Concerted Economic Action,* Geneva Research Centre, Geneva Special Studies, Vol. II, No. 2 (February, 1931).

Wright, Philip G. *Trade and Trade Barriers in the Pacific* (Stanford University: Stanford University Press, 1935).

Wright, Stanley F. *China's Struggle for Tariff Autonomy, 1843–1938* (Shanghai: Kelly & Walsh, 1938).

Yanson, J. D. *Foreign Trade in the U.S.S.R.* (London: Victor Gollancz, 1934).

II. ARTICLES

Abel, Wilhelm. "Der Preis in der landwirtschaftlichen Marktordnung," *Jahrbücher für Nationalökonomie und Statistik,* CXLV (1937), 22–50.

Allix, Edgard. "La clause de la nation la plus favorisée," *Revue d'Économie Politique,* XLVII (1933), 466–82.

Amark, Karl. "Die Entwicklung des schwedischen Aussenhandels und der schwedischen Handelspolitik nach dem Kriege," *Weltwirtschaftliches Archiv,* XXXI (1930), 108–31.

Bachfeld, Hellmuth. "Das Kompensationsgeschäft in der Praxis," *Die Wirtschaftskurve,* XIII (1934), 213–23.

Bailey, S. H. "The Political Aspect of Discrimination in International Economic Relations," *Economica,* XII (1932), 89–115 and 160–79.

—— "Reciprocity and the Most-Favored-Nation Clause," *Economica,* XIII (1933), 428–56.

Balogh, Thomas. "The National Economy of Germany," *Economic Journal,* XLVIII (1938), 461–97.

—— "Some Theoretical Aspects of the Central European Credit and Transfer Crisis," *International Affairs: Journal of the Royal Institute of International Affairs,* XI (1932), 346–69.

Barber, Alvin. "Six Years of Economic Planning in Netherlands India," *Far Eastern Survey,* VIII (1939), 195–203.

Belshaw, H. "Guaranteed Prices for New Zealand Exports," *Economic Record,* XIII (1937), 168–88.

Benning, B. "Der 'Neue Plan' und die Neuordnung der deutschen Aussenwirtschaft," *Jahrbücher für Nationalökonomie und Statistik,* CXLII (1935), 35–62.

Bevin, Ernest. "Impressions of the British Commonwealth Conference,

1938," *International Affairs: Journal of the Royal Institute of International Affairs,* XVIII (1939), 56–76.

Bidwell, Percy W. "Latin America, Germany and the Hull Program," *International Conciliation,* No. 347 (February, 1939), pp. 95–112.

────── "Our Invisible Tariff," *Foreign Affairs,* XVII (1939), 774–87.

────── "Prospects of a Trade Agreement with England," *Foreign Affairs,* XVI (1937), 103–14.

────── "Trade, Tariffs, the Depression," *Foreign Affairs,* X (1932), 391–402.

Bloch, Kurt. "Inflation and Prices in the Yen Bloc," *Far Eastern Survey,* VIII (1939), 183–90.

Bonnet, Georges. "The Economic Reconstruction of Central and South-Eastern Europe," *International Affairs: Journal of the Royal Institute of International Affairs,* XII (1933), 37–59.

Bopp, Karl R. "Die Politik der deutschen Reichsbank seit der Stabilisierung," *Weltwirtschaftliches Archiv,* XLII (1935), 445–83.

Brandt, Karl. "Farm Relief in Germany," *Social Research,* I (1934), 185–98.

────── "German Agricultural Policy—Some Selected Lessons," *Journal of Farm Economics,* XIX (1937), 287–99.

────── "Recent Agrarian Policies in Germany and the United States," *Social Research,* III (1936), 167–201.

Bratter, Herbert M. "Foreign Exchange Control in Latin America," *Foreign Policy Reports,* XIV (1939), 274–88.

Bresler, Harvey J. "Trade Barriers and the League of Nations," *Foreign Policy Reports,* VII (1931), 205–18.

Brinkmann, Carl. "Meistbegünstigungsklausel und Kontingent," *Weltwirtschaftliches Archiv,* XXXIX (1934), 67–79.

Brocard, Lucien. "Nouveaux fondements du protectionnisme industriel," *Revue d'Économie Politique,* XLVII (1933), 380–402.

────── "Die Tendenz zur Nationalwirtschaft und die internationalen Beziehungen," *Weltwirtschaftliches Archiv,* XXXVIII (1933), 317–33.

Campbell, R. M. "Empire Free Trade," *Economic Journal,* XXXIX (1929), 371–78.

Candace, G. "Le régime douanier de la France et ses colonies," *Revue Politique et Parlementaire,* CLX (1934), 58–75.

Carroll, Mitchell B. "Double Taxation—A Trade Barrier," Svenska Handelsbanken, *Index,* VIII (1933), 162–69.

Chalmers, Henry. "Control of Foreign Trade," *American Yearbook,* 1927, pp. 307–11.

────── "Current Trends in Foreign Commercial Policy," *Annals of the American Academy of Political and Social Science,* CL (1930), 126–45.

────── "The Depression and Foreign Trade Barriers," *Annals of the American Academy of Political and Social Science,* CLXXIV (1934), 88–106.

────── "International Trade Control," *American Yearbook,* 1927, pp.

440–46. [Also articles bearing same title in *American Yearbook*, 1928, pp. 331–34, and 1929, pp. 316–20.]

—— "The Post-War Drift in European Commercial Policy," *American Economic Review*, XIV, Supplement (March, 1924), 14–25.

—— "The World Economic Conference," *American Yearbook*, 1927, pp. 297–300.

Chancellor, Christopher. "Japan in China," *International Affairs: Journal of the Royal Institute of International Affairs*, XVIII (1939), 601–22.

Ch.-Walden, E. A. "The Sino-Japanese War and the Open Door," *International Affairs: Journal of the Royal Institute of International Affairs*, XVII (1938), 629–54.

Cole, G. D. H. "Planning International Trade," *Foreign Affairs*, XII (1934), 231–43.

Colegrove, Kenneth. "The German-Polish Rye Agreement," *Journal of Political Economy*, XXXIX (1931), 213–28.

Condliffe, J. B. "Some Problems of International Economic Equilibrium," Svenska Handelsbanken, *Index*, VIII (1933), 226–37.

—— "The Value of International Trade," *Economica*, New Series, V (1938), 123–37.

"Consultative Meeting of Foreign Ministers of the American Republics, September 23 to October 3, 1939: Text of Final Act and Statement by Sumner Welles, Under Secretary of State," *International Conciliation*, No. 356 (January, 1940), pp. 3–32.

Corcelle, Charles. "Les échanges commerciaux franco-canadiens," *Revue Économique internationale*, XXXI (1939), 285–346.

Czechowicz, P. "Die Exportpolitik und das Problem der Exportfähigkeit der U. d. S.S.R.," *Weltwirtschaftliches Archiv*, XXXV (1932), 475–513.

Davis, Eric. "Some Aspects of the Marketing of Farm Products in South Africa," *South African Journal of Economics*, I (1933), 167–87.

Davis, Joseph S. "The Export Debenture Plan for Aid to Agriculture," *Quarterly Journal of Economics*, XLIII (1929), 250–77.

—— "Pacific Northwest Wheat Problems and the Export Subsidy," *Wheat Studies*, X (1933–34), 353–426.

Dean, Vera M. "European Efforts for Economic Collaboration," *Foreign Policy Reports*, VII (1931), 219–40.

Delaisi, Francis. "Après les conférences agraires de l'Europe centrale," *Revue d'Économie Politique*, XLIV (1930), 1329–48.

Dietrich, Ethel B. "British Export Credit Insurance," *American Economic Review*, XXV (1935), 236–49.

—— "French Import Quotas," *American Economic Review*, XXIII (1933), 661–74.

—— "The New Model Trade Agreement," *Journal of Political Economy*, XLII (1934), 595–612.

von Dietze, C. "Zwangssyndikate als Mittel der Agrarpreispolitik," *Jahrbücher für Nationalökonomie und Statistik*, CXLV (1937), 129–42.

Digby, Margaret. "Genossenschaftswesen und gegenwärtige Agrarpolitik in Grossbritannien," *Jahrbücher für Nationalökonomie und Statistik,* CXLV (1937), 58–65.

Dillner, Günther. "Einzelstudien über Marktregulierungen. III. Die Marktregulierungen in der tschechoslowakischen Getreidewirtschaft," *Weltwirtschaftliches Archiv,* XLIV (1936), 549–79.

Döblin, Ernst. "Internationale Konjunkturabhängigkeit und Autarkie," *Archiv für Sozialwissenschaft und Sozialpolitik,* LXVII (1932), 283–313.

van Dorp, E. C. "Die Freihandelsgedanke in der Welt nach dem Kriege," *Weltwirtschaftliches Archiv,* XXX (1929), 212–40.

Durand, E. Dana. "Measurement of Effects of Reciprocal Trade Agreements," *Journal of the American Statistical Association,* XXXII (1937), 50–64.

"Economic Nationalism in Europe as Applied to Wheat," *Wheat Studies,* VIII (1931–32), 261–76.

Edminster, Lynn R. "Agriculture's Stake in the British Agreement and the Trade Agreements Program," *International Conciliation,* No. 347 (February, 1939), pp. 77–94.

———— "The Trade Agreements Program and American Agriculture," *American Economic Review,* XXVI, Supplement (March, 1936), 129–40.

"Eighth International Conference of American States: Explanatory Introduction by George A. Finch and Texts of Declarations, Resolutions, and Recommendations Adopted by the Conference," *International Conciliation,* No. 349 (April, 1939), pp. 143–249.

Eiteman, W. J. "The Rise and Decline of Orthodox Tariff Propaganda," *Quarterly Journal of Economics,* XLV (1930), 22–39.

Ellis, Howard S. "The Equilibrium Rate of Exchange," in *Explorations in Economics: Notes and Essays Contributed in Honor of F. W. Taussig* (New York and London: McGraw-Hill, 1936).

———— "Exchange Control in Austria and Hungary," a special supplement to the *Quarterly Journal of Economics,* LIV (November, 1939, Part II), 1–188.

Eulenburg, Franz. "Europäische Handelspolitik," *Zeitschrift für schweizerische Statistik und Volkswirtschaft,* LXXI (1935), 473–92.

Farley, Miriam S. "The Impact of War on Japan's Foreign Trade," *Far Eastern Survey,* VIII (1939), 123–28.

———— "Japan between Two Wars," *Far Eastern Survey,* VIII (1939), 243–48.

Fay, Harold van V. "Commercial Policy in Post-War Europe: Reciprocity versus Most-favored-nation Treatment," *Quarterly Journal of Economics,* XLI (1927), 441–70.

Feiler, Arthur. "Current Tendencies in Commercial Policy," *American Economic Review,* XXVII, Supplement (March, 1937), 29–42.

———— "International Trade under Totalitarian Governments," *Social Research,* V (1938), 424–41.

Feis, Herbert. "Raw Materials and Foreign Policy," *Foreign Affairs*, XVI (1938), 574–86.

Fox, Albert M. "Quantitative and Qualitative Changes in International Trade during the Depression," *American Economic Review*, XXVII, Supplement (March, 1937), 12–28.

Frankel, S. Herbert. "Some Comments on Price and Marketing Control in South African Agriculture," *South African Journal of Economics*, II (1934), 324–31.

Fromont, Pierre. "Staatliche Massnahmen in der französischen Landwirtschaft," *Weltwirtschaftliches Archiv*, XLIV (1936), 84–121.

Gabriel, S. L. "Der Gutertarif der Eisenbahnen als Mittel der Aussenhandelspolitik," *Jahrbücher für Nationalökonomie und Statistik*, CXLI (1935), 668–86.

Gheorgui, D. I. "La politique douanière et commerciale de la Roumanie après la Guerre," Société belge d'études et d'expansion, Liege, *Bulletin périodique*, No. 70 (April, 1929), pp. 244–50.

"Government Measures for the Relief of Agriculture in Sweden since 1930," Svenska Handelsbanken, *Index*, XIV, Supplement (March, 1939), 3–32.

Grady, Henry F. "The New Trade Policy of the United States," *Foreign Affairs*, XIV (1936), 283–96.

———— "Tariff and Trade: The New American Law and the Pacific," *Pacific Affairs*, III (1930), 719–34.

Grau, Román Perpiñá. "Der Wirtschaftsaufbau Spaniens und die Problematik seiner Aussenhandelspolitik," *Weltwirtschaftliches Archiv*, XLI (1935), 61–131.

Green, James F. "Britain's Foreign Trade Policy," *Foreign Policy Reports*, XIII (1938), 250–64.

Gross, Herbert, "Ausgangspunkte, Formen und Wirkungen der Devisenzwangswirtschaft," *Archiv für Sozialwissenschaft und Sozialpolitik*, LXIX (1933), 49–79.

———— "Industriewirtschaftliche Wirkungen einer deutsch-österreichischen Zollunion," *Weltwirtschaftliches Archiv*, XXXIV (1931), 41–99.

Häfner, Kurt. "Die Politik der mengenmässigen Einfuhrregulierung," *Weltwirtschaftliches Archiv*, XL (1934), 18–59.

———— "Zur Theorie der mengenmässigen Einfuhrregulierung," *Weltwirtschaftliches Archiv*, XLI (1935), 190–223.

Halkema-Kohl, J. F. "Belgisch-niederländisch-luxemburgisch Wirtschaftskooperation: Der Vertrag von Ouchy vom 18 Juli 1932," *Weltwirtschaftliches Archiv*, XXXVI (1932), 620–29.

Hall, Noel F. " 'Trade Diversion'—An Australian Interlude," *Economica* New Series, V (1938), 1–11.

Hansen, Simon G. "The Argentine Grain Board," *Journal of Political Economy*, XLIV (1936), 240–47.

Hantos, Elemér (or Helemer). "Der Donauraum in der Weltwirtschaft," *Weltwirtschaftliches Archiv*, XXXIX (1934), 256–315.

———— "Le régionalisme économique en Europe," *Revue Économique internationale*, XXXI (1939), 63–100.

Hanwell, Norman. "Economic Disruption in Occupied China," *Far Eastern Survey*, VIII (1939), 61–66.

Harris, Seymour E. "Measures of Currency Overvaluation and Stabilization," in *Explorations in Economics: Notes and Essays Contributed in Honor of F. W. Taussig* (New York and London: McGraw-Hill, 1936).

Helander, S. "Merkantilistische Verkehrspolitik," *Weltwirtschaftliches Archiv*, XLVIII (1938), 420–51.

Heuser, Heinrich. "The German Method of Combined Debt Liquidation and Export Stimulation," *Review of Economic Studies*, I (1934), 210–17.

Hilgerdt, Folke. "The Approach to Bilateralism—A Change in the Structure of World Trade," Svenska Handelsbanken, *Index*, X (1935), 175–88.

Hodson, H. V. "Before Ottawa," *Foreign Affairs*, X (1932), 589–99.

———— "Imperial Economic Policy," *International Affairs: Journal of the Royal Institute of International Affairs*, XIV (1935), 531–50.

Huhle, Fritz. "Die Behandlung der gesperrten Auslandsguthaben in der deutschen Wirtschaftspolitik," *Jahrbücher für Nationalökonomie und Statistik*, CXLVII (1938), 55–81.

———— "Das Clearingswesen im Aussenhandel vom deutschen Standpunkt aus," *Jahrbücher für Nationalökonomie und Statistik*, CXLVI (1937), 171–205.

———— "Das Kompensationsgeschäft im Rahmen der deutschen Handelspolitik seit der Wirtschaftkrise," *Jahrbücher für Nationalökonomie und Statistik*, CXLV (1937), 181–214.

———— "Die Meistbegünstigung in der Aussenhandelspolitik der deutschen Nationalwirtschaft," *Jahrbücher für Nationalökonomie und Statistik*, CXLVIII (1938), 202–35.

Ischboldin, Boris. "Donaueuropa und die Mitteleuropäische Zukunft. Ein Beitrag zum Problem der Grossraumwirtschaft," *Jahrbücher für Nationalökonomie und Statistik*, CXLV (1937), 641–63.

———— "Die neue Aussenhandelspolitik des französischen Imperiums," *Weltwirtschaftliches Archiv*, XLI (1935), 174–89.

Iversen, Carl. "Probleme der dänischen Währungspolitik," *Archiv für Sozialwissenschaft und Sozialpolitik*, LXVII (1932), 641–69.

Jessen, Jens. "Le Plan Quadriennal allemand," *Revue Économique internationale*, XXIX (1937), 465–80.

de Leener, G. "Les systèmes de contingentement douanier," *Bulletin d'information et de documentation de la Banque Nationale de Belgique*, VII (1932), 65–70.

Leguizamon, G. E. "An Argentine View of the Problem of Exchange Restrictions," *International Affairs: Journal of the Royal Institute of International Affairs*, XII (1933), 504–17.

SELECTED BIBLIOGRAPHY 503

Lèvy, Roger. "A French Ottawa—The Imperial Conference," *Pacific Affairs*, IX (1936), 94–101.

Low, H. B. "The Growth of Control of Butter Marketing within New Zealand," *Economic Record*, XV (1939), 60–67.

MacDonnell, J. M. "After the Ottawa Conference," *Foreign Affairs*, XI (1933), 331–46.

McFadyean, Sir Andrew. "International Repercussions of the Ottawa Agreements," *International Affairs: Journal of the Royal Institute of International Affairs*, XII (1933), 19–36.

Machlup, Fritz. "Die Theorie der Kapitalflucht," *Weltwirtschaftliches Archiv*, XXXVI (1932), 512–29.

Mackenroth, Gerhard. "Neue Formen der Weltwirtschaft," *Weltwirtschaftliches Archiv*, XLI (1935), 1–19.

Martin, William. "The Tariff Truce," Svenska Handelsbanken, *Index*, V (1930), 45–49.

Marvaux, A. "La politique commerciale de la France," *Revue Économique internationale*, XXVI (1934), 245–68.

Maspétiol, Roland. "L'office français du blé," *Revue Économique internationale*, XXIX (1937), 523–46.

Mauldon, F. R. E. "Die äussere Wirtschaftspolitik Australiens," *Weltwirtschaftliches Archiv*, XXXVIII (1933), 442–70.

Meyer, Fritz. "Devisenbewirtschaftung als neue Währungsform," *Weltwirtschaftliches Archiv*, XLIX (1939), 415–72.

Mitnitzky, Mark. "Germany's Trade Monopoly in Eastern Europe," *Social Research*, VI (1939), 22–39.

Morgenstern, Oskar. "La introduzione e la abolizione del controllo dei cambi esteri in Austria (1931–34)," *Rivista di Storia economica*, II (1937), 312–43.

Muhlbach, Walter. "Tariff Devices to Meet a Problem of Depreciating Currencies," *Journal of Political Economy*, XXXIII (1925), 293–317.

Naudin, Jean. "La politique douanière et les accords commerciaux," *Revue d'Économie Politique*, XLVIII (1934), 937–49.

Ogata, Shigeyuki. "Probleme der Exportkontrolle in Japan," *Weltwirtschaftliches Archiv*, XLIII (1936), 472–507.

Ohlin, Bertil. "Mechanisms and Objectives of Exchange Control," *American Economic Review*, XXVII, Supplement (March, 1937), 141–50.

"Ottawa Supplement," *The Economist*, Supplement, October 22, 1932.

Passow, Luise. "Zwischenstaatliche Regulierung des Weizenangebots auf dem Weltmarkt," *Weltwirtschaftliches Archiv*, XLV (1937), 171–99.

Pasvolsky, Leo. "Bilateralism in International Commercial Relations," *Harvard Business Review*, XIV (1936), 279–89.

Peffer, Nathaniel. "Would Japan Shut the Open Door in China?" *Foreign Affairs*, XVII (1938), 37–50.

Pertot, Vladimir. "Einzelstudien über Marktregulierungen. V. Die Weizenregulierungen in Jugoslawien," *Weltwirtschaftliches Archiv*, XLV (1937), 628–59.

Planche, L. "La Conférence économique de la France métropolitaine et d'outre-mer," *Journal des Économistes*, XCIII (1934), 828–34.

"Planning and Control in Agriculture," (Symposium), *South African Journal of Economics*, VI (1938), 280–312 and 418–28.

Plant, Arnold. "The Anti-Dumping Regulations of the South African Tariff," *Economica*, XI (1931), 63–102.

Plummer, Alfred. "The British Wheat Act, 1932," *Quarterly Journal of Economics*, XLVII (1932), 63–77.

Reedman, J. N. "Some Notes on the Theoretical Aspects of Import Quotas," *South African Journal of Economics*, IV (1936), 425–35.

Richards, C. S. "The 'New Despotism' in Agriculture: Some Reflections on the Marketing Bill," *South African Journal of Economics*, IV (1936), 469–504.

―――― "Subsidies, Quotas, Tariffs, and the Excess Cost of Agriculture in South Africa," *South African Journal of Economics*, III (1935), 365–403.

Riedl, Richard. "Innereuropäische Handelspolitik," *Weltwirtschaftliches Archiv*, XXXIX (1934), 13–66.

―――― "International Trade Policy," Svenska Handelsbanken, *Index*, No. 40 (April, 1929), pp. 2–9.

Ritter, Karl. "Germany's Experience with Clearing Agreements," *Foreign Affairs*, XIV (1936), 465–76.

Robertson, Dennis H. "The Future of International Trade," *Economic Journal*, XLVIII (1938), 1–15.

Rodwell, H. R. "Economic Aspects of Empire Tariff Preference," *Economic Record*, VIII (1932), 1–18.

Rosenstiel, F. "Ausländische Sperrguthaben in Deutschland," *Die Wirtschaftskurve*, XIV (1936), 297–311.

Rowe, J. W. F. "Artificial Control Schemes and the World's Staples," Svenska Handelsbanken, *Index*, X (1935), 75–89.

Schiller, Karl. "Einzelstudien über Marktregulierungen. I. Das niederländische Marktregulierungssystem für Weizen und Weizenprodukte," *Weltwirtschaftliches Archiv*, XLIV (1936), 335–71.

―――― "Einzelstudien über Marktregulierungen. VII. Die Regulierung der niederländischen Schweinewirtschaft," *Weltwirtschaftliches Archiv*, XLVI (1937), 515–44.

Schürmann-Mack, Fridel. "Einzelstudien über Marktregulierungen. VIII. Die Marktregulierungen in der dänischen Vieh- und Fleischwirtschaft," *Weltwirtschaftliches Archiv*, XLVI (1937), 544–68.

Schuster, Sir George. "Empire Trade before and after Ottawa," *The Economist*, Supplement, November 3, 1934.

Schüttauf, A. W. "Einzelstudien über Marktregulierungen. II. Strukturpolitik und Marktregulierungen in der italienischen Weizenwirtschaft," *Weltwirtschaftliches Archiv*, XLIV (1936), 530–48.

Sehlberg, Nils. "Guiding Principles in Sweden's Trade Policy," Svenska Handelsbanken, *Index*, XI (1936), 206–13.

SELECTED BIBLIOGRAPHY 505

―――― "Indirect Protection," Svenska Handelsbanken, *Index,* No. 42 (June, 1929), pp. 9–16.

Seraphim, Peter-Heinz. "Wirkungen der Neustaatenbildung in Nachkriegs-europa auf Wirtschaftsstruktur und Wirtschaftsniveau," *Weltwirtschaftliches Archiv,* XLI (1935), 385–402.

Smith, James G. "Development of Policy under the Trade Agreements Program," *Quarterly Journal of Economics,* L (1936), 297–312.

―――― "Economic Nationalism and International Trade," *Economic Journal,* XLV (1935), 619–48.

Smith, Lawrence. "Suspension of Gold Standard in Raw Material Exporting Countries," *American Economic Review,* XXIV (1934), 430–49.

Sommer, Louise. "Die Vorgeschichte der Weltwirtschaftskonferenz (Genf, 1927)," *Weltwirtschaftliches Archiv,* XXVIII (1928), 340–418.

―――― "Die Wirtschaftsstrukturellen Voraussetzungen des Kampfes gegen die Meistbegünstigungsklausel," *Zeitschrift für schweizerische Statistik und Volkswirtschaft,* LXXII (1936), 29–47.

Soudek, J. "Devisenbewirtschaftung und Goldwährung," *Die Wirtschaftskurve,* XI (1932), 121–29.

Stewart, Maxwell S. "American Commercial Policy and the World Crisis," *Foreign Policy Reports,* VIII (1932), 68–78.

―――― "The Ottawa Conference," *Foreign Policy Reports,* VIII (1932), 244–54.

―――― "Problems before the World Economic Conference," *Foreign Policy Reports,* IX (1933), 82–92.

―――― "The Work of the London Economic Conference," *Foreign Policy Reports,* IX (1933), 198–208.

Stewart, R. B. "Anglo-Argentine Trade Agreements," *Canadian Journal of Economics and Political Science,* II (1936), 16–26.

―――― "Great Britain's Foreign Loan Policy," *Economica,* New Series, V (1938), 45–60.

Takidani, Zen-ichi. "The Development of the Japanese Commercial Policy," *Journal of the Kobe University of Commerce,* I (May, 1938), 1–40.

Taniguchi, K. "The Link System in Japan," *Kyoto University Economic Review,* XIV (April, 1939), 33–54.

―――― "The Development of the Commodity Link System in Japan," *Kyoto University Economic Review,* XIV (July, 1939), 1–22.

Taussig, Frank W. "Necessary Changes in Our Commercial Policy," *Foreign Affairs,* XI (1933), 397–405.

―――― "The Tariff, 1929–30," *Quarterly Journal of Economics,* XLIV (1930), 175–204.

―――― "The Tariff Act of 1930," *Quarterly Journal of Economics,* XLV (1930), 1–21.

Tocker, A. H. "Exchange Policy and Economic Recovery in New Zealand," *Economic Record,* XII (1936), 86–91.

Trueblood, Howard J. "Trade Rivalries in Latin America," *Foreign Policy Reports*, XIII (1937), 154–64.

Upgren, A. P. "Triangular Trade," *Journal of Political Economy*, XLIII (1935), 653–73.

"Verrechnungsverträge in Varianten," *Die Wirtschaftskurve*, XIII (1934), 298–301.

Viner, Jacob. "The Commercial Policy and the Foreign Trade of the United States," Svenska Handelsbanken, *Index*, No. 37 (January, 1929), pp. 3–17.

—— "The Most Favored Nation Clause in American Commercial Treaties," *Journal of Political Economy*, XXXII (1924), 101–29.

—— "The Most-favoured-nation Clause," Svenska Handelsbanken, *Index*, VI (1931), 2–17.

"Von der Zahlungsüberwachen zur Einfuhrgenehmigung," *Die Wirtschaftskurve*, XIII (1934), 170–72.

Wallace, B. B., and Fay, H. v. V. "Die jüngste Handelspolitik der Vereinigten Staaten," *Weltwirtschaftliches Archiv*, XLIV (1936), 10–83.

Weiller, Jean. "Essai sur le mouvement protectionniste en Grand-Bretagne," *Revue d'Économie Politique*, XLV (1931), 1403–38.

Welk, William G. "League Sanctions and Foreign Trade Restrictions in Italy," *American Economic Review*, XXVII (1937), 96–107.

"Die Welthandelsentwicklung und das Problem der deutschen Ausfuhrpolitik," *Weltwirtschaftliches Archiv*, XXXVI (1932), 24–58.

Wertheimer, Mildred S. "The Lausanne Reparation Settlement," *Foreign Policy Reports*, VIII (1932), 220–30.

White, Horace G., Jr. "Blocked Commercial Balances in American Foreign Policy," *American Economic Review*, XXIX (1939), 74–91.

Whittlesey, Charles R. "Exchange Control," *American Economic Review*, XXII (1932), 585–604.

—— "Excise Taxes as a Substitute for Tariffs," *American Economic Review*, XXVII (1937), 667–79.

—— "Five Years of the Export-Import Bank," *American Economic Review*, XXIX (1939), 487–502.

—— "Governmental Controls and the Theory of International Trade and Finance," *Quarterly Journal of Economics*, LI (1936), 90–105.

—— "Import Quotas in the United States," *Quarterly Journal of Economics*, LII (1937), 37–65.

de Wilde, John C. "German Trade Drive in South-Eastern Europe," *Foreign Policy Reports*, XII (1936), 214–20.

—— "Germany's Controlled Economy," *Foreign Policy Reports*, XIV (1939), 290–304.

—— "Raw Materials in World Politics," *Foreign Policy Reports*, XII (1936), 162–76.

—— "Sugar: An International Problem," *Foreign Policy Reports*, IX (1933), 162–72.

Wolfgang, E., and Cahnmann, E. "Schuldentilgung durch Anleiherück-käufe," *Die Wirtschaftskurve*, XII (1933), 43–53.
Yomoto, Toyokichi. "Wandlungen der japanischen Devisen- und Zoll-politik," *Weltwirtschaftliches Archiv*, XXXVIII (1933), 170–94.
Zimmern, Alfred. "The Open Door and Reciprocity: As Illustrated by Developments within the British Colonial Empire," Svenska Handels-banken, *Index*, VIII (1933), 123–35.

III. Bank Publications

Banco Central de Chile. *Monthly Report on Credit and Business Conditions.*
Banco Central de la Republica Argentina. *Annual Report.*
Banco de la Nacion Argentina. *Economic Review.*
Bank for International Settlements. *Annual Report.*
—— *Foreign Exchange Regulations in the Different Countries* (Basle, 1931–).
Banque Nationale de Belgique. *Bulletin d'information et de documentation.*
District Bank, Ltd., London. *Review of Principal Foreign Exchange Regulations throughout the World.*
Export-Import Bank of Washington. *General Policy Statement*, June 15, 1938.
Narodní Banka Ceskoslovenska (National Bank of Czechoslovakia). *Bulletin*, Supplements giving foreign exchange regulations in Czechoslovakia, October, 1931, and later numbers.
Reichsbank (Germany). *Verwaltungsbericht.*
Reichs-Kredit-Gesellschaft, Berlin. *Germany's Economic Development*, semi-annual report (title varies).

IV. Official Documents

CANADA

Imperial Economic Conference, 1932. *Report of the Conference* (Ottawa: Acland).
Ministry of Trade and Commerce. *Commercial Intelligence Journal* (Ottawa: Gov't Printing Office).

FRANCE

Journal Officiel de la République française (Paris).
Ministère du commerce et de l'industrie. *Moniteur officiel du commerce et de l'industrie* (Paris).

508 SELECTED BIBLIOGRAPHY

GERMANY

Auswärtiges Amt. *Materialen zu der Übersicht über die handelspolitische Lage Deutschlands Ende 1932* (Berlin: Reichsdruckerei, 1933).
Reichsgesetzblatt.
Reichsstelle für den Aussenhandel. *Ein- und Ausfuhrverbote des deutschen Reichs nach den Stand von Ende Dezember, 1935* (Berlin: Reichsdruckerei, 1935).
Reichswirtschaftsministerium. *Deutsches Handels-Archiv.*
Wirtschaft und Statistik.

GREAT BRITAIN

(All printed documents published by H. M. Stationery Office, London.)
Board of Trade. *Board of Trade Journal.*
——— *Report on the Import Duties Act Inquiry (1933).*
Committee on Commercial and Industrial Policy after the War. *Final Report,* Cmd. 9035 (1918).
Committee on Finance and Industry. *Report,* Cmd. 3897 (1931).
Committee on National Expenditure. *Report,* Cmd. 3920 (1931).
Department of Overseas Trade. Reports on economic conditions in individual British and foreign countries, issued irregularly at intervals of a year or more.
Foreign Office. *List of Commercial Treaties, etc., with Foreign Powers,* annual.
——— *Treaty Series.*
Parliamentary Papers. *The Final Act of the Lausanne Conference,* Cmd. 4126 (1932).
——— *Further Documents Relating to the Settlement Reached at the Lausanne Conference,* Cmd. 4129 (1932).
——— *Papers respecting the German Transfer Moratorium,* Cmd. 4260 (1934).
——— *Imperial Economic Conference at Ottawa, 1932: Appendices to the Summaries of Proceedings,* Cmd. 4175 (1932).
——— *Imperial Economic Conference at Ottawa, 1932: Summary of Proceedings and Copies of Trade Agreements,* Cmd. 4174 (1932).
——— *Report Presented by Monsieur van Zeeland to the Governments of the United Kingdom and France on the Possibility of Obtaining a General Reduction of the Obstacles to International Trade, January 28, 1938,* Misc. No. 1 (1938), Cmd. 5648 (1938).
——— *Safeguarding of Industries—Procedure and Enquiries,* Cmd. 2327 (1925).

ITALY

Gazetta Ufficiale del Regno d'Italia (Rome).

LEAGUE OF NATIONS

(Unless otherwise noted, all documents published by the League
in Geneva.)

Balances of Payments, annual.
Chronology of International Treaties and Legislative Matters.
Commission of Enquiry for European Union. *Report by the Stresa Conference for the Economic Restoration of Central and Eastern Europe, submitted to the Commission of Enquiry for European Union*, VII. Political 1932. VII. 11. (C. 666. M. 321. 1932. VII.) (C.E.U.E. 77.)
Committee for the Study of the Problem of Raw Materials. *Report*, II. Econ. & Fin. 1937. II. B. 7. (A. 27. 1937. II. B.).
Conference of Wheat Exporting and Importing Countries (London, Aug. 21–25, 1933). *Final Act, Signed at London, Aug. 25, 1933, with Appendices and Minutes of Final Meeting*, II. B. Economic Relations Section. 1933. II. B. 4. (C. 511. M. 256. 1933. II. B.)
The Course and Phases of the World Economic Depression, Report presented to the Assembly of the League of Nations (1st rev. ed.), II. A. Econ. & Fin. 1931. II. A. 21. (A. 22. 1931. II. A.)
Economic and Financial Section. *Memorandum on Discriminatory Tariff Classifications*, II. Econ. & Fin. 1927. II. 27. (C.E.C.P. 96.)
———— *Memorandum on European Bargaining Tariffs*, by W. T. Page, II. Econ. & Fin. 1927. II. 28. (C.E.C.P. 97.)
Economic Committee. *The Agricultural Crisis* (2 vols.), II. B. Econ. Relations Section. 1931. II. B. 12/1–2. (C. 239. M. 105. 1931. II. B.)
———— *Considerations on the Present Evolution of Agricultural Protectionism*, II. Econ. & Fin. 1935. II. B. 7. (C. 178. M. 97. 1935. II. B.)
———— *Equality of Treatment in the Present State of International Commercial Relations. The Most-Favoured-Nation Clause*, II. Econ. & Fin. 1936. II. B. 9. (C. 379. M. 250. 1936. II. B.)
———— *Observations on the Present Prospects of Commercial Policy*, II. Econ. & Fin. 1939. II. B. 3. (C. 179. M. 108. 1939. II. B.)
———— *Remarks on the Present Phase of International Economic Relations*, II. Econ. & Fin. 1935. II. B. 11. (C. 344. M. 174. 1935. II. B.)
[Also later documents bearing similar title.]
———— Reports to the Council.
———— *Survey of Tourist Traffic considered as an International Economic Factor*, II. Econ. & Fin. 1936. II. B. 1. (C. 3. M. 3. 1936. II. B.)
Economic Organization, Consultative Committee. *Application of the Recommendations of the International Economic Conference*, Report on the period May, 1927, to May, 1928. II. Econ. & Fin. 1928. II. 16. (C.C.E. 7.)
———— *Application of the Recommendations of the International Economic Conference*, Report on the period May, 1928, to May, 1929. II. Econ. & Fin. 1929. II. 12. (C. 130. M. 45. 1929. II.) (C.C.E. 53.)
Economic Work of the League of Nations. *Report and Draft Resolutions*

Presented by the Second Committee to the Assembly, II. Econ. & Fin. 1929. II. 40. (A. 68. 1929. II.) and II. Econ. & Fin. 1930. II. 37. A. 79. 1930. II.)

Enquiry into Clearing Agreements, II. Econ. & Fin. 1935. II. B. 6. (C. 153. M. 83. 1935. II. B.)

Evolution of Economic and Commercial Policy (Autonomous, Contractual and Collective) since the Tenth Assembly, II. B. Econ. & Fin. 1931. II. B. 13. (C.E.U.E./E.E./5.)

Financial Committee. Reports to the Council.

Financial Situation of Austria. Reports, quarterly, 1931—.

Financial Situation of Bulgaria. Reports, quarterly (in French), 1926—.

Financial Position of Hungary. Reports, quarterly, 1931—.

International Conference for the Abolition of Import and Export Prohibitions and Restrictions, Oct. 17–Nov. 8, 1927. *Convention and Protocol and Erratum,* II. Econ. & Fin. 1929. II. 1. (C. 14. M. 11. 1929. II.) (C.I.A.P. 19(3). 1927.)

—— *Final Act,* II. Econ. & Fin. 1927. II. 71. (C. 559. M. 201. 1927. II.) (C.I.A.P. 19(1). 1927.)

—— *Proceedings,* II. Econ. & Fin. 1928. II. 7. (C. 21. M. 12. 1928. II.)

International Economic Conference. Documentation. *Commercial Treaties, Tariff Systems and Contractual Methods,* II. Econ. & Fin. 1927. II. 26. (C.E.I. 31)

—— 1. *Direct and Indirect Subsidies; 2. Differential Taxes on Circulation, Consumption, or Handling of Foreign Imported Goods; 3. Regulation of Quantities of Imports and Exports Admitted,* II. Econ. & Fin. 1927. II. 35. (C.E.I. 42.)

—— *Export Duties,* II. Econ. & Fin. 1927. II. 14.

—— *Stability of Customs Tariffs,* II. Econ. & Fin. 1927. II. 17. (C.E.C.P. 71 (1).)

—— *System of Fixing Export Prices; Dependence of Trade on Control of Foreign Exchange; Methods of Assessment of ad valorem Duties; Variations in Tariffs; Consular Charges,* II. Econ. & Fin. 1927. II. 20. (C.E.I. 28.)

—— *Tariff Level Indices,* II. Econ. & Fin. 1927. II. 34. (C.E.I. 37.)

International Financial Conference, Brussels, 1920. *Papers of the Conference, Exchange Control,* No. XI, II. Econ. & Fin. 1920. (London, 1920.)

International Sugar Conference, London, April 5 to May 6, 1937. I. *Text of the Agreement.* II. *Proceedings and Documents of the Conference,* II. Econ. & Fin. 1937. II. B. 8. (C. 289. M. 190. 1937. II. B.)

International Trade Statistics, annual.

Memorandum on Dumping, by Jacob Viner, II. Econ. & Fin. 1926. II. 63. (C.E.C.P. 36.)

Memorandum on the Legislation of Different States for the Prevention of Dumping, by Ernst Trendelenburg, II. Econ. & Fin. 1926. II. 66. (C.E.I. 7.)

Monetary and Economic Conference. *Addendum to the Reports Approved by the Conference on July 27, 1933,* II. Special. 1933. II. Spec. 4. Addendum. (C. 435. M. 220. 1933. II. Addendum.) (Conf. M. E. 22(1). Addendum.)

—— *Draft Annotated Agenda: Submitted by the Preparatory Commission of Experts,* II. Special. 1933. II. Spec. 1. (C. 48. M. 18. 1933. II.) (Conf. M.E. 1.)

—— *Journal of the Conference* (London, 1933).

—— *Reports Approved by the Conference on July 27, 1933, and Resolutions Adopted by the Bureau and Executive Committee,* II. Special. 1933. II. Spec. 4 (C. 435. M. 220. 1933. II.) (Conf. M. E. 22 (1)) (London, 1933).

Money and Banking. 2 vols., annual, I. *Monetary Review,* II. *Commercial Banks.*

Preliminary Conference with a view to Concerted Economic Action, Feb. 17 to Mar. 24, 1930. *Commercial Convention (with Protocol); Protocol regarding the Program of Future Negotiations; Final Act, Mar. 24, 1930,* II. Econ. & Fin. 1930. II. 15. (C. 203. M. 96. 1930. II.)

Proceedings of the Second International Conference with a view to Concerted Economic Action (1st sess.), Geneva, Nov. 17–28, 1930, II. Econ. & Fin. 1931. II. B. 3. (C. 149. M. 48. 1931. II. B.)

Proceedings of the Second International Conference with a view to Concerted Economic Action (2d sess.), Geneva, Mar. 16–18, 1931, II. Econ. & Fin. 1931. II. B. 10. (C. 269. M. 124. 1931. II. B.)

Recommendations of the Economic Committee relating to Tariff Policy and the Most-Favoured-Nation Clause, II. B. Econ. & Fin. 1933. II. B. I. (E. 805.)

Recommendations of the Economic Committee Relating to Commercial Policy, II. Econ. & Fin. 1929. II. 15. (C. 138. M. 55. 1929. II.)

Report of the Trade Barriers Committee of the International Chamber of Commerce, II Econ. & Fin. 1926. II. 62. (C.E.I. 5.)

Report on Exchange Control, II. Econ. & Fin. 1938. II. A. 10. (C. 232. M. 131. 1938. II. A.)

Review of World Trade, annual.

Treaty Series.

The World Economic Conference. *Final Report,* II. Econ. & Fin. 1927. II. 46(a). (C.E.I. 44 (1))

World Economic Survey, annual.

SWITZERLAND

Feuille officielle suisse du commerce.

Recueil Officiel des Lois et Ordonnances de la Confédération suisse (Berne).

UNION OF SOUTH AFRICA

Department of Agriculture and Forestry. *The Marketing Act, 1937, in Summary* (Mimeo.; Pretoria, 1937).

Office of Census and Statistics. *Official Yearbook of the Union* (Pretoria).

UNITED STATES

(Printed documents published by the Government Printing Office, Washington.)

Chalmers, Henry. "European Tariff Policies since the War," *Trade Information Bulletin,* No. 228 (1924).

—— "Foreign Tariffs and Trade-Control Movements, 1930–31," *Commerce Reports,* April 20, 1931. [Also articles with similar titles for later years in *Commerce Reports,* February 22, 1932; *Trade Information Bulletin,* No. 812 (1933); and *Commerce Reports,* February 24, 1934; February 9, 1935; February 15, 1936; February 6, 1937; January 29, 1938; February 4, 1939; February 3, 1940.]

Congress. House of Representatives. Committee on Ways and Means. *Extending Reciprocal Foreign Trade Agreement Act,* Hearings on H. J. Res. 96, 75th Congr., 1st Sess. (1937).

—— —— —— *Reciprocal Trade Agreements,* Hearings on H. R. 8430, 73d Congr., 2d Sess. (1934).

—— —— —— *Report to Accompany Bill to Amend the Tariff Act of 1930: Reciprocal Trade Agreements,* 73d Congr., 2d Sess. (1934).

—— Senate. Committee on Agriculture and Forestry. *Causes of the Loss of Export Trade and the Means of Recovery,* Hearings, 74th Congr., 1st Sess. (1935).

—— —— —— *World Trade Barriers in Relation to American Agriculture,* Sen. Doc. No. 70, 73d Congr., 1st Sess. (1933).

—— —— Committee on Finance. *Extending Reciprocal Trade Agreements Act,* Hearings on H. J. Res. 96, 75th Congr., 1st Sess. (1937).

—— —— —— *Reciprocal Trade Agreements,* Hearings on H. R. 8687, 73d Congr., 2d Sess. (1934).

—— —— —— *Report to Accompany Bill to Provide for Reciprocal Trade Agreements,* 73d Congr., 2d Sess. (1934).

Department of Agriculture. Agricultural Adjustment Administration. *Information for the Press.*

—— Bureau of Agricultural Economics. *Foreign Agriculture,* monthly, 1937—.

Department of Commerce. Bureau of Foreign and Domestic Commerce. *Commerce Reports,* weekly.

—— —— *The Netherlands: Basic Data on Import Trade and Trade Barriers, Part A, Factors Affecting Imports from the United States* (1935).

—— —— *Sweden. Basic Data on Import Trade and Trade Barriers* (1935).

—— —— Finance Division. *Foreign Financial News: European Financial Notes,* semi-monthly, 1925—.

—— —— —— *Foreign Financial News: Far Eastern Financial Notes,* semi-monthly, 1926—.

—— —— —— *Foreign Financial News: Latin American Financial Notes,* semi-monthly, 1925—.

—— —— —— *Foreign Financial News: Special Circular,* issued at irregular intervals, 1923—.

Department of State. *Analysis of the Trade Agreement with Belgium, February 27, 1935.* [Also analyses of other trade agreements.]

—— *Bulletin.*

—— *Commercial Policy Series.*

—— *Executive Agreement Series.*

—— *Press Releases.*

—— *Reciprocal Trade Agreement between the United States and Cuba, and Exchange of Notes,* August 24, 1934. [Also texts of other trade agreements; see list on p. 395.]

—— *Reports of the Delegates of the United States of America to the International Conferences of American States.*

—— *Treaty Information Bulletin.*

Federal Trade Commission. *Antidumping Legislation and Other Import Regulations in the United States and Foreign Countries,* Sen. Doc. No. 112, 73d Congr., 2d Sess. (1934).

Margold, S. K. *Export Credit in Europe Today, 1934,* Sen. Doc. No. 225, 73d Congr., 2d Sess. (1934).

Tariff Commission. *Annual Reports.*

—— *Changes in Import Duties since the Passage of the Tariff Act of 1930* (1939).

—— *Colonial Tariff Policies* (1922).

—— *Concessions Granted by the United States in the Trade Agreement with Canada* (1936). [Also publications with similar titles dealing with other trade agreements.]

—— *Digest of Trade Agreement with Belgium* (1935). [Also publications with similar titles dealing with other trade agreements.]

—— *Economic Analysis of the Foreign Trade of the United States in Relation to the Tariff,* Sen. Doc. No. 180, 72d Congr., 2d Sess. (1934).

—— *Extent of Equal Tariff Treatment in Foreign Countries* (1937).

—— *Reciprocal Trade: A Current Bibliography* (3d ed.; 1937).

—— *Reciprocity and Commercial Treaties* (1919).

—— *Regulation of Tariffs in Foreign Countries by Administrative Action* (1934).

—— *Tariff Bargaining under Most-favored-nation Treaties,* Report to U. S. Senate in response to paragraphs 10 and 11 of Senate Resolution No. 325, 72d Congr. 2d Sess. (1933).

—— *The Tariff and Its History* (1934).

—— *The Tariff: A Bibliography* (1934).

Temporary National Economic Committee. *Transcript of Testimony of Dr. Theodore J. Kreps on Cartels, January 15, 1940* (1940).

INDEX

Abel, W., 311n.
"Additional" exports, *see* "Supplementary" exports
Afghanistan: exchange control, 208; import quotas, 249
Agricultural commodities, and import quotas, 253f.
Agricultural prices, 30
Agricultural tariffs, 219
Agriculture: and commercial policy, 285–90; and Ottawa agreements, 463; export subsidies, 321f., 328; preferential tariffs, 447–49; trade control, 480
Albania: Balkan regional cooperation, 453f.; import quotas, 248n.
Aluminum, international control, 437
Animal and dairy products, export subsidies, 335f.
Anti-dumping duties, 225–27
Anti-dumping legislation, 17, 329
Argentina: and American Trade Agreements, 395, 406, 466; and British quotas, 281; anti-dumping duties, 226; "bilateral balancing," 201; capital exports, 28; clearing agreements, 130, 133; commercial treaties, 211n.; compensation agreements, 187; currency depreciation, 41; exchange control, 54, 67, 76, 77, 80, 105–10, 116; export promotion, 106, 109; foreign debts, 87; gold standard, 40; Grain Board, 106, 108, 333; payments agreements, 130, 190f., 194f., 197, 198; post-war industrialization, 20; preferential treatment, 468n.; relations with Great Britain, 410–14; stabilization fund, 107f., 110; Sterling area, 44; tariff rates, 209
Asiatic countries, *see* Orient and individual countries
Askimark system, 178–85

Atwater, E., 354n.
Australia: and American Trade Agreements, 399; capital exports, 28; exchange control, 55n.; export control, 361; export subsidies, 331f.; gold standard, 30, 38, 40; import quotas, 248n.; multiple-column tariffs, 224; Ottawa agreements, 458–63; post-war industrialization, 20; tariff rates, 32, 209, 462
Austria: Austro-German union, 35; blocked accounts, 96; clearing agreements, 120, 126, 130, 141, 148; collapse of the Credit Anstalt, 35; exchange control, 54, 66, 67, 70, 75, 100; export control, 358; export restrictions, 353; gold standard, 40, 41; import quotas, 14n.; import restrictions, 253; payments agreements, 130; private clearings, 100–102; regional negotiations, 447–51; Rome agreements, 337, 451–53; tariff rates, 17, 19, 209
Autarky, *see* Self-sufficiency

Bachfeld, H., 179
Bacon, export restrictions, 357
Bailey, S. H., 370n.
Balance of trade, *see* Trade balances, "Bilateral balancing," and Compensation clauses
Balkan countries: export control, 357f.; relations with Germany, 159–65; regional cooperation, 453f.
Balogh, T., 57n.
Baltic states, most-favored-nation clause, 372
Barber, A., 474n.
Barter, *see* Compensation transactions
Basch, A., 58n.
"Base period" formula, 402, 416
Bataille, J., 186n.

515

INDEX

523